CAMBRIDGE LIB

*Books of end*

## Literary Studies

This series provides a high-quality selection of early printings of literary works, textual editions, anthologies and literary criticism which are of lasting scholarly interest. Ranging from Old English to Shakespeare to early twentieth-century work from around the world, these books offer a valuable resource for scholars in reception history, textual editing, and literary studies.

## The Life of Charles Dickens

John Forster (1812–76), an exact contemporary of Charles Dickens, was one of his closest friends, and acted for him (as for many other authors) as advisor, editor, proofreader, agent and marketing manager: according to Thackeray, 'whenever anyone is in a scrape we all fly to him for refuge. He is omniscient and works miracles.' Forster was Dickens' literary executor, and was left the manuscripts of many of the novels, which he in turn left (along with the rest of his magnificent library) to the South Kensington Museum (later the Victoria and Albert Museum). He was ideally placed to write a biography of Dickens, having known him since the 1830s, and having been involved in deeply private matters such as Dickens' separation from his wife. This three-volume account was first published between 1872 and 1874; the version of Volume 3 reissued here is the first edition.

Cambridge University Press has long been a pioneer in the reissuing of out-of-print titles from its own backlist, producing digital reprints of books that are still sought after by scholars and students but could not be reprinted economically using traditional technology. The Cambridge Library Collection extends this activity to a wider range of books which are still of importance to researchers and professionals, either for the source material they contain, or as landmarks in the history of their academic discipline.

Drawing from the world-renowned collections in the Cambridge University Library, and guided by the advice of experts in each subject area, Cambridge University Press is using state-of-the-art scanning machines in its own Printing House to capture the content of each book selected for inclusion. The files are processed to give a consistently clear, crisp image, and the books finished to the high quality standard for which the Press is recognised around the world. The latest print-on-demand technology ensures that the books will remain available indefinitely, and that orders for single or multiple copies can quickly be supplied.

The Cambridge Library Collection will bring back to life books of enduring scholarly value (including out-of-copyright works originally issued by other publishers) across a wide range of disciplines in the humanities and social sciences and in science and technology.

# The Life of Charles Dickens

Volume 3: 1852–1870

John Forster

CAMBRIDGE UNIVERSITY PRESS

Cambridge, New York, Melbourne, Madrid, Cape Town,
Singapore, São Paolo, Delhi, Tokyo, Mexico City

Published in the United States of America by Cambridge University Press, New York

www.cambridge.org
Information on this title: www.cambridge.org/9781108039376



This edition first published 1874
This digitally printed version 2011

ISBN 978-1-108-03937-6 Paperback

# THE LIFE

OF

Photᵈ. in America. J.C. Armytage.

CHARLES DICKENS.

ÆT. 56.

# THE LIFE

OF

# CHARLES DICKENS.

BY JOHN FORSTER.

VOLUME THE THIRD.

1852—1870.

LONDON:
CHAPMAN AND HALL, 193, PICCADILLY.
1874.

LONDON:
BRADBURY, AGNEW, & CO., PRINTERS, WHITEFRIARS.

## ILLUSTRATIONS.

# TABLE OF CONTENTS.

## CHAPTER I. 1850-1853.

Pages 1–30.

DAVID COPPERFIELD AND BLEAK HOUSE. ÆT. 38-41.



## CHAPTER II. 1853–1855.

Pages 31–54.

HOME INCIDENTS AND HARD TIMES. ÆT. 41–43.

## CHAPTER III. 1853.

Pages 55–74.

SWITZERLAND AND ITALY REVISITED. ÆT. 41.



## CHAPTER IV. 1853, 1854, and 1856.

Pages 75-98.

THREE SUMMERS AT BOULOGNE. ÆT. 41, 42, 44.



## CHAPTER V. 1855, 1856.

Pages 99–130.

RESIDENCE IN PARIS. ÆT. 43-44.

## CHAPTER VI. 1855-1857.

Pages 131–152.

LITTLE DORRIT, AND A LAZY TOUR. ÆT. 43–45.



## CHAPTER VII. 1857-1858.

Pages 153–176.

WHAT HAPPENED AT THIS TIME. ÆT. 45–46.



## CHAPTER VIII. 1856–1870.

Pages 177–195.

GADSHILL PLACE. ÆT. 44–58.

## CHAPTER IX. 1858–1859.

Pages 196–210.

First Paid Readings. Æt. 46-47.



## CHAPTER X. 1859–1861.

Pages 211–225.

All the Year Round and the Uncommercial Traveller. Æt. 47-49.



## CHAPTER XI. 1861–1863.

Pages 226–244.

Second Series of Readings. Æt. 49-51.

## CHAPTER XV. 1867.

Pages 353-371.

AMERICA REVISITED. NOVEMBER AND DECEMBER, 1867. ÆT. 55.

## CHAPTER XVI. 1868.

Pages 372–407.

AMERICA REVISITED. JANUARY TO APRIL, 1868. ÆT. 56.



## CHAPTER XVII. 1868-1870.

Pages 408–423.

LAST READINGS. ÆT. 56–58.



## CHAPTER XVIII. 1869-1870.

Pages 424–439.

LAST BOOK. ÆT. 57–58.

## CHAPTER XIX. 1836-1870.

Pages 440–486.

PERSONAL CHARACTERISTICS.

ÆT. 24–58.



## CHAPTER XX. 1869-1870.

Pages 487–504.

THE END. ÆT. 57–58.

THE

# LIFE OF CHARLES DICKENS.

## CHAPTER I.

### DAVID COPPERFIELD AND BLEAK HOUSE.

1850—1853.

LONDON: 1850.

DICKENS never stood so high in reputation as at the completion of *Copperfield*. The popularity it obtained at the outset increased to a degree not approached by any previous book excepting *Pickwick*. 'You gratify me more 'than I can tell you,' he wrote to Bulwer Lytton (July 1850), 'by what you say about *Copperfield*, because I 'hope myself that some heretofore deficient qualities are 'there.' If the power was not greater than in *Chuzzlewit*, the subject had more attractiveness; there was more variety of incident, with a freer play of character; and there was withal a suspicion, which though general and vague had sharpened interest not a little, that underneath the fiction lay something of the author's life. How much, was not known by the world until he had passed away.

Interest of *Copperfield*.

To be acquainted with English literature is to know,

LONDON: 1850.

that, into its most famous prose fiction, autobiography has entered largely in disguise, and that the characters most familiar to us in the English novel had originals in actual life. Smollett never wrote a story that was not in some degree a recollection of his own adventures; and Fielding, who put something of his wife into all his heroines, had been as fortunate in finding, not Trulliber only, but Parson Adams himself, among his living experiences. To come later down, there was hardly any one ever known to Scott of whom his memory had not treasured up something to give minuter reality to the people of his fancy; and we know exactly whom to look for in Dandie Dinmont and Jonathan Oldbuck, in the office of Alan Fairford and the sick room of Crystal Croftangry. We are to observe also that it is never anything complete that is thus taken from life by a genuine writer, but only leading traits, or such as may give greater finish; that the fine artist will embody in his portraiture of one person his experiences of fifty; and that this would have been Fielding's answer to Trulliber if he had objected to the pigstye, and to Adams if he had sought to make a case of scandal out of the affair in Mrs. Slipslop's bedroom. Such questioning befell Dickens repeatedly in the course of his writings, where he freely followed, as we have seen, the method thus common to the masters in his art; but there was an instance of alleged wrong in the course of *Copperfield* where he felt his vindication to be hardly complete, and what he did thereupon was characteristic.

Real people in novels.

Scott, Smollett, and Fielding.

A complaint.

'I have had the queerest adventure this morning,' he wrote (28th of December 1849) on the eve of his tenth

LONDON: 1850.

number, 'the receipt of the enclosed from Miss Moucher! 'It is serio-comic, but there is no doubt one is wrong in 'being tempted to such a use of power.' Thinking a grotesque little oddity among his acquaintance to be safe from recognition, he had done what Smollett did sometimes, but never Fielding, and given way, in the first outburst of fun that had broken out around the fancy, to the temptation of copying too closely peculiarities of figure and face amounting in effect to deformity. He was shocked at discovering the pain he had given, and a copy is before me of the assurances by way of reply which he at once sent to the complainant. That he was grieved and surprised beyond measure. That he had not intended her altogether. That all his characters, being made up out of many people, were composite, and never individual. That the chair (for table) and other matters were undoubtedly from her, but that other traits were not hers at all; and that in Miss Moucher's 'Ain't I volatile' his friends had quite correctly recognized the favourite utterance of a different person. That he felt nevertheless he had done wrong, and would now do anything to repair it. That he had intended to employ the character in an unpleasant way, but he would, whatever the risk or inconvenience, change it all, so that nothing but an agreeable impression should be left. The reader will remember how this was managed, and that the thirty-second chapter went far to undo what the twenty-second had done.

Too close to the Real.

Confession and atonement.

A much earlier instance is the only one known to me where a character in one of his books intended to be odious was copied wholly from a living original. The use

LONDON: 1850.

of such material, never without danger, might have been justifiable here if anywhere, and he had himself a satisfaction in always admitting the identity of Mr. Fang in *Oliver Twist* with Mr. Laing of Hatton-garden. But the avowal of his purpose in that case, and his mode of setting about it, mark strongly a difference of procedure from that which, following great examples, he adopted in his later books. An allusion to a common friend in one of his letters of the present date—'A dreadful thought occurs 'to me! how brilliant in a book!'—expresses both the continued strength of his temptations and the dread he had brought himself to feel of immediately yielding to them; but he had no such misgivings in the days of *Oliver Twist*. Wanting an insolent and harsh police-magistrate, he bethought him of an original ready to his hand in one of the London offices; and instead of pursuing his later method of giving a personal appearance that should in some sort render difficult the identification of mental peculiarities, he was only eager to get in the whole man complete upon his page, figure and face as well as manners and mind.

Earlier and later methods.

A want for *Oliver Twist*.

He wrote accordingly (from Doughty-street on the 3rd of June 1837) to Mr. Haines,* a gentleman who then had general supervision over the police reports for the daily papers. 'In my next number of *Oliver Twist* I must have 'a magistrate; and, casting about for a magistrate whose 'harshness and insolence would render him a fit subject 'to be *shown up*, I have as a necessary consequence stum- 'bled upon Mr. Laing of Hatton-garden celebrity. I know

Mr. Laing for Mr. Fang.

* This letter is now in the possession of S. R. Goodman Esq. of Brighton.

'the man's character perfectly well; but as it would be 'necessary to describe his personal appearance also, I ought 'to have seen him, which (fortunately or unfortunately as 'the case may be) I have never done. In this dilemma 'it occurred to me that perhaps I might under your aus-'pices be smuggled into the Hatton-garden office for a few 'moments some morning. If you can further my object I 'shall be really very greatly obliged to you.' The opportunity was found; the magistrate was brought up before the novelist; and shortly after, on some fresh outbreak of intolerable temper, the home-secretary found it an easy and popular step to remove Mr. Laing from the bench.

Dickens at Hatton-garden (1837).

This was a comfort to everybody, saving only the principal person; but the instance was highly exceptional, and it rarely indeed happens that to the individual objection natural in every such case some consideration should not be paid. In the book that followed *Copperfield*, two characters appeared having resemblances in manner and speech to two distinguished writers too vivid to be mistaken by their personal friends. To Lawrence Boythorn, under whom Landor figured, no objection was made; but Harold Skimpole, recognizable for Leigh Hunt, led to much remark; the difference being, that ludicrous traits were employed in the first to enrich without impairing an attractive person in the tale, whereas to the last was assigned a part in the plot which no fascinating foibles or gaieties of speech could redeem from contempt. Though a want of consideration was thus shown to the friend whom the character would be likely to recall to many readers, it is nevertheless very certain that the intention of Dickens was not at first,

Originals of Boythorn and Skimpole.

LONDON: 1850.

or at any time, an unkind one. He erred from thoughtlessness only. What led him to the subject at all, he has himself stated. Hunt's philosophy of moneyed obligations, always, though loudly, half jocosely proclaimed, and his ostentatious wilfulness in the humouring of that or any other theme on which he cared for the time to expatiate,* had so often seemed to Dickens to be whimsical and attractive that, wanting an 'airy quality' for the man he invented, this of Hunt occurred to him; and 'partly for that 'reason, and partly, he has since often grieved to think, for 'the pleasure it afforded to find a delightful manner repro-'ducing itself under his hand, he yielded to the temptation 'of too often making the character speak like his old

Yielding to temptation.

* Here are two passages taken from Hunt's writing in the *Tatler* (a charming little paper which it was one of the first ventures of the young firm of Chapman and Hall to attempt to establish for Hunt in 1830), to which accident had unluckily attracted Dickens's notice:—'Supposing us to be in want 'of patronage, and in possession of talent enough to make it an honour to 'notice us, we would much rather have some great and comparatively private 'friend, rich enough to assist us, and amiable enough to render obligation 'delightful, than become the public property of any man, or of any govern-'ment. . . . . If a divinity had given us our choice we should have said—'make us La Fontaine, who goes and lives twenty years with some rich friend, 'as innocent of any harm in it as a child, and who writes what he thinks 'charming verses, sitting all day under a tree.' Such sayings will not bear to be deliberately read and thought over, but any kind of extravagance or oddity came from Hunt's lips with a curious fascination. There was surely never a man of so sunny a nature, who could draw so much pleasure from common things, or to whom books were a world so real, so exhaustless, so delightful. I was only seventeen when I derived from him the tastes which have been the solace of all subsequent years, and I well remember the last time I saw him at Hammersmith, not long before his death in 1859, when, with his delicate, worn, but keenly intellectual face, his large luminous eyes, his thick shock of wiry grey hair, and a little cape of faded black silk over his shoulders, he looked like an old French abbé. He was buoyant and pleasant as ever; and was busy upon a vindication of Chaucer and Spenser from Cardinal Wiseman, who had attacked them for alleged sensuous and voluptuous qualities.

Sayings from Hunt's *Tatler*.

Last glimpse of Leigh Hunt (1859).

LONDON: 1850.

'friend.' This apology was made* after Hunt's death, and mentioned a revision of the first sketch, so as to render it less like, at the suggestion of two other friends of Hunt. The friends were Procter (Barry Cornwall) and myself; the feeling having been mine from the first that the likeness was too like. Procter did not immediately think so, but a little reflection brought him to that opinion. 'You 'will see from the enclosed,' Dickens wrote (17th of March 1852), 'that Procter is much of my mind. I will never-'theless go through the character again in the course of the 'afternoon, and soften down words here and there.' But before the day closed Procter had again written to him, and next morning this was the result. 'I have again gone 'over every part of it very carefully, and I think I have 'made it much less like. I have also changed Leonard 'to Harold. I have no right to give Hunt pain, and I am 'so bent upon not doing it that I wish you would look at 'all the proof once more, and indicate any particular place 'in which you feel it particularly like. Whereupon I will 'alter that place.'

Friends consulted.

Changes made in Skimpole.

Upon the whole the alterations were considerable, but the radical wrong remained. The pleasant sparkling airy talk, which could not be mistaken, identified with odious qualities a friend only known to the writer by attractive ones; and for this there was no excuse. Perhaps the only person acquainted with the original who failed to recognize the copy, was the original himself (a common case); but good-natured friends in time told Hunt everything, and painful explanations followed, where nothing

The wrong not remedied.

* In a paper in *All the Year Round*.

LONDON: 1850.

was possible to Dickens but what amounted to a friendly evasion of the points really at issue. The time for redress had gone. I yet well remember with what eager earnestness, on one of these occasions, he strove to set Hunt up again in his own esteem. 'Separate in your own 'mind,' he said to him, 'what you see of yourself from what 'other people tell you that they see. As it has given you 'so much pain, I take it at its worst, and say I am deeply 'sorry, and that I feel I did wrong in doing it. I should 'otherwise have taken it at its best, and ridden off upon 'what I strongly feel to be the truth, that there is nothing 'in it that *should* have given you pain. Every one in 'writing must speak from points of his experience, and so 'I of mine with you: but when I have felt it was going too 'close I stopped myself, and the most blotted parts of my 'MS. are those in which I have been striving hard to make 'the impression I was writing from, *un*like you. The 'diary-writing I took from Haydon, not from you. I now 'first learn from yourself that you ever set anything to 'music, and I could not have copied *that* from you. The 'character is not you, for there are traits in it common to 'fifty thousand people besides, and I did not fancy you 'would ever recognize it. Under similar disguises my own 'father and mother are in my books, and you might as well 'see your likeness in Micawber.' The distinction is that the foibles of Mr. Micawber and of Mrs. Nickleby, however laughable, make neither of them in speech or character less loveable; and that this is not to be said of Skimpole's. The kindly or unkindly impression makes all the difference where liberties are taken with a friend; and even this

C. D. to Leigh Hunt.

Self-defence.

Relatives put into books.

entirely favourable condition will not excuse the practice to many, where near relatives are concerned. LONDON: 1850.

For what formerly was said of the Micawber resemblances, Dickens has been sharply criticized; and in like manner it was thought objectionable in Scott that for the closing scenes of Crystal Croftangry he should have found the original of his fretful patient at the death-bed of his own father. Lockhart, who tells us this, adds with a sad significance that he himself lived to see the curtain fall at Abbotsford upon even such another scene. But to no purpose will such objections still be made. All great novelists will continue to use their experiences of nature and fact, whencesoever derivable; and a remark made to Lockhart by Scott himself suggests their vindication. 'If 'a man will paint from nature, he will be most likely to 'interest and amuse those who are daily looking at it.'

Scott and his father.

Scott to Lockhart.

The Micawber offence otherwise was not grave. We have seen in what way Dickens was moved or inspired by the rough lessons of his boyhood, and the groundwork of the character was then undoubtedly laid; but the rhetorical exuberance impressed itself upon him later, and from this, as it expanded and developed in a thousand amusing ways, the full-length figure took its great charm. Better illustration of it could not perhaps be given than by passages from letters of Dickens, written long before Micawber was thought of, in which this peculiarity of his father found frequent and always agreeable expression. Several such have been given in this work from time to time, and one or two more may here be added. It is proper to preface them by saying that no one could know the elder Dickens

Dickens and his father.

LONDON: 1850.

without secretly liking him the better for these flourishes of speech, which adapted themselves so readily to his gloom as well as to his cheerfulness, that it was difficult not to fancy they had helped him considerably in both, and had rendered more tolerable to him, if also more possible, the shade and sunshine of his chequered life. 'If you should 'have an opportunity *pendente lite*, as my father would 'observe—indeed did on some memorable ancient occa-'sions when he informed me that the ban-dogs would 'shortly have him at bay'—Dickens wrote in December 1847. 'I have a letter from my father' (May 1841) 'lamenting the fine weather, invoking congenial tempests, 'and informing me that it will not be possible for him to 'stay more than another year in Devonshire, as he must 'then proceed to Paris to consolidate Augustus's French.' 'There has arrived,' he writes from the Peschiere in September 1844, 'a characteristic letter for Kate from my 'father. He dates it Manchester, and says he has reason 'to believe that he will be in town with the pheasants, on 'or about the first of October. He has been with Fanny 'in the Isle of Man for nearly two months: finding there, 'as he goes on to observe, troops of friends, and every 'description of continental luxury at a cheap rate.' Describing in the same year the departure from Genoa of an English physician and acquaintance, he adds: 'We are 'very sorry to lose the benefit of his advice—or, as my 'father would say, to be deprived, to a certain extent, of 'the concomitant advantages, whatever they may be, re-'sulting from his medical skill, such as it is, and his pro-'fessional attendance, in so far as it may be so considered.'

Flourishes of speech.

i. 161.

Micawber flights.

LONDON: 1850.

Sayings of John Dickens.

Thus also it delighted Dickens to remember that it was of one of his connections his father wrote a celebrated sentence; 'And I must express my tendency to believe that 'his longevity is (to say the least of it) extremely proble-'matical:' and that it was to another, who had been insisting somewhat obtrusively on dissenting and nonconformist superiorities, he addressed words which deserve to be no less celebrated; 'The Supreme Being must be an entirely 'different individual from what I have every reason to 'believe him to be, if He would care in the least for the 'society of your relations.' There was a laugh in the enjoyment of all this, no doubt, but with it much personal fondness; and the feeling of the creator of Micawber as he thus humoured and remembered the foibles of his original, found its counterpart in that of his readers for the creation itself, as its part was played out in the story. Nobody likes Micawber less for his follies; and Dickens liked his father more, the more he recalled his whimsical qualities. 'The longer I live, the better man I think 'him,' he exclaimed afterwards. The fact and the fancy had united whatever was most grateful to him in both.

Humouring a foible.

No harm done.

It is a tribute to the generally healthful and manly tone of the story of *Copperfield* that such should be the outcome of the eccentricities of this leading personage in it; and the superiority in this respect of Micawber over Skimpole is one of many indications of the inferiority of *Bleak House* to its predecessor. With leading resemblances that make it difficult to say which character best represents the principle or no principle of impecuniosity, there cannot be any doubt which has the advantage in moral

LONDON: 1850.

Resemblances and differences.

and intellectual development. It is genuine humour against personal satire. Between the worldly circumstances of the two, there is nothing to choose; but as to everything else it is the difference between shabbiness and greatness. Skimpole's sunny talk might be expected to please as much as Micawber's gorgeous speech, the design of both being to take the edge off poverty. But in the one we have no relief from attendant meanness or distress, and we drop down from the airiest fancies into sordidness and pain; whereas in the other nothing pitiful or merely selfish ever touches us. At its lowest depth of what is worst, we never doubt that something better must turn up; and of a man who sells his bedstead that he may entertain his friend, we altogether refuse to think nothing but badly. This is throughout the free and cheery style of *Copperfield*. The masterpieces of Dickens's humour are not in it; but he has nowhere given such variety of play to his invention, and the book is unapproached among his writings for its completeness of effect and uniform pleasantness of tone.

Skimpole and Micawber.

What has to be said hereafter of those writings generally, will properly restrict what is said here, as in previous instances, mainly to personal illustration. The *Copperfield* disclosures formerly made will for ever connect the book with the author's individual story; but too much has been assumed, from those revelations, of a full identity of Dickens with his hero, and of a supposed intention that his own character as well as parts of his career should be expressed in the narrative. It is right to warn the reader as to this. He can judge for himself how far the childish experiences

Dickens and David.

are likely to have given the turn to Dickens's genius; whether their bitterness had so burnt into his nature, as, in the hatred of oppression, the revolt against abuse of power, and the war with injustice under every form displayed in his earliest books, to have reproduced itself only; and to what extent mere compassion for his own childhood may account for the strange fascination always exerted over him by child-suffering and sorrow. But, many as are the resemblances in Copperfield's adventures to portions of those of Dickens, and often as reflections occur to David which no one intimate with Dickens could fail to recognize as but the reproduction of his, it would be the greatest mistake to imagine anything like a complete identity of the fictitious novelist with the real one, beyond the Hungerford scenes; or to suppose that the youth, who then received his first harsh schooling in life, came out of it as little harmed or hardened as David did. The language of the fiction reflects only faintly the narrative of the actual fact; and the man whose character it helped to form was expressed not less faintly in the impulsive impressionable youth, incapable of resisting the leading of others, and only disciplined into self-control by the later griefs of his entrance into manhood. Here was but another proof how thoroughly Dickens understood his calling, and that to weave fact with fiction unskilfully would be only to make truth less true.

Outcome of early trials.

Self-portraiture not attempted.

Compare i. 30-50 with 11th chapter of *Copperfield*.

The character of the hero of the novel finds indeed his right place in the story he is supposed to tell, rather by unlikeness than by likeness to Dickens, even where intentional resemblance might seem to be prominent. Take

LONDON: 1850.

The auto-biographic form.

autobiography as a design to show that any man's life may be as a mirror of existence to all men, and the individual career becomes altogether secondary to the variety of experiences received and rendered back in it. This particular form in imaginative literature has too often led to the indulgence of mental analysis, metaphysics, and sentiment, all in excess: but Dickens was carried safely over these

Its dangers avoided.

allurements by a healthy judgment and sleepless creative fancy; and even the method of his narrative is more simple here than it generally is in his books. His imaginative growths have less luxuriance of underwood, and the crowds of external images always rising so vividly before him are more within control.

Consider Copperfield thus in his proper place in the story, and sequence as well as connection will be given to the varieties of its childish adventure. The first warm nest of love in which his vain fond mother, and her quaint kind servant, cherish him; the quick-following contrast of

Consistent drawing.

hard dependence and servile treatment; the escape from that premature and dwarfed maturity by natural relapse into a more perfect childhood; the then leisurely growth of emotions and faculties into manhood; these are component parts of a character consistently drawn. The sum of its achievement is to be a successful cultivation of letters; and often as such imaginary discipline has been the theme of fiction, there are not many happier conceptions of it. The ideal and real parts of the boy's nature receive development in the proportions which contribute best to the end desired; the readiness for impulsive attachments that had put him into the leading of others, has underneath it

London: 1850.

a base of truthfulness on which at last he rests in safety; the practical man is the outcome of the fanciful youth; and a more than equivalent for the graces of his visionary days, is found in the active sympathies that life has opened to him. Many experiences have come within its range, and his heart has had room for all. Our interest in him cannot but be increased by knowing how much he expresses of what the author had himself gone through; but David includes far less than this, and infinitely more.

Design of David's character.

That the incidents arise easily, and to the very end connect themselves naturally and unobtrusively with the characters of which they are a part, is to be said perhaps more truly of this than of any other of Dickens's novels. There is a profusion of distinct and distinguishable people, and a prodigal wealth of detail; but unity of drift or purpose is apparent always, and the tone is uniformly right. By the course of the events we learn the value of self-denial and patience, quiet endurance of unavoidable ills, strenuous effort against ills remediable; and everything in the fortunes of the actors warns us, to strengthen our generous emotions and to guard the purities of home. It is easy thus to account for the supreme popularity of *Copperfield*, without the addition that it can hardly have had a reader, man or lad, who did not discover that he was something of a Copperfield himself. Childhood and youth live again for all of us in its marvellous boy-experiences. Mr. Micawber's presence must not prevent my saying that it does not take the lead of the other novels in humorous creation; but in the use of humour to bring out prominently the ludicrous in any object or incident without excluding

Tone of the novel.

Its boy-life.

Humour and sentiment.

LONDON: 1850.

or weakening its most enchanting sentiment, it stands decidedly first. It is the perfection of English mirth. We are apt to resent the exhibition of too much goodness, but it is here so qualified by oddity as to become not merely palatable but attractive; and even pathos is heightened by what in other hands would only make it comical. That there are also faults in the book is certain, but none that are incompatible with the most masterly qualities.; and a book becomes everlasting by the fact, not that faults are not in it, but that genius nevertheless is there.

Why books continue.

Of its method, and its author's generally, in the delineation of character, something will have to be said on a later page. The author's own favourite people in it, I think, were the Peggotty group; and perhaps he was not far wrong. It has been their fate, as with all the leading figures of his invention, to pass their names into the language, and become types; and he has nowhere given happier embodiment to that purity of homely goodness, which, by the kindly and all-reconciling influences of humour, may exalt into comeliness and even grandeur the clumsiest forms of humanity. What has been indicated in the style of the book as its greatest charm is here felt most strongly. The ludicrous so helps the pathos, and the humour so uplifts and refines the sentiment, that mere rude affection and simple manliness in these Yarmouth boatmen, passed through the fires of unmerited suffering and heroic endurance, take forms half-chivalrous half-sublime. It is one of the cants of critical superiority to make supercilious mention of the serious passages in this great writer; but the storm and shipwreck at the close of *Copperfield*, when

The Peggottys.

LONDON: 1850.

The storm and shipwreck.

the body of the seducer is flung dead upon the shore amid the ruins of the home he has wasted and by the side of the man whose heart he has broken, the one as unconscious of what he had failed to reach as the other of what he has perished to save, is a description that may compare with the most impressive in the language. There are other people drawn into this catastrophe who are among the failures of natural delineation in the book. But though Miss Dartle is curiously unpleasant, there are some natural traits in her (which Dickens's least life-like people are never without); and it was from one of his lady friends, very familiar to him indeed, he copied her peculiarity of never saying anything outright, but hinting it merely, and making more of it that way. Of Mrs. Steerforth it may also be worth remembering that Thackeray had something of a fondness for her. 'I knew how it would be when I began,' says a pleasant letter all about himself written immediately after she appeared in the story. 'My letters to my mother are 'like this, but then she likes 'em—like Mrs. Steerforth: 'don't you like Mrs. Steerforth?'

Miss Dartle.

Mrs. Steerforth.

Turning to another group there is another elderly lady to be liked without a shadow of misgiving; abrupt, angular, extravagant, but the very soul of magnanimity and rectitude; a character thoroughly made out in all its parts; a gnarled and knotted piece of female timber, sound to the core; a woman Captain Shandy would have loved for her startling oddities, and who is linked to the gentlest of her sex by perfect womanhood. Dickens has done nothing better, for solidness and truth all round, than Betsey Trotwood. It is one of her oddities to have a fool

Betsey Trotwood.

LONDON: 1850.

for a companion; but this is one of them that has also most pertinence and wisdom. By a line thrown out in *Wilhelm Meister*, that the true way of treating the insane was, in all respects possible, to act to them as if they were sane, Goethe anticipated what it took a century to apply to the most terrible disorder of humanity; and what Mrs. Trotwood does for Mr. Dick goes a step farther, by showing how often asylums might be dispensed with, and how large might be the number of deficient intellects manageable with patience in their own homes. Characters hardly less distinguishable for truth as well as oddity are the kind old nurse and her husband the carrier, whose vicissitudes alike of love and of mortality are condensed into the three words since become part of universal speech, *Barkis is willin'*. There is wholesome satire of much utility in the conversion of the brutal schoolmaster of the earlier scenes into the tender Middlesex magistrate at the close. Nor is the humour anywhere more subtle than in the country undertaker, who makes up in fullness of heart for scantness of breath, and has so little of the vampire propensity of the town undertaker in *Chuzzlewit*, that he dares not even inquire after friends who are ill for fear of unkindly misconstruction. The test of a master in creative fiction, according to Hazlitt, is less in contrasting characters that are unlike than in distinguishing those that are like; and to many examples of the art in Dickens, such as the Shepherd and Chadband, Creakle and Squeers, Charley Bates and the Dodger, the Guppys and the Wemmicks, Mr. Jaggers and Mr. Vholes, Sampson Brass and Conversation Kenge, Jack Bunsby, Captain Cuttle, and Bill Barley,

Wise hint of Goethe's.

Truths in oddities.

A country undertaker.

the Perkers and Pells, the Dodsons and Fogs, Sarah Gamp and Betsy Prig, and a host of others, is to be added the nicety of distinction between those eminent furnishers of funerals, Mr. Mould and Messrs. Omer and Joram. All the mixed mirth and sadness of the story are skilfully drawn into the handling of this portion of it; and, amid wooings and preparations for weddings and church-ringing bells for baptisms, the steadily-going rat-tat of the hammer on the coffin is heard.

Characters like yet unlike.

Of the heroines who divide so equally between them the impulsive, easily swayed, not disloyal but sorely distracted affections of the hero, the spoilt foolishness and tenderness of the loving little child-wife, Dora, is more attractive than the too unfailing wisdom and self-sacrificing goodness of the angel-wife, Agnes. The scenes of the courtship and housekeeping are matchless; and the glimpses of Doctors' Commons, opening those views, by Mr. Spenlow, of man's vanity of expectation and inconsistency of conduct in neglecting the sacred duty of making a will, on which he largely moralizes the day before he dies intestate, form a background highly appropriate to David's domesticities. This was among the reproductions of personal experience in the book; but it was a sadder knowledge that came with the conviction some years later, that David's contrasts in his earliest married life between his happiness enjoyed and his happiness once anticipated, the 'vague unhappy loss or 'want of something' of which he so frequently complains, reflected also a personal experience which had not been supplied in fact so successfully as in fiction. (A closing word may perhaps be allowed, to connect with Devonshire-terrace

The two heroines.

Doctors' Commons experience.

LONDON: 1853.

the last book written there. On the page opposite is engraved a drawing by Maclise of the house where so many of Dickens's masterpieces were composed, done on the first anniversary of the day when his daughter Kate was born.)

Contrast of Esther and David.

*Bleak House* followed *Copperfield,* which in some respects it copied in the autobiographical form by means of extracts from the personal relation of its heroine. But the distinction between the narrative of David and the diary of Esther, like that between Micawber and Skimpole, marks the superiority of the first to its successor. To represent a storyteller as giving the most surprising vividness to manners, motives, and characters of which we are to believe her, all the time, as artlessly unconscious, as she is also entirely ignorant of the good qualities in herself she is naïvely revealing in the story, was a difficult enterprise, full of hazard in any case, not worth success, and certainly not successful. Ingenuity is more apparent than freshness, the invention is neither easy nor unstrained, and though the old marvellous power over the real is again abundantly manifest, there is some alloy of the artificial. Nor can this be said of Esther's relation without some general application to the book of which it forms so large a part. The novel is nevertheless, in the very important particular of construction, perhaps the best thing done by Dickens.

Risks not worth running.

In his later writings he had been assiduously cultivating this essential of his art, and here he brought it very nearly to perfection. Of the tendency of composing a story piecemeal to induce greater concern for the part than for the whole, he had been always conscious; but I remember a remark also made by him to the effect that to read a story

LONDON: 1840.

DEVONSHIRE-TERRACE: 29th October 1840.

LONDON: 1853.

Writing and reading in parts.

in parts had no less a tendency to prevent the reader's noticing how thoroughly a work so presented might be calculated for perusal as a whole. Look back from the last to the first page of the present novel, and not even in the highest examples of this kind of elaborate care will it be found, that event leads more closely to event, or that the separate incidents have been planned with a more studied consideration of the bearing they are severally to have on the general result. Nothing is introduced at random, everything tends to the catastrophe, the various lines of the plot converge and fit to its centre, and to the larger interest all the rest is irresistibly drawn. The heart of the story is a Chancery suit. On this the plot hinges and on incidents connected with it, trivial or important, the passion and suffering turn exclusively. Chance words, or the deeds of chance people, to appearance irrelevant, are found everywhere influencing the course taken by a train of incidents of which the issue is life or death, happiness or misery, to men and women perfectly unknown to them, and to whom they are unknown. Attorneys of all possible grades, law clerks of every conceivable kind, the copyist, the law stationer, the usurer, all sorts of money lenders, suitors of every description, haunters of the Chancery court and their victims, are for ever moving round about the lives of the chief persons in the tale, and drawing them on insensibly, but very certainly, to the issues that await them. Even the fits of the little law-stationer's servant help directly in the chain of small things that lead indirectly to Lady Dedlock's death. One strong chain of interest holds together Chesney Wold and its inmates,

Plot of the story.

Constructive art.

Incidents and persons interwoven.

LONDON: 1853.

Bleak House and the Jarndyce group, Chancery with its sorry and sordid neighbourhood. The characters multiply as the tale advances, but in each the drift is the same. 'There's no great odds betwixt my noble and learned 'brother and myself,' says the grotesque proprietor of the rag and bottle shop under the wall of Lincoln's-inn, 'they 'call me Lord Chancellor and my shop Chancery, and we 'both of us grub on in a muddle.' *Edax rerum* the motto of both, but with a difference. Out of the lumber of the shop emerge slowly some fragments of evidence by which the chief actors in the story are sensibly affected, and to which Chancery itself might have succumbed if its devouring capacities had been less complete. But by the time there is found among the lumber the will which puts all to rights in the Jarndyce suit, it is found to be too late to put anything to rights. The costs have swallowed up the estate, and there is an end of the matter.

Two Chancery shops.

Shells of the oyster.

What in one sense is a merit however may in others be a defect, and this book has suffered by the very completeness with which its Chancery moral is worked out. The didactic in Dickens's earlier novels derived its strength from being merely incidental to interest of a higher and more permanent kind, and not in a small degree from the playful sportiveness and fancy that lighted up its graver illustrations. Here it is of sterner stuff, too little relieved, and all-pervading. The fog so marvellously painted in the opening chapter has hardly cleared away when there arises, in *Jarndyce* v. *Jarndyce*, as bad an atmosphere to breathe in; and thenceforward to the end, clinging round the people of the story as they come or go, in dreary mist

Defects of *Bleak House.*

LONDON: 1853.

or in heavy cloud, it is rarely absent. Dickens has himself described his purpose to have been to dwell on the romantic side of familiar things. But it is the romance of discontent and misery, with a very restless dissatisfied moral, and is too much brought about by agencies disagreeable and sordid. The Guppys, Weevles, Snagsbys, Chadbands, Krooks, and Smallweeds, even the Kenges, Vholeses, and Tulkinghorns, are much too real to be pleasant; and the necessity becomes urgent for the reliefs and contrasts of a finer humanity. These last are not wanting; yet it must be said that we hardly escape, even with them, into the old freedom and freshness of the author's imaginative worlds, and that the too conscious unconsciousness of Esther flings something of a shade on the radiant goodness of John Jarndyce himself. Nevertheless there are very fine delineations in the story. The crazed little Chancery lunatic, Miss Flite; the loud-voiced tender-souled Chancery victim, Gridley; the poor good-hearted youth Richard, broken up in life and character by the suspense of the Chancery suit on whose success he is to 'begin the world,' believing himself to be saving money when he is stopped from squandering it, and thinking that having saved it he is entitled to fling it away; trooper George, with the Bagnets and their household, where the most ludicrous points are more forcible for the pathetic touches underlying them; the Jellyby interior, and its philanthropic strong-minded mistress, placid and smiling amid a household muddle outmuddling Chancery itself; the model of deportment, Turveydrop the elder, whose relations to the young people, whom he so superbly patronizes by being dependent on

Too little relief.

Set-offs.

Successes in character.

them for everything, touch delightfully some subtle points of truth; the inscrutable Tulkinghorn, and the immortal Bucket; all these, and especially the last, have been added by this book to the list of people more intimately and permanently known to us than the scores of actual familiar acquaintance whom we see around us living and dying.

LONDON: 1853.

Praise with a grudge.

But how do we know them? There are plenty to tell us that it is by vividness of external observation rather than by depth of imaginative insight, by tricks of manner and phrase rather than by truth of character, by manifestation outwardly rather than by what lies behind. Another opportunity will present itself for some remark on this kind of criticism, which has always had a special pride in the subtlety of its differences from what the world may have shown itself prone to admire. 'In my father's 'library,' wrote Landor to Southey's daughter Edith, 'was 'the *Critical Review* from its commencement; and it 'would have taught me, if I could not even at a very early 'age teach myself better, that Fielding, Sterne, and Goldsmith were really worth nothing.' It is a style that will never be without cultivators, and its frequent application to Dickens will be shown hereafter. But in speaking of a book in which some want of all the freshness of his genius first became apparent, it would be wrong to omit to add that his method of handling a character is as strongly impressed on the better portions of it as on the best of his writings. It is difficult to say when a peculiarity becomes too grotesque, or an extravagance too farcical, to be within the limits of art, for it is the truth of these as of graver things that they exist in the world in just the proportions and

Value of critical judgments.

What Art has room for.

LONDON: 1853.

degree in which genius can discover them. But no man had ever so surprising a faculty as Dickens of becoming himself what he was representing; and of entering into mental phases and processes so absolutely, in conditions of life the most varied, as to reproduce them completely in dialogue without need of an explanatory word. (He only departed from this method once, with a result which will then be pointed out.) In speaking on a former page of the impression of reality thus to a singular degree conveyed by him, it was remarked that where characters so revealed themselves the author's part in them was done; and in the book under notice there is none, not excepting those least attractive which apparently present only prominent or salient qualities, in which it will not be found that the characteristic feature embodied, or the main idea personified, contains as certainly also some human truth universally applicable. To expound or discuss his creations, to lay them psychologically bare, to analyse their organisms, to subject to minute demonstration their fibrous and other tissues, was not at all Dickens's way. His genius was his fellow feeling with his race; his mere personality was never the bound or limit to his perceptions, however strongly sometimes it might colour them; he never stopped to dissect or anatomize his own work; but no man could better adjust the outward and visible oddities in a delineation to its inner and unchangeable veracities. The rough estimates we form of character, if we have any truth of perception, are on the whole correct: but men touch and interfere with one another by the contact of their extremes, and it may very often become necessarily

Mastery in dialogue.

Handling of character.

The contact of extremes.

LONDON: 1853.

the main business of a novelist to display the salient points, the sharp angles, or the prominences merely.

Pathetic touches.

The pathetic parts of *Bleak House* do not live largely in remembrance, but the deaths of Richard and of Gridley, the wandering fancies of Miss Flite, and the extremely touching way in which the gentleman-nature of the pompous old baronet, Dedlock, asserts itself under suffering, belong to a high order of writing. There is another most affecting example, taking the lead of the rest, in the poor street-sweeper Jo; which has made perhaps as deep an impression as anything in Dickens. 'We have been reading *Bleak House* 'aloud,' the good Dean Ramsay wrote to me very shortly before his death. 'Surely it is one of his most powerful 'and successful! What a triumph is Jo! Uncultured 'nature is *there* indeed; the intimations of true heart-'feeling, the glimmerings of higher feeling, all are there; 'but everything still consistent and in harmony. Won-'derful is the genius that can show all this, yet keep it 'only and really part of the character itself, low or common 'as it may be, and use no morbid or fictitious colouring. 'To my mind, nothing in the field of fiction is to be found 'in English literature surpassing the death of Jo!' What occurs at and after the inquest is as worth remembering. Jo's evidence is rejected because he cannot exactly say what will be done to him after he is dead if he should tell a lie;* but he manages to say afterwards very exactly

Dean Ramsay on *Bleak House* and Jo.

The inquest.

* 'O! Here's the boy, gentlemen! Here he is, very muddy, very hoarse, 'very ragged. Now, boy!—But stop a minute. Caution. This boy must be 'put through a few preliminary paces. Name, Jo. Nothing else that he 'knows on. Don't know that everybody has two names. Never heerd of sich 'a think. Don't know that Jo is short for a longer name. Thinks it long

LONDON: 1853.

What Jo cannot say exactly.

What he remembers very exactly.

Town graves.

what the deceased while he lived did to him. That one cold winter night, when he was shivering in a doorway near his crossing, a man turned to look at him, and came back, and, having questioned him and found he had not a friend in the world, said 'Neither have I. Not one!' and gave him the price of a supper and a night's lodging. That the man had often spoken to him since, and asked him if he slept of a night, and how he bore cold and hunger, or if he ever wished to die; and would say in passing 'I am as poor as you to-day, Jo' when he had no money, but when he had any would always give some. 'He wos 'wery good to me,' says the boy, wiping his eyes with his wretched sleeve. 'Wen I see him a-layin' so stritched out 'just now, I wished he could have heerd me tell him so. 'He wos werry good to me, he wos!' The inquest over, the body is flung into a pestiferous churchyard in the next street, houses overlooking it on every side, and a reeking little tunnel of a court giving access to its iron gate. 'With 'the night, comes a slouching figure through the tunnel-'court, to the outside of the iron gate. It holds the gate 'with its hands, and looks in within the bars; stands look-'ing in, for a little while. It then, with an old broom it

'enough for *him*. *He* don't find no fault with it. Spell it? No. *He* can't 'spell it. No father, no mother, no friends. Never been to school. What's 'home? Knows a broom's a broom, and knows it's wicked to tell a lie. 'Don't recollect who told him about the broom, or about the lie, but knows 'both. Can't exactly say what'll be done to him arter he's dead if he tells a 'lie to the gentleman here, but believes it'll be something wery bad to punish 'him, and serve him right—and so he'll tell the truth. "This won't do, '"gentlemen," says the coroner, with a melancholy shake of the head. . . . '"*Can't exactly say* won't do, you know. . . It's terrible depravity. Put '"the boy aside." Boy put aside; to the great edification of the audience;—'especially of Little Swills, the Comic Vocalist.'

LONDON: 1853.

'carries, softly sweeps the step, and makes the archway 'clean. It does so, very busily, and trimly; looks in again, 'a little while; and so departs.' These are among the things in Dickens that cannot be forgotten; and if *Bleak House* had many more faults than have been found in it, such salt and savour as this might freshen it for some generations.

One last friend.

The first intention was to have made Jo more prominent in the story, and its earliest title was taken from the tumbling tenements in Chancery, 'Tom-all-Alone's,' where he finds his wretched habitation; but this was abandoned. On the other hand, Dickens was encouraged and strengthened in his design of assailing Chancery abuses and delays by receiving, a few days after the appearance of his first number, a striking pamphlet on the subject containing details so apposite that he took from them, without change in any material point, the memorable case related in his fifteenth chapter. Any one who examines the tract* will see how exactly true is the reference to it made by Dickens in his preface. 'The case of Gridley is in no essential 'altered from one of actual occurrence, made public by a 'disinterested person who was professionally acquainted 'with the whole of the monstrous wrong from beginning 'to end.' The suit, of which all particulars are given, affected a single farm, in value not more than £1200, but all that its owner possessed in the world, against which a

Originals of Chancery abuses.

The truth of Gridley's case.

* By W. Challinor Esq. of Leek in Staffordshire, by whom it has been obligingly sent to me, with a copy of Dickens's letter acknowledging the receipt of it from the author on the 11th of March 1852. On the first of that month the first number of *Bleak House* had appeared, but two numbers of it were then already written.

London: 1853.

bill had been filed for a £300 legacy left in the will bequeathing the farm. In reality there was only one defendant, but in the bill, by the rule of the Court, there were seventeen; and, after two years had been occupied over the seventeen answers, everything had to begin over again because an eighteenth had been accidentally omitted. 'What a mockery of justice this is,' says Mr. Challinor, 'the facts speak for themselves, and I can personally vouch 'for their accuracy. The costs already incurred in reference 'to this £300 legacy are not less than from £800 to £900, 'and the parties are no forwarder. Already near five years 'have passed by, and the plaintiff would be glad to give 'up his chance of the legacy if he could escape from his 'liability to costs, while the defendants who own the little 'farm left by the testator, have scarce any other prospect 'before them than ruin.'

An actual occurrence.

# CHAPTER II.

## HOME INCIDENTS AND HARD TIMES.

### 1853—1854—1855.

*DAVID COPPERFIELD* had been written, in Devonshire-terrace for the most part, between the opening of 1849 and October 1850, its publication covering that time; and its sale, which has since taken the lead of all his books but *Pickwick*, never then exceeding twenty-five thousand. But though it remained thus steady for the time, the popularity of the book added largely to the sale of its successor. *Bleak House* was begun in his new abode of Tavistock House at the end of November 1851; was carried on, amid. the excitements of the Guild performances, through the following year; was finished at Boulogne in the August of 1853; and was dedicated to 'his 'friends and companions in the Guild of Literature and 'Art.'

LONDON: 1852.

*Bleak House* sale, ii. 417.

Completion. Aug. 1853.

In March 1852 the first number appeared,* and its sale

Proposed titles.

* I subjoin the dozen titles successively proposed for *Bleak House.* 1. 'Tom-all-Alone's. The Ruined House;' 2. 'Tom-all-Alone's. The Solitary 'House that was always shut up;' 3. 'Bleak House Academy;' 4. 'The 'East Wind; 5. 'Tom-all-Alone's. The Ruined [House, Building, Factory, 'Mill] that got into Chancery and never got out;' 6. 'Tom-all-Alone's. The 'Solitary House where the Grass grew;' 7. 'Tom-all-Alone's. The Solitary

LONDON: 1852.

was mentioned in the same letter from Tavistock House (7th of March) which told of his troubles in the story at its outset, and of other anxieties incident to the common lot and inseparable equally from its joys and sorrows, through which his life was passing at the time. 'My 'Highgate journey yesterday was a sad one. Sad to think 'how all journeys tend that way. I went up to the ceme- 'tery to look for a piece of ground. In no hope of a 'Government bill,* and in a foolish dislike to leaving the 'little child shut up in a vault there, I think of pitching 'a tent under the sky. . . Nothing has taken place here: 'but I believe, every hour, that it must next hour. Wild 'ideas are upon me of going to Paris—Rouen—Switzer- 'land—somewhere—and writing the remaining two-thirds 'of the next No. aloft in some queer inn room. I have 'been hanging over it, and have got restless. Want a 'change I think. Stupid. We were at 30,000 when I 'last heard. . . I am sorry to say that after all kinds of 'evasions, I am obliged to dine at Lansdowne House to- 'morrow. But maybe the affair will come off to-night 'and give me an excuse! I enclose proofs of No. 2. Browne 'has done Skimpole, and helped to make him singularly 'unlike the great original. Look it over, and say what

Grave at Highgate, ii. 461.

Restless.

Sale of his novel.

Skimpole portrait.

'House that was always shut up and never Lighted;' 8. 'Tom-all-Alone's. 'The Ruined Mill, that got into Chancery and never got out;' 9. 'Tom-all- 'Alone's. The Solitary House where the Wind howled;' 10. 'Tom-all-Alone's. 'The Ruined House that got into Chancery and never got out;' 11. 'Bleak 'House and the East Wind. How they both got into Chancery and never 'got out;' 12. 'Bleak House.'

* He was greatly interested in the movement for closing town and city graves (see the close of the 11th chapter of *Bleak House*), and providing places of burial under State supervision.

'occurs to you. . . Don't you think Mrs. Gaskell charming? 'With one ill-considered thing that looks like a want of 'natural perception, I think it masterly.' His last allusion

LONDON: 1852.

TAVISTOCK HOUSE.

is to the story by a delightful writer then appearing in *Household Words;* and of the others it only needs to say that the family affair which might have excused his absence at the Lansdowne dinner did not come off until four days later. On the 13th of March his last child was born; and

Last child born.

DOVER: 1852.

the boy, his seventh son, bears his godfather's distinguished name, Edward Bulwer Lytton.

The inability to 'grind sparks out of his dull blade,' as he characterized his present labour at *Bleak House*, still fretting him, he struck out a scheme for Paris. 'I could 'not get to Switzerland very well at this time of year. 'The Jura would be covered with snow. And if I went 'to Geneva I don't know where I might *not* go to.' It ended at last in a flight to Dover; but he found time before he left, amid many occupations and some anxieties, for a good-natured journey to Walworth to see a youth rehearse who was supposed to have talents for the stage, and he was able to gladden Mr. Toole's friends by thinking favourably of his chances of success. 'I remember 'what I once myself wanted in that way,' he said, 'and I 'should like to serve him.'

Unsettled.

Young stage-aspirant.

At one of the last dinners in Tavistock House before his departure, Mr. Watson of Rockingham was present; and he was hardly settled in Camden-crescent, Dover, when he had news of the death of that excellent friend. 'Poor 'dear Watson! It was this day two weeks when you 'rode with us and he dined with us. We all remarked 'after he had gone how happy he seemed to have got over 'his election troubles, and how cheerful he was. He was 'full of Christmas plans for Rockingham, and was very 'anxious that we should get up a little French piece I 'had been telling him the plot of. He went abroad next 'day to join Mrs. Watson and the children at Homburg, 'and then go to Lausanne, where they had taken a house 'for a month. He was seized at Homburg with violent

Death of a friend.

Mr. Watson of Rockingham.

DOVER: 1852.

internal inflammation, and died—without much pain—'in four days. . . . I was so fond of him that I am 'sorry you didn't know him better. I believe he was as 'thoroughly good and true a man as ever lived; and I am 'sure I can have felt no greater affection for him than he 'felt for me. When I think of that bright house, and his 'fine simple honest heart, both so open to me, the blank 'and loss are like a dream.' Other deaths followed. 'Poor 'd'Orsay!' he wrote after only seven days (8th of August). 'It is a tremendous consideration that friends should fall 'around us in such awful numbers as we attain middle 'life. What a field of battle it is!' Nor had another month quite passed before he lost, in Mrs. Macready, a very dear family friend. 'Ah me! ah me!' he wrote. 'This tremendous sickle certainly does cut deep into the 'surrounding corn, when one's own small blade has ripened. 'But *this* is all a Dream, may be, and death will wake us.'

Count d'Orsay's death.

Loss of another friend.

Able at last to settle to his work, he stayed in Dover three months; and early in October, sending home his family caravan, crossed to Boulogne to try it as a resort for seaside holiday. 'I never saw a better instance of our 'countrymen than this place. Because it is accessible it 'is genteel to say it is of no character, quite English, 'nothing continental about it, and so forth. It is as quaint, 'picturesque, good a place as I know; the boatmen and 'fishing-people quite a race apart, and some of their villages 'as good as the fishing-villages on the Mediterranean. The 'Haute Ville, with a walk all round it on the ramparts, 'charming. The country walks, delightful. It is the best 'mixture of town and country (with sea air into the bar-

BOULOGNE.

Liking for Boulogne.

BOULOGNE: 1852.

'gain) I ever saw; everything cheap, everything good; and 'please God I shall be writing on those said ramparts next 'July!'

Publishing agreements ii. 65–6.

Before the year closed, the time to which his publishing arrangements with Messrs. Bradbury and Evans were limited had expired, but at his suggestion the fourth share in such books as he might write, which they had now received for eight years, was continued to them on the understanding that the publishers' per-centage should no longer be charged in the partnership accounts, and with a power reserved to himself to withdraw when he pleased.

BIRMINGHAM: 1853.

In the new year his first adventure was an ovation in Birmingham, where a silver-gilt salver and a diamond ring were presented to him, as well for eloquent service specially rendered to the Institution, as in general testimony of 'varied literary acquirements, genial philosophy, and high 'moral teaching.'

A banquet and a promise.

A great banquet followed on Twelfth Night, made memorable by an offer* to give a couple of readings from his books at the following Christmas, in aid of the new Midland Institute. It might seem to have been drawn from him as a grateful return for the enthusiastic greeting of his entertainers, but it was in his mind before he left London. It was his first formal undertaking to read in public.

His eldest son had now left Eton, and, the boy's wishes

C. D. to Mr. Ryland.

* The promise was formally conveyed next morning in a letter to one who took the lead then and since in all good work for Birmingham, Mr. Arthur Ryland. The reading would, he said in this letter (7th of Jan. 1853), 'take 'about two hours, with a pause of ten minutes half way through. There 'would be some novelty in the thing, as I have never done it in public, though 'I have in private, and (if I may say so) with a great effect on the hearers.'

pointing at the time to a mercantile career, he was sent to Leipzig for completion of his education.* At this date it seemed to me that the overstrain of attempting too much, brought upon him by the necessities of his weekly periodical, became first apparent in Dickens. Not unfrequently a complaint strange upon his lips fell from him. 'Hypochondriacal whisperings tell me that I am rather 'overworked. The spring does not seem to fly back again 'directly, as it always did when I put my own work aside, 'and had nothing else to do. Yet I have everything to keep 'me going with a brave heart, Heaven knows!' Courage and hopefulness he might well derive from the increasing sale of *Bleak House,* which had risen to nearly forty thousand; but he could no longer bear easily what he carried so lightly of old, and enjoyments with work were too much for him. 'What with *Bleak House,* and *Household Words,* and '*Child's History*' (he dictated from week to week the papers which formed that little book, and cannot be said to have quite hit the mark with it), 'and Miss Coutts's 'Home, and the invitations to feasts and festivals, I really 'feel as if my head would split like a fired shell if I re-'mained here.' He tried Brighton first, but did not find it answer, and returned.† A few days of unalloyed enjoy-

LONDON: 1853.

Eldest son's education.

Self-changes.

Over-doing it.

* Baron Tauchnitz, describing to me his long and uninterrupted friendly intercourse with Dickens, has this remark: 'I give also a passage from one of 'his letters written at the time when he sent his son Charles, through my 'mediation, to Leipzig. He says in it what he desires for his son. "I want '"him to have all interest in, and to acquire a knowledge of, the life around '"him, and to be treated like a gentleman though pampered in nothing. By '"punctuality in all things, great or small, I set great store."'

Baron Tauchnitz.

† From one of his letters while there I take a passage of observation full of character. 'Great excitement here about a wretched woman who has mur-

LONDON: 1853.

ment were afterwards given to the visit of his excellent American friend Felton; and on the 13th of June he was again in Boulogne, thanking heaven for escape from a breakdown. 'If I had substituted anybody's knowledge 'of myself for my own, and lingered in London, I never 'could have got through.'

BOULOGNE: 1853.

What befell him in Boulogne will be given, with the incidents of his second and third summer visits to the place, on a later page. He completed, by the third week of August, his novel of *Bleak House;* and it was resolved to celebrate the event by a two months' trip to Italy, in company with Mr. Wilkie Collins and Mr. Augustus Egg. The start was to be made from Boulogne in the middle of October, when he would send his family home; and he described the intervening weeks as a fearful 'reaction and prostration of 'laziness' only broken by the *Child's History.* At the end of September he wrote: 'I finished the little *History* yes'terday, and am trying to think of something for the 'Christmas number. After which I shall knock off; 'having had quite enough to do, small as it would have

Projected trip to Italy.

Non sum qualis eram.

'dered her child. Apropos of which I observed a curious thing last night. 'The newspaper offices (local journals) had placards like this outside:

'CHILD MURDER IN BRIGHTON.
'INQUEST.
'COMMITTAL OF THE MURDERESS.

'I saw so many common people stand profoundly staring at these lines for 'half-an-hour together—and even go back to stare again—that I feel quite 'certain they had not the power of thinking about the thing at all connectedly 'or continuously, without having something about it before their sense of 'sight. Having got that, they were considering the case, wondering how the 'devil they had come into that power. I saw one man in a smock frock lose 'the said power the moment he turned away, and bring his hob-nails back 'again.'

Seeing is believing.

'seemed to me at any other time, since I finished *Bleak* 'House.' He added, a week before his departure: 'I get 'letters from Genoa and Lausanne as if I were going 'to stay in each place at least a month. If I were to mea-'sure my deserts by people's remembrance of me, I should 'be a prodigy of intolerability. Have recovered my Ita-'lian, which I had all but forgotten, and am one entire and 'perfect chrysolite of idleness.'

BOULOGNE: 1853.

From this trip, of which the incidents have an interest independent of my ordinary narrative, Dickens was home again in the middle of December 1853, and kept his promise to his Birmingham friends by reading in their Town Hall his *Christmas Carol* on the 27th,* and his *Cricket on the Hearth* on the 29th. The enthusiasm was great, and he consented to read his *Carol* a second time, on Friday the 30th, if seats were reserved for working men at prices within their means. The result was an addition of between four and five hundred pounds to the funds for establishment of the new Institute; and a prettily worked flower-basket in silver, presented to Mrs. Dickens, commemorated these first public readings 'to nearly six 'thousand people,' and the design they had generously helped. Other applications then followed to such extent that limits to compliance had to be put; and a letter of the 16th of May 1854 is one of many that express both the difficulty in which he found himself, and his much desired expedient for solving it. 'The objection you 'suggest to paid public lecturing does not strike me at all.

BIRMINGHAM: 1853.

First public readings.

Desire to become a public reader: ii. 149, 257.

* The reading occupied nearly three hours: double the time devoted to it in the later years.

LONDON: 1854.

'It is worth consideration, but I do not think there is any-'thing in it. On the contrary, if the lecturing would have 'any motive power at all (like my poor father this, in the 'sound!) I believe it would tend the other way. In the Colchester matter I had already received a letter from a 'Colchester magnate; to whom I had honestly replied 'that I stood pledged to Christmas readings at Bradford * 'and at Reading, and could in no kind of reason do more 'in the public way.' The promise to the people of Reading was for Talfourd's sake; the other was given after the Birmingham nights, when an institute in Bradford asked similar help, and offered a fee of fifty pounds. At first this was entertained; but was abandoned, with some reluctance, upon the argument that to become publicly a reader must alter without improving his position publicly as a writer, and that it was a change to be justified only when the higher calling should have failed of the old success. Thus yielding for the time, he nevertheless soon found the question rising again with the same importunity; his own position to it being always that of a man assenting against his will that it should rest in abeyance. But nothing farther was resolved on yet. The readings mentioned came off as promised, in aid of public objects; † and besides others

Promises made.

Argument against paid Readings.

* 'After correspondence with all parts of England, and every kind of refusal 'and evasion on my part, I am now obliged to decide this question—whether 'I shall read two nights at Bradford for a hundred pounds. If I do, I may 'take as many hundred pounds as I choose.' 27th of Jan. 1854.

Offer from Bradford.

† On the 28th of Dec. 1854 he wrote from Bradford: 'The hall is enormous, 'and they expect to seat 3700 people to night! Notwithstanding which, it 'seems to me a tolerably easy place—except that the width of the platform is 'so very great to the eye at first.' From Folkestone, on his way to Paris, he wrote in the autumn of 1855: '16th of Sept. I am going to read for them

two years later for the family of a friend, he had given the like liberal help to institutes in Folkestone, Chatham, and again in Birmingham, Peterborough, Sheffield, Coventry, and Edinburgh, before the question settled itself finally in the announcement for paid public readings issued by him in 1858.

LONDON: 1854.

Children's theatricals.

Carrying memory back to his home in the first half of 1854, there are few things that rise more pleasantly in connection with it than the children's theatricals. These began with the first Twelfth Night at Tavistock House, and were renewed until the principal actors ceased to be children. The best of the performances were *Tom Thumb* and *Fortunio*, in '54 and '55; Dickens now joining first in the revel, and Mr. Mark Lemon bringing into it his own clever children and a very mountain of child-pleasing fun in himself. Dickens had become very intimate with him, and his merry genial ways had given him unbounded popularity with the 'young 'uns,' who had no such favourite as 'Uncle 'Mark.' In Fielding's burlesque he was the giantess Glumdalca, and Dickens was the ghost of Gaffer Thumb; the names by which they respectively appeared being the Infant Phenomenon and the Modern Garrick. But the

Big actors.

'here, on the 5th of next month, and have answered in the last fortnight 'thirty applications to do the like all over England, Ireland, and Scotland. 'Fancy my having to come from Paris in December, to do this, at Peter-'borough, Birmingham, and Sheffield—old promises.' Again: 23rd of Sept. 'I 'am going to read here, next Friday week. There are (as there are everywhere) 'a Literary Institution and a Working Men's Institution, which have not the 'slightest sympathy or connexion. The stalls are five shillings, but I have 'made them fix the working men's admission at threepence, and I hope it 'may bring them together. The event comes off in a carpenter's shop, as the 'biggest place that can be got.' In 1857, at Paxton's request, he read his *Carol* at Coventry for the Institute.

Gratuitous Readings.

LONDON: 1854.

Small actors.

younger actors carried off the palm. There was a Lord Grizzle, at whose ballad of Miss Villikins, introduced by desire, Thackeray rolled off his seat in a burst of laughter that became absurdly contagious. Yet even this, with hardly less fun from the Noodles, Doodles, and King Arthurs, was not so good as the pretty, fantastic, comic grace of Dollalolla, Huncamunca, and Tom. The girls wore steadily the grave airs irresistible when put on by little children; and an actor not out of his fourth year, who went through the comic songs and the tragic exploits without a wrong note or a victim unslain, represented the small helmeted hero. He was in the bills as Mr. H——, but bore in fact the name of the illustrious author whose conception he embodied; and who certainly would have hugged him for Tom's opening song, delivered in the arms of Huncamunca, if he could have forgiven the later master in his own craft for having composed it afresh to the air of a ditty then wildly popular at the 'Coal Hole.'* The encores were frequent, and for the most part the little fellow responded to them; but the misplaced enthusiasm that took similar form at the heroic intensity with which he stabbed Dollalolla, he rebuked by going gravely on to the close. His Fortunio, the next Twelfth Night, was not so great; yet when, as a prelude to getting the better of the Dragon, he adulterated his drink (Mr. Lemon played the Dragon) with sherry, the sly relish with which he watched the demora-

Henry Fielding Dickens.

Acting of Fortunio.

* My name it is Tom Thumb,
Small my size,
Small my size,
My name it is Tom Thumb,
Small my size.
Yet though I am so sma
I have kill'd the giants tall;
And now I'm paid for all,
Small my size,
Small my size;
And now I'm paid for all,
Small my size.

LONDON: 1855.

lization, by this means, of his formidable adversary into a helpless imbecility, was perfect. Here Dickens played the testy old Baron, and took advantage of the excitement against the Czar raging in 1855 to denounce him (in a song) as no other than own cousin to the very Bear that Fortunio had gone forth to subdue. He depicted him, in his desolation of autocracy, as the Robinson Crusoe of absolute state, who had at his court many a show-day and many a high-day, but hadn't in all his dominions a Friday.* The bill, which attributed these interpolations to 'the Dramatic 'Poet of the Establishment,' deserves also mention for the fun of the six large-lettered announcements which stood at the head of it, and could not have been bettered by Mr. Crummles himself. 'Re-engagement of that irresistible 'comedian' (the performer of Lord Grizzle) 'Mr. Ainger!' 'Reappearance of Mr. H. who created so powerful an im- 'pression last year!' 'Return of Mr. Charles Dickens Junior 'from his German engagements!' 'Engagement of Miss 'Kate, who declined the munificent offers of the Manage-

Dickens and the Czar.

Mr. Crummles.

* This finds mention, I observe, in a pleasant description of 'Mr. Dickens's 'Amateur Theatricals,' which appeared in *Macmillan's Magazine* two years ago, by one who had been a member of the Juvenile Company. I quote a passage, recommending the whole paper as very agreeably written, with some shrewd criticism. 'Mr. Planché had in one portion of the extravaganza 'put into the mouth of one of the characters for the moment a few lines of 'burlesque upon Macbeth, and we remember Mr. Dickens's unsuccessful at- 'tempts to teach the performer how to imitate Macready, whom he (the per- 'former) had never seen! And after the performance, when we were restored 'to our evening-party costumes, and the school-room was cleared for dancing, 'still a stray "property" or two had escaped the vigilant eye of the property- 'man, for Douglas Jerrold had picked up the horse's head (Fortunio's faithful 'steed *Comrade*), and was holding it up before the greatest living animal 'painter, who had been one of the audience, with "Looks as if it knew *you*, '"Edwin!"'

Account by one of the actors.

LONDON: 1855.

'ment last season!' 'Mr. Passé, Mr. Mudperiod, Mr. 'Measly Servile, and Mr. Wilkini Collini!' 'First appear-'ance on any stage of Mr. Plornishmaroontigoonter (who 'has been kept out of bed at a vast expense).' The last performer mentioned * was yet at some distance from the third year of his age. Dickens was Mr. Passé.

Smallest of the comedians.

Gravities were mixed with these gaieties. 'I wish you 'would look' (20th of January 1854) 'at the enclosed titles 'for the *H. W.* story, between this and two o'clock or so, 'when I will call. It is my usual day, you observe, on which 'I have jotted them down—Friday! It seems to me that 'there are three very good ones among them. I should 'like to know whether you hit upon the same.' On the paper enclosed was written: 1. According to Cocker. 2. Prove it. 3. Stubborn Things. 4. Mr. Gradgrind's Facts. 5. The Grindstone. 6. Hard Times. 7. Two and Two are Four. 8. Something Tangible. 9. Our Hard-headed Friend. 10. Rust and Dust. 11. Simple Arithmetic. 12. A Matter of Calculation. 13. A Mere Question of Figures. 14. The

Titles for a new story.

From a Boulogne jest-book.

* He went with the rest to Boulogne in the summer, and an anecdote transmitted in one of his father's letters will show that he maintained the reputation as a comedian which his early debut had awakened. 'ORIGINAL ANECDOTE 'OF THE PLORNISHGHENTER. This distinguished wit, being at Boulogne with 'his family, made a close acquaintance with his landlord, whose name was 'M. Beaucourt—the only French word with which he was at that time 'acquainted. It happened that one day he was left unusually long in a 'bathing-machine when the tide was making, accompanied by his two young 'brothers and little English nurse, without being drawn to land. The little 'nurse, being frightened, cried "M'soo! M'soo!" The two young brothers 'being frightened, cried "Ici! Ici!" Our wit, at once perceiving that his 'English was of no use to him under the foreign circumstances, immediately 'fell to bawling "Beau-court!" which he continued to shout at the utmost 'pitch of his voice and with great gravity, until rescued.—*New Boulogne Jest 'Book*, page 578.'

Gradgrind Philosophy.* The three selected by me were 2, 6, and 11; the three that were his own favourites were 6, 13, and 14; and as 6 had been chosen by both, that title was taken.

LONDON: 1854.

'Hard 'Times' chosen.

It was the first story written by him for *Household Words;* and in the course of it the old troubles of the *Clock* came back, with the difference that the greater brevity of the weekly portions made it easier to write them up to time, but much more difficult to get sufficient interest into each. 'The difficulty of the space,' he wrote after a few weeks' trial, 'is CRUSHING. Nobody can have 'an idea of it who has not had an experience of patient 'fiction-writing with some elbow-room always, and open 'places in perspective. In this form, with any kind of 'regard to the current number, there is absolutely no such 'thing.' He went on, however; and, of the two designs he started with, accomplished one very perfectly and the other at least partially. He more than doubled the circulation of his journal; and he wrote a story which, though not among his best, contains things as characteristic as any he has written. I may not go as far as Mr. Ruskin in giving it a high place; but to anything falling from that writer, however one may differ from it, great respect is due, and every word here said of Dickens's intention is in the most strict sense just.† 'The essential value and truth

i. 180.

Difficulties of weekly publication.

What was proposed and what was done.

* To show the pains he took in such matters I will give other titles also thought of for this tale. 1. Fact; 2. Hard-headed Gradgrind; 3. Hard Heads and Soft Hearts; 4. Heads and Tales; 5. Black and White.

† It is well to remember, too, what he wrote about the story to Charles Knight. It had no design, he said, to damage the really useful truths of Political Economy, but was wholly directed against 'those who see figures and averages, 'and nothing else; who would take the average of cold in the Crimea during

Dickens to Charles Knight.

LONDON: 1854.

*Unto this End*: note to First Essay, 14-15.

'of Dickens's writings,' he says, 'have been unwisely lost 'sight of by many thoughtful persons, merely because he 'presents his truth with some colour of caricature. Unwisely, because Dickens's caricature, though often gross, 'is never mistaken. Allowing for his manner of telling 'them, the things he tells us are always true. I wish that 'he could think it right to limit his brilliant exaggeration 'to works written only for public amusement; and when 'he takes up a subject of high national importance, such 'as that which he handled in *Hard Times*, that he would 'use severer and more accurate analysis. The usefulness of that work (to my mind, in several respects, the 'greatest he has written) is with many persons seriously 'diminished, because Mr. Bounderby is a dramatic monster, 'instead of a characteristic example of a worldly master; 'and Stephen Blackpool a dramatic perfection, instead of 'a characteristic example of an honest workman. But let 'us not lose the use of Dickens's wit and insight, because 'he chooses to speak in a circle of stage fire. He is entirely 'right in his main drift and purpose in every book he has 'written; and all of them, but especially *Hard Times*, 'should be studied with close and earnest care by persons 'interested in social questions. They will find much that 'is partial, and, because partial, apparently unjust; but if 'they examine all the evidence on the other side, which 'Dickens seems to overlook, it will appear, after all their

Mr. Ruskin on *Hard Times*.

'twelve months as a reason for clothing a soldier in nankeen on a night when 'he would be frozen to death in fur; and who would comfort the labourer in 'travelling twelve miles a day to and from his work, by telling him that the 'average distance of one inhabited place from another, on the whole area of 'England, is not more than four miles.'

'trouble, that his view was the finally right one, grossly 'and sharply told.'* The best points in it, out of the circle of stage fire (an expression of wider application to this part of Dickens's life than its inventor supposed it to be), were the sketches of the riding-circus people and the Bounderby household; but it is a wise hint of Mr. Ruskin's that there may be, in the drift of a story, truths of sufficient importance to set against defects of workmanship; and here they challenged wide attention. You cannot train any one properly, unless you cultivate the fancy, and allow fair scope to the affections. You cannot govern men on a principle of averages; and to buy in the cheapest and sell in the dearest market is not the *summum bonum* of life. You cannot treat the working man fairly unless, in dealing with his wrongs and his delusions, you take equally into account the simplicity and tenacity of his nature, arising partly from limited knowledge, but more from honesty and singleness of intention. Fiction cannot

Best things in the tale.

Truths enforced.

* It is curious that with as strong a view in the opposite direction, and with an equally mistaken exaltation, above the writer's ordinary level, of a book which on the whole was undoubtedly below it, Mr. Taine speaks of *Hard Times* as that one of Dickens's romances which is a summary of all the rest: exalting instinct above reason, and the intuitions of the heart above practical knowledge; attacking all education based on statistic figures and facts; heaping sorrow and ridicule on the practical mercantile people; fighting against the pride, hardness, and selfishness of the merchant and noble; cursing the manufacturing towns for imprisoning bodies in smoke and mud, and souls in falsehood and factitiousness;—while it contrasts, with that satire of social oppression, lofty eulogy of the oppressed; and searches out poor workmen, jugglers, foundlings, and circus people, for types of good sense, sweetness of disposition, generosity, delicacy, and courage, to perpetual confusion of the pretended knowledge, pretended happiness, pretended virtue, of the rich and powerful who trample upon them! This is a fair specimen of the exaggerations with which exaggeration is rebuked, in Mr. Taine's and much similar criticism.

Exaggerated rebuke of exaggeration.

BOULOGNE: 1854.

Uses of fiction.

prove a case, but it can express forcibly a righteous sentiment; and this is here done unsparingly upon matters of universal concern. The book was finished at Boulogne in the middle of July,* and is inscribed to Carlyle.

Horse-riding scenes.

An American admirer accounted for the vivacity of the circus-scenes by declaring that Dickens had 'arranged with 'the master of Astley's Circus to spend many hours behind 'the scenes with the riders and among the horses;' a thing just as likely as that he went into training as a stroller to qualify for Mr. Crummles in *Nickleby*. Such successes belonged to the experiences of his youth; he had nothing to add to what his marvellous observation had made familiar from almost childish days; and the glimpses we get of them in the *Sketches by Boz* are in these points as perfect as anything his later experience could supply. There was one thing nevertheless which the choice of his subject made him anxious to verify while *Hard Times* was in hand; and this was a strike in a manufacturing town. He went to Preston to see one at the end of January, and was somewhat disappointed. 'I am afraid I shall not be able 'to get much here. Except the crowds at the street-'corners reading the placards pro and con; and the cold 'absence of smoke from the mill-chimneys; there is very

PRESTON.

Manufacturing town on strike.

* Here is a note at the close. 'Tavistock House. Look at that! 'Boulogne, of course. Friday, 14th of July, 1854. I am three parts mad, and 'the fourth delirious, with perpetual rushing at *Hard Times*. I have done 'what I hope is a good thing with Stephen, taking his story as a whole; and 'hope to be over in town with the end of the book on Wednesday night. . . 'I have been looking forward through so many weeks and sides of paper to 'this Stephen business, that now—as usual—it being over, I feel as if nothing 'in the world, in the way of intense and violent rushing hither and thither, 'could quite restore my balance.'

PRESTON: 1854.

'little in the streets to make the town remarkable. I am 'told that the people "sit at home and mope." The dele-'gates with the money from the neighbouring places come 'in to-day to report the amounts they bring; and to-'morrow the people are paid. When I have seen both 'these ceremonies, I shall return. It is a nasty place (I 'thought it was a model town); and I am in the Bull 'Hotel, before which some time ago the people assembled 'supposing the masters to be here, and on demanding to 'have them out were remonstrated with by the landlady 'in person. I saw the account in an Italian paper, in 'which it was stated that "the populace then environed '"the Palazzo Bull, until the padrona of the Palazzo heroi-'"cally appeared at one of the upper windows and addressed '"them!" One can hardly conceive anything less likely 'to be represented to an Italian mind by this description, 'than the old, grubby, smoky, mean, intensely formal red 'brick house with a narrow gateway and a dingy yard, to 'which it applies. At the theatre last night I saw *Hamlet*, 'and should have done better to "sit at home and mope" 'like the idle workmen. In the last scene, Laertes on 'being asked how it was with him replied (verbatim) '"Why, like a woodcock—on account of my treachery"' (29th Jan.)

Palazzo Bull.

*Hamlet* at Preston.

LONDON: 1855.

The home incidents of the summer and autumn of 1855 may be mentioned briefly. It was a year of much unsettled discontent with him, and upon return from a short trip to Paris with Mr. Wilkie Collins, he flung himself rather hotly into agitation with the administrative reformers,*

* 'I have hope of Mr. Morley—whom one cannot see without knowing to

LONDON: 1855.

Speaking at Drury-lane.

and spoke at one of the great meetings in Drury-lane Theatre. In the following month (April) he took occasion, even from the chair of the General Theatrical Fund, to give renewed expression to political dissatisfactions.* In the summer he threw open to many friends his Tavistock House Theatre, having secured for its 'lessee and manager Mr. 'Crummles;' for its poet Mr. Wilkie Collins, in 'an en-'tirely new and original domestic melodrama;' and for its scene-painter 'Mr. Stanfield, R.A.'† *The Lighthouse,* by Mr. Wilkie Collins, was then produced, its actors being Mr. Crummles the manager (Dickens in other words), the Author

Tavistock House theatricals.

Administrative reformers.

'be a straightforward, earnest man. Travers, too, I think a man of the 'Anti-corn-law-league order. I also think Higgins will materially help them. 'Generally I quite agree with you that they hardly know what to be at; but 'it is an immensely difficult subject to start, and they must have every allow-'ance. At any rate, it is not by leaving them alone and giving them no help, 'that they can be urged on to success.' 29th of March 1855.

* 'The Government hit took immensely, but I'm afraid to look at the 'report, these things are so ill done. It came into my head as I was walking 'about at Hampstead yesterday . . . On coming away I told B. we must have 'a toastmaster in future less given to constant drinking while the speeches 'are going on. B. replied "Yes sir, you are quite right sir, he has no head '"whatever sir, look at him now sir"—Toastmaster was weakly contemplat-'ing the coats and hats "do you not find it difficult to keep your hands off '"him sir, he ought to have his head knocked against the wall sir,—and he '"should sir, I assure you sir, if he was not in too debased a condition to be '"aware of it sir."' April 3rd 1855.

Tavern-keeper and toast-master.

Clarkson Stanfield, R.A.

† For the scene of the Eddystone Lighthouse at this little play, afterwards placed in a frame in the hall at Gadshill, a thousand guineas was given at the Dickens sale. It occupied the great painter only one or two mornings, and Dickens will tell how it originated. Walking on Hampstead Heath to think over his Theatrical Fund speech, he met Mr. Lemon, and they went together to Stanfield. 'He has been very ill, and he told us that large pictures are too 'much for him, and he must confine himself to small ones. But I would not 'have this, I declared he must paint bigger ones than ever, and what would 'he think of beginning upon an act-drop for a proposed vast theatre at Tavi-'stock House? He laughed and caught at this, we cheered him up very much, 'and he said he was quite a man again.' April 1855.

LONDON: 1855.

of the play, Mr. Lemon and Mr. Egg, and the manager's sister-in-law and eldest daughter. It was followed by the Guild farce of *Mr. Nightingale's Diary*, in which besides the performers named, and Dickens in his old personation part, the manager's youngest daughter and Mr. Frank Stone assisted. The success was wonderful; and in the three delighted audiences who crowded to what the bills described as 'the smallest theatre in the world,' were not a few of the notabilities of London. Mr. Carlyle compared Dickens's wild picturesqueness in the old lighthouse keeper to the famous figure in Nicholas Poussin's bacchanalian dance in the National Gallery; and at one of the joyous suppers that followed on each night of the play, Lord Campbell told the company that he had much rather have written *Pickwick* than be Chief Justice of England and a peer of parliament.*

ii. 367.

Mr. Carlyle.

Lord Campbell.

Then came the beginning of *Nobody's Fault*, as *Little Dorrit* continued to be called by him up to the eve of its publication; a flight to Folkestone to help his sluggish fancy; and his return to London in October to preside at a dinner to Thackeray on his going to lecture in America. It was a muster of more than sixty admiring entertainers, and Dickens's speech gave happy expression to the spirit that animated all, telling Thackeray not alone how much

Dinner to Thackeray.

* Sitting at Nisi Prius not long before, the Chief Justice, with the same eccentric liking for literature, had committed what was called at the time a breach of judicial decorum. (Such indecorums were less uncommon in the great days of the Bench.) 'The name,' he said, 'of the illustrious Charles 'Dickens has been called on the jury, but he has not answered. If his great 'Chancery suit had been still going on, I certainly would have excused him, 'but, as that is over, he might have done us the honour of attending here, 'that he might have seen how we went on at common law.'

LONDON: 1855.

his friendship was prized by those present, and how proud they were of his genius, but offering him in the name of the tens of thousands absent who had never touched his hand or seen his face, life-long thanks for the treasures of mirth, wit, and wisdom within the yellow-covered numbers of *Pendennis* and *Vanity Fair*. Peter Cunningham, one of the sons of Allan, was secretary to the banquet; and for many pleasures given to the subject of this memoir, who had a hearty regard for him, should have a few words to his memory.

Peter Cunningham.

His presence was always welcome to Dickens, and indeed to all who knew him, for his relish of social life was great, and something of his keen enjoyment could not but be shared by his company. His geniality would have carried with it a pleasurable glow even if it had stood alone, and it was invigorated by very considerable acquirements. He had some knowledge of the works of eminent authors and artists; and he had an eager interest in their lives and haunts, which he had made the subject of minute and novel enquiry. This store of knowledge gave substance to his talk, yet never interrupted his buoyancy and pleasantry, because only introduced when called for, and not made matter of parade or display. But the happy combination of qualities that rendered him a favourite companion, and won him many friends, proved in the end injurious to himself. He had done much while young in certain lines of investigation which he had made almost his own, and there was every promise that, in the department of biographical and literary research, he would have produced much weightier works with advancing years. This however

LONDON: 1855.

A life wasted.

was not to be. The fascinations of good fellowship encroached more and more upon literary pursuits, until he nearly abandoned his former favourite studies, and sacrificed all the deeper purposes of his life to the present temptation of a festive hour. Then his health gave way, and he became lost to friends as well as to literature. But the impression of the bright and amiable intercourse of his better time survived, and his old associates never ceased to think of Peter Cunningham with regret and kindness.

Incident of a November night.

Dickens went to Paris early in October, and at its close was brought again to London by the sudden death of a friend, much deplored by himself, and still more so by a distinguished lady who had his loyal service at all times. An incident before his return to France is worth brief relation. He had sallied out for one of his night walks, full of thoughts of his story, one wintery rainy evening (the 8th of November), and 'pulled himself up,' outside the door of Whitechapel Workhouse, at a strange sight which arrested him there. Against the dreary enclosure of the house were leaning, in the midst of the downpouring rain and storm, what seemed to be seven heaps of rags: 'dumb, wet, silent 'horrors' he described them, 'sphinxes set up against that 'dead wall, and no one likely to be at the pains of solving 'them until the General Overthrow.' He sent in his card to the Master. Against him there was no ground of complaint; he gave prompt personal attention; but the casual ward was full, and there was no help. The rag-heaps were all girls, and Dickens gave each a shilling. One girl, 'twenty or so,' had been without food a day and night. 'Look at me,' she said, as she clutched the shilling, and

Outside Whitechapel workhouse.

LONDON: 1855.

without thanks shuffled off. So with the rest. There was not a single 'thank you.' A crowd meanwhile, only less poor than these objects of misery, had gathered round the scene; but though they saw the seven shillings given away they asked for no relief to themselves, they recognized in their sad wild way the other greater wretchedness, and made room in silence for Dickens to walk on.

Degrees in misery.

Not more tolerant of the way in which laws meant to be most humane are too often administered in England, he left in a day or two to resume his *Little Dorrit* in Paris. But before his life there is described, some sketches from his holiday trip to Italy with Mr. Wilkie Collins and Mr. Augustus Egg, and from his three summer visits to Boulogne, claim to themselves two intervening chapters.

## CHAPTER III.

### SWITZERLAND AND ITALY REVISITED.

1853.

THE first news of the three travellers was from Chamounix, on the 20th of October; and in it there was little made of the fatigue, and much of the enjoyment, of their Swiss travel. Great attention and cleanliness at the inns, very small windows and very bleak passages, doors opening to wintery blasts, overhanging eaves and external galleries, plenty of milk, honey, cows, and goats, much singing towards sunset on mountain sides, mountains almost too solemn to look at—that was the picture of it, with the country everywhere in one of its finest aspects, as winter began to close in. They had started from Geneva the previous morning at four, and in their day's travel Dickens had again noticed what he spoke of formerly, the ill-favoured look of the people in the valleys owing to their hard and stern climate. 'All the women were like used-up men, 'and all the men like a sort of fagged dogs. But the good, 'genuine, grateful Swiss recognition of the commonest kind 'word—not too often thrown to them by our countrymen—'made them quite radiant. I walked the greater part of 'the way, which was like going up the Monument.' On

CHAMOUNIX: 1853.

Swiss people.

CHAMOUNIX: 1853.

the day the letter was written they had been up to the Mer de Glace, finding it not so beautiful in colour as in summer, but grander in its desolation; the green ice, like the greater part of the ascent, being covered with snow. 'We 'were alarmingly near to a very dismal accident. We were 'a train of four mules and two guides, going along an im-'mense height like a chimney-piece, with sheer precipice 'below, when there came rolling from above, with fearful

Narrow escape.

'velocity, a block of stone about the size of one of the foun-'tains in Trafalgar-square, which Egg, the last of the party, 'had preceded by not a yard, when it swept over the ledge, 'breaking away a tree, and rolled and tumbled down into 'the valley. It had been loosened by the heavy rains, or 'by some woodcutters afterwards reported to be above.'

Berne.

The only place new to Dickens was Berne: 'a surprisingly 'picturesque old Swiss town, with a view of the Alps from 'the outside of it singularly beautiful in the morning light.' Everything else was familiar to him: though at that winter season, when the inns were shutting up, and all who could afford it were off to Geneva, most things in the valley struck him with a new aspect. From such of his old friends as he found at Lausanne, where a day or two's rest was taken, he

Lausanne.

had the gladdest of greetings; 'and the wonderful manner 'in which they turned out in the wettest morning ever 'beheld for a Godspeed down the Lake was really quite 'pathetic.'

He had found time to see again the deaf, dumb, and blind youth at Mr. Haldimand's Institution who had aroused so deep an interest in him seven years before, but, in his brief present visit, the old associations would not reawaken.

LAUSANNE: 1853.

An old friend.

'Tremendous efforts were made by Hertzel to impress him 'with an idea of me, and the associations belonging to me; 'but it seemed in my eyes quite a failure, and I much 'doubt if he had the least perception of his old acquaint-'ance. According to his custom, he went on muttering 'strange eager sounds like Town and Down and Mown, 'but nothing more. I left ten francs to be spent in cigars 'for my old friend. If I had taken one with me, I think 'I could, more successfully than his master, have estab-'lished my identity.' The child similarly afflicted, the little girl whom he saw at the same old time, had been after some trial discharged as an idiot.

ii. 209-214.

Genoa.

Before October closed, the travellers had reached Genoa, having been thirty-one consecutive hours on the road from Milan. They arrived in somewhat damaged condition, and took up their lodging in the top rooms of the Croce di Malta, 'overlooking the port and sea pleasantly and 'airily enough, but it was no joke to get so high, and the 'apartment is rather vast and faded.' The warmth of personal greeting that here awaited Dickens was given no less to the friends who accompanied him, and though the reader may not share in such private confidences as would show the sensation created by his reappearance, and the jovial hours that were passed among old associates, he will perhaps be interested to know how far the intervening years had changed the aspect of things and places made pleasantly familiar to us in his former letters. He wrote to his sister-in-law that the old walks were pretty much the same as ever except that there had been building behind the Peschiere up the San Bartolomeo hill, and the

Personal greetings.

GENOA: 1853.

whole town towards San Pietro d'Arena had been quite changed. The Bisagno looked just the same, stony just then, having very little water in it; the vicoli were fragrant with the same old flavour of 'very rotten cheese kept in 'very hot blankets;' and everywhere he saw the mezzaro as of yore. The Jesuits' College in the Strada Nuova was become, under the changed government, the Hôtel de Ville, and a splendid caffè with a terrace-garden had arisen between it and Palaviccini's old palace. 'Pal him-'self has gone to the dogs.' Another new and handsome caffè had been built in the Piazza Carlo Felice, between the old one of the Bei Arti and the Strada Carlo Felice; and the Teatro Diurno had now stone galleries and seats, like an ancient amphitheatre. 'The beastly gate and 'guardhouse in the Albaro road are still in their dear old 'beastly state; and the whole of that road is just as it 'was. The man without legs is still in the Strada Nuova; 'but the beggars in general are all cleared off, and our old 'one-arm'd Belisario made a sudden evaporation a year or 'two ago. I am going to the Peschiere to-day.' To myself he described his former favourite abode as converted into a girls' college; all the paintings of gods and goddesses canvassed over, and the gardens gone to ruin; 'but O! what 'a wonderful place!' He observed an extraordinary increase everywhere else, since he was last in the splendid city, of 'life, growth, and enterprise;' and he declared his old conviction to be confirmed that for picturesque beauty and character there was nothing in Italy, Venice excepted, 'near brilliant old Genoa.'

Old and new places.

Owner of the Peschiere.

Peschiere revisited. ii. 114-116.

The voyage thence to Naples, written from the latter

LEGHORN: 1853.

place, is too capital a description to be lost. The steamer in which they embarked was 'the new express English 'ship,' but they found her to be already more than full of passengers from Marseilles (among them an old friend, Sir Emerson Tennent, with his family), and everything in confusion. There were no places at the captain's table, dinner had to be taken on deck, no berth or sleeping accommodation was available, and heavy first-class fares had to be paid. Thus they made their way to Leghorn, where worse awaited them. The authorities proved to be not favourable to the 'crack' English-officered vessel (she had just been started for the India mail); and her papers not being examined in time, it was too late to steam away again that day, and she had to lie all night long off the lighthouse. 'The scene 'on board beggars description. Ladies on the tables; gen'tlemen under the tables; bed-room appliances not usually 'beheld in public airing themselves in positions where 'soup-tureens had been lately developing themselves; and 'ladies and gentlemen lying indiscriminately on the open 'deck, arranged like spoons on a sideboard. No mattresses, 'no blankets, nothing. Towards midnight attempts were 'made, by means of awning and flags, to make this latter 'scene remotely approach an Australian encampment; and 'we three (Collins, Egg, and self) lay together on the bare 'planks covered with our coats. We were all gradually 'dozing off, when a perfectly tropical rain fell, and in a 'moment drowned the whole ship. The rest of the night 'we passed upon the stairs, with an immense jumble of 'men and women. When anybody came up for any pur'pose we all fell down, and when anybody came down we

On the way to Naples.

Scene on board steamship.

LEGHORN: 1853.

'all fell up again. Still, the good-humour in the English 'part of the passengers was quite extraordinary. . . There 'were excellent officers aboard, and, in the morning, the 'first mate lent me his cabin to wash in—which I after- 'wards lent to Egg and Collins. Then we, the Emerson 'Tennents, the captain, the doctor, and the second officer, 'went off on a jaunt together to Pisa, as the ship was to 'lie all day at Leghorn. The captain was a capital fellow, 'but I led him, facetiously, such a life the whole day, that 'I got most things altered at night. Emerson Tennent's 'son, with the greatest amiability, insisted on turning out 'of his state-room for me, and I got a good bed there. 'The store-room down by the hold was opened for Collins 'and Egg; and they slept with the moist sugar, the cheese 'in cut, the spices, the cruets, the apples and pears, in a 'perfect chandler's shop—in company with what a friend 'of ours would call a hold gent, who had been so horribly 'wet through over night that his condition frightened the 'authorities; a cat; and the steward, who dozed in an arm- 'chair, and all-night-long fell head foremost, once every 'five minutes, on Egg, who slept on the counter or dresser. 'Last night, I had the steward's own cabin, opening on 'deck, all to myself. It had been previously occupied by 'some desolate lady who went ashore at Civita Vecchia. 'There was little or no sea, thank Heaven, all the trip; 'but the rain was heavier than any I have ever seen, and 'the lightning very constant and vivid. We were, with the 'crew, some 200 people—provided with boats, at the utmost 'stretch, for one hundred perhaps. I could not help think- 'ing what would happen if we met with any accident: the

A jaunt to Pisa.

Night on board.

'crew being chiefly Maltese, and evidently fellows who 'would cut off alone in the largest boat, on the least alarm; 'the speed very high; and the running, thro' all the nar-'row rocky channels. Thank God, however, here we are.'

A whimsical postscript closed the amusing narrative. 'We towed from Civita Vecchia the entire Greek navy, 'I believe; consisting of a little brig of war with no 'guns, fitted as a steamer, but disabled by having burnt 'the bottoms of her boilers out, in her first run. She was 'just big enough to carry the captain and a crew of six or 'so: but the captain was so covered with buttons and gold 'that there never would have been room for him on board 'to put those valuables away, if he hadn't worn them—'which he consequently did, all night. Whenever any-'thing was wanted to be done, as slackening the tow-rope 'or anything of that sort, our officers roared at this miser-'able potentate, in violent English, through a speaking 'trumpet; of which he couldn't have understood a word 'in the most favourable circumstances. So he did all the 'wrong things first, and the right thing always last. The 'absence of any knowledge of anything but English on the 'part of the officers and stewards was most ridiculous. I 'met an Italian gentleman on the cabin steps yesterday 'morning, vainly endeavouring to explain that he wanted 'a cup of tea for his sick wife. And when we were coming 'out of the harbour at Genoa, and it was necessary to 'order away that boat of music you remember, the chief 'officer (called "aft" for the purpose, as "knowing some-'"thing of Italian") delivered himself in this explicit and 'clear Italian to the principal performer—"Now Signora,

A Greek war-ship.

English officers and stewards.

English Italian.

NAPLES: 1853.

'"if you don't sheer off you'll be run down, so you had '"better trice up that guitar of yours and put about."'

At Naples some days were passed very merrily; going up Vesuvius and into the buried cities, with Layard who had joined them, and with the Tennents. Here a small adventure befell Dickens specially, in itself extremely unimportant, but told by him with delightful humour in a letter to his sister-in-law. The old idle Frenchman, to whom all things are possible, with his snuff-box and dusty umbrella, and all the delicate and kindly observation, would have enchanted Leigh Hunt, and made his way to the heart of Charles Lamb. After mentioning Mr. Lowther, then English chargé d'affaires in Naples, as a very agreeable fellow who

ii. 449.

had been at the Rockingham play, he alludes to a meeting at his house. 'We had an exceedingly pleasant dinner of 'eight, preparatory to which I was near having the ridiculous 'adventure of not being able to find the house and coming 'back dinnerless. I went in an open carriage from the hotel 'in all state, and the coachman to my surprise pulled up

Going out to dinner.

'at the end of the Chiaja. "Behold the house," says he, '"of Il Signor Larthoor!"—at the same time pointing with 'his whip into the seventh heaven where the early stars 'were shining. "But the Signor Larthorr," says I, "lives '"at Pausilippo." "It is true," says the coachman (still 'pointing to the evening star), "but he lives high up the '"Salita Sant' Antonio where no carriage ever yet '"ascended, and that is the house" (evening star as afore-'said), "and one must go on foot. Behold the Salita

Difficult road.

'"Sant' Antonio!" I went up it, a mile and a half I should think. I got into the strangest places among the 'wildest Neapolitans; kitchens, washing-places, archways, 'stables, vineyards; was baited by dogs, and answered, in 'profoundly unintelligible language, from behind lonely 'locked doors in cracked female voices, quaking with fear; 'but could hear of no such Englishman, nor any Eng- 'lishman. Bye and bye, I came upon a polenta-shop in 'the clouds, where an old Frenchman with an umbrella 'like a faded tropical leaf (it had not rained in Naples 'for six weeks) was staring at nothing at all, with a snuff- 'box in his hand. To him I appealed, concerning the 'Signor Larthoor. "Sir," said he, with the sweetest polite- 'ness, "can you speak French?" "Sir," said I, "a little." '"Sir," said he, "I presume the Signor Loothere"—you 'will observe that he changed the name according to the 'custom of his country—"is an Englishman?" I ad- 'mitted that he was the victim of circumstances and had 'that misfortune. "Sir," said he, "one word more. '"*Has* he a servant with a wooden leg?" "Great heaven, '"sir," said I, "how do I know? I should think not, but '"it is possible." "It is always," said the Frenchman, '"possible. Almost all the things of the world are always '"possible." "Sir," said I—you may imagine my con- 'dition and dismal sense of my own absurdity, by this 'time—"that is true." He then took an immense pinch 'of snuff, wiped the dust off his umbrella, led me to an 'arch commanding a wonderful view of the Bay of Naples, 'and pointed deep into the earth from which I had 'mounted. "Below there, near the lamp, one finds an '"Englishman with a servant with a wooden leg. It is '"always possible that he is the Signor Loothore." I

NAPLES: 1853.

Old Frenchman at the polenta-shop.

All things possible.

NAPLES: 1853.

'had been asked at six o'clock, and it was now getting 'on for seven. I went back in a state of perspiration and 'misery not to be described, and without the faintest 'hope of finding the spot. But as I was going farther 'down to the lamp, I saw the strangest staircase up a 'dark corner, with a man in a white waistcoat (evidently 'hired) standing on the top of it fuming. I dashed in at 'a venture, found it was the house, made the most of the 'whole story, and achieved much popularity. The best of 'it was that as nobody ever did find the place, Lowther 'had put a servant at the bottom of the Salita to wait '"for an English gentleman;" but the servant (as he pre- 'sently pleaded), deceived by the moustache, had allowed 'the English gentleman to pass unchallenged.'

A waiter in distress.

Dinner at last.

From Naples they went to Rome, where they found Lockhart, 'fearfully weak and broken, yet hopeful of him- 'self too' (he died the following year); smoked and drank punch with David Roberts, then painting everyday with Louis Haghe in St. Peter's; and took the old walks. The Coliseum, Appian Way, and Streets of Tombs, seemed desolate and grand as ever; but generally, Dickens adds, 'I discovered the Roman antiquities to be *smaller* than my 'imagination in nine years had made them. The Electric 'Telegraph now goes like a sunbeam through the cruel 'old heart of the Coliseum—a suggestive thing to think 'about, I fancied. The Pantheon I thought even nobler 'than of yore.' The amusements were of course an attrac- tion; and nothing at the Opera amused the party of three English more, than another party of four Americans who sat behind them in the pit. 'All the seats are numbered

Old friends.

Time's changes.

ROME: 1853.

'arm-chairs, and you buy your number at the pay-place, 'and go to it with the easiest direction on the ticket itself. 'We were early, and the four places of the Americans were 'on the next row behind us—all together. After looking 'about them for some time, and seeing the greater part of 'the seats empty (because the audience generally wait in 'a caffè which is part of the theatre), one of them said '"Waal I dunno—I expect we aint no call to set so nigh '"to one another neither—will you scatter Kernel, will you '"scatter sir?—" Upon this the Kernel "scattered" some 'twenty benches off; and they distributed themselves (for 'no earthly reason apparently but to get rid of one another) 'all over the pit. As soon as the overture began, in came 'the audience in a mass. Then the people who had got 'the numbers into which they had "scattered," had to get 'them out; and as they understood nothing that was said 'to them, and could make no reply but "A-mericani," you 'may imagine the number of cocked hats it took to dis-'lodge them. At last they were all got back into their right 'places, except one. About an hour afterwards when Moses '(*Moses in Egypt* was the opera) was invoking the dark-'ness, and there was a dead silence all over the house, 'unwonted sounds of disturbance broke out from a distant 'corner of the pit, and here and there a beard got up to 'look. "What is it neow sir?" said one of the Americans 'to another;—"some person seems to be getting along, '"again streeem." "Waal sir" he replied "I dunno. But '"I xpect 'tis the Kernel sir, a holdin on." So it was. 'The Kernel was ignominiously escorted back to his right 'place, not in the least disconcerted, and in perfectly good

At the Opera.

A 'scatter-'ing' party.

The Colonel holding on.

ROME: 1853.

'spirits and temper.' The opera was excellently done, and the price of the stalls one and threepence English. At Milan, on the other hand, the Scala was fallen from its old estate, dirty, gloomy, dull, and the performance execrable.

Another theatre of the smallest pretension Dickens sought out with avidity in Rome, and eagerly enjoyed. He had heard it said in his old time in Genoa that the finest Marionetti were here; and now, after great difficulty, he discovered the company in a sort of stable attached to a decayed palace. 'It was a wet night, and there was no 'audience but a party of French officers and ourselves. We 'all sat together. I never saw anything more amazing 'than the performance—altogether only an hour long, but 'managed by as many as ten people, for we saw them all 'go behind, at the ringing of a bell. The saving of a young 'lady by a good fairy from the machinations of an en'chanter, coupled with the comic business of her servant 'Pulcinella (the Roman Punch) formed the plot of the first 'piece. A scolding old peasant woman, who always leaned 'forward to scold and put her hands in the pockets of her 'apron, was incredibly natural. Pulcinella, so airy, so 'merry, so life-like, so graceful, he was irresistible. To 'see him carrying an umbrella over his mistress's head in 'a storm, talking to a prodigious giant whom he met in 'the forest, and going to bed with a pony, were things 'never to be forgotten. And so delicate are the hands of 'the people who move them, that every puppet was an 'Italian, and did exactly what an Italian does. If he 'pointed at any object, if he saluted anybody, if he laughed,

Performance of puppets.

Pulcinella, giant, and pony.

'if he cried, he did it as never Englishman did it since 'Britain first at Heaven's command arose—arose—arose, '&c. There was a ballet afterwards, on the same scale, and 'we really came away quite enchanted with the delicate 'drollery of the thing. French officers more than ditto.'

Of the great enemy to the health of the now capital of the kingdom of Italy, Dickens remarked in the same letter. 'I have been led into some curious speculations by the 'existence and progress of the Malaria about Rome. Isn't 'it very extraordinary to think of its encroaching and en-'croaching on the Eternal City as if it were commissioned 'to swallow it up. This year it has been extremely bad, 'and has long outstayed its usual time. Rome has been 'very unhealthy, and is not free now. Few people care to 'be out at the bad times of sunset and sunrise, and the 'streets are like a desert at night. There is a church, a 'very little way outside the walls, destroyed by fire some '16 or 18 years ago, and now restored and re-created at an 'enormous expense. It stands in a wilderness. For any 'human creature who goes near it, or can sleep near it, after 'nightfall, it might as well be at the bottom of the upper-'most cataract of the Nile. Along the whole extent of the 'Pontine Marshes (which we came across the other day), 'no creature in Adam's likeness lives, except the sallow 'people at the lonely posting-stations. I walk out from the 'Coliseum through the Street of Tombs to the ruins of the 'old Appian Way—pass no human being, and see no human 'habitation but ruined houses from which the people have 'fled, and where it is Death to sleep: these houses being 'three miles outside a gate of Rome at its farthest extent.

Malaria.

Desolation.

ROME: 1853.

'Leaving Rome by the opposite side, we travel for many 'many hours over the dreary Campagna, shunned and 'avoided by all but the wretched shepherds. Thirteen

At Bolsena.

'hours' good posting brings us to Bolsena (I slept there 'once before), on the margin of a stagnant lake whence the 'workpeople fly as the sun goes down—where it is a risk 'to go; where from a distance we saw a mist hang on the 'place; where, in the inconceivably wretched inn, no 'window can be opened; where our dinner was a pale ghost 'of a fish with an oily omelette, and we slept in great 'mouldering rooms tainted with ruined arches and heaps

Plague-smitten tract.

'of dung—and coming from which we saw no colour in the 'cheek of man, woman, or child for another twenty miles. 'Imagine this phantom knocking at the gates of Rome; 'passing them; creeping along the streets; haunting the 'aisles and pillars of the churches; year by year more 'encroaching, and more impossible of avoidance.'

VENICE: November.

From Rome they posted to Florence, reaching it in three days and a half, on the morning of the 20th of November; having then been out six weeks, with only three days' rain; and in another week they were at Venice. 'The fine 'weather has accompanied us here,' Dickens wrote on the 28th of November, 'the place of all others where it is 'necessary, and the city has been a blaze of sunlight and 'blue sky (with an extremely clear cold air) ever since we 'have been in it. If you could see it at this moment you

ii. 140.

'would never forget it. We live in the same house that I 'lived in nine years ago, and have the same sitting-room '—close to the Bridge of Sighs and the Palace of the 'Doges. The room is at the corner of the house, and

VENICE: 1853.

'there is a narrow street of water running round the side: 'so that we have the Grand Canal before the two front 'windows, and this wild little street at the corner window: 'into which, too, our three bedrooms look. We established 'a gondola as soon as we arrived, and we slide out of the 'hall on to the water twenty times a day. The gondoliers 'have queer old customs that belong to their class, and 'some are sufficiently disconcerting. . . It is a point of 'honour with them, while they are engaged, to be always 'at your disposal. Hence it is no use telling them they 'may go home for an hour or two—for they won't go. 'They roll themselves in shaggy capuccins, great coats 'with hoods, and lie down on the stone or marble pave-'ment until they are wanted again. So that when I come 'in or go out, on foot—which can be done from this house 'for some miles, over little bridges and by narrow ways—'I usually walk over the principal of my vassals, whose 'custom it is to snore immediately across the doorway. 'Conceive the oddity of the most familiar things in this 'place, from one instance: Last night we go downstairs at 'half-past eight, step into the gondola, slide away on the 'black water, ripple and plash swiftly along for a mile or two, 'land at a broad flight of steps, and instantly walk into 'the most brilliant and beautiful theatre conceivable—all 'silver and blue, and precious little fringes made of glittering 'prisms of glass. There we sit until half-past eleven, come 'out again (gondolier asleep outside the box-door), and in 'a moment are on the black silent water, floating away 'as if there were no dry building in the world. It stops, 'and in a moment we are out again, upon the broad solid

Gondola hired.

Habits of gondoliers.

At the theatre.

VENICE: 1853. 'Piazza of St. Mark, brilliantly lighted with gas, very like 'the Palais Royal at Paris, only far more handsome, and 'shining with no end of caffès. The two old pillars and the 'enormous bell-tower are as gruff and solid against the 'exquisite starlight as if they were a thousand miles from 'the sea or any undermining water; and the front of the 'cathedral, overlaid with golden mosaics and beautiful 'colours, is like a thousand rainbows even in the night.'

ii. 142-4. His formerly expressed notions as to art and pictures in Italy received confirmation at this visit. 'I am more than 'ever confirmed in my conviction that one of the great uses 'of travelling is to encourage a man to think for himself, 'to be bold enough always to declare without offence that 'he *does* think for himself, and to overcome the villainous 'meanness of professing what other people have professed 'when he knows (if he has capacity to originate an opinion) 'that his profession is untrue. The intolerable nonsense 'against which genteel taste and subserviency are afraid to 'rise, in connection with art, is astounding. Egg's honest 'amazement and consternation when he saw some of the 'most trumpeted things was what the Americans call "a '"caution." In the very same hour and minute there were 'scores of people falling into conventional raptures with that 'very poor Apollo, and passing over the most beautiful little 'figures and heads in the whole Vatican because they were 'not expressly set up to be worshipped. So in this place. 'There are pictures by Tintoretto in Venice, more delight-'ful and masterly than it is possible sufficiently to express. 'His Assembly of the Blest I do believe to be, take it all in 'all, the most wonderful and charming picture ever painted.

Uses of travel.

A painter among paintings.

Tintoretto.

'Your guide-book writer, representing the general swarm-'ing of humbugs, rather patronizes Tintoretto as a man 'of some sort of merit; and (bound to follow Eustace, 'Forsyth, and all the rest of them) directs you, on pain of 'being broke for want of gentility in appreciation, to go 'into ecstacies with things that have neither imagination, 'nature, proportion, possibility, nor anything else in them. 'You immediately obey, and tell your son to obey. He 'tells his son, and he tells his, and so the world gets at 'three-fourths of its frauds and miseries.'

VENICE: 1853.

Conventional praises.

The last place visited was Turin, where the travellers arrived on the 5th of December, finding it, with a brightly shining sun, intensely cold and freezing hard. 'There are 'double windows to all the rooms, but the Alpine air comes 'down and numbs my feet as I write (in a cap and shawl) 'within six feet of the fire.' There was yet something better than this to report of that bracing Alpine air. To Dickens's remarks on the Sardinian race, and to what he says of the exile of the noblest Italians, the momentous events of the few following years gave striking comment; nor could better proof be afforded of the judgment he brought to the observation of what passed before him. The letter had in all respects much interest and attractiveness. 'This is a remarkably agreeable place. A beau-'tiful town, prosperous, thriving, growing prodigiously, as 'Genoa is; crowded with busy inhabitants; full of noble 'streets and squares. The Alps, now covered deep with 'snow, are close upon it, and here and there seem almost 'ready to tumble into the houses. The contrast this part 'of Italy presents to the rest, is amazing. Beautifully

TURIN: December.

Liking for the Sardinians.

TURIN: 1853.

Contrasts.

'made railroads, admirably managed; cheerful, active 'people; spirit, energy, life, progress. In Milan, in every 'street, the noble palace of some exile is a barrack, and 'dirty soldiers are lolling out of the magnificent windows '—it seems as if the whole place were being gradually 'absorbed into soldiers. In Naples, something like a hun- 'dred thousand troops. "I knew," I said to a certain Nea- 'politan Marchese there whom I had known before, and 'who came to see me the night after I arrived, "I knew '"a very remarkable gentleman when I was last here; '"who had never been out of his own country, but was '"perfectly acquainted with English literature, and had '"taught himself to speak English in that wonderful '"manner that no one could have known him for a foreigner; '"I am very anxious to see him again, but I forget his '"name."—He named him, and his face fell directly. '"Dead?" said I.—"In exile."—"O dear me!" said I, '"I had looked forward to seeing him again, more than '"any one I was acquainted with in the country!"— '"What would you have!" says the Marchese in a low 'voice. "He was a remarkable man—full of knowledge, '"full of spirit, full of generosity. Where should he be '"but in exile! Where could he be!" We said not 'another word about it, but I shall always remember the 'short dialogue.'

Enquiry after friends.

Noblest in exile.

On the other hand there were incidents of the Austrian occupation as to which Dickens thought the ordinary style of comment unfair; and his closing remark on their police is well worth preserving. 'I am strongly inclined to think 'that our countrymen are to blame in the matter of the

'Austrian vexations to travellers that have been complained 'of. Their manner is so very bad, they are so extraordinarily 'suspicious, so determined to be done by everybody, and 'give so much offence. Now, the Austrian police are very 'strict, but they really know how to do business, and they 'do it. And if you treat them like gentlemen, they will 'always respond. When we first crossed the Austrian 'frontier, and were ushered into the police office, I took 'off my hat. The officer immediately took off his, and 'was as polite — still doing his duty, without any com- 'promise—as it was possible to be. When we came to 'Venice, the arrangements were very strict, but were so 'business-like that the smallest possible amount of incon- 'venience consistent with strictness ensued. Here is the 'scene. A soldier has come into the railway carriage (a 'saloon on the American plan) some miles off, has touched 'his hat, and asked for my passport. I have given it. 'Soldier has touched his hat again, and retired as from 'the presence of superior officer. Alighted from carriage, 'we pass into a place like a banking-house, lighted up 'with gas. Nobody bullies us or drives us there, but we 'must go, because the road ends there. Several soldierly 'clerks. One very sharp chief. My passport is brought 'out of an inner room, certified to be en règle. Very sharp 'chief takes it, looks at it (it is rather longer, now, than '*Hamlet*), calls out—" Signor Carlo Dickens!" "Here I '" am sir." "Do you intend remaining long in Venice '" sir?" "Probably four days sir!" "Italian is known '" to you sir. You have been in Venice before?" "Once '" before sir." "Perhaps you remained longer then sir?"

Austrian police.

Police arrangements.

Dickens and the Austrian.

ITALY: 1853.

'"No indeed; I merely came to see, and went as I came." '"Truly sir? Do I infer that you are going by Trieste?" '"No. I am going to Parma, and Turin, and by Paris '"home." "A cold journey sir, I hope it may be a '"pleasant one." "Thank you."—He gives me one very 'sharp look all over, and wishes me a very happy night. 'I wish *him* a very happy night and it's done. The thing 'being done at all, could not be better done, or more politely '—though I dare say if I had been sucking a gentish cane 'all the time, or talking in English to my compatriots, it 'might not unnaturally have been different. At Turin and 'at Genoa there are no such stoppages at all; but in any 'other part of Italy, give me an Austrian in preference to a 'native functionary. At Naples it is done in a beggarly, 'shambling, bungling, tardy, vulgar way; but I am

An old dislike.

'strengthened in my old impression that Naples is one of 'the most odious places on the face of the earth. The 'general degradation oppresses me like foul air.'

# CHAPTER IV.

## THREE SUMMERS AT BOULOGNE.

### 1853, 1854, AND 1856.

Boulogne: 1853.

DICKENS was in Boulogne, in 1853, from the middle of June to the end of September, and for the next three months, as we have seen, was in Switzerland and Italy. In the following year he went again to Boulogne in June, and stayed, after finishing *Hard Times*, until far into October. In February of 1855 he was for a fortnight in Paris with Mr. Wilkie Collins; not taking up his more prolonged residence there until the winter. From November 1855 to the end of April 1856 he made the French capital his home, working at *Little Dorrit* during all those months. Then, after a month's interval in Dover and London, he took up his third summer residence in Boulogne, whither his younger children had gone direct from Paris; and stayed until September, finishing *Little Dorrit* in London in the spring of 1857.

Visits to France.

Of the first of these visits, a few lively notes of humour and character out of his letters will tell the story sufficiently. The second and third had points of more attractiveness. Those were the years of the French-English alliance, of the great exposition of English paintings, of

BOULOGNE: 1853.

the return of the troops from the Crimea, and of the visit of the Prince Consort to the Emperor; such interest as Dickens took in these several matters appearing in his letters with the usual vividness, and the story of his continental life coming out with amusing distinctness in the successive pictures they paint with so much warmth and colour. Another chapter will be given to Paris. This deals only with Boulogne.

His first residence.

For his first summer residence, in June 1853, he had taken a house on the high ground near the Calais road; an odd French place with the strangest little rooms and halls, but standing in the midst of a large garden, with wood and waterfall, a conservatory opening on a great bank of roses, and paths and gates on one side to the ramparts, on the other to the sea. Above all there was a capital proprietor and landlord, by whom the cost of keeping up gardens and wood (which he called a forest) was defrayed, while he gave his tenant the whole range of both and all the flowers for nothing, sold him the garden produce as it was wanted, and kept a cow on the estate to supply the family milk. 'If this were but 300 miles 'farther off,' wrote Dickens, 'how the English would rave 'about it! I do assure you that there are picturesque 'people, and town, and country, about this place, that 'quite fill up the eye and fancy. As to the fishing people '(whose dress can have changed neither in colour nor in 'form for many many years), and their quarter of the town 'cobweb-hung with great brown nets across the narrow 'up-hill streets, they are as good as Naples, every bit.' His description both of house and landlord, of which I

The 'forest.'

Fisherman's quarter.

tested the exactness when I visited him, was in the old pleasant vein; requiring no connection with himself to give it interest, but, by the charm and ease with which everything picturesque or characteristic was disclosed, placed in the domain of art.

Villa des Moulineaux.

'O the rain here yesterday!' (26th of June.) 'A great 'sea-fog rolling in, a strong wind blowing, and the rain com'ing down in torrents all day long. . . This house is on 'a great hill-side, backed up by woods of young trees. It 'faces the Haute Ville with the ramparts and the unfinished 'cathedral—which capital object is exactly opposite the 'windows. On the slope in front, going steep down to the 'right, all Boulogne is piled and jumbled about in a very 'picturesque manner. The view is charming—closed in at 'last by the tops of swelling hills; and the door is within 'ten minutes of the post-office, and within quarter of an 'hour of the sea. The garden is made in terraces up the 'hill-side, like an Italian garden; the top walks being in the 'before-mentioned woods. The best part of it begins at 'the level of the house, and goes up at the back, a couple 'of hundred feet perhaps. There are at present thousands 'of roses all about the house, and no end of other flowers. 'There are five great summer-houses, and (I think) fifteen 'fountains—not one of which (according to the invariable 'French custom) ever plays. The house is a doll's house 'of many rooms. It is one story high, with eight and 'thirty steps up and down—tribune wise—to the front 'door: the noblest French demonstration I have ever seen 'I think. It is a double house; and as there are only 'four windows and a pigeon-hole to be beheld in front,

Garden and fountains.

A doll's house.

BOULOGNE: 1853.

'you would suppose it to contain about four rooms. Being 'built on the hill-side, the top story of the house at the 'back—there are two stories there—opens on the level of 'another garden. On the ground floor there is a very 'pretty hall, almost all glass; a little dining-room opening 'on a beautiful conservatory, which is also looked into 'through a great transparent glass in a mirror-frame over 'the chimney-piece, just as in Paxton's room at Chats-'worth; a spare bed-room, two little drawing-rooms open-'ing into one another, the family bed-rooms, a bath-room, 'a glass corridor, an open yard, and a kind of kitchen with 'a machinery of stoves and boilers. Above, there are 'eight tiny bed-rooms all opening on one great room in 'the roof, originally intended for a billiard-room. In the 'basement there is an admirable kitchen with every con-'ceivable requisite in it, a noble cellar, first-rate man's 'room and pantry; coach-house, stable, coal-store and 'wood-store; and in the garden is a pavilion, containing 'an excellent spare bed-room on the ground floor. The 'getting-up of these places, the looking-glasses, clocks, 'little stoves, all manner of fittings, must be seen to be 'appreciated. The conservatory is full of choice flowers 'and perfectly beautiful.'

Rooms.

Offices.

Then came the charm of the letter, his description of his landlord, lightly sketched by him in print as M. Loyal-Devasseur, but here filled in with the most attractive touches his loving hand could give. 'But the landlord—M. Beau-'court—is wonderful. Everybody here has two surnames (I 'cannot conceive why), and M. Beaucourt, as he is always 'called, is by rights M. Beaucourt-Mutuel. He is a portly

Landlord.

Wife's name and his own.

'jolly fellow with a fine open face; lives on the hill 'behind, just outside the top of the garden; and was a 'linen draper in the town, where he still has a shop, but 'is supposed to have mortgaged his business and to be in 'difficulties—all along of this place, which he has planted 'with his own hands; which he cultivates all day; and 'which he never on any consideration speaks of but as '"the Property." He is extraordinarily popular in Bou-'logne (the people in the shops invariably brightening up 'at the mention of his name, and congratulating us on 'being his tenants), and really seems to deserve it. He is 'such a liberal fellow that I can't bear to ask him for 'anything, since he instantly supplies it whatever it is. 'The things he has done in respect of unreasonable bed-'steads and washing-stands, I blush to think of. I observed 'the other day in one of the side gardens—there are gar-'dens at each side of the house too—a place where I 'thought the Comic Countryman' (a name he was giving just then to his youngest boy) 'must infallibly trip over, 'and make a little descent of a dozen feet. So I said, '"M. Beaucourt"—who instantly pulled off his cap and 'stood bareheaded—"there are some spare pieces of wood '"lying by the cow-house, if you would have the kind-'"ness to have one laid across here I think it would be '"safer." "Ah, mon dieu sir," said M. Beaucourt, "it must '"be iron. This is not a portion of the property where '"you would like to see wood." "But iron is so expen-'"sive," said I, "and it really is not worth while——" '"Sir, pardon me a thousand times," said M. Beaucourt, '"it shall be iron. Assuredly and perfectly it shall be

BOULOGNE: 1853.

Bon garçon.

i. 159. ii. 221, 288.

Tenant and landlord.

BOULOGNE: 1853.

'"iron." "Then M. Beaucourt," said I, "I shall be glad '"to pay a moiety of the cost." "Sir," said M. Beaucourt, '"Never!" Then to change the subject, he slided from 'his firmness and gravity into a graceful conversational 'tone, and said, "In the moonlight last night, the flowers '"on the property appeared, O Heaven, to be *bathing* '"*themselves in the sky.* You like the property?" "M. '"Beaucourt," said I, "I am enchanted with it; I am '"more than satisfied with everything." "And I sir," 'said M. Beaucourt, laying his cap upon his breast, and 'kissing his hand—"I equally!" Yesterday two black- 'smiths came for a day's work, and put up a good solid 'handsome bit of iron-railing, morticed into the stone 'parapet. . . If the extraordinary things in the house defy 'description, the amazing phenomena in the gardens never 'could have been dreamed of by anybody but a French- 'man bent upon one idea. Besides a portrait of the house 'in the dining-room, there is a plan of the property in the 'hall. It looks about the size of Ireland; and to every 'one of the extraordinary objects, there is a reference 'with some portentous name. There are fifty-one such 'references, including the Cottage of Tom Thumb, the 'Bridge of Austerlitz, the Bridge of Jena, the Hermitage, 'the Bower of the Old Guard, the Labyrinth (I have no idea 'which is which); and there is guidance to every room in 'the house, as if it were a place on that stupendous scale 'that without such a clue you must infallibly lose your 'way, and perhaps perish of starvation between bedroom 'and bedroom.' *

Mr. Beaucourt and the 'pro- 'perty.'

Making the most of it.

* Prices are reported in one of the letters; and, considering what they have

On the 3rd of July there came a fresh trait of the good fellow of a landlord. 'Fancy what Beaucourt told me last 'night. When he "conceived the inspiration" of planting 'the property ten years ago, he went over to England to 'buy the trees, took a small cottage in the market-gardens 'at Putney, lived there three months, held a symposium 'every night attended by the principal gardeners of Ful-'ham, Putney, Kew, and Hammersmith (which he calls 'Hamsterdam), and wound up with a supper at which the 'market-gardeners rose, clinked their glasses, and exclaimed 'with one accord (I quote him exactly) VIVE BEAUCOURT! 'He was a captain in the National Guard, and Cavaignac 'his general. Brave Capitaine Beaucourt! said Cavaignac, 'you must receive a decoration. My General, said Beau-'court, No! It is enough for me that I have done my duty. 'I go to lay the first stone of a house upon a Property I 'have—that house shall be my decoration. (Regard that 'house!)' Addition to the picture came in a letter of the 24th of July: with a droll glimpse of Shakespeare at the theatre, and of the Saturday's pig-market.

BOULOGNE: 1853.

Beaucourt's visit to England.

Among the Putney market-gardeners.

'I may mention that the great Beaucourt daily changes 'the orthography of this place. He has now fixed it, by 'having painted up outside the garden gate, "Entrée par-'"ticulière de la Villa des Moulineaux." On another gate

been since, the touch of disappointment hinted at may raise a smile. 'Pro-'visions are scarcely as cheap as I expected, though very different from London: 'besides which, a pound weight here, is a pound and a quarter English. So 'that meat at 7*d*. a pound, is actually a fourth less. A capital dish of 'asparagus costs us about fivepence; a fowl, one and threepence; a duck, a 'few halfpence more; a dish of fish, about a shilling. The very best wine at 'tenpence that I ever drank—I used to get it very good for the same money 'in Genoa, but not so good. The common people very engaging and obliging.'

Prices.

BOULOGNE: 1853.

Pride in the Property.

'a little higher up, he has had painted "Entrée des Ecuries "de la Villa des Moulineaux." On another gate a little 'lower down (applicable to one of the innumerable build-'ings in the garden), "Entrée du Tom Pouce." On the 'highest gate of the lot, leading to his own house, "Entrée "du Château Napoléonienne." All of which inscriptions 'you will behold in black and white when you come. I see 'little of him now, as, all things being "bien arrangées," 'he is delicate of appearing. His wife has been making a 'trip in the country during the last three weeks, but (as 'he mentioned to me with his hat in his hand) it was 'necessary that he should remain here, to be continually 'at the disposition of the tenant of the Property. (The 'better to do this, he has had roaring dinner parties of 'fifteen daily; and the old woman who milks the cows has 'been fainting up the hill under vast burdens of champagne.)

Absence of Madame B.

Shakespearian performance.

'We went to the theatre last night, to see the *Mid-'summer Night's Dream*—of the Opera Comique. It is 'a beautiful little theatre now, with a very good company; 'and the nonsense of the piece was done with a sense quite 'confounding in that connexion. Willy Am Shay Kes 'Peer; Sirzhon Foll Stayffe; Lor Lattimeer; and that 'celebrated Maid of Honour to Queen Elizabeth, Meees 'Oleeveeir—were the principal characters.

Preparations for the Fair.

'Outside the old town, an army of workmen are (and 'have been for a week or so, already) employed upon an 'immense building which I supposed might be a Fort, or 'a Monastery, or a Barrack, or other something designed 'to last for ages. I find it is for the annual fair, which 'begins on the fifth of August and lasts a fortnight. Almost

BOULOGNE: 1853.

'every Sunday we have a fête, where there is dancing in 'the open air, and where immense men with prodigious 'beards revolve on little wooden horses like Italian irons, 'in what we islanders call a roundabout, by the hour to-'gether. But really the good humour and cheerfulness 'are very delightful. Among the other sights of the place, 'there is a pig-market every Saturday, perfectly insup-'portable in its absurdity. An excited French peasant, 'male or female, with a determined young pig, is the most 'amazing spectacle. I saw a little Drama enacted yester-'day week, the drollery of which was perfect. *Dram. Pers.* '1. A pretty young woman with short petticoats and trim 'blue stockings, riding a donkey with two baskets and a 'pig in each. 2. An ancient farmer in a blouse, driving 'four pigs, his four in hand, with an enormous whip—and 'being drawn against walls and into smoking shops by any 'one of the four. 3. A cart, with an old pig (manacled) 'looking out of it, and terrifying six hundred and fifty 'young pigs in the market by his terrific grunts. 4. Col-'lector of Octroi in an immense cocked hat, with a stream 'of young pigs running, night and day, between his mili-'tary boots and rendering accounts impossible. 5. Inimit-'able, confronted by a radiation of elderly pigs, fastened 'each by one leg to a bunch of stakes in the ground. '6. John Edmund Reade, poet, expressing eternal devotion 'to and admiration of Landor, unconscious of approaching 'pig recently escaped from barrow. 7. Priests, peasants, 'soldiers, &c. &c.'

Pictures at the Pig-market.

He had meanwhile gathered friendly faces round him. Frank Stone went over with his family to a house taken

BOULOGNE: 1853.

English friends.

for him on the St. Omer road by Dickens, who was joined in the chateau by Mr. and Mrs. Leech and Mr. Wilkie Collins. 'Leech says that when he stepped from the boat 'after their stormy passage, he was received by the congre-'gated spectators with a distinct round of applause as by 'far the most intensely and unutterably miserable looking 'object that had yet appeared. The laughter was tumul-'tuous, and he wishes his friends to know that altogether he 'made an immense hit.' So passed the summer months: excursions with these friends to Amiens and Beauvais relieving the work upon his novel, and the trip to Italy, already described, following on its completion.

June 1854.

In June, 1854, M. Beaucourt had again received his famous tenant, but in another cottage or chateau (to him convertible terms) on the much cherished property, placed on the very summit of the hill with a private road leading out to the Column, a really pretty place, rooms larger than in the other house, a noble sea view, everywhere nice prospects, good garden, and plenty of sloping turf.* It was called the Villa du Camp de Droite, and here Dickens stayed, as I have intimated, until the eve of his winter residence in Paris.

Change of Villa on 'the pro-'perty.'

Ante, 48.

The formation of the Northern Camp at Boulogne began the week after he had finished *Hard Times*, and he watched

Thackeray.

* Besides the old friends before named, Thackeray and his family were here in the early weeks, living 'in a melancholy but very good chateau on the 'Paris road, where their landlord (a Baron) has supplied them, T. tells me, 'with one milk-jug as the entire crockery of the establishment.' Our friend soon tired of this, going off to Spa, and on his return, after ascending the hill to smoke a farewell cigar with Dickens, left for London and Scotland in October.

its progress, as it increased and extended itself along the cliffs towards Calais, with the liveliest amusement. At first he was startled by the suddenness with which soldiers overran the roads, became billeted in every house, made the bridges red with their trowsers, and 'sprang upon the 'pier like fantastic mustard and cress when boats were 'expected, many of them never having seen the sea before.' But the good behaviour of the men had a reconciling effect, and their ingenuity delighted him. The quickness with which they raised whole streets of mud-huts, less picturesque than the tents,* but (like most unpicturesque things) more comfortable, was like an Arabian Nights' tale. 'Each 'little street holds 144 men, and every corner-door has 'the number of the street upon it as soon as it is put up; 'and the postmen can fall to work as easily as in the Rue 'de Rivoli at Paris.' His patience was again a little tried when he found baggage-wagons ploughing up his favourite walks, and trumpeters in twos and threes teaching newly-recruited trumpeters in all the sylvan places, and making the echoes hideous. But this had its amusement too. 'I 'met to-day a weazen sun-burnt youth from the south with 'such an immense regimental shako on, that he looked like 'a sort of lucifer match-box, evidently blowing his life 'rapidly out, under the auspices of two magnificent creatures 'all hair and lungs, of such breadth across the shoulders 'that I couldn't see their breast-buttons when I stood in 'front of them.'

BOULOGNE: 1854.

Northern Camp.

Mud-huts and tents.

A trumpeter recruit.

* Another of his letters questioned even the picturesqueness a little, for he discovered that on a sunny day the white tents, seen from a distance, looked exactly like an immense washing establishment with all the linen put out to dry.

BOULOGNE: 1854.

Visit of Prince Albert.

The interest culminated as the visit of the Prince Consort approached with its attendant glories of illuminations and reviews. Beaucourt's excitement became intense. The Villa du Camp de Droite was to be a blaze of triumph on the night of the arrival; Dickens, who had carried over with him the meteor flag of England and set it streaming over a haystack in his field,* now hoisted the French colours over the British Jack in honour of the national alliance; the Emperor was to subside to the station of a general officer, so that all the rejoicings should be in honour of the Prince; and there was to be a review in the open country near Wimereux, when 'at one stage of the 'maneuvres (I am too excited to spell the word but you 'know what I mean)' the whole hundred thousand men in the camp of the North were to be placed before the Prince's eyes, to show him what a division of the French army might be. 'I believe everything I hear,' said Dickens. It was the state of mind of Hood's country gentleman after the fire at the Houses of Parliament. 'Beaucourt, as one 'of the town council, receives summonses to turn out and 'debate about something, or receive somebody, every five 'minutes. Whenever I look out of window, or go to the 'door, I see an immense black object at Beaucourt's porch 'like a boat set up on end in the air with a pair of white 'trowsers below it. This is the cocked hat of an official 'Huissier, newly arrived with a summons, whose head is 'thrown back as he is in the act of drinking Beaucourt's 'wine.' The day came at last, and all Boulogne turned

Grand review.

Beaucourt's excitement.

* 'Whence it can be seen for miles and miles, to the glory of England and 'the joy of Beaucourt.'

BOULOGNE: 1854.

out for its holiday; 'but I' Dickens wrote, 'had by this 'cooled down a little, and, reserving myself for the illumi-'nations, I abandoned the great men and set off upon my 'usual country walk. See my reward. Coming home by 'the Calais road, covered with dust, I suddenly find myself 'face to face with Albert and Napoleon, jogging along in 'the pleasantest way, a little in front, talking extremely 'loud about the view, and attended by a brilliant staff of 'some sixty or seventy horsemen, with a couple of our royal 'grooms with their red coats riding oddly enough in the 'midst of the magnates. I took off my wide-awake with-'out stopping to stare, whereupon the Emperor pulled off 'his cocked hat; and Albert (seeing, I suppose, that it was 'an Englishman) pulled off his. Then we went our several 'ways. The Emperor is broader across the chest than in 'the old times when we used to see him so often at Gore-'House, and stoops more in the shoulders. Indeed his 'carriage thereabouts is like Fonblanque's.' * The town he described as 'one great flag' for the rest of the visit; and to the success of the illuminations he contributed largely himself by leading off splendidly with a hundred and twenty wax candles blazing in his seventeen front windows, and visible from that great height over all the place. 'On the first eruption Beaucourt *danced and 'screamed* on the grass before the door; and when he was

Meeting the great.

Emperor, Prince, and Dickens.

The illuminations.

* The picture had changed drearily in less than a year and a half, when (17th of Feb. 1856) Dickens thus wrote from Paris. 'I suppose mortal man 'out of bed never looked so ill and worn as the Emperor does just now. He 'passed close by me on horseback, as I was coming in at the door on Friday, 'and I never saw so haggard a face. Some English saluted him, and he lifted 'his hand to his hat as slowly, painfully, and laboriously, as if his arm were 'made of lead. I think he *must* be in pain.'

A changed Emperor.

BOULOGNE: 1854.

'more composed, set off with Madame Beaucourt to look at 'the house from every possible quarter, and, he said, collect 'the suffrages of his compatriots.'

Their suffrages seem to have gone, however, mainly in another direction. 'It was wonderful,' Dickens wrote, 'to behold about the streets the small French soldiers of 'the line seizing our Guards by the hand and embracing 'them. It was wonderful, too, to behold the English 'sailors in the town, shaking hands with everybody and 'generally patronizing everything. When the people could 'not get hold of either a soldier or a sailor, they rejoiced 'in the royal grooms, and embraced *them*. I don't think 'the Boulogne people were surprised by anything so much, 'as by the three cheers the crew of the yacht gave when 'the Emperor went aboard to lunch. The prodigious volume 'of them, and the precision, and the circumstance that no 'man was left straggling on his own account either before 'or afterwards, seemed to strike the general mind with 'amazement. Beaucourt said it was *like boxing*.' That was written on the 10th of September; but in a very few days Dickens was unwillingly convinced that whatever the friendly disposition to England might be, the war with Russia was decidedly unpopular. He was present when the false report of the taking of Sebastopol reached the Emperor and Empress. 'I was at the Review' (8th of October) 'yesterday week, very near the Emperor and 'Empress, when the taking of Sebastopol was announced. 'It was a magnificent show on a magnificent day; and if 'any circumstance could make it special, the arrival of the 'telegraphic despatch would be the culminating point one

Jack-Tars.

English cheers.

'Like 'boxing.'

Supposed fall of Sebastopol.

'might suppose. It quite disturbed and mortified me to 'find how faintly, feebly, miserably, the men responded to 'the call of the officers to cheer, as each regiment passed 'by. Fifty excited Englishmen would make a greater 'sign and sound than a thousand of these men do. . . The 'Empress was very pretty, and her slight figure sat capi-'tally on her grey horse. When the Emperor gave her the 'despatch to read, she flushed and fired up in a very plea-'sant way, and kissed it with as natural an impulse as one 'could desire to see.'

BOULOGNE: 1854.

On the night of that day Dickens went up to see a play acted at a café at the camp, and found himself one of an audience composed wholly of officers and men, with only four ladies among them, officers' wives. The steady, work-ing, sensible faces all about him told their own story; 'and 'as to kindness and consideration towards the poor actors, 'it was real benevolence.' Another attraction at the camp was a conjuror, who had been called to exhibit twice before the imperial party, and whom Dickens always afterwards referred to as the most consummate master of legerdemain he had seen. Nor was he a mean authority as to this, being himself, with his tools at hand, a capital conjuror;* but the Frenchman scorned help, stood among the company without any sort of apparatus, and, by the mere force of sleight of hand and an astonishing memory, performed feats having no likeness to anything Dickens had ever seen done, and totally inexplicable to his most vigilant reflec-

A play at the Camp.

A French conjuror.

* I permit myself to quote from the bill of one of his entertainments in the old merry days at Bonchurch (ii. 394—406), of course drawn up by him-self, whom it describes as 'The Unparalleled Necromancer RHIA RHAMA 'RHOOS, educated cabalistically in the Orange Groves of Salamanca and the

BOULOGNE: 1854.

Legerdemain in perfection.

tion. 'So far as I know, a perfectly original genius, and 'that puts any sort of knowledge of legerdemain, such as 'I supposed that I possessed, at utter defiance.' The account he gave dealt with two exploits only, the easiest to describe,

'Ocean Caves of Alum Bay,' some of whose proposed wonders it thus prefigures:

### THE LEAPING CARD WONDER.

Two Cards being drawn from the Pack by two of the company, and placed, with the Pack, in the Necromancer's box, will leap forth at the command of any lady of not less than eight, or more than eighty, years of age.

*** *This wonder is the result of nine years' seclusion in the mines of Russia.*

### THE PYRAMID WONDER.

Conjuring by Dickens.

A shilling being lent to the Necromancer by any gentleman of not less than twelve months, or more than one hundred years, of age, and carefully marked by the said gentleman, will disappear from within a brazen box at the word of command, and pass through the hearts of an infinity of boxes, which will afterwards build themselves into pyramids and sink into a small mahogany box, at the Necromancer's bidding.

*** *Five thousand guineas were paid for the acquisition of this wonder, to a Chinese Mandarin, who died of grief immediately after parting with the secret.*

### THE CONFLAGRATION WONDER.

A Card being drawn from the Pack by any lady, not under a direct and positive promise of marriage, will be immediately named by the Necromancer, destroyed by fire, and reproduced from its own ashes.

*** *An annuity of one thousand pounds has been offered to the Necromancer by the Directors of the Sun Fire Office for the secret of this wonder—and refused!!!*

### THE LOAF OF BREAD WONDER.

The watch of any truly prepossessing lady, of any age, single or married, being locked by the Necromancer in a strong box, will fly at the word of command from within that box into the heart of an ordinary half-quartern loaf, whence it shall be cut out in the presence of the whole company, whose cries of astonishment will be audible at a distance of some miles.

*** *Ten years in the Plains of Tartary were devoted to the study of this wonder.*

### THE TRAVELLING DOLL WONDER.

The travelling doll is composed of solid wood throughout, but, by putting on a travelling dress of the simplest construction, becomes invisible, performs enormous journeys in half a minute, and passes from visibility to invisibility with an expedition so astonishing that no eye can follow its transformations.

*** *The Necromancer's attendant usually faints on beholding this wonder, and is only to be revived by the administration of brandy and water.*

### THE PUDDING WONDER.

The company having agreed among themselves to offer to the Necromancer, by way of loan, the hat of any gentleman whose head has arrived at maturity of size, the Necromancer, without removing that hat for an instant from before the eyes of the delighted company, will light a fire in it, make a plum-pudding in his magic saucepan, boil it over the said fire, produce it in two minutes, thoroughly done, cut it, and dispense it in portions to the whole company, for their consumption then and there; returning the hat at last, wholly uninjured by fire, to its lawful owner.

*** *The extreme liberality of this wonder awakening the jealousy of the beneficent Austrian Government, when exhibited in Milan, the Necromancer had the honour to be seized, and confined for five years in the fortress of that city.*

and, not being with cards, not the most remarkable; for he would also say of this Frenchman that he transformed cards into very demons. He never saw a human hand touch them in the same way, fling them about so amazingly, or change them in his, one's own, or another's hand, with a skill so impossible to follow.

BOULOGNE: 1854.

Making demons of cards.

'You are to observe that he was *with the company*, 'not in the least removed from them; and that we occu-'pied the front row. He brought in some writing paper 'with him when he entered, and a black-lead pencil; and 'he wrote some words on half-sheets of paper. One of 'these half-sheets he folded into two, and gave to Catherine 'to hold. Madame, he says aloud, will you think of any 'class of objects? I have done so.—Of what class, Madame? 'Animals.—Will you think of a particular animal, Madame? 'I have done so.—Of what animal? The Lion.—Will 'you think of another class of objects, Madame? I have 'done so.—Of what class? Flowers.—The particular 'flower? The Rose.—Will you open the paper you hold 'in your hand? She opened it, and there was neatly and 'plainly written in pencil—*The Lion. The Rose.* No-'thing whatever had led up to these words, and they were 'the most distant conceivable from Catherine's thoughts 'when she entered the room. He had several common 'school-slates about a foot square. He took one of these to 'a field-officer from the camp, decoré and what not, who sat 'about six from us, with a grave saturnine friend next him. 'My General, says he, will you write a name on this slate, 'after your friend has done so? Don't show it to me. 'The friend wrote a name, and the General wrote a name.

Examples of a conjuror's art.

BOULOGNE: 1854.

'The conjuror took the slate rapidly from the officer, threw 'it violently down on the ground with its written side to 'the floor, and asked the officer to put his foot upon it and 'keep it there: which he did. The conjuror considered 'for about a minute, looking devilish hard at the General. '—My General, says he, your friend wrote Dagobert, upon 'the slate under your foot. The friend admits it.—And 'you, my General, wrote Nicholas. General admits it, and 'everybody laughs and applauds.—My General, will you 'excuse me, if I change that name into a name expressive of 'the power of a great nation, which, in happy alliance with 'the gallantry and spirit of France will shake that name 'to its centre? Certainly I will excuse it.—My General, 'take up the slate and read. General reads: DAGOBERT, 'VICTORIA. The first in his friend's writing; the second 'in a new hand. I never saw anything in the least like 'this; or at all approaching to the absolute certainty, the 'familiarity, quickness, absence of all machinery, and actual 'face-to-face, hand-to-hand fairness between the conjuror 'and the audience, with which it was done. I have not 'the slightest idea of the secret.—One more. He was 'blinded with several table napkins, and then a great 'cloth was bodily thrown over them and his head too, so 'that his voice sounded as if he were under a bed. Perhaps 'half a dozen dates were written on a slate. He takes the 'slate in his hand, and throws it violently down on the 'floor as before, remains silent a minute, seems to become 'agitated, and bursts out thus: "What is this I see? A '"great city, but of narrow streets and old-fashioned houses, '"many of which are of wood, resolving itself into ruins!

The conjuror compliments England;

and sees London in 1666.

'"How is it falling into ruins? Hark! I hear the crack-'"ling of a great conflagration, and, looking up, I behold '"a vast cloud of flame and smoke. The ground is covered '"with hot cinders too, and people are flying into the '"fields and endeavouring to save their goods. This great '"fire, this great wind, this roaring noise! This is the '"great fire of London, and the first date upon the slate '"must be one, six, six, six—the year in which it hap-'"pened!" And so on with all the other dates. There! 'Now, if you will take a cab and impart these mysteries 'to Rogers, I shall be very glad to have his opinion of 'them.' Rogers had taxed our credulity with some wonderful clairvoyant experiences of his own in Paris to which here was a parallel at last!

BOULOGNE: 1854.

June 1856.

When leaving Paris for his third visit to Boulogne, at the beginning of June 1856, he had not written a word of the ninth number of his new book, and did not expect for another month to 'see land from the running sea of *Little 'Dorrit*.' He had resumed the house he first occupied, the cottage or villa 'des Moulineaux,' and after dawdling about his garden for a few days with surprising industry in a French farmer garb of blue blouse, leathern belt, and military cap, which he had mounted as 'the only one for complete comfort,' he wrote to me that he was getting 'Now to work again—'to work! The story lies before me, I hope, strong and clear. 'Not to be easily told; but nothing of that sort IS to be 'easily done that *I* know of.' At work it became his habit to sit late, and then, putting off his usual walk until night, to lie down among the roses reading until after tea ('middle-aged Love in a blouse and belt'), when he went

Old residence resumed.

BOULOGNE: 1856.

The Pier at evening.

down to the pier. 'The said pier at evening is a phase of 'the place we never see, and which I hardly knew. But 'I never did behold such specimens of the youth of my 'country, male and female, as pervade that place. They 'are really, in their vulgarity and insolence, quite dis-'heartening. One is so fearfully ashamed of them, and 'they contrast so very unfavourably with the natives.' Mr. Wilkie Collins was again his companion in the summer weeks, and the presence of Jerrold for the greater part of the time added much to his enjoyment.

Last of the Camp.

The last of the camp was now at hand. It had only a battalion of men in it, and a few days would see them out. At first there was horrible weather, 'storms of wind, rushes 'of rain, heavy squalls, cold airs, sea fogs, banging shutters, 'flapping doors, and beaten down rose-trees by the hun-'dred;' but then came a delightful week among the corn fields and bean fields, and afterwards the end. 'It looks 'very singular and very miserable. The soil being sand, 'and the grass having been trodden away these two years, 'the wind from the sea carries the sand into the chinks 'and ledges of all the doors and windows, and chokes 'them;—just as if they belonged to Arab huts in the 'desert. A number of the non-commissioned officers made 'turf-couches outside their huts, and there were turf or-'chestras for the bands to play in; all of which are fast 'getting sanded over in a most Egyptian manner. The 'Fair is on, under the walls of the haute ville over the way.

Crimean exploits at a Fair.

'At one popular show, the Malakhoff is taken every half-'hour between 4 and 11. Bouncing explosions announce 'every triumph of the French arms (the English have 'nothing to do with it); and in the intervals a man outside blows a railway whistle—straight into the dining-room. Do you know that the French soldiers call the 'English medal "The Salvage Medal"—meaning that they 'got it for saving the English army? I don't suppose there 'are a thousand people in all France who believe that we 'did anything but get rescued by the French. And I am 'confident that the no-result of our precious Chelsea enquiry 'has wonderfully strengthened this conviction. Nobody at 'home has yet any adequate idea, I am deplorably sure, 'of what the Barnacles and the Circumlocution Office have 'done for us. But whenever we get into war again, the 'people will begin to find out.'

BOULOGNE: 1856.

Old grudges.

His own household had got into a small war already, of which the commander-in-chief was his man-servant 'French,' the bulk of the forces engaged being his children, and the invaders two cats. Business brought him to London on the hostilities breaking out, and on his return after a few days the story of the war was told. 'Dick,' it should be said, was a canary very dear both to Dickens and his eldest daughter, who had so tamed to her loving hand its wild little heart that it was become the most docile of companions.* 'The only thing new in this garden is that war 'is raging against two particularly tigerish and fearful cats '(from the mill, I suppose), which are always glaring in 'dark corners, after our wonderful little Dick. Keeping 'the house open at all points, it is impossible to shut them 'out, and they hide themselves in the most terrific manner:

A household war.

'Dick' in danger.

The two invaders.

* Dick died at Gadshill in 1866, in the sixteenth year of his age, and was honoured with a small tomb and epitaph.

BOULOGNE: 1856.

Feline foes.

'hanging themselves up behind draperies, like bats, and 'tumbling out in the dead of night with frightful cater-'waulings. Hereupon, French borrows Beaucourt's gun, 'loads the same to the muzzle, discharges it twice in vain 'and throws himself over with the recoil, exactly like a 'clown. But at last (while I was in town) he aims at the 'more amiable cat of the two, and shoots that animal dead. 'Insufferably elated by this victory, he is now engaged 'from morning to night in hiding behind bushes to get 'aim at the other. He does nothing else whatever. All 'the boys encourage him and watch for the enemy—on 'whose appearance they give an alarm which immediately 'serves as a warning to the creature, who runs away. They 'are at this moment (ready dressed for church) all lying on 'their stomachs in various parts of the garden. Horrible 'whistles give notice to the gun what point it is to ap-'proach. I am afraid to go out, lest I should be shot. Mr. 'Plornish says his prayers at night in a whisper, lest the 'cat should overhear him and take offence. The trades-'men cry out as they come up the avenue, "Me voici! '"C'est moi—boulanger—ne tirez pas, Monsieur Franche!" 'It is like living in a state of siege; and the wonderful 'manner in which the cat preserves the character of being 'the only person not much put out by the intensity of this 'monomania, is most ridiculous.' (6th of July.) . . . 'About 'four pounds of powder and half a ton of shot have been '(13th of July) fired off at the cat (and the public in general) 'during the week. The finest thing is that immediately 'after I have heard the noble sportsman blazing away at 'her in the garden in front, I look out of my room door

Household troops.

State of siege.

'into the drawing-room, and am pretty sure to see her 'coming in after the birds, in the calmest manner, by the 'back window. Intelligence has been brought to me from 'a source on which I can rely, that French has newly con-'ceived the atrocious project of tempting her into the coach-'house by meat and kindness, and there, from an elevated 'portmanteau, blowing her head off. This I mean sternly 'to interdict, and to do so to-day as a work of piety.'

BOULOGNE: 1856.

Indifference of the enemy.

Besides the graver work which Mr. Wilkie Collins and himself were busy with, in these months, and by which *Household Words* mainly was to profit, some lighter matters occupied the leisure of both. There were to be, at Christmas, theatricals again at Tavistock House; in which the children, with the help of their father and other friends, were to follow up the success of the *Lighthouse* by again acquitting themselves as grown-up actors; and Mr. Collins was busy preparing for them a new drama to be called *The Frozen Deep*, while Dickens was sketching a farce for Mr. Lemon to fill in. But this pleasant employment had sudden and sad interruption.

Preparing for Christmas.

An epidemic broke out in the town, affecting the children of several families known to Dickens, among them that of his friend Mr. Gilbert A'Becket; who, upon arriving from Paris, and finding a favourite little son stricken dangerously, sank himself under an illness from which he had been suffering, and died two days after the boy. 'He had for three days shown symptoms of rallying, and 'we had some hope of his recovery; but he sank and 'died, and never even knew that the child had gone before 'him. A sad, sad story.' Dickens meanwhile had sent

Deaths in the town.

Gilbert A'Becket.

BOULOGNE: 1856.

Leaving for England.

M. Beaucourt's grief.

his own children home with his wife, and the rest soon followed. Poor M. Beaucourt was inconsolable. 'The desolation of the place is wretched. When Mamey and Katey 'went, Beaucourt came in and wept. He really is almost 'broken-hearted about it. He had planted all manner of 'flowers for next month, and has thrown down the spade 'and left off weeding the garden, so that it looks something like a dreary bird-cage with all manner of grasses 'and chickweeds sticking through the bars and lying in 'the sand. "Such a loss too," he says, "for Monsieur '"Dickens!" Then he looks in at the kitchen window '(which seems to be his only relief), and sighs himself up 'the hill home.' *

The interval of residence in Paris between these two last visits to Boulogne is now to be described.

The goodness of M. Beaucourt.

* I cannot take leave of M. Beaucourt without saying that I am necessarily silent as to the most touching traits recorded of him by Dickens, because they refer to the generosity shown by him to an English family in occupation of another of his houses, in connection with whom his losses must have been considerable, but for whom he had nothing but help and sympathy. Replying to some questions about them, put by Dickens one day, he had only enlarged on their sacrifices and self-denials. 'Ah that family, unfortunate! "And '"you, Monsieur Beaucourt," I said to him, "you are unfortunate too, God '"knows!" Upon which he said in the pleasantest way in the world, Ah, 'Monsieur Dickens, thank you, don't speak of it!—And backed himself down 'the avenue with his cap in his hand, as if he were going to back himself 'straight into the evening star, without the ceremony of dying first. I never 'did see such a gentle, kind heart.'

# CHAPTER V.

## RESIDENCE IN PARIS.

### 1855—1856.

PARIS: 1855-6.

IN Paris Dickens's life was passed among artists, and in the exercise of his own art. His associates were writers, painters, actors, or musicians, and when he wanted relief from any strain of work he found it at the theatre. The years since his last residence in the great city had made him better known, and the increased attentions pleased him. He had to help in preparing for a translation of his books into French; and this, with continued labour at the story he had in hand, occupied him as long as he remained. It will be all best told by extracts from his letters; in which the people he met, the theatres he visited, and the incidents, public or private, that seemed to him worthy of mention, reappear with the old force and liveliness.

Actors and dramas.

Nor is anything better worth preserving from them than choice bits of description of an actor or a drama, for this perishable enjoyment has only so much as may survive out of such recollections to witness for itself to another generation; and an unusually high place may be challenged for the subtlety and delicacy of what is said in these letters of things theatrical, when the writer was especially attracted

PARIS: 1855-6.

Ante, 75.

by a performer or a play. Frédéric Lemaitre has never had a higher tribute than Dickens paid to him during his few days' earlier stay at Paris in the spring.

Criticism of Frédéric Lemaitre.

'Incomparably the finest acting I ever saw, I saw last 'night at the Ambigu. They have revived that old piece, 'once immensely popular in London under the name of '*Thirty Years of a Gambler's Life.* Old Lemaitre plays 'his famous character,* and never did I see anything, in art, 'so exaltedly horrible and awful. In the earlier acts he was 'so well made up, and so light and active, that he really 'looked sufficiently young. But in the last two, when he 'had grown old and miserable, he did the finest things, I 'really believe, that are within the power of acting. Two 'or three times, a great cry of horror went all round the 'house. When he met, in the inn yard, the traveller whom 'he murders, and first saw his money, the manner in which 'the crime came into his head—and eyes—was as truthful 'as it was terrific. This traveller, being a good fellow, gives 'him wine. You should see the dim remembrance of his 'better days that comes over him as he takes the glass, and 'in a strange dazed way makes as if he were going to touch 'the other man's, or do some airy thing with it; and then 'stops and flings the contents down his hot throat, as if he 'were pouring it into a lime-kiln. But this was nothing to 'what follows after he has done the murder, and comes 'home, with a basket of provisions, a ragged pocket full of 'money, and a badly-washed bloody right hand—which

* Twenty-one years before this date, in this same part, Lemaitre had made a deep impression in London; and now, eighteen years later, he is appearing in one of the revivals of Victor Hugo in Paris. (1873.)

PARIS: 1855-6.

'his little girl finds out. After the child asked him if he 'had hurt his hand, his going aside, turning himself round, 'and looking over all his clothes for spots, was so inex-'pressibly dreadful that it really scared one. He called 'for wine, and the sickness that came upon him when he 'saw the colour, was one of the things that brought out 'the curious cry I have spoken of, from the audience. 'Then he fell into a sort of bloody mist, and went on to 'the end groping about, with no mind for anything, except 'making his fortune by staking this money, and a faint 'dull kind of love for the child. It is quite impossible to 'satisfy one's-self by saying enough of such a magnificent 'performance. I have never seen him come near its finest 'points, in anything else. He said two things in a way 'that alone would put him far apart from all other actors. 'One to his wife, when he has exultingly shewn her the 'money and she has asked him how he got it—"I found '"it"—and the other to his old companion and tempter, 'when he charged him with having killed that traveller, 'and he suddenly went headlong mad and took him by 'the throat and howled out, "It wasn't I who murdered '"him—it was Misery!" And such a dress; such a face; 'and, above all, such an extraordinary guilty wicked thing 'as he made of a knotted branch of a tree which was his 'walking-stick, from the moment when the idea of the 'murder came into his head! I could write pages about 'him. It is an impression quite ineffaceable. He got 'half-boastful of that walking-staff to himself, and half-'afraid of it; and didn't know whether to be grimly pleased 'that it had the jagged end, or to hate it and be horrified

Last scene in the *Gambler's Life* described.

PARIS: 1855-6.

'at it. He sat at a little table in the inn-yard, drinking 'with the traveller; and this horrible stick got between 'them like the Devil, while he counted on his fingers the 'uses he could put the money to.'

That was at the close of February. In October, Dickens's longer residence began. He betook himself with his family, after two unsuccessful attempts in the new region of the Rue Balzac and Rue Lord Byron, to an apartment in the Avenue des Champs Elysées. Over him was an English bachelor with an establishment consisting of an English groom and five English horses. 'The concierge and his wife 'told us that his name was *Six*, which drove me nearly 'mad until we discovered it to be *Sykes*.' The situation was a good one, very cheerful for himself and with amusement for his children. It was a quarter of a mile above Franconi's on the other side of the way, and within a door or two of the Jardin d'Hiver. The Exposition was just below; the Barrière de l'Etoile from a quarter to half a mile below; and all Paris, including Emperor and Empress coming from and returning to St. Cloud, thronged past the windows in open carriages or on horseback, all day long. Now it was he found himself more of a celebrity than when he had wintered in the city nine years before;* the

Bachelor 'Six.'

Increase of celebrity.

* 'It is surprising what a change nine years have made in my notoriety 'here. So many of the rising French generation now read English (and *Chuz-'zlewit* is now being translated daily in the *Moniteur*), that I can't go into a 'shop and give my card without being acknowledged in the pleasantest way 'possible. A curiosity-dealer brought home some little knick-knacks I had 'bought, the other night, and knew all about my books from beginning to end 'of 'em. There is much of the personal friendliness in my readers, here, that is 'so delightful at home; and I have been greatly surprised and pleased by the 'unexpected discovery.' To this I may add a line from one of his letters six

Personal attentions.

feuilleton of the *Moniteur* was filled daily with a translation of *Chuzzlewit;* and he had soon to consider the proposal I have named, to publish in French his collected novels and tales.* Before he had been a week in his new abode, Ary Scheffer, 'a frank and noble fellow,' had made his acquaintance; introduced him to several distinguished Frenchmen; and expressed the wish to paint him. To Scheffer was also due an advantage obtained for my friend's two little daughters of which they may always keep the memory with

PARIS: 1855-6.

Ary Scheffer.

Daniel Manin.

years later. 'I see my books in French at every railway station great and 'small.'—13th of Oct. 1862.

* 'I forget whether' (6th of Jan. 1856) 'I have already told you that I have 'received a proposal from a responsible bookselling house here, for a complete 'edition, authorized by myself, of a French translation of all my books. The 'terms involve questions of space and amount of matter; but I should say, 'at a rough calculation, that I shall get about £300 by it—perhaps £50 'more.' 'I have arranged' (30th of Jan.) 'with the French bookselling house 'to receive, by monthly payments of £40, the sum of £440 for the right to 'translate all my books: that is, what they call my Romances, and what I 'call my Stories. This does not include the Christmas Books, *American Notes*, '*Pictures from Italy*, or the *Sketches;* but they are to have the right to 'translate them for extra payments if they choose. In consideration of this 'venture as to the unprotected property, I cede them the right of translating 'all future Romances at a thousand francs (£40) each. Considering that I 'get so much for what is otherwise worth nothing, and get my books before 'so clever and important a people, I think this is not a bad move?' The first friend with whom he advised about it, I should mention, was the famous Leipzig publisher, M. Tauchnitz, in whose judgment, as well as in his honour and good faith, he had implicit reliance, and who thought the offer fair. On the 17th of April he wrote: 'On Monday I am going to dine with all my 'translators at Hachette's, the bookseller who has made the bargain for the 'complete edition, and who began this week to pay his monthly £40 for a 'year. I don't mean to go out any more. Please to imagine me in the 'midst of my French dressers.' He wrote an address for the Edition in which he praised the liberality of his publishers and expressed his pride in being so presented to the French people whom he sincerely loved and honoured. Another word may be added. 'It is rather appropriate that the French 'translation edition will pay my rent for the whole year, and travelling 'charges to boot.'—24th of Feb. 1856.

French translation of Dickens.

M. von Tauchnitz.

PARIS: 1855-6.

pride. 'Mamey and Katey are learning Italian, and their 'master is Manin of Venetian fame, the best and the noblest 'of those unhappy gentlemen. He came here with a wife 'and a beloved daughter, and they are both dead. Scheffer 'made him known to me, and has been, I understand, won- 'derfully generous and good to him.' Nor may I omit to state the enjoyment afforded him, not only by the presence in Paris during the winter of Mr. Wilkie Collins and of Mr. and Mrs. White of Bonchurch, but by the many friends from England whom the Art Exposition brought over. Sir Alexander Cockburn was one of these; Edwin Landseer, Charles Robert Leslie, and William Boxall, were others. Macready left his retreat at Sherborne to make him a visit of several days. Thackeray went to and fro all the time between London and his mother's house, also in the Champs Elysées, where his daughters were. And Paris for the time was the home of Robert Lytton, who belonged to the Embassy, of the Sartorises, of the Brownings, and of others whom Dickens liked and cared for.

English friends. ii. 394-5.

At the first play he went to, the performance was stopped while the news of the last Crimean engagement, just issued in a supplement to the *Moniteur*, was read from the stage. 'It made not the faintest effect upon the 'audience; and even the hired claqueurs, who had been 'absurdly loud during the piece, seemed to consider the 'war not at all within their contract, and were as stagnant 'as ditch-water. The theatre was full. It is quite impos- 'sible to see such apathy, and suppose the war to be popu- 'lar, whatever may be asserted to the contrary.' The day before, he had met the Emperor and the King of Sardinia

Unpopularity of the war.

Victor Emmanuel's visit.

in the streets, 'and, as usual, no man touching his hat, and 'very very few so much as looking round.'

The success of a most agreeable little piece by our old friend Regnier took him next to the Français, where Plessy's acting enchanted him. 'Of course the interest of it 'turns upon a flawed piece of living china (*that* seems to be 'positively essential), but, as in most of these cases, if you 'will accept the position in which you find the people, you 'have nothing more to bother your morality about.' The theatre in the Rue Richelieu, however, was not generally his favourite resort. He used to talk of it whimsically as a kind of tomb, where you went, as the Eastern people did in the stories, to think of your unsuccessful loves and dead relations. 'There is a dreary classicality at that establish-'ment calculated to freeze the marrow. Between ourselves, 'even one's best friends there are at times very aggravating. 'One tires of seeing a man, through any number of acts, 'remembering everything by patting his forehead with the 'flat of his hand, jerking out sentences by shaking himself, 'and piling them up in pyramids over his head with his 'right forefinger. And they have a generic small comedy-'piece, where you see two sofas and three little tables, to 'which a man enters with his hat on, to talk to another 'man—and in respect of which you know exactly when 'he will get up from one sofa to sit on the other, and 'take his hat off one table to put it upon the other—'which strikes one quite as ludicrously as a good farce.*

Flawed pieces of china.

Classicality.

Conventionalities of the Français.

* He wrote a short and very comical account of one of these stock performances at the Français in which he brought out into strong relief all their conventionalities and formal habits, their regular surprises surprising nobody,

PARIS: 1855-6.

'... There seems to be a good piece at the Vaudeville, on 'the idea of the *Town and Country Mouse.* It is too 'respectable and inoffensive for me to-night, but I hope to 'see it before I leave... I have a horrible idea of making 'friends with Franconi, and sauntering when I am at work 'into their sawdust green-room.'

*Michel Cervantes.*

At a theatre of a yet heavier school than the Français he had a drearier experience. 'On Wednesday we went to 'the Odéon to see a new piece, in four acts and in verse, 'called *Michel Cervantes.* I suppose such an infernal dose of 'ditch water never was concocted. But there were certain 'passages, describing the suppression of public opinion in 'Madrid, which were received with a shout of savage 'application to France that made one stare again! And 'once more, here again, at every pause, steady, compact, 'regular as military drums, the Ça Ira!' On another night, even at the Porte St. Martin, drawn there doubtless by the attraction of repulsion, he supped full with the horrors of classicality at a performance of *Orestes* versified by Alexandre Dumas. 'Nothing have I ever seen so weighty and so ridiculous. If I had not already learnt to tremble at 'the sight of classic drapery on the human form, I should 'have plumbed the utmost depths of terrified boredom in 'this achievement. The chorus is not preserved otherwise 'than that bits of it are taken out for characters to speak. 'It is really so bad as to be almost good. Some of the 'Frenchified classical anguish struck me as so unspeakably 'ridiculous that it puts me on the broad grin as I write.'

Dumas' *Orestes.*

and their mysterious disclosures of immense secrets known to everybody beforehand, which he meant for *Household Words;* but it occurred to him that it might give pain to Regnier, and he destroyed it.

At the same theatre, in the early spring, he had a somewhat livelier entertainment. 'I was at the Porte St. Martin 'last night, where there is a rather good melodrama called '*Sang Melé*, in which one of the characters is an English 'Lord—Lord William Falkland—who is called throughout 'the piece Milor Williams Fack Lorn, and is a hundred 'times described by others and described by himself as 'Williams. He is admirably played; but two English 'travelling ladies are beyond expression ridiculous, and 'there is something positively vicious in their utter want 'of truth. One "set," where the action of a whole act is 'supposed to take place in the great wooden verandah of a 'Swiss hotel overhanging a mountain ravine, is the best 'piece of stage carpentering I have seen in France. Next 'week we are to have at the Ambigu *Paradise Lost*, with 'the murder of Abel, and the Deluge. The wildest rumours 'are afloat as to the un-dressing of our first parents.' Anticipation far outdoes a reality of this kind; and at the fever-pitch to which rumours raised it here, Dickens might vainly have attempted to get admission on the first night, if Mr. Webster, the English manager and comedian, had not obtained a ticket for him. He went with Mr. Wilkie Collins. 'We were rung in (out of the café below 'the Ambigu) at 8, and the play was over at half-past 1: 'the waits between the acts being very much longer than 'the acts themselves. The house was crammed to excess 'in every part, and the galleries awful with Blouses, who 'again, during the whole of the waits, beat with the regu'larity of military drums the revolutionary tune of famous 'memory—Ça Ira! The play is a compound of *Paradise*

PARIS: 1855-6.

Milor Williams Fack Lorn.

*Paradise Lost* at the Ambigu.

Ça Ira!

PARIS: 1855-6.

'*Lost* and Byron's *Cain;* and some of the controversies between the archangel and the devil, when the 'celestial power argues with the infernal in conversational 'French, as "Eh bien! Satan, crois-tu donc que notre '"Seigneur t'aurait exposé aux tourments que t'endures à '"présent, sans avoir prévu," &c. &c. are very ridiculous.

Natural and supernatural.

'All the supernatural personages are alarmingly natural '(as theatre nature goes), and walk about in the stupidest 'way. Which has occasioned Collins and myself to institute a perquisition whether the French ever have shown 'any kind of idea of the supernatural; and to decide this 'rather in the negative. The people are very well dressed, 'and Eve very modestly. All Paris and the provinces had 'been ransacked for a woman who had brown hair that would 'fall to the calves of her legs—and she was found at last 'at the Odéon. There was nothing attractive until the 4th 'act, when there was a pretty good scene of the children 'of Cain dancing in, and desecrating, a temple, while Abel 'and his family were hammering hard at the Ark, outside,

Profane nonsense.

'in all the pauses of the revel. The Deluge in the fifth 'act was up to about the mark of a drowning scene at the 'Adelphi; but it had one new feature. When the rain 'ceased, and the ark drove in on the great expanse of 'water, then lying waveless as the mists cleared and the 'sun broke out, numbers of bodies drifted up and down. 'These were all real men and boys, each separate, on a 'new kind of horizontal sloat. They looked horrible and 'real. Altogether, a merely dull business; but I dare say 'it will go for a long while.'

A piece of honest farce is a relief from these profane

absurdities. 'An uncommonly droll piece with an original 'comic idea in it has been in course of representation here. 'It is called *Les Cheveux de ma Femme.* A man who is 'dotingly fond of his wife, and who wishes to know whether 'she loved anybody else before they were married, cuts off 'a lock of her hair by stealth, and takes it to a great mes- 'meriser, who submits it to a clairvoyante who never was 'wrong. It is discovered that the owner of this hair has 'been up to the most frightful dissipations, insomuch that 'the clairvoyante can't mention half of them. The dis- 'tracted husband goes home to reproach his wife, and she 'then reveals that she wears a wig, and takes it off.'

PARIS: 1855-6.

Good farce.

The last piece he went to see before leaving Paris was a French version of *As You Like It;* but he found two acts of it to be more than enough. 'In *Comme il vous Plaira* 'nobody had anything to do but to sit down as often as 'possible on as many stones and trunks of trees as possible. 'When I had seen Jacques seat himself on 17 roots of trees, 'and 25 grey stones, which was at the end of the second act, 'I came away.' Only one more sketch taken in a theatre, and perhaps the best, I will give from these letters. It simply tells us what is necessary to understand a particular 'tag' to a play, but it is related so prettily that the thing it celebrates could not have a nicer effect than is produced by this account of it. The play in question, *Mémoires du Diable,* and another piece of enchanting interest, the *Médecin des Enfants,** were his favourites among all he

French *As You Like It.*

* Before he saw this he wrote: 'That piece you spoke of (the *Médecin des* '*Enfants*) is one of the very best melodramas I have ever read. Situations, 'admirable. I will send it to you by Landseer. I am very curious indeed to 'go and see it; and it is an instance to me of the powerful emotions from which

*Médecin des Enfants.*

PARIS: 1855–6.

saw at this time. 'As I have no news, I may as well tell 'you about the tag that I thought so pretty to the *Mémoires 'du Diable;* in which piece by the way, there is a most 'admirable part, most admirably played, in which a man 'says merely "Yes" or "No" all through the piece, until 'the last scene. A certain M. Robin has got hold of the 'papers of a deceased lawyer, concerning a certain estate 'which has been swindled away from its rightful owner, a 'Baron's widow, into other hands. They disclose so much 'roguery that he binds them up into a volume lettered '"Mémoires du Diable." The knowledge he derives from 'these papers not only enables him to unmask the hypo'crites all through the piece (in an excellent manner), but 'induces him to propose to the Baroness that if he restores 'to her her estate and good name—for even her marriage 'to the deceased Baron is denied—she shall give him her 'daughter in marriage. The daughter herself, on hearing 'the offer, accepts it; and a part of the plot is, her going to 'a masked ball, to which he goes as the Devil, to see how 'she likes him (when she finds, of course, that she likes 'him very much). The country people about the Château 'in dispute, suppose him to be really the Devil, because of 'his strange knowledge, and his strange comings and goings;

Story of a French drama.

'art is shut out in England by the conventionalities.' After seeing it he writes: 'The low cry of excitement and expectation that goes round the house 'when any one of the great situations is felt to be coming, is very remarkable 'indeed. I suppose there has not been so great a success of the genuine and 'worthy kind (for the authors have really taken the French dramatic bull by 'the horns, and put the adulterous wife in the right position), for many 'years. When you come over and see it, you will say you never saw anything 'so admirably done. There is one actor, Bignon (M. Delormel), who has a 'good deal of Macready in him; sometimes looks very like him; and who 'seems to me the perfection of manly good sense.' 17th of April 1856.

PARIS: 1855-6.

*Mémoires du Diable.*

'and he, being with this girl in one of its old rooms, in 'the beginning of the 3rd act, shews her a little coffer on 'the table with a bell in it. "They suppose," he tells her, '"that whenever this bell is rung, I appear and obey the '"summons. Very ignorant, isn't it? But, if you ever '"want me particularly—very particularly—ring the little '"bell and try." The plot proceeds to its development. 'The wrong-doers are exposed; the missing document, 'proving the marriage, is found; everything is finished; 'they are all on the stage; and M. Robin hands the paper 'to the Baroness. "You are reinstated in your rights, '"Madame; you are happy; I will not hold you to a com-'"pact made when you didn't know me; I release you and '"your fair daughter; the pleasure of doing what I have '"done, is my sufficient reward; I kiss your hand and take '"my leave. Farewell!" He backs himself courteously out; 'the piece seems concluded, everybody wonders, the girl '(little Mdlle. Luther) stands amazed; when she suddenly 'remembers the little bell. In the prettiest way possible, 'she runs to the coffer on the table, takes out the little 'bell, rings it, and he comes rushing back and folds her to 'his heart. I never saw a prettier thing in my life. It 'made me laugh in that most delightful of ways, with the 'tears in my eyes; so that I can never forget it, and must 'go and see it again.'

Delightful close to a play.

But great as was the pleasure thus derived from the theatre, he was, in the matter of social intercourse, even more indebted to distinguished men connected with it by authorship or acting. At Scribe's he was entertained frequently; and 'very handsome and pleasant' was his account

At M. Scribe's.

PARIS: 1855-6.

of the dinners, as of all the belongings, of the prolific dramatist—a charming place in Paris, a fine estate in the country, capital carriage, handsome pair of horses, 'all 'made, as he says, by his pen.' One of the guests the first evening was Auber, 'a stolid little elderly man, rather 'petulant in manner,' who told Dickens he had once lived 'at Stock Noonton' (Stoke Newington) to study English, but had forgotten it all. 'Louis Philippe had invited him 'to meet the Queen of England, and when L. P. presented 'him, the Queen said "We are such old acquaintances '"through M. Auber's works, that an introduction is quite '"unnecessary."' They met again a few nights later, with the author of the *History of the Girondins*, at the hospitable table of M. Pichot, to whom Lamartine had expressed a strong desire again to meet Dickens as 'un des 'grands amis de son imagination.' 'He continues to be 'precisely as we formerly knew him, both in appearance 'and manner; highly propossessing, and with a sort of 'calm passion about him, very taking indeed. We talked 'of De Foe* and Richardson, and of that wonderful genius

Auber and Queen Victoria.

Lamartine.

ii. 303.

* I subjoin from another of these French letters of later date a remark on *Robinson Crusoe*. 'You remember my saying to you some time ago how curious 'I thought it that *Robinson Crusoe* should be the only instance of an universally popular book that could make no one laugh and could make no one cry. 'I have been reading it again just now, in the course of my numerous refreshings at those English wells, and I will venture to say that there is not in 'literature a more surprising instance of an utter want of tenderness and sentiment, than the death of Friday. It is as heartless as *Gil Blas*, in a very 'different and far more serious way. But the second part altogether will not 'bear enquiry. In the second part of *Don Quixote* are some of the finest 'things. But the second part of *Robinson Crusoe* is perfectly contemptible, 'in the glaring defect that it exhibits the man who was 30 years on that 'desert island with no visible effect made on his character by that experience. 'De Foe's women too—Robinson Crusoe's wife for instance—are terrible dull

*Robinson Crusoe.*

PARIS: 1855-6.

'for the minutest details in a narrative, which has given 'them so much fame in France. I found him frank and 'unaffected, and full of curious knowledge of the French 'common people. He informed the company at dinner 'that he had rarely met a foreigner who spoke French so 'easily as your inimitable correspondent, whereat your 'correspondent blushed modestly, and almost immediately 'afterwards so nearly choked himself with the bone of a 'fowl (which is still in his throat), that he sat in torture 'for ten minutes with a strong apprehension that he was 'going to make the good Pichot famous by dying like the 'little Hunchback at his table. Scribe and his wife were 'of the party, but had to go away at the ice-time because 'it was the first representation at the Opéra Comique of a 'new opera by Auber and himself, of which very great ex-'pectations have been formed. It was very curious to see 'him—the author of 400 pieces—getting nervous as the 'time approached, and pulling out his watch every minute. 'At last he dashed out as if he were going into what a 'friend of mine calls a plunge-bath. Whereat she rose 'and followed. She is the most extraordinary woman I 'ever beheld; for her eldest son must be thirty, and she 'has the figure of five-and-twenty, and is strikingly hand-'some. So graceful too, that her manner of rising, curt-'seying, laughing, and going out after him, was pleasanter 'than the pleasantest thing I have ever seen done on the 'stage.' The opera Dickens himself saw a week later, and

A compliment and its result.

Scribe's author-anxieties.

Madame Scribe.

'commonplace fellows without breeches; and I have no doubt he was a pre-'cious dry and disagreeable article himself—I mean De Foe: not Robinson. 'Poor dear Goldsmith (I remember as I write) derived the same impression.'

PARIS: 1855-6.

wrote of it as 'most charming. Delightful music, an excellent story, immense stage tact, capital scenic arrangements, and the most delightful little prima donna ever seen or heard, in the person of Marie Cabel. It is called

*Manon Lescaut.*

'*Manon Lescaut*—from the old romance—and is charming throughout. She sings a laughing song in it which is received with madness, and which is the only real laughing song that ever was written. Auber told me that when it was first rehearsed, it made a great effect upon the orchestra; and that he could not have had a better compliment upon its freshness than the musical director paid him, in coming and clapping him on the shoulder with "Bravo, jeune homme! Cela promet bien!"'

At M. Regnier's.

At dinner at Regnier's he met M. Legouvet, in whose tragedy Rachel, after its acceptance, had refused to act Medea; a caprice which had led not only to her condemnation in costs of so much a night until she did act it, but to a quasi rivalry against her by Ristori, who was now on her way to Paris to play it in Italian. To this performance Dickens and Macready subsequently went together, and pronounced it to be hopelessly bad. 'In the day enter-

Ristori.

'tainments, and little melodrama theatres, of Italy, I have seen the same thing fifty times, only not at once so conventional and so exaggerated. The papers have all been in fits respecting the sublimity of the performance, and the genuineness of the applause—particularly of the bouquets; which were thrown on at the most preposterous times in the midst of agonizing scenes, so that the characters had to pick their way among them, and a certain stout gentleman who played King Creon was obliged to keep a 'wary eye, all night, on the proscenium boxes, and dodge 'them as they came down. Now Scribe, who dined here next 'day (and who follows on the Ristori side, being offended, 'as everybody has been, by the insolence of Rachel), could 'not resist the temptation of telling us, that, going round 'at the end of the first act to offer his congratulations, he 'met all the bouquets coming back in men's arms to be 'thrown on again in the second act. . . . By the bye, I 'see a fine actor lost in Scribe. In all his pieces he has 'everything done in his own way; and on that same night 'he was showing what Rachel did not do, and wouldn't do, 'in the last scene of Adrienne Lecouvreur, with extraordi-'nary force and intensity.'

PARIS: 1855-6.

Serviceable bouquets.

An actor lost in Scribe.

At the house of another great artist, Madame Viardot,* the sister of Malibran, Dickens dined to meet Georges Sand, that lady having appointed the day and hour for the interesting festival, which came off duly on the 10th of

Meets Georges Sand.

* When in Paris six years later Dickens saw this fine singer in an opera by Gluck, and the reader will not be sorry to have his description of it. 'Last night 'I saw Madame Viardot do Gluck's Orphée. It is a most extraordinary per-'formance—pathetic in the highest degree, and full of quite sublime acting. 'Though it is unapproachably fine from first to last, the beginning of it, at 'the tomb of Eurydice, is a thing that I cannot remember at this moment of 'writing, without emotion. It is the finest presentation of grief that I can 'imagine. And when she has received hope from the Gods, and encouragement 'to go into the other world and seek Eurydice, Viardot's manner of taking the 'relinquished lyre from the tomb and becoming radiant again, is most noble. 'Also she recognizes Eurydice's touch, when at length the hand is put in hers 'from behind, like a most transcendant genius. And when, yielding to Eury-'dice's entreaties she has turned round and slain her with a look, her despair 'over the body is grand in the extreme. It is worth a journey to Paris to 'see, for there is no such Art to be otherwise looked upon. Her husband 'stumbled over me by mere chance, and took me to her dressing-room. Nothing 'could have happened better as a genuine homage to the performance, for I 'was disfigured with crying.'—30th of November 1862.

Viardot in Orphée.

Paris: 1855-6.

January. 'I suppose it to be impossible to imagine anybody more unlike my preconceptions than the illustrious 'Sand. Just the kind of woman in appearance whom you 'might suppose to be the Queen's monthly nurse. Chubby, 'matronly, swarthy, black-eyed. Nothing of the blue-'stocking about her, except a little final way of settling 'all your opinions with hers, which I take to have been 'acquired in the country where she lives, and in the domi-'nation of a small circle. A singularly ordinary woman in 'appearance and manner. The dinner was very good and 'remarkably unpretending. Ourselves, Madame and her 'son, the Scheffers, the Sartorises, and some Lady some-'body (from the Crimea last) who wore a species of paletot, 'and smoked. The Viardots have a house away in the 'new part of Paris, which looks exactly as if they had 'moved into it last week and were going away next. 'Notwithstanding which, they have lived in it eight years. 'The opera the very last thing on earth you would associate 'with the family. Piano not even opened. Her husband 'is an extremely good fellow, and she is as natural as it is 'possible to be.'

Madame Dudevant at the Viardots.

Dickens was hardly the man to take fair measure of Madame Dudevant in meeting her thus. He was not familiar with her writings, and had no very special liking for such of them as he knew. But no disappointment, nothing but amazement, awaited him at a dinner that followed soon after. Emile de Girardin gave a banquet in his honour. His description of it, which he declares to be strictly prosaic, sounds a little Oriental, but not inappropriately so. 'No man unacquainted with my deter-

Banquet at Girardin's.

'mination never to embellish or fancify such accounts, 'could believe in the description I shall let off when we 'meet of dining at Emile Girardin's—of the three gorgeous 'drawing rooms with ten thousand wax candles in golden 'sconces, terminating in a dining-room of unprecedented 'magnificence with two enormous transparent plate-glass 'doors in it, looking (across an ante-chamber full of clean 'plates) straight into the kitchen, with the cooks in their 'white paper caps dishing the dinner. From his seat in 'the midst of the table, the host (like a Giant in a Fairy 'story) beholds the kitchen, and the snow-white tables, 'and the profound order and silence there prevailing. 'Forth from the plate-glass doors issues the Banquet—the 'most wonderful feast ever tasted by mortal: at the pre'sent price of Truffles, that article alone costing (for eight 'people) at least five pounds. On the table are ground 'glass jugs of peculiar construction, laden with the finest 'growth of Champagne and the coolest ice. With the third 'course is issued Port Wine (previously unheard of in a 'good state on this continent), which would fetch two 'guineas a bottle at any sale. The dinner done, Oriental 'flowers in vases of golden cobweb are placed upon the 'board. With the ice is issued Brandy, buried for 100 'years. To that succeeds Coffee, brought by the brother of 'one of the convives from the remotest East, in exchange 'for an equal quantity of Californian gold dust. The com'pany being returned to the drawing-room—tables roll in 'by unseen agency, laden with Cigarettes from the Hareem 'of the Sultan, and with cool drinks in which the flavour of 'the Lemon arrived yesterday from Algeria, struggles volup-

Dining-room.

Kitchen.

Truffles.

Dessert.

Cigarettes.

PARIS: 1855-6.

'tuously with the delicate Orange arrived this morning 'from Lisbon. That period past, and the guests reposing 'on Divans worked with many-coloured blossoms, big table 'rolls in, heavy with massive furniture of silver, and breath- 'ing incense in the form of a little present of Tea direct 'from China—table and all, I believe; but cannot swear to 'it, and am resolved to be prosaic. All this time the host 'perpetually repeats "Ce petit dîner-ci n'est que pour faire '"la connaissance de Monsieur Dickens; il ne compte '"pas; ce n'est rien." And even now I have forgotten to 'set down half of it—in particular the item of a far larger 'plum pudding than ever was seen in England at Christ- 'mas time, served with a celestial sauce in colour like the 'orange blossom, and in substance like the blossom pow- 'dered and bathed in dew, and called in the carte (carte 'in a gold frame like a little fish-slice to be handed about) '"Hommage à l'illustre écrivain d'Angleterre." That illus- 'trious man staggered out at the last drawing-room door, 'speechless with wonder, finally; and even at that moment 'his host, holding to his lips a chalice set with precious 'stones and containing nectar distilled from the air that 'blew over the fields of beans in bloom for fifteen summers, 'remarked "Le diner que nous avons eu, mon cher, n'est '"rien—il ne compte pas—il a été tout-à-fait en famille— '"il faut dîner (en vérité, dîner) bientôt. Au plaisir! Au '"revoir! Au dîner!"'

What the host thought of the dinner.

National and personal compliment.

Au revoir.

The second dinner came, wonderful as the first; among the company were Regnier, Jules Sandeau, and the new Director of the Français; and his host again played Lucullus in the same style, with success even more con-

Second banquet.

Paris: 1855-6.

summate. The only absolutely new incident however was that 'After dinner he asked me if I would come into an-'other room and smoke a cigar? and on my saying Yes, 'coolly opened a drawer, containing about 5000 inestimable 'cigars in prodigious bundles—just as the Captain of the 'Robbers in *Ali Baba* might have gone to a corner of the 'cave for bales of brocade. A little man dined who was 'blacking shoes 8 years ago, and is now enormously rich—'the richest man in Paris—having ascended with rapidity 'up the usual ladder of the Bourse. By merely observing 'that perhaps he might come down again, I clouded so many 'faces as to render it very clear to me that *everybody pre-'sent* was at the same game for some stake or other!' He returned to that subject in a letter a few days later. 'If 'you were to see the steps of the Bourse at about 4 in the 'afternoon, and the crowd of blouses and patches among the 'speculators there assembled, all howling and haggard with 'speculation, you would stand aghast at the consideration of 'what must be going on. Concierges and people like that 'perpetually blow their brains out, or fly into the Seine, '"à cause des pertes sur la Bourse." I hardly ever take 'up a French paper without lighting on such a paragraph. 'On the other hand, thoroughbred horses without end, and 'red velvet carriages with white kid harness on jet black 'horses, go by here all day long; and the pedestrians who 'turn to look at them, laugh, and say "C'est la Bourse!" 'Such crashes must be staved off every week as have not 'been seen since Law's time.'

One of the guests.

The Bourse and its victims.

Type of the Empire.

Another picture connects itself with this, and throws light on the speculation thus raging. The French loans

PARIS: 1855-6.

connected with the war, so much puffed and praised in England at the time for the supposed spirit in which they were taken up, had in fact only ministered to the commonest and lowest gambling; and the war had never in the least been popular. 'Emile Girardin,' wrote Dickens on the 23rd of March, 'was here yesterday, and he says that Peace 'is to be formally announced at Paris to-morrow amid general 'apathy.' But the French are never wholly apathetic to their own exploits; and a display with a touch of excitement in it had been witnessed a couple of months before on the entry of the troops from the Crimea,* when the Zouaves, as they marched past, pleased Dickens most. 'A 'remarkable body of men,' he wrote, 'wild, dangerous, and 'picturesque. Close-cropped head, red skull cap, Greek 'jacket, full red petticoat trowsers trimmed with yellow, 'and high white gaiters—the most sensible things for the 'purpose I know, and coming into use in the line. A man 'with such things on his legs is always free there, and 'ready for a muddy march; and might flounder through

Feeling as to the war.

Entry of troops from Crimea.

* Here is another picture of Regiments in the Streets of which the date is the 30th of January. 'It was cold this afternoon, as bright as Italy, and 'these Elysian Fields crowded with carriages, riders, and foot passengers. All 'the fountains were playing, all the Heavens shining. Just as I went out at '4 o'clock, several regiments that had passed out at the Barrière in the morn- 'ing to exercise in the country, came marching back, in the straggling French 'manner, which is far more picturesque and real than anything you can imagine 'in that way. Alternately great storms of drums played, and then the most 'delicious and skilful bands, "Trovatore" music, "Barber of Seville" music, 'all sorts of music with well-marked melody and time. All bloused Paris '(led by the Inimitable, and a poor cripple who works himself up and down 'all day in a big-wheeled car) went at quick march down the avenue, in a 'sort of hilarious dance. If the colours with the golden eagle on the top had 'only been unfurled, we should have followed them anywhere, in any cause— 'much as the children follow Punches in the better cause of Comedy. Napoleon 'on the top of the Column seemed up to the whole thing, I thought.'

Regiments in the streets.

Paris: 1855-6.

'roads two feet deep in mud, and, simply by changing his 'gaiters (he has another pair in his haversack), be clean 'and comfortable and wholesome again, directly. Plenty 'of beard and moustache, and the musket carried reverse-'wise with the stock over the shoulder, make up the sun-'burnt Zouave. He strides like Bobadil, smoking as he 'goes; and when he laughs (they were under my window 'for half-an-hour or so), plunges backward in the wildest 'way, as if he were going to throw a sommersault. They 'have a black dog belonging to the regiment, and, when 'they now marched along with their medals, this dog marched 'after the one non-commissioned officer he invariably 'follows with a profound conviction that he was decorated. 'I couldn't see whether he had a medal, his hair being 'long; but he was perfectly up to what had befallen his 'regiment; and I never saw anything so capital as his way 'of regarding the public. Whatever the regiment does, he 'is always in his place; and it was impossible to mistake 'the air of modest triumph which was now upon him. A 'small dog corporeally, but of a great mind.'* On that night there was an illumination in honour of the army, when the 'whole of Paris, bye streets and lanes and all sorts of 'out of the way places, was most brilliantly illuminated. It 'looked in the dark like Venice and Genoa rolled into one, 'and split up through the middle by the Corso at Rome in 'the carnival time. The French people certainly do know 'how to honour their own countrymen, in a most marvel-'lous way.' It was the festival time of the New Year, and

The Zouave.

Dog of the regiment.

Paris illuminated.

* Apropos of this, I may mention that the little shaggy white terrier who came with him from America, so long a favourite in his household, had died of old age a few weeks before (5th of Oct. 1855) in Boulogne.

Timber's death. ii. 4.

PARIS: 1855-6.

Dickens was fairly lost in a mystery of amazement at where the money could come from that everybody was spending on the étrennes they were giving to everybody else. All the famous shops on the Boulevards had been blockaded for more than a week. 'There is now a line of 'wooden stalls, three miles long, on each side of that 'immense thoroughfare; and wherever a retiring house 'or two admits of a double line, there it is. All sorts of 'objects from shoes and sabots, through porcelain and 'crystal, up to live fowls and rabbits which are played for 'at a sort of dwarf skittles (to their immense disturbance, 'as the ball rolls under them and shakes them off their 'shelves and perches whenever it is delivered by a vigorous 'hand), are on sale in this great Fair. And what you may 'get in the way of ornament for twopence, is astounding.' Unhappily there came dark and rainy weather, and one of the improvements of the Empire ended, as so many others did, in slush and misery.*

Streets on New Year's Day.

Results of Imperial improvement.

Round the walls.

* 'We have wet weather here—and dark too for these latitudes—and oceans 'of mud. Although numbers of men are perpetually scooping and sweeping 'it away in this thoroughfare, it accumulates under the windows so fast, and 'in such sludgy masses, that to get across the road is to get half over one's 'shoes in the first outset of a walk.' . . . 'It is difficult,' he added (20th of Jan.) 'to picture the change made in this place by the removal of the paving stones '(too ready for barricades), and macadamization. It suits neither the climate 'nor the soil. We are again in a sea of mud. One cannot cross the road of 'the Champs Elysées here, without being half over one's boots.' A few more days brought a welcome change. 'Three days ago the weather changed here 'in an hour, and we have had bright weather and hard frost ever since. All 'the mud disappeared with marvellous rapidity, and the sky became Italian. 'Taking advantage of such a happy change, I started off yesterday morning '(for exercise and meditation) on a scheme I have taken into my head, to walk 'round the walls of Paris. It is a very odd walk, and will make a good 'description. Yesterday I turned to the right when I got outside the Barrière 'de l'Etoile, walked round the wall till I came to the river, and then entered

PARIS: 1855-6.

Some sketches connected with the Art Exposition in the winter of 1855, and with the fulfilment of Ary Scheffer's design to paint the portrait of Dickens, may close these Paris pictures. He did not think that English art showed to advantage beside the French. It seemed to him small, shrunken, insignificant, 'niggling.' He thought the general absence of ideas horribly apparent; 'and even when one 'comes to Mulready, and sees two old men talking over a 'much-too-prominent table-cloth, and reads the French 'explanation of their proceedings, "La discussion sur les '"principes de Docteur Whiston," one is dissatisfied. 'Somehow or other they don't tell. Even Leslie's Sancho 'wants go, and Stanny is too much like a set-scene. It is 'of no use disguising the fact that what we know to be 'wanting in the men is wanting in their works—character, fire, purpose, and the power of using the vehicle 'and the model as mere means to an end. There is a 'horrible respectability about most of the best of them—a 'little, finite, systematic routine in them, strangely expressive to me of the state of England itself. As a mere fact, 'Frith, Ward, and Egg, come out the best in such pictures 'as are here, and attract to the greatest extent. The first, 'in the picture from the Good-natured Man; the second, 'in the Royal Family in the Temple; the third, in the 'Peter the Great first seeing Catherine—which I always 'thought a good picture, and in which foreigners evidently 'descry a sudden dramatic touch that pleases them. There 'are no end of bad pictures among the French, but, Lord!

Art-Exposition.

English and French art.

Popular English pictures.

'Paris beyond the site of the Bastille. To-day I mean to turn to the left when 'I get outside the Barrière, and see what comes of that.'

PARIS: 1855-6.

'the goodness also!—the fearlessness of them; the bold 'drawing; the dashing conception; the passion and action 'in them!* The Belgian department is full of merit. It 'has the best landscape in it, the best portrait, and the 'best scene of homely life, to be found in the building.

What English Art wants.

'Don't think it a part of my despondency about public 'affairs, and my fear that our national glory is on the de-'cline, when I say that mere form and conventionalities 'usurp, in English art, as in English government and 'social relations, the place of living force and truth. I 'tried to resist the impression yesterday, and went to the 'English gallery first, and praised and admired with great 'diligence; but it was of no use. I could not make any-'thing better of it than what I tell you. Of course this is 'between ourselves. Friendship is better than criticism, 'and I shall steadily hold my tongue. Discussion is worse 'than useless when you cannot agree about what you are 'going to discuss.'

French and English nature.

French nature is all wrong, said the English artists whom Dickens talked to; but surely not because it is French, was his reply. The English point of view is not the only one to take men and women from. The French pictures are 'theatrical,' was the rejoinder. But the French themselves are a demonstrative and gesticulating people,

The Emperor and Edwin Landseer.

* This was much the tone of Edwin Landseer also, whose praise of Horace Vernet was nothing short of rapture; and how well I remember the humour of his description of the Emperor on the day when the prizes were given, and, as his old friend the great painter came up, the comical expression in his face that said plainly 'What a devilish odd thing this is altogether, isn't it?' composing itself to gravity as he took Edwin by the hand, and said in cordial English 'I am very glad to see you.' He stood, Landseer told us, in a recess so arranged as to produce a clear echo of every word he said, and this had a startling effect. In the evening of that day Dickens, Landseer, Boxall, Leslie 'and three others' dined together in the Palais Royal.

PARIS. 1855-6.

was Dickens's retort ; and what thus is rendered by their artists is the truth through an immense part of the world. 'I never saw anything so strange. They seem to me to 'have got a fixed idea that there is no natural manner but 'the English manner (in itself so exceptional that it is a 'thing apart, in all countries); and that unless a French-'man—represented as going to the guillotine for example '—is as calm as Clapham, or as respectable as Richmond-'hill, he cannot be right.'

Sitting to Ary Scheffer;

To the sittings at Ary Scheffer's some troubles as well as many pleasures were incident, and both had mention in his letters. 'You may faintly imagine what I have 'suffered from sitting to Scheffer every day since I came 'back. He is a most noble fellow, and I have the greatest 'pleasure in his society, and have made all sorts of 'acquaintances at his house; but I can scarcely express 'how uneasy and unsettled it makes me to have to sit, sit, 'sit, with *Little Dorrit* on my mind, and the Christmas 'business too—though that is now happily dismissed. On 'Monday afternoon, *and all day on Wednesday,* I am 'going to sit again. And the crowning feature is, that I 'do not discern the slightest resemblance, either in his 'portrait or his brother's! They both peg away at me at 'the same time.' The sittings were varied by a special entertainment, when Scheffer received some sixty people in his 'long atelier'—'including a lot of French who *say* '(but I don't believe it) that they know English'—to whom Dickens, by special entreaty, read his *Cricket on the Hearth.*

and to Henri Scheffer.

A Reading in Scheffer's studio.

That was at the close of November. January came, and the end of the sittings was supposed to be at hand. 'The

PARIS: 1855-6.

'nightmare portrait is nearly done; and Scheffer promises 'that an interminable sitting next Saturday, beginning at '10 o'clock in the morning, shall finish it. It is a fine 'spirited head, painted at his very best, and with a very 'easy and natural appearance in it. But it does not look 'to me at all like, nor does it strike me that if I saw it in 'a gallery I should suppose myself to be the original. It 'is always possible that I don't know my own face. It is 'going to be engraved here, in two sizes and ways—the 'mere head and the whole thing.' A fortnight later, the interminable sitting came. 'Imagine me if you please 'with No. 5 on my head and hands, sitting to Scheffer 'yesterday four hours! At this stage of a story, no one 'can conceive how it distresses me.' Still this was not the last. March had come before the portrait was done. 'Scheffer finished yesterday; and Collins, who has a good 'eye for pictures, says that there is no man living who 'could do the painting about the eyes. As a work of art 'I see in it spirit combined with perfect ease, and yet I 'don't see myself. So I come to the conclusion that I 'never *do* see myself. I shall be very curious to know the 'effect of it upon you.' March had then begun; and at its close Dickens, who had meanwhile been in England, thus wrote: 'I have not seen Scheffer since I came back, 'but he told Catherine a few days ago that he was not 'satisfied with the likeness after all, and thought he must 'do more to it. My own impression of it, you remember?' In these few words he anticipated the impression made upon myself. I was not satisfied with it. The picture had much merit, but not as a portrait. From its very resem-

Doubts of the likeness.

More sittings. January.

Scheffer's own opinion.

PARIS: 1855-6.

blance in the eyes and mouth one derived the sense of a general unlikeness. But the work of the artist's brother, Henri Scheffer, painted from the same sittings, was in all ways greatly inferior.

A Duchess murdered.

Before Dickens left Paris in May he had sent over two descriptions that the reader most anxious to follow him to a new scene would perhaps be sorry to lose. A Duchess was murdered in the Champs Elysées. 'The murder over 'the way (the third or fourth event of that nature in the 'Champs Elysées since we have been here) seems to dis-'close the strangest state of things. The Duchess who is 'murdered lived alone in a great house which was always 'shut up, and passed her time entirely in the dark. In a 'little lodge outside lived a coachman (the murderer), and 'there had been a long succession of coachmen who had 'been unable to stay there, and upon whom, whenever 'they asked for their wages, she plunged out with an 'immense knife, by way of an immediate settlement. The 'coachman never had anything to do, for the coach hadn't 'been driven out for years; neither would she ever allow 'the horses to be taken out for exercise. Between the 'lodge and the house, is a miserable bit of garden, all over-'grown with long rank grass, weeds, and nettles; and in 'this, the horses used to be taken out to swim—in a dead 'green vegetable sea, up to their haunches. On the day 'of the murder, there was a great crowd, of course; and 'in the midst of it up comes the Duke her husband (from 'whom she was separated), and rings at the gate. The 'police open the grate. "C'est vrai donc," says the Duke, '"que Madame la Duchesse n'est plus?"—"C'est trop

Arrival of the Duke.

PARIS: 1855-6.

'"vrai, Monseigneur."—"Tant mieux," says the Duke, and 'walks off deliberately, to the great satisfaction of the 'assemblage.'

Truth stranger than fiction.

The second description relates an occurrence in England of only three years previous date, belonging to that wildly improbable class of realities which Dickens always held, with Fielding, to be (properly) closed to fiction. Only, he would add, critics should not be so eager to assume that what had never happened to themselves could not, by any human possibility, ever be supposed to have happened to anybody else. 'B. was with me the other day, and, among other 'things that he told me, described an extraordinary adven- 'ture in his life, at a place not a thousand miles from my '"property" at Gadshill, three years ago. He lived at the 'tavern and was sketching one day when an open carriage 'came by with a gentleman and lady in it. He was sitting 'in the same place working at the same sketch, next day, 'when it came by again. So, another day, when the gen- 'tleman got out and introduced himself. Fond of art; 'lived at the great house yonder, which perhaps he knew; 'was an Oxford man and a Devonshire squire, but not 'resident on his estate, for domestic reasons; would be 'glad to see him to dinner to-morrow. He went, and found 'among other things a very fine library. "At your dispo- '"sition," said the Squire, to whom he had now described 'himself and his pursuits. "Use it for your writing and '"drawing. Nobody else uses it." He stayed in the house '*six months*. The lady was a mistress, aged five-and-twenty, 'and very beautiful, drinking her life away. The Squire 'was drunken, and utterly depraved and wicked; but an

A chance encounter:

and what came of it.

Guest and entertainers.

'excellent scholar, an admirable linguist, and a great 'theologian. Two other mad visitors stayed the six months. 'One, a man well known in Paris here, who goes about 'the world with a crimson silk stocking in his breast pocket, 'containing a tooth-brush and an immense quantity of 'ready money. The other, a college chum of the Squire's, 'now ruined; with an insatiate thirst for drink; who con-'stantly got up in the middle of the night, crept down to 'the dining-room, and emptied all the decanters . . . B. 'stayed on in the place, under a sort of devilish fascination 'to discover what might come of it . . . Tea or coffee never 'seen in the house, and very seldom water. Beer, cham-'pagne, and brandy, were the three drinkables. Break-'fast: leg of mutton, champagne, beer, and brandy. Lunch: 'shoulder of mutton, champagne, beer, and brandy. Dinner: 'every conceivable dish (Squire's income, £7,000 a-year), 'champagne, beer, and brandy. The Squire had married 'a woman of the town from whom he was now separated, 'but by whom he had a daughter. The mother, to spite 'the father, had bred the daughter in every conceivable 'vice. Daughter, then 13, came from school once a month. 'Intensely coarse in talk, and always drunk. As they drove 'about the country in two open carriages, the drunken mis-'tress would be perpetually tumbling out of one, and the 'drunken daughter perpetually tumbling out of the other. 'At last the drunken mistress drank her stomach away, and 'began to die on the sofa. Got worse and worse, and was 'always raving about Somebody's where she had once been 'a lodger, and perpetually shrieking that she would cut 'somebody else's heart out. At last she died on the sofa,

PARIS: 1855-6.

A strange interior.

Persons composing it.

End of the drama.

Paris: 1855-6.

'and, after the funeral, the party broke up. A few months 'ago, B. met the man with the crimson silk stocking at 'Brighton, who told him that the Squire was dead "of '"a broken heart"; that the chum was dead of delirium 'tremens; and that the daughter was heiress to the fortune. 'He told me all this, which I fully believe to be true, with'out any embellishment—just in the off-hand way in which 'I have told it to you.'

What became of the actors.

Dickens left Paris at the end of April, and, after the summer in Boulogne which has been described, passed the winter in London, giving to his theatrical enterprise nearly all the time that *Little Dorrit* did not claim from him. His book was finished in the following spring; was inscribed to Clarkson Stanfield; and now claims to have something said about it.

# CHAPTER VI.

## LITTLE DORRIT, AND A LAZY TOUR.

1855—1857.

LONDON: 1855-7.

BETWEEN *Hard Times* and *Little Dorrit*, Dickens's principal literary work had been the contribution to *Household Words* of two tales for Christmas (1854 and 1855) which his readings afterwards made widely popular, the Story of Richard Doubledick,* and Boots at the Holly-Tree Inn. In the latter was related, with a charming naturalness and spirit, the elopement, to get married at Gretna Green, of two little children of the mature respective ages of eight and seven. At Christmas 1855 came out the first number of *Little Dorrit*, and in April 1857 the last.

Christmas tales.

The book took its origin from the notion he had of a

* The framework for this sketch was a graphic description, also done by Dickens, of the celebrated Charity at Rochester founded in the sixteenth century by Richard Watts, 'for six poor travellers, who, not being Rogues or Proctors, 'may receive gratis for one night, lodging, entertainment, and fourpence each.' A quaint monument to Watts is the most prominent object on the wall of the south-west transept of the cathedral, and underneath it is now placed a brass thus inscribed: 'CHARLES DICKENS. Born at Portsmouth, seventh of February 1812. 'Died at Gadshill Place by Rochester, ninth of June 1870. Buried in Westminster Abbey. To connect his memory with the scenes in which his earliest 'and his latest years were passed, and with the associations of Rochester 'Cathedral and its neighbourhood which extended over all his life, this Tablet, 'with the sanction of the Dean and Chapter, is placed by his Executors.'

Brass tablet to Dickens in Rochester Cathedral.

LONDON: 1855-7.

*Nobody's Fault.*

leading man for a story who should bring about all the mischief in it, lay it all on Providence, and say at every fresh calamity, 'Well it's a mercy, however, nobody was 'to blame you know!' The title first chosen, out of many suggested, was *Nobody's Fault;* and four numbers had been written, of which the first was on the eve of appearance, before this was changed. When about to fall to work he excused himself from an engagement he should have kept because 'the story is breaking out all round me, 'and I am going off down the railroad to humour it.' The humouring was a little difficult, however; and such indi-

Difficulties.

cations of a droop in his invention as presented themselves in portions of *Bleak House,* were noticeable again. 'As to 'the story I am in the second number, and last night and 'this morning had half a mind to begin again, and work

Aug. 19th, 1855.

'in what I have done, afterwards.' It had occurred to him, that, by making the fellow-travellers at once known to each other, as the opening of the story stands, he had missed an effect. 'It struck me that it would be a new 'thing to show people coming together, in a chance way, 'as fellow-travellers, and being in the same place, ignorant

A proposed opening.

'of one another, as happens in life; and to connect them 'afterwards, and to make the waiting for that connection 'a part of the interest.' The change was not made; but the mention of it was one of several intimations to me of the altered conditions under which he was writing, and that the old, unstinted, irrepressible flow of fancy had received temporary check. In this view I have found it very interesting to compare the original notes, which as usual he prepared for each number of the tale, and which

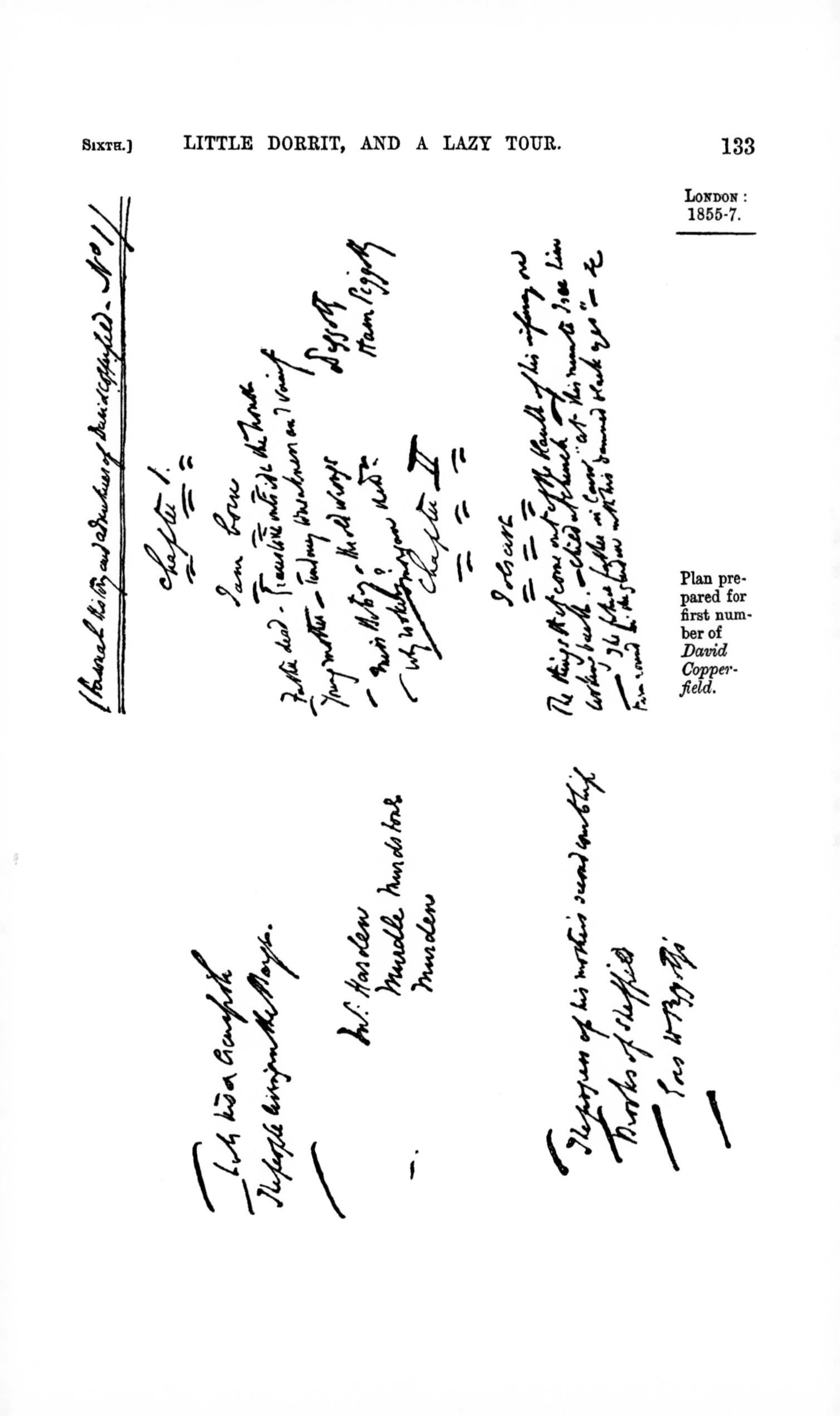

LONDON: 1855-7.

Plan prepared for first number of *David Copperfield.*

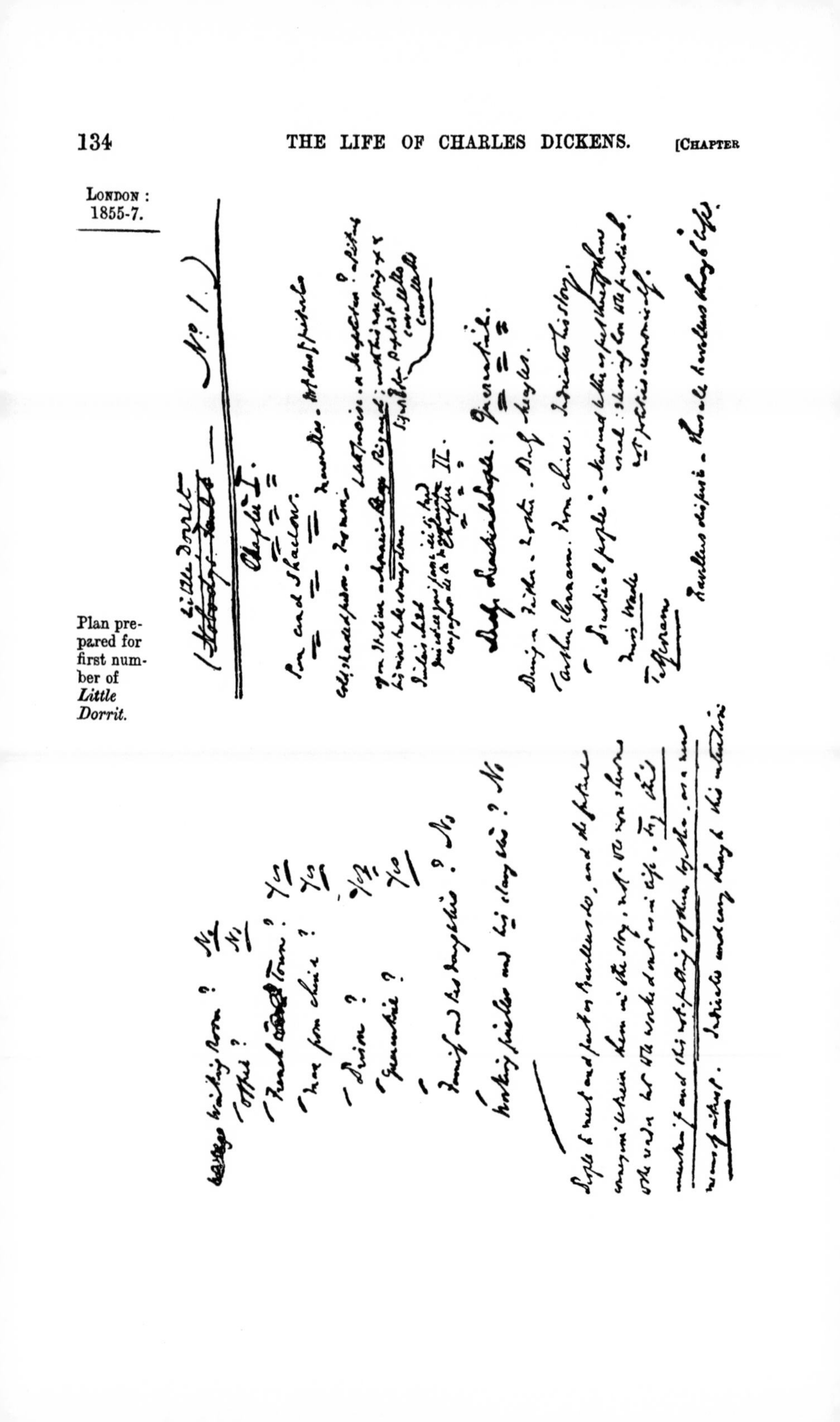

LONDON:
1855-7.

Plan prepared for first number of *Little Dorrit*.

with the rest are in my possession, with those of *Chuzzlewit* or *Copperfield;* observing in the former the labour and pains, and in the latter the lightness and confidence of handling.* 'I am just now getting to work on number 'three: sometimes enthusiastic, more often dull enough. 'There is an enormous outlay in the Father of the Mar-'shalsea chapter, in the way of getting a great lot of matter 'into a small space. I am not quite resolved, but I have 'a great idea of overwhelming that family with wealth. 'Their condition would be very curious. I can make Dorrit 'very strong in the story, I hope.' The Marshalsea part of the tale undoubtedly was excellent, and there was masterly treatment of character in the contrasts of the brothers Dorrit; but of the family generally it may be said that its least important members had most of his genius in them. The younger of the brothers, the scapegrace son, and 'Fanny dear,' are perfectly real people in what makes them unattractive; but what is meant for attractiveness in the heroine becomes often tiresome by want of reality.

How the story grew.

Sept. 16th (Folkestone).

The Dorrits.

The first number appeared in December 1855, and on the 2nd there was an exultant note. '*Little Dorrit* has 'beaten even *Bleak House* out of the field. It is a most 'tremendous start, and I am overjoyed at it;' to which he added, writing from Paris on the 6th of the month following, 'You know that they had sold 35,000 of number two 'on new year's day.' He was still in Paris on the day of the appearance of that portion of the tale by which it

Dec. 2nd.

Sale of the book.

* So curious a contrast, taking *Copperfield* for the purpose, I have thought worth giving in fac-simile; and can assure the reader that the examples taken express very fairly the general character of the Notes to the two books respectively.

LONDON: 1856-7.

will always be most vividly remembered, and thus wrote on the 30th of January 1856: 'I have a grim pleasure upon 'me to-night in thinking that the Circumlocution Office 'sees the light, and in wondering what effect it will make. 'But my head really stings with the visions of the book, 'and I am going, as we French say, to disembarrass it by 'plunging out into some of the strange places I glide into 'of nights in these latitudes.' The Circumlocution heroes led to the Society scenes, the Hampton-court dowager-sketches, and Mr. Gowan; all parts of one satire levelled against prevailing political and social vices. Aim had been taken, in the course of it, at some living originals, disguised sufficiently from recognition to enable him to make his thrust more sure; but there was one exception self-revealed. 'I had the general idea,' he wrote while engaged on the sixth number, 'of the Society business 'before the Sadleir affair, but I shaped Mr. Merdle him-'self out of that precious rascality. Society, the Cir-'cumlocution Office, and Mr. Gowan, are of course three 'parts of one idea and design. Mr. Merdle's complaint, 'which you will find in the end to be fraud and forgery, 'came into my mind as the last drop in the silver cream-'jug on Hampstead-heath. I shall beg, when you have 'read the present number, to enquire whether you consider '"Bar" an instance, in reference to K F, of a suggested 'likeness in not many touches?' The likeness no one could mistake; and, though that particular Bar has since been moved into a higher and happier sphere, Westminster-hall is in no danger of losing 'the insinuating Jury-'droop, and persuasive double-eyeglass,' by which this keen

Circumlocution Office.

Satirical scenes:

Parts of general design.

From the life.

observer could express a type of character in half a dozen words. LONDON: 1856-7.

Of the other portions of the book that had a strong personal interest for him I have spoken on a former page, and I will now only add an allusion of his own. 'There are 'some things in Flora in number seven that seem to me 'to be extraordinarily droll, with something serious at the 'bottom of them after all. Ah, well! was there *not* some- 'thing very serious in it once? I am glad to think of being 'in the country with the long summer mornings as I 'approach number ten, where I have finally resolved to 'make Dorrit rich. It should be a very fine point in the 'story . . . Nothing in Flora made me laugh so much 'as the confusion of ideas between gout flying upwards, 'and its soaring with Mr. F—— to another sphere.' He had himself no inconsiderable enjoyment also of Mr. F.'s aunt; and in the old rascal of a patriarch, the smooth-surfaced Casby, and other surroundings of poor Flora, there was fun enough to float an argosy of second-rates, assuming such to have formed the staple of the tale. It would be far from fair to say they did. The defect in the book was less the absence of excellent character or keen observation, than the want of ease and coherence among the figures of the story, and of a central interest in the plan of it. The agencies that bring about its catastrophe, too, are less agreeable even than in *Bleak House*; and, most unlike that well-constructed story, some of the most deeply considered things that occur in it have really little to do with the tale itself. The surface-painting of both Miss Wade and Tattycoram, to take an instance, is anything but

i. 71-74.

April 7th, 1856.

Flora and her surroundings.

Weak points in the book.

LONDON: 1856-7.

Characters good but not essential.

attractive, yet there is under it a rare force of likeness in the unlikeness between the two which has much subtlety of intention; and they must both have had, as well as Mr. Gowan himself, a striking effect in the novel, if they had been made to contribute in a more essential way to its interest or development. The failure nevertheless had not been for want of care and study, as well of his own design as of models by masters in his art. A happier hint of apology, for example, could hardly be given for Fielding's introduction of such an episode as the Man of the Hill between the youth and manhood of Blifil and Tom Jones, than is suggested by what Dickens wrote of the least interesting part of *Little Dorrit.* In the mere form, Fielding of course was only following the lead of Cervantes and Le Sage; but Dickens rightly judged his purpose also to have been, to supply a kind of connection between the episode and the story. 'I don't see the practicability of making 'the History of a Self-Tormentor, with which I took great 'pains, a written narrative. But I do see the possibility' (he saw the other practicability before the number was published) 'of making it a chapter by itself, which might 'enable me to dispense with the necessity of the turned 'commas. Do you think that would be better? I have no 'doubt that a great part of Fielding's reason for the 'introduced story, and Smollett's also, was, that it is 'sometimes really impossible to present, in a full book, the 'idea it contains (which yet it may be on all accounts de-'sirable to present), without supposing the reader to be pos-'sessed of almost as much romantic allowance as would put 'him on a level with the writer. In Miss Wade I had

Episodes in novels.

'an idea, which I thought a new one, of making the intro-'duced story so fit into surroundings impossible of separa-'tion from the main story, as to make the blood of the book 'circulate through both. But I can only suppose, from what 'you say, that I have not exactly succeeded in this.'

LONDON: 1856-7.

Miss Wade's narrative.

Shortly after the date of his letter he was in London on business connected with the purchase of Gadshill Place, and he went over to the Borough to see what traces were left of the prison of which his first impression was taken in his boyhood, which had played so important a part in this latest novel, and every brick and stone of which he had been able to rebuild in his book by the mere vividness of his marvellous memory. 'Went to the Borough yesterday 'morning before going to Gadshill, to see if I could find 'any ruins of the Marshalsea. Found a great part of the 'original building—now "Marshalsea Place." Found the 'rooms that have been in my mind's eye in the story. 'Found, nursing a very big boy, a very small boy, who, 'seeing me standing on the Marshalsea pavement, looking 'about, told me how it all used to be. God knows how he 'learned it (for he was a world too young to know anything 'about it), but he was right enough. . . There is a room 'there—still standing, to my amazement—that I think of 'taking! It is the room through which the ever-memorable 'signers of Captain Porter's petition filed off in my boy-'hood. The spikes are gone, and the wall is lowered, 'and anybody can go out now who likes to go, and is not 'bedridden; and I said to the boy "Who lives there?" 'and he said, "Jack Pithick." "Who is Jack Pithick?" 'I asked him. And he said, "Joe Pithick's uncle."'

Coming to the close.

Remains of Marshalsea visited.

A scene of his boy-trials. i. 45-6.

LONDON: 1856-7.

Mention was made of this visit in the preface that appeared with the last number; and all it is necessary to add of the completed book will be, that, though in the humour and satire of its finer parts not unworthy of him, and though it had the clear design, worthy of him in an especial degree, of contrasting, both in private and in public life, and in poverty equally as in wealth, duty done and duty not done, it made no material addition to his reputation. His public, however, showed no falling-off in its enormous numbers; and what is said in one of his letters, noticeable for this touch of character, illustrates his anxiety to avoid any set-off from the disquiet that critical discourtesies might give. 'I was ludicrously foiled here the other night 'in a resolution I have kept for twenty years not to know 'of any attack upon myself, by stumbling, before I could 'pick myself up, on a short extract in the *Globe* from '*Blackwood's Magazine*, informing me that *Little Dorrit* 'is "Twaddle." I was sufficiently put out by it to be angry 'with myself for being such a fool, and then pleased with 'myself for having so long been constant to a good resolu- 'tion.' There was a scene that made itself part of history not four months after his death, which, if he could have lived to hear of it, might have more than consoled him. It was the meeting of Bismarck and Jules Favre under the walls of Paris. The Prussian was waiting to open fire on the city; the Frenchman was engaged in the arduous task of showing the wisdom of not doing it; and 'we learn,' say the papers of the day, 'that while the two eminent 'statesmen were trying to find a basis of negotiation, Von 'Moltke was seated in a corner reading *Little Dorrit*.'

Reception of the novel.

Criticism and its set-off.

*Pall Mall Gazette* of 3rd of Oct. Paris letter of 25th of Sept. 1870.

Who will doubt that the chapter on HOW NOT TO DO IT was then absorbing the old soldier's attention?

LONDON: 1856-7.

---

Christmas theatricals preparing

Preparations for the private play had gone on incessantly up to Christmas, and, in turning the schoolroom into a theatre, sawing and hammering worthy of Babel continued for weeks. The priceless help of Stanfield had again been secured, and I remember finding him one day at Tavistock House in the act of upsetting some elaborate arrangements by Dickens, with a proscenium before him made up of chairs, and the scenery planned out with walking-sticks. But Dickens's art in a matter of this kind was to know how to take advice; and no suggestion came to him that he was not ready to act upon, if it presented the remotest likelihood. In one of his great difficulties of obtaining more space, for audience as well as actors, he was told that Mr. Cooke of Astley's was a man of much resource in that way; and to Mr. Cooke he applied, with the following result. 'One of the finest things' (18th of October 1856) 'I have ever seen in my life of that kind was the arrival 'of my friend Mr. Cooke one morning this week, in an 'open phaeton drawn by two white ponies with black 'spots all over them (evidently stencilled), who came in 'at the gate with a little jolt and a rattle, exactly as 'they come into the Ring when they draw anything, and 'went round and round the centre bed of the front court, 'apparently looking for the clown. A multitude of boys 'who felt them to be no common ponies rushed up in a 'breathless state—twined themselves like ivy about the 'railings—and were only deterred from storming the en-

A visit from Astley's.

Outside Tavistock House.

LONDON: 1856-7.

'closure by the glare of the Inimitable's eye. Some of 'these boys had evidently followed from Astley's. I grieve 'to add that my friend, being taken to the point of diffi-'culty, had no sort of suggestion in him; no gleam of an 'idea; and might just as well have been the popular 'minister from the Tabernacle in Tottenham Court Road. 'All he could say was—answering me, posed in the garden, 'precisely as if I were the clown asking him a riddle at 'night—that two of their stable tents would be home in 'November, and that they were "20 foot square," and I 'was heartily welcome to 'em. Also, he said, "You might '"have half a dozen of my trapezes, or my middle-distance-'"tables, but they're all 6 foot and all too low sir." Since 'then, I have arranged to do it in my own way, and with 'my own carpenter. You will be surprised by the look of 'the place. It is no more like the schoolroom than it is 'like the sign of the Salutation Inn at Ambleside in 'Westmoreland. The sounds in the house remind me, as 'to the present time, of Chatham Dockyard—as to a remote 'epoch, of the building of Noah's ark. Joiners are never 'out of the house, and the carpenter appears to be un-'settled (or settled) for life.'

Dickens and his visitor.

Theatre-making.

Of course time did not mend matters, and as Christmas approached the house was in a state of siege. 'All day 'long, a labourer heats size over the fire in a great crucible. 'We eat it, drink it, breathe it, and smell it. Seventy 'paint-pots (which came in a van) adorn the stage; and 'thereon may be beheld, Stanny, and three Dansons (from 'the Surrey Zoological Gardens), all painting at once!! 'Meanwhile, Telbin, in a secluded bower in Brewer-street,

Scene-painting.

'Golden-square, plies *his* part of the little undertaking.' How worthily it turned out in the end, the excellence of the performances and the delight of the audiences, became known to all London; and the pressure for admittance at last took the form of a tragi-comedy, composed of ludicrous makeshifts and gloomy disappointments, with which even Dickens's resources could not deal. 'My audience is now 93,' he wrote one day in despair, 'and at least 10 will neither 'hear nor see.' There was nothing for it but to increase the number of nights; and it was not until the 20th of January he described 'the workmen smashing the last atoms of the theatre.'

LONDON: 1856-7.

Rush for places.

His book was finished soon after at Gadshill Place, to be presently described, which he had purchased the previous year, and taken possession of in February; subscribing himself, in the letter announcing the fact, as 'the Kentish Freeholder on his native heath, his name Protection.' * The new abode occupied him in various ways in the early part of the summer; and Hans Andersen the Dane had just arrived upon a visit to him there, when Douglas Jerrold's unexpected death befell. It was a shock to every one, and an especial grief to Dickens. Jerrold's wit, and the bright shrewd intellect that had so many triumphs, need no celebration from me; but the keenest of satirists was one of the kindliest of men, and Dickens had a fondness for

At Gadshill.

Douglas Jerrold

* In the same letter was an illustration of the ruling passion in death, which, even in so undignified a subject, might have interested Pope. 'You 'remember little Wieland who did grotesque demons so well. Did you ever 'hear how he died? He lay very still in bed with the life fading out of him— 'suddenly sprung out of it, threw what is professionally called a flip-flap, and 'fell dead on the floor.'

Ruling passion in death.

LONDON: 1856-7.

Jerrold as genuine as his admiration for him. 'I chance to 'know a good deal about the poor fellow's illness, for I was 'with him on the last day he was out. It was ten days 'ago, when we dined at a dinner given by Russell at Green- 'wich. He was complaining much when we met, said he had 'been sick three days, and attributed it to the inhaling of 'white paint from his study window. I did not think much 'of it at the moment, as we were very social; but while 'we walked through Leicester-square he suddenly fell into 'a white, hot, sick perspiration, and had to lean against 'the railings. Then, at my urgent request, he was to let me 'put him in a cab and send him home; but he rallied a little 'after that, and, on our meeting Russell, determined to 'come with us. We three went down by steamboat that 'we might see the great ship, and then got an open fly and 'rode about Blackheath: poor Jerrold mightily enjoying 'the air, and constantly saying that it set him up. He was 'rather quiet at dinner—sat next Delane—but was very 'humorous and good, and in spirits, though he took hardly 'anything. We parted with references to coming down 'here' (Gadshill) 'and I never saw him again. Next 'morning he was taken very ill when he tried to get up. 'On the Wednesday and Thursday he was very bad, but 'rallied on the Friday, and was quite confident of getting 'well. On the Sunday he was very ill again, and on the 'Monday forenoon died; "at peace with all the world" 'he said, and asking to be remembered to friends. He 'had become indistinct and insensible, until for but a few 'minutes at the end. I knew nothing about it, except that 'he had been ill and was better, until, going up by railway

Last meeting of Jerrold and Dickens.

Jerrold's death.

LONDON: 1856-7.

'yesterday morning, I heard a man in the carriage, unfold- 'ing his newspaper, say to another "Douglas Jerrold is '"dead." I immediately went up there, and then to 'Whitefriars . . . I propose that there shall be a night at a 'theatre when the actors (with old Cooke) shall play the '*Rent Day* and *Black-ey'd Susan;* another night else- 'where, with a lecture from Thackeray; a day reading by 'me; a night reading by me; a lecture by Russell; and a 'subscription performance of the *Frozen Deep*, as at Tavis- 'tock House. I don't mean to do it beggingly; but merely 'to announce the whole series, the day after the funeral, '"In memory of the late Mr. Douglas Jerrold," or some 'such phrase. I have got hold of Arthur Smith as the best 'man of business I know, and go to work with him to- 'morrow morning—inquiries being made in the meantime 'as to the likeliest places to be had for these various pur- 'poses. My confident hope is that we shall get close upon 'two thousand pounds.'

Proposed memorial tribute.

The friendly enterprise was carried to the close with a vigour, promptitude, and success, that well corresponded with this opening. In addition to the performances named, there were others in the country also organized by Dickens, in which he took active personal part; and the result did not fall short of his expectations. The sum was invested ultimately for our friend's unmarried daughter, who still receives the income from myself, the last surviving trustee.

Exertions of Dickens and result.

So passed the greater part of the summer,* and when

* One of its incidents made such an impression on him that it will be worth while to preserve his description of it. "I have been (by mere accident) see- 'ing the serpents fed to-day, with the live birds, rabbits, and guinea pigs—a 'sight so very horrible that I cannot get rid of the impression, and am, at

Seeing the serpents fed.

LONDON: 1856-7.

the country performances were over at the end of August I had this intimation. 'I have arranged with Collins that 'he and I will start next Monday on a ten or twelve days' 'expedition to out-of-the-way places, to do (in inns and 'coast-corners) a little tour in search of an article and in 'avoidance of railroads. I must get a good name for it, 'and I propose it in five articles, one for the beginning of 'every number in the October part.' Next day: 'Our 'decision is for a foray upon the fells of Cumberland; I 'having discovered in the books some promising moors and 'bleak places thereabout.' Into the lake-country they went accordingly; and The Lazy Tour of Two Idle Apprentices, contributed to *Household Words,* was a narrative of the trip. But his letters had descriptive touches,

Lazy Tour projected.

'this present, imagining serpents coming up the legs of the table, with their 'infernal flat heads, and their tongues like the Devil's tail (evidently taken 'from that model, in the magic lanterns and other such popular representa- 'tions), elongated for dinner. I saw one small serpent, whose father was 'asleep, go up to a guinea pig (white and yellow, and with a gentle eye—every 'hair upon him erect with horror); corkscrew himself on the tip of his tail; 'open a mouth which couldn't have swallowed the guinea pig's nose; dilate a 'throat which wouldn't have made him a stocking; and show him what his 'father meant to do with him when he came out of that ill-looking Hookah into 'which he had resolved himself. The guinea pig backed against the side of 'the cage—said "I know it, I know it!"—and his eye glared and his coat 'turned wiry, as he made the remark. Five small sparrows crouching 'together in a little trench at the back of the cage, peeped over the brim of 'it, all the time; and when they saw the guinea pig give it up, and the young 'serpent go away looking at him over about two yards and a quarter of 'shoulder, struggled which should get into the innermost angle and be seized 'last. Everyone of them then hid his eyes in another's breast, and then they 'all shook together like dry leaves—as I daresay they may be doing now, for 'old Hookah was as dull as laudanum . . . . Please to imagine two small 'serpents, one beginning on the tail of a white mouse, and one on the head, 'and each pulling his own way, and the mouse very much alive all the time, 'with the middle of him madly writhing.'

At the Zoological Gardens.

CUMBERLAND: 1857.

and some whimsical personal experiences, not in the published account.

Scene chosen.

Looking over the *Beauties of England and Wales* before he left London, his ambition was fired by mention of Carrick Fell, 'a gloomy old mountain 1500 feet high,' which he secretly resolved to go up. 'We came straight 'to it yesterday' (9th of September). 'Nobody goes up. 'Guides have forgotten it. Master of a little inn, excellent 'north-countryman, volunteered. Went up, in a tremendous rain. C. D. beat Mr. Porter (name of landlord) in 'half a mile. Mr. P. done up in no time. Three never'theless went on. Mr. P. again leading; C. D. and C.' (Mr. Wilkie Collins) 'following. Rain terrific, black mists, 'darkness of night. Mr. P. agitated. C. D. confident. C. '(a long way down in perspective) submissive. All wet 'through. No poles. Not so much as a walking-stick in 'the party. Reach the summit, at about one in the day. 'Dead darkness as of night. Mr. P. (excellent fellow to the 'last) uneasy. C. D. produces compass from pocket. Mr. 'P. reassured. Farm-house where dog-cart was left, N.N.W. 'Mr. P. complimentary. Descent commenced. C. D. with 'compass triumphant, until compass, with the heat and wet 'of C. D.'s pocket, breaks. Mr. P. (who never had a com'pass), inconsolable, confesses he has not been on Carrick 'Fell for twenty years, and he don't know the way down. 'Darker and darker. Nobody discernible, two yards off, by 'the other two. Mr. P. makes suggestions, but no way. It 'becomes clear to C. D. and to C. that Mr. P. is going round 'and round the mountain, and never coming down. Mr. P. 'sits on angular granite, and says he is "just fairly doon."

Up Carrick Fell.

Summit reached.

Way lost in coming down.

CUMBERLAND: 1857.

'C. D. revives Mr. P. with laughter, the only restorative 'in the company. Mr. P. again complimentary. Descent 'tried once more. Mr. P. worse and worse. Council of 'war. Proposals from C. D. to go "slap down." Seconded 'by C. Mr. P. objects, on account of precipice called The 'Black Arches, and terror of the country-side. More wan-'dering. Mr. P. terror-stricken, but game. Watercourse, 'thundering and roaring, reached. C. D. suggests that it 'must run to the river, and had best be followed, subject to 'all gymnastic hazards. Mr. P. opposes, but gives in. Water-'course followed accordingly. Leaps, splashes, and tumbles, 'for two hours. C. lost. C. D. whoops. Cries for assist-'ance from behind. C. D. returns. C. with horribly sprained 'ankle, lying in rivulet!'

Accident to Wilkie Collins.

All the danger was over when Dickens sent his description; but great had been the trouble in binding up the sufferer's ankle and getting him painfully on, shoving, shouldering, carrying alternately, till terra firma was reached. 'We got down at last in the wildest place, pre-'posterously out of the course; and, propping up C. against 'stones, sent Mr. P. to the other side of Cumberland for 'dog-cart, so got back to his inn, and changed. Shoe or 'stocking on the bad foot, out of the question. Foot 'tumbled up in a flannel waistcoat. C. D. carrying C. 'melo-dramatically (Wardour to the life!)* everywhere; 'into and out of carriages; up and down stairs; to bed; 'every step. And so to Wigton, got doctor, and here we 'are!! A pretty business, we flatter ourselves!'

Down at last.

* There was a situation in the *Frozen Deep* where Richard Wardour, played by Dickens, had thus to carry about Frank Aldersley in the person of Wilkie Collins.

CUMBERLAND: 1857.

At Wigton.

Wigton, Dickens described as a place of little houses all in half-mourning, yellow stone or white stone and black, with the wonderful peculiarity that though it had no population, no business, and no streets to speak of, it had five linendrapers within range of their single window, one linendraper's next door, and five more linendrapers round the corner. 'I ordered a night light in my bed-room. A 'queer little old woman brought me one of the common 'Child's night lights, and, seeming to think that I looked 'at it with interest, said, "It's joost a vara keeyourious '"thing, sir, and joost new coom oop. It'll burn awt hoors '"a' end, and no gootther, nor no waste, nor ony sike a '"thing, if you can creedit what I say, seein' the airticle."' In these primitive quarters there befell a difficulty about letters, which Dickens solved in a fashion especially his own. 'The day after Carrick there was a mess about our 'letters, through our not going to a place called Mayport. 'So, while the landlord was planning how to get them (they 'were only twelve miles off), I walked off, to his great 'astonishment, and brought them over.' The night after leaving Wigton they were at the Ship-hotel in Allonby.

Wonders of a night-light.

A difficulty solved.

At Allonby.

Allonby his letters presented as a small untidy outlandish place; rough stone houses in half mourning, a few coarse yellow-stone lodging houses with black roofs (bills in all the windows), five bathing-machines, five girls in straw hats, five men in straw hats (wishing they had not come); very much what Broadstairs would have been if it had been born Irish, and had not inherited a cliff. 'But 'this is a capital little homely inn, looking out upon the 'sea; with the coast of Scotland, mountainous and romantic,

CUMBERLAND: 1857.

'over against the windows; and though I can just stand 'upright in my bedroom, we are really well lodged. It is 'a clean nice place in a rough wild country, and we have a 'very obliging and comfortable landlady.' He had found indeed, in the latter, an acquaintance of old date. 'The 'landlady at the little inn at Allonby, lived at Greta-Bridge 'in Yorkshire when I went down there before *Nickleby;* 'and was smuggled into the room to see me, after I was 'secretly found out. She is an immensely fat woman now. '"But I could tuck my arm round her waist then, Mr. '"Dickens," the landlord said when she told me the story 'as I was going to bed the night before last. "And can't '"you do it now?" I said. "You insensible dog! Look at '"me! Here's a picture!" Accordingly I got round as 'much of her as I could; and this gallant action was the 'most successful I have ever performed, on the whole.'

An old acquaintance.

A picture.

At Doncaster.

On their way home the friends were at Doncaster, and this was Dickens's first experience of the St. Leger and its saturnalia. His companion had by this time so far recovered as to be able, doubled-up, to walk with a thick stick; in which condition, 'being exactly like the gouty admiral 'in a comedy I have given him that name.' The impressions received from the race-week were not favourable. It was noise and turmoil all day long, and a gathering of vagabonds from all parts of the racing earth. Every bad face that had ever caught wickedness from an innocent horse had its representative in the streets; and as Dickens, like Gulliver looking down upon his fellow-men after coming from the horse-country, looked down into Doncaster High-street from his inn-window, he seemed to see everywhere a

The race-week.

then notorious personage who had just poisoned his betting-companion. 'Everywhere I see the late Mr. Palmer with 'his betting-book in his hand. Mr. Palmer sits next me at 'the theatre; Mr. Palmer goes before me down the street; 'Mr. Palmer follows me into the chemist's shop where I 'go to buy rose water after breakfast, and says to the 'chemist "Give us soom sal volatile or soom damned thing '"o' that soort, in wather—my head's bad!" And I look at 'the back of his bad head repeated in long, long lines on 'the race course, and in the betting stand and outside the 'betting rooms in the town, and I vow to God that I can 'see nothing in it but cruelty, covetousness, calculation, 'insensibility, and low wickedness.'

DONCASTER: 1857.

Betting-men.

Even a half-appalling kind of luck was not absent from my friend's experiences at the race course, when, what he called a 'wonderful, paralysing, coincidence' befell him. He bought the card; facetiously wrote down three names for the winners of the three chief races (never in his life having heard or thought of any of the horses, except that the winner of the Derby, who proved to be nowhere, had been mentioned to him); 'and, if you can believe it without your 'hair standing on end, those three races were won, one after 'another, by those three horses!!!' That was the St. Leger-day, of which he also thought it noticeable, that, though the losses were enormous, nobody had won, for there was nothing but grinding of teeth and blaspheming of ill-luck. Nor had matters mended on the Cup-day, after which celebration 'a groaning phantom' lay in the doorway of his bed-room and howled all night. The landlord came up in the morning to apologise, 'and said it was a gentleman

Racing prophecy by Dickens!

The 'horrors.'

DONCASTER: 1857.

'who had lost £1500 or £2000; and he had drunk a 'deal afterwards; and then they put him to bed, and then 'he—took the 'orrors, and got up, and yelled till morning.'* Dickens might well believe, as he declared at the end of his letter, that if a boy with any good in him, but with a dawning propensity to sporting and betting, were but brought to the Doncaster races soon enough, it would cure him.

A performance of *Money*.

* The mention of a performance of Lord Lytton's *Money* at the theatre will supply the farce to this tragedy. 'I have rarely seen anything finer than Lord 'Glossmore, a chorus-singer in bluchers, drab trowsers, and a brown sack; and 'Dudley Smooth, in somebody else's wig, hindside before. Stout also, in any-'thing he could lay hold of. The waiter at the club had an immense moustache, 'white trowsers, and a striped jacket; and he brought everybody who came in, 'a vinegar-cruet. The man who read the will began thus: "I so-and-so, being '"of unsound mind but firm in body.." In spite of all this, however, the real 'character, humour, wit, and good writing of the comedy, made themselves 'apparent; and the applause was loud and repeated, and really seemed genuine. 'Its capital things were not lost altogether. It was succeeded by a Jockey 'Dance by five ladies, who put their whips in their mouths and worked imagi-'nary winners up to the float—an immense success.'

## CHAPTER VII.

### WHAT HAPPENED AT THIS TIME.

1857—1858.

AN unsettled feeling greatly in excess of what was usual with Dickens, more or less observable since his first residence at Boulogne, became at this time almost habitual, and the satisfactions which home should have supplied, and which indeed were essential requirements of his nature, he had failed to find in his home. He had not the alternative that under this disappointment some can discover in what is called society. It did not suit him, and he set no store by it. No man was better fitted to adorn any circle he entered, but beyond that of friends and equals he rarely passed. He would take as much pains to keep out of the houses of the great as others take to get into them. Not always wisely, it may be admitted. Mere contempt for toadyism and flunkeyism was not at all times the prevailing motive with him which he supposed it to be. Beneath his horror of those vices of Englishmen in his own rank of life, there was a still stronger resentment at the social inequalities that engender them, of which he was not so conscious and to which he owned less freely. Not the less it served secretly to justify what he might other-

LONDON: 1857.

**Disappointments and distastes.**

LONDON: 1857.

wise have had no mind to. To say he was not a gentleman would be as true as to say he was not a writer; but if any one should assert his occasional preference for what was even beneath his level over that which was above it, this would be difficult of disproof. It was among those defects of temperament for which his early trials and his early successes were accountable in perhaps equal measure. He was sensitive in a passionate degree to praise and blame, which yet he made it for the most part a point of pride to assume indifference to; the inequalities of rank which he secretly resented took more galling as well as glaring prominence from the contrast of the necessities he had gone through with the fame that had come to him; and when the forces he most affected to despise assumed the form of barriers he could not easily overleap, he was led to appear frequently intolerant (for he very seldom was really so) in opinions and language. His early sufferings brought with them the healing powers of energy, will, and persistence, and taught him the inexpressible value of a determined resolve to live down difficulties; but the habit, in small as in great things, of renunciation and self-sacrifice, they did not teach; and, by his sudden leap into a world-wide popularity and influence, he became master of everything that might seem to be attainable in life, before he had mastered what a man must undergo to be equal to its hardest trials.

What we seem and are.

Contrasted influences.

Nothing of all this has yet presented itself to notice, except in occasional forms of restlessness and desire of change of place, which were themselves, when his books were in progress, so incident as well to the active requirements of his fancy as to call, thus far, for no other explanation. Up

LONDON: 1857.

Compensations of art.

to the date of the completion of *Copperfield* he had felt himself to be in possession of an all-sufficient resource. Against whatever might befall he had a set-off in his imaginative creations, a compensation derived from his art that never failed him, because there he was supreme. It was the world he could bend to his will, and make subserve to all his desires. He had otherwise, underneath his exterior of a singular precision, method, and strictly orderly arrangement in all things, and notwithstanding a temperament to which home and home interests were really a necessity, something in common with those eager, impetuous, somewhat overbearing natures, that rush at existence without heeding the cost of it, and are not more ready to accept and make the most of its enjoyments than to be easily and quickly overthrown by its burdens.* But the world he had called into being had thus far borne him safely through these perils. He had his own creations always by his side. They were living, speaking companions. With them only he was everywhere thoroughly identified.

Hidden perils.

* Anything more completely opposed to the Micawber type could hardly be conceived, and yet there were moments (really and truly only moments) when the fancy would arise that if the conditions of his life had been reversed, something of a vagabond existence (using the word in Goldsmith's meaning) might have supervened. It would have been an unspeakable misery to him, but it might have come nevertheless. The question of hereditary transmission had a curious attraction for him, and considerations connected with it were frequently present to his mind. Of a youth who had fallen into a father's weaknesses without the possibility of having himself observed them for imitation, he thus wrote on one occasion: 'It suggests the strangest consideration 'as to which of our own failings we are really responsible, and as to which 'of them we cannot quite reasonably hold ourselves to be so. What A. 'evidently derived from his father cannot in his case be derived from association and observation, but must be in the very principles of his individuality 'as a living creature.'

Hereditary transmission.

LONDON: 1857.

He laughed and wept with them; was as much elated by their fun as cast down by their grief; and brought to the consideration of them a belief in their reality as well as in the influences they were meant to exercise, which in every circumstance sustained him.

Misgivings.

It was during the composition of *Little Dorrit* that I think he first felt a certain strain upon his invention which brought with it other misgivings. In a modified form this was present during the later portions of *Bleak House*, of which not a few of the defects might be traced to the acting excitements amid which it was written; but the succeeding book made it plainer to him; and it is remarkable that in the interval between them he resorted for the first and only time in his life to a practice, which he abandoned at the close of his next and last story published in the twenty-number form, of putting down written 'Memoranda' of suggestions for characters or incidents by way of resource to him in his writing. Never before had his teeming fancy seemed to want such help; the need being less to contribute to its fullness than to check its overflowing; but it is another proof that he had been secretly bringing before himself, at least, the possibility that what had ever been his great support might some day desert him. It was strange that he should have had such doubt, and he would hardly have confessed it openly; but apart from that wonderful world of his books, the range of his thoughts was not always proportioned to the width and largeness of his nature. His ordinary circle of activity, whether in likings or thinkings, was full of such surprising animation, that one was apt to believe it more comprehensive than it really

Written suggestions for stories.

LONDON: 1857.

was; and again and again, when a wide horizon might seem to be ahead of him, he would pull up suddenly and stop short, as though nothing lay beyond. For the time, though each had its term and change, he was very much a man of one idea, each having its turn of absolute predominance; and this was one of the secrets of the thoroughness with which everything he took in hand was done. As to the matter of his writings, the actual truth was that his creative genius never really failed him. Not a few of his inventions of character and humour, up to the very close of his life, his Marigolds, Lirripers, Gargerys, Pips, Sapseas and many others, were as fresh and fine as in his greatest day. He had however lost the free and fertile method of the earlier time. He could no longer fill a wide-spread canvas with the same facility and certainty as of old; and he had frequently a quite unfounded apprehension of some possible break-down, of which the end might be at any moment beginning. There came accordingly, from time to time, intervals of unusual impatience and restlessness, strange to me in connection with his home; his old pursuits were too often laid aside for other excitements and occupations; he joined a public political agitation, set on foot by administrative reformers; he got up various quasi-public private theatricals, in which he took the leading place; and though it was but part of his always generous devotion in any friendly duty to organize the series of performances on his friend Jerrold's death, yet the eagerness with which he flung himself into them, so arranging them as to assume an amount of labour in acting and travelling that might have appalled an experienced comedian, and carrying them on week after week

A defect and a merit.

Unfounded fear.

Restlessness and impatience.

LONDON: 1857.

Jerrold performances.

unceasingly in London and the provinces, expressed but the craving which still had possession of him to get by some means at some change that should make existence easier. What was highest in his nature had ceased for the time to be highest in his life, and he had put himself at the mercy of lower accidents and conditions. The mere effect of the strolling wandering ways into which this acting led him could not be other than unfavourable. But remonstrance as yet was unavailing.

Reply to a remonstrance.

To one very earnestly made in the early autumn of 1857, in which opportunity was taken to compare his recent rush up Carrick Fell to his rush into other difficulties, here was the reply. 'Too late to say, put the curb on, and don't rush 'at hills—the wrong man to say it to. I have now no relief 'but in action. I am become incapable of rest. I am quite 'confident I should rust, break, and die, if I spared myself. 'Much better to die, doing. What I am in that way, nature 'made me first, and my way of life has of late, alas! con'firmed. I must accept the drawback—since it is one—'with the powers I have; and I must hold upon the tenure 'prescribed to me.' Something of the same sad feeling, it is right to say, had been expressed from time to time, in connection also with home dissatisfactions and misgivings, through the three years preceding; but I attributed it to other causes, and gave little attention to it. During his absences abroad for the greater part of 1854, '55, and '56, while the elder of his children were growing out of childhood, and his books were less easy to him than in his earlier manhood, evidences presented themselves in his letters of the old 'unhappy loss or want of something' to which he had given a pervading prominence in *Copperfield*. In the first of those years he made express allusion to the kind of experience which had been one of his descriptions in that favourite book, and, mentioning the drawbacks of his present life, had first identified it with his own: 'the 'so happy and yet so unhappy existence which seeks its 'realities in unrealities, and finds its dangerous comfort in 'a perpetual escape from the disappointment of heart 'around it.'

LONDON: 1857.

Dangerous comfort.

Later in the same year he thus wrote from Boulogne: 'I have had dreadful thoughts of getting away somewhere 'altogether by myself. If I could have managed it, I think 'possibly I might have gone to the Pyreennees (you know 'what I mean that word for, so I won't re-write it) for six 'months! I have put the idea into the perspective of 'six months, but have not abandoned it. I have visions 'of living for half a year or so, in all sorts of inaccessible 'places, and opening a new book therein. A floating idea 'of going up above the snow-line in Switzerland, and 'living in some astonishing convent, hovers about me. If '*Household Words* could be got into a good train, in short, 'I don't know in what strange place, or at what remote 'elevation above the level of the sea, I might fall to work 'next. *Restlessness*, you will say. Whatever it is, it is 'always driving me, and I cannot help it. I have rested 'nine or ten weeks, and sometimes feel as if it had been a 'year—though I had the strangest nervous miseries before 'I stopped. If I couldn't walk fast and far, I should just 'explode and perish.' Again, four months later he wrote: 'You will hear of me in Paris, probably next Sunday, and

Visions of places to write books in.

LONDON: 1857.

'I *may* go on to Bordeaux. Have general ideas of emi-'grating in the summer to the mountain-ground between 'France and Spain. Am altogether in a dishevelled state 'of mind—motes of new books in the dirty air, miseries of 'older growth threatening to close upon me. Why is it, 'that as with poor David, a sense comes always crushing 'on me now, when I fall into low spirits, as of one happiness 'I have missed in life, and one friend and companion I 'have never made?'

One happiness missed.

Early in 1856 (20th of January) the notion revisited him of writing a book in solitude. 'Again I am beset by 'my former notions of a book whereof the whole story 'shall be on the top of the Great St. Bernard. As I accept 'and reject ideas for *Little Dorrit*, it perpetually comes 'back to me. Two or three years hence, perhaps you'll 'find me living with the Monks and the Dogs a whole 'winter—among the blinding snows that fall about that 'monastery. I have a serious idea that I shall do it, if I 'live.' He was at this date in Paris; and during the visit to him of Macready in the following April, the self-revelations were resumed. The great actor was then living in retirement at Sherborne, to which he had gone on quitting the stage; and Dickens gave favourable report of his enjoyment of the change to his little holiday at Paris. Then, after recurring to his own old notion of having some slight idea of going to settle in Australia, only he could not do it until he should have finished *Little Dorrit*, he went on to say that perhaps Macready, if he could get into harness again, would not be the worse for some such troubles as were worrying himself. 'It fills me with pity to think of

More book projects.

An old friend retired.

'him away in that lonely Sherborne place. I have always 'felt of myself that I must, please God, die in harness, but 'I have never felt it more strongly than in looking at, and 'thinking of, him. However strange it is to be never at 'rest, and never satisfied, and ever trying after something 'that is never reached, and to be always laden with plot 'and plan and care and worry, how clear it is that it must 'be, and that one is driven by an irresistible might until 'the journey is worked out! It is much better to go on 'and fret, than to stop and fret. As to repose—for some 'men there's no such thing in this life. The foregoing has 'the appearance of a small sermon; but it is so often in 'my head in these days that it cannot help coming out. 'The old days—the old days! Shall I ever, I wonder, get 'the frame of mind back as it used to be then? Some-'thing of it perhaps—but never quite as it used to be. I 'find that the skeleton in my domestic closet is becoming 'a pretty big one.'

LONDON: 1857.

Homily on life.

Fruitless aspirations.

It would be unjust and uncandid not to admit that these and other similar passages in the letters that extended over the years while he lived abroad, had served in some degree as a preparation for what came after his return to England in the following year. It came with a great shock nevertheless; because it told plainly what before had never been avowed, but only hinted at more or less obscurely. The opening reference is to the reply which had been made to a previous expression of his wish for some confidences as in the old time. I give only what is strictly necessary to account for what followed, and even this with deep reluctance. 'Your letter of yesterday was

What lay behind.

LONDON: 1857.

'so kind and hearty, and sounded so gently the many 'chords we have touched together, that I cannot leave it 'unanswered, though I have not much (to any purpose) to 'say. My reference to "confidences" was merely to the 'relief of saying a word of what has long been pent up in 'my mind. Poor Catherine and I are not made for each 'other, and there is no help for it. It is not only that she 'makes me uneasy and unhappy, but that I make her so 'too—and much more so. She is exactly what you know, 'in the way of being amiable and complying; but we are 'strangely ill-assorted for the bond there is between us. 'God knows she would have been a thousand times happier 'if she had married another kind of man, and that her 'avoidance of this destiny would have been at least equally 'good for us both. I am often cut to the heart by thinking 'what a pity it is, for her own sake, that I ever fell in her 'way; and if I were sick or disabled to-morrow, I know 'how sorry she would be, and how deeply grieved myself, 'to think how we had lost each other. But exactly the 'same incompatibility would arise, the moment I was well 'again; and nothing on earth could make her understand 'me, or suit us to each other. Her temperament will not 'go with mine. It mattered not so much when we had 'only ourselves to consider, but reasons have been growing 'since which make it all but hopeless that we should even 'try to struggle on. What is now befalling me I have seen 'steadily coming, ever since the days you remember when 'Mary was born; and I know too well that you cannot, 'and no one can, help me. Why I have even written I 'hardly know; but it is a miserable sort of comfort that

Confidences.

Sorrowful convictions.

Hopeless of help.

LONDON: 1857.

'you should be clearly aware how matters stand. The mere 'mention of the fact, without any complaint or blame of 'any sort, is a relief to my present state of spirits—and 'I can get this only from you, because I can speak of 'it to no one else.' In the same tone was his rejoinder to my reply. 'To the most part of what you say—Amen! 'You are not so tolerant as perhaps you might be of 'the wayward and unsettled feeling which is part (I 'suppose) of the tenure on which one holds an imagi'native life, and which I have, as you ought to know well, 'often only kept down by riding over it like a dragoon '—but let that go by. I make no maudlin complaint. 'I agree with you as to the very possible incidents, 'even not less bearable than mine, that might and must 'often occur to the married condition when it is entered 'into very young. I am always deeply sensible of the 'wonderful exercise I have of life and its highest sensa'tions, and have said to myself for years, and have honestly 'and truly felt, This is the drawback to such a career, 'and is not to be complained of. I say it and feel it now 'as strongly as ever I did; and, as I told you in my last, 'I do not with that view put all this forward. But the 'years have not made it easier to bear for either of us; 'and, for her sake as well as mine, the wish will force itself 'upon me that something might be done. I know too 'well it is impossible. There is the fact, and that is all 'one can say. Nor are you to suppose that I disguise from 'myself what might be urged on the other side. I claim 'no immunity from blame. There is plenty of fault on 'my side, I dare say, in the way of a thousand uncertain-

Rejoinder to a reply.

Tenure of imaginative life.

No complaint made.

No desire for immunity from blame.

LONDON: 1857.

'ties, caprices, and difficulties of disposition; but only one 'thing will alter all that, and that is, the end which alters 'everything.'

It will not seem to most people that there was anything here which in happier circumstances might not have been susceptible of considerate adjustment; but all the circumstances were unfavourable, and the moderate middle course which the admissions in that letter might wisely have prompted and wholly justified, was unfortunately not taken. Compare what before was said of his temperament, with what is there said by himself of its defects, and the explanation will not be difficult. Every counteracting influence against the one idea which now predominated over him had been so weakened as to be almost powerless. His elder children were no longer children; his books had lost for the time the importance they formerly had over every other consideration in his life; and he had not in himself the resource that such a man, judging him from the surface, might be expected to have had. Not his genius only, but his whole nature, was too exclusively made up of sympathy for, and with, the real in its most intense form, to be sufficiently provided against failure in the realities around him. There was for him no 'city 'of the mind' against outward ills, for inner consolation and shelter. It was in and from the actual he still stretched forward to find the freedom and satisfactions of an ideal, and by his very attempts to escape the world he was driven back into the thick of it. But what he would have sought there, it supplies to none; and to get the infinite out of anything so finite, has broken many a stout heart.

Opportunity missed.

Counteracting influences weakened.

What the world cannot give.

At the close of that last letter from Gadshill (5th of September) was this question—'What do you think of my 'paying for this place, by reviving that old idea of some 'Readings from my books. I am very strongly tempted. 'Think of it.' The reasons against it had great force, and took, in my judgment, greater from the time at which it was again proposed. The old ground of opposition remained. It was a substitution of lower for higher aims; a change to commonplace from more elevated pursuits; and it had so much of the character of a public exhibition for money as to raise, in the question of respect for his calling as a writer, a question also of respect for himself as a gentleman. This opinion, now strongly reiterated, was referred ultimately to two distinguished ladies of his acquaintance, who decided against it.* Yet not without such mo-

Old project revived.

*Ante*, 40.

Objections to it.

* 'You may as well know' (20th of March 1858) 'that I went on' (I designate the ladies by A and B respectively) 'and propounded the matter 'to A, without any preparation. Result.—"I am surprised, and I should '"have been surprised if I had seen it in the newspaper without previous '"confidence from you. But nothing more. N—no. Certainly not. Nothing '"more. I don't see that there is anything derogatory in it, even now when '"you ask me that question. I think upon the whole that most people would '"be glad you should have the money, rather than other people. It might be '"misunderstood here and there, at first; but I think the thing would very '"soon express itself, and that your own power of making it express itself '"would be very great." As she wished me to ask B, who was in another 'room, I did so. She was for a moment tremendously disconcerted, "*under* '"*the impression that it was to lead to the stage*" (!!). Then, without know- 'ing anything of A's opinion, closely followed it. That absurd association 'had never entered my head or yours; but it might enter some other heads 'for all that. Take these two opinions for whatever they are worth. A '(being very much interested and very anxious to help to a right conclusion) 'proposed to ask a few people of various degrees who know what the Readings 'are, what *they* think—not compromising me, but suggesting the project afar- 'off, as an idea in somebody else's mind. I thanked her, and said "Yes," 'of course.'

Opinions asked and given.

LONDON: 1857-8.

mentary misgiving in the direction of 'the stage,' as pointed strongly to the danger, which, by those who took the opposite view, was most of all thought incident to the particular time of the proposal. It might be a wild exaggeration to fear that he was in danger of being led to adopt the stage as a calling, but he was certainly about to place himself within reach of not a few of its drawbacks and disadvantages. To the full extent he perhaps did not himself know, how much his eager present wish to become a public reader was but the outcome of the restless domestic discontents of the last four years; and that to indulge it, and the unsettled habits inseparable from it, was to abandon every hope of resettling his disordered home. There is nothing, in its application to so divine a genius as Shakespeare, more affecting than his expressed dislike to a profession, which, in the jealous self-watchfulness of his noble nature, he feared might hurt his mind.* The long subsequent line of actors admirable in private as in public life, and all the gentle and generous associations of the histrionic art, have not weakened the testimony of its greatest name against its less favourable influences; against the

Disadvantages of public reading.

The profession of the stage.

Shakespeare on the actor's calling.

* Oh ! for my sake do you with Fortune chide
The guilty goddess of my harmful deeds,
That did not better for my life provide
Than public means which public manners breeds.
Thence comes it that my name receives a brand;
And almost thence my nature is subdu'd
To what it works in, like the dyer's hand. . .
Pity me, then, and wish I were renew'd. . .
Sonnet cxi.

And in the preceding Sonnet cx.

Alas, 'tis true I have gone here and there,
And made myself a motley to the view,
Gor'd mine own thoughts, sold cheap what is most dear. . .

LONDON: 1857-8.

laxity of habits it may encourage; and its public manners, bred of public means, not always compatible with home felicities and duties. But, freely open as Dickens was to counsel in regard of his books, he was, for reasons formerly stated,* less accessible to it on points of personal conduct; and when he had neither self-distrust nor self-denial to hold him back, he would push persistently forward to whatever object he had in view.

Hospital for sick children. 1858.

An occurrence of the time hastened the decision in this case. An enterprise had been set on foot for establishment of a hospital for sick children; † a large old-fashioned mansion in Great Ormond-street, with spacious garden, had been fitted up with more than thirty beds; during the four or five years of its existence, outdoor and indoor relief had been afforded by it to nearly fifty thousand children, of whom thirty thousand were under five years of age; but, want of funds having threatened to arrest the merciful work, it was resolved to try a public dinner by way of charitable appeal, and for president the happy choice was

* Vol. I. p. 52-3. I repeat from that passage one or two sentences, though it is hardly fair to give them without the modifications that accompany them. 'A too great confidence in himself, a sense that everything was possible to the 'will that would make it so, laid occasionally upon him self-imposed burdens 'greater than might be borne by any one with safety. In that direction there 'was in him, at such times, something even hard and aggressive; in his 'determinations a something that had almost the tone of fierceness; something 'in his nature that made his resolves insuperable, however hasty the opinions 'on which they had been formed.'

Deaths of little children.

† The Board of Health returns, showing that out of every annual thousand of deaths in London, the immense proportion of four hundred were those of children under four years old, had established the necessity for such a scheme. Of course the stress of this mortality fell on the children of the poor, 'dragged 'up rather than brought up,' as Charles Lamb expressed it, and perishing unhelped by the way.

LONDON: 1858.

Help asked from Dickens.

made of one who had enchanted everybody with the joys and sorrows of little children. Dickens threw himself into the service heart and soul. There was a simple pathos in his address from the chair quite startling in its effect at such a meeting; and he probably never moved any audience so much as by the strong personal feeling with which he referred to the sacrifices made for the Hospital by the very poor themselves: from whom a subscription of fifty pounds, contributed in single pennies, had come to the treasurer during almost every year it had been open. The whole speech, indeed, is the best of the kind spoken by him; and two little pictures from it, one of the misery he had witnessed, the other of the remedy he had found, should not be absent from the picture of his own life.

Charities of the poor.

Speech for Child's Hospital.

'Some years ago, being in Scotland, I went with one of 'the most humane members of the most humane of profes- 'sions, on a morning tour among some of the worst lodged 'inhabitants of the old town of Edinburgh. In the closes 'and wynds of that picturesque place (I am sorry to remind 'you what fast friends picturesqueness and typhus often 'are), we saw more poverty and sickness in an hour than 'many people would believe in, in a life. Our way lay 'from one to another of the most wretched dwellings, 'reeking with horrible odours; shut out from the sky and 'from the air, mere pits and dens. In a room in one of 'these places, where there was an empty porridge-pot on 'the cold hearth, a ragged woman and some ragged children 'crouching on the bare ground near it,—and, I remember 'as I speak, where the very light, refracted from a high 'damp-stained wall outside, came in trembling, as if the

A sad scene.

LONDON: 1858.

'fever which had shaken everything else had shaken even 'it,—there lay, in an old egg-box which the mother had 'begged from a shop, a little, feeble, wan, sick child. 'With his little wasted face, and his little hot worn hands 'folded over his breast, and his little bright attentive eyes, 'I can see him now, as I have seen him for several years, 'looking steadily at us. There he lay in his small frail 'box, which was not at all a bad emblem of the small body 'from which he was slowly parting—there he lay, quite 'quiet, quite patient, saying never a word. He seldom 'cried, the mother said; he seldom complained; "he lay '"there, seemin' to woonder what it was a' aboot." God 'knows, I thought, as I stood looking at him, he had his 'reasons for wondering . . . Many a poor child, sick and 'neglected, I have seen since that time in London; many 'have I also seen most affectionately tended, in unwhole-'some houses and hard circumstances where recovery was 'impossible: but at all such times I have seen my little 'drooping friend in his egg-box, and he has always ad-'dressed his dumb wonder to me what it meant, and why, 'in the name of a gracious God, such things should be! . . 'But, ladies and gentlemen,' Dickens added, 'such things 'need NOT be, and will not be, if this company, which is a 'drop of the life-blood of the great compassionate public 'heart, will only accept the means of rescue and prevention 'which it is mine to offer. Within a quarter of a mile of 'this place where I speak, stands a once courtly old house, 'where blooming children were born, and grew up to be men 'and women, and married, and brought their own blooming 'children back to patter up the old oak staircase which

A small patient.

Unsolved mysteries.

Hospital described.

LONDON: 1858.

'stood but the other day, and to wonder at the old oak 'carvings on the chimney-pieces. In the airy wards into 'which the old state drawing-rooms and family bedcham-'bers of that house are now converted, are lodged such small 'patients that the attendant nurses look like reclaimed 'giantesses, and the kind medical practitioner like an 'amiable Christian ogre. Grouped about the little low 'tables in the centre of the rooms, are such tiny convales-'cents that they seem to be playing at having been ill. 'On the doll's beds are such diminutive creatures that each 'poor sufferer is supplied with its tray of toys: and, look-'ing round, you may see how the little tired flushed cheek 'has toppled over half the brute creation on its way into the ark; or how one little dimpled arm has mowed down '(as I saw myself) the whole tin soldiery of Europe. On 'the walls of these rooms are graceful, pleasant, bright, 'childish pictures. At the beds' heads, hang representa-'tions of the figure which is the universal embodiment of all 'mercy and compassion, the figure of Him who was once a 'child Himself, and a poor one. But alas! reckoning up 'the number of beds that are there, the visitor to this Child's 'Hospital will find himself perforce obliged to stop at very 'little over thirty; and will learn, with sorrow and surprise, 'that even that small number, so forlornly, so miserably 'diminutive compared with this vast London, cannot pos-'sibly be maintained unless the Hospital be made better 'known. I limit myself to saying better known, because 'I will not believe that in a Christian community of fathers 'and mothers, and brothers and sisters, it can fail, being 'better known, to be well and richly endowed.' It was a

See Ch. ix. of *Our Mutual Friend.*

Appeal for sick children.

Success of appeal.

brave and true prediction. The Child's Hospital has never since known want. That night alone added greatly more than three thousand pounds to its funds, and Dickens put the crown to his good work by reading on its behalf, shortly afterwards, his *Christmas Carol;* when the sum realized, and the urgent demand that followed for a repetition of the pleasure given by the reading, bore down farther opposition to the project of his engaging publicly in such readings for himself.

Reading for the Hospital.

The Child's Hospital night was the 9th of February, its Reading was appointed for the 15th of April, and, nearly a month before, renewed efforts at remonstrance had been made. 'Your view of the reading matter,' Dickens replied, 'I still think is unconsciously taken from your own par-'ticular point. You don't seem to me to get out of your-'self in considering it. A word more upon it. You are not 'to think I have made up my mind. If I had, why should 'I not say so? I find very great difficulty in doing so be-'cause of what you urge, because I know the question to 'be a balance of doubts, and because I most honestly feel 'in my innermost heart, in this matter (as in all others for 'years and years), the honour of the calling by which I 'have always stood most conscientiously. But do you 'quite consider that the public exhibition of oneself takes 'place equally, whosoever may get the money? And have 'you any idea that at this moment—this very time—half 'the public at least supposes me to be paid? My dear F, 'out of the twenty or five-and-twenty letters a week that 'I get about Readings, twenty will ask at what price, or on 'what terms, it can be done. The only exceptions, in truth,

Reasons for and against paid readings.

LONDON: 1858.

'are when the correspondent is a clergyman, or a banker, 'or the member for the place in question. Why, at this 'very time half Scotland believes that I am paid for going 'to Edinburgh!—Here is Greenock writes to me, and asks 'could it be done for a hundred pounds? There is Aber- 'deen writes, and states the capacity of its hall, and says, 'though far less profitable than the very large hall in 'Edinburgh, is it not enough to come on for? W. answers 'such letters continually. (—At this place, enter Beale. 'He called here yesterday morning, and then wrote to 'ask if I would see him to-day. I replied "Yes," so here

A proposal from Mr. Beale.

'he came in. With long preface called to know whether 'it was possible to arrange anything in the way of Readings 'for this autumn—say, six months. Large capital at com- 'mand. Could produce partners, in such an enterprise, also 'with large capital. Represented such. Returns would be 'enormous. Would I name a sum? a minimum sum that 'I required to have, in any case? Would I look at it as a 'Fortune, and in no other point of view? I shook my 'head, and said, my tongue was tied on the subject for the 'present; I might be more communicative at another 'time. Exit Beale in confusion and disappointment.)—You 'will be happy to hear that at one on Friday, the Lord 'Provost, Dean of Guild, Magistrates, and Council of the 'ancient city of Edinburgh will wait (in procession) on their

i. 232.

'brother freeman, at the Music Hall, to give him hospit- 'able welcome. Their brother freeman has been cursing 'their stars and his own, ever since the receipt of solemn 'notification to this effect.' But very grateful, when it came, was the enthusiasm of the greeting, and welcome the gift

LONDON: 1858.

Edinburgh reading and gift.

of the silver wassail-bowl which followed the reading of the *Carol*. 'I had no opportunity of asking any one's advice 'in Edinburgh,' he wrote on his return. 'The crowd was 'too enormous, and the excitement in it much too great. 'But my determination is all but taken. I must do *some-'thing*, or I shall wear my heart away. I can see no better 'thing to do that is half so hopeful in itself, or half so well 'suited to my restless state.'

Nearer and nearer.

What is pointed at in those last words had been taken as a ground of objection, and thus he turned it into an argument the other way. During all these months many sorrowful misunderstandings had continued in his home, and the relief sought from the misery had but the effect of making desperate any hope of a better understanding. 'It becomes necessary,' he wrote at the end of March, 'with a view to the arrangements that would have to be 'begun next month if I decided on the Readings, to con-'sider and settle the question of the Plunge. Quite dis-'miss from your mind any reference whatever to present 'circumstances at home. Nothing can put *them* right, 'until we are all dead and buried and risen. It is not, with 'me, a matter of will, or trial, or sufferance, or good humour, 'or making the best of it, or making the worst of it, any 'longer. It is all despairingly over. Have no lingering 'hope of, or for, me in this association. A dismal failure 'has to be borne, and there an end. Will you then 'try to think of this reading project (as I do) apart from 'all personal likings and dislikings, and solely with a view 'to its effect on that peculiar relation (personally affec-'tionate, and like no other man's) which subsists between

Question of the Plunge.

LONDON: 1858.

'me and the public? I want your most careful consideration. If you would like, when you have gone over it in 'your mind, to discuss the matter with me and Arthur 'Smith (who would manage the whole of the Business, 'which I should never touch); we will make an appointment. But I ought to add that Arthur Smith plainly 'says, "Of the immense return in money, I have no doubt. '"Of the Dash into the new position, however, I am not '"so good a judge." I enclose you a rough note * of my 'project, as it stands in my mind.'

Doubt and no doubt.

Mr. Arthur Smith.

Mr. Arthur Smith, a man possessed of many qualities

First rough note as to readings.

* Here is the rough note: in which the reader will be interested to observe the limits originally placed to the proposal. The first Readings were to comprise only the *Carol*, and for others a new story was to be written. He had not yet the full confidence in his power or versatility as an actor which subsequent experience gave him. 'I propose to announce in a short and plain advertise-'ment (what is quite true) that I cannot so much as answer the numerous 'applications that are made to me to read, and that compliance with ever so 'few of them is, in any reason, impossible. That I have therefore resolved 'upon a course of readings of the *Christmas Carol* both in town and country, 'and that those in London will take place at St. Martin's Hall on certain even-'ings. Those evenings will be either four or six Thursdays, in May and the 'beginning of June . . . I propose an Autumn Tour, for the country, extend-'ing through August, September, and October. It would comprise the Eastern 'Counties, the West, Lancashire, Yorkshire, and Scotland. I should read from '35 to 40 times in this tour, at the least. At each place where there was a 'great success, I would myself announce that I should come back, on the turn 'of Christmas, to read a new Christmas story written for that purpose. This 'story I should first read a certain number of times in London. I have the 'strongest belief that by April in next year, a very large sum of money 'indeed would be gained by these means. Ireland would be still untouched, 'and I conceive America alone (if I could resolve to go there) to be worth Ten 'Thousand Pounds. In all these proceedings, the Business would be wholly 'detached from me, and I should never appear in it. I would have an office, 'belonging to the Readings and to nothing else, opened in London; I would 'have the advertisements emanating from it, and also signed by some one be-'longing to it; and they should always mention me as a third person—just as 'the Child's Hospital, for instance, in addressing the public, mentions me.'

that justified the confidence Dickens placed in him, might not have been a good judge of the 'Dash' into the new position, but no man knew better every disadvantage incident to it, or was less likely to be disconcerted by any. His exact fitness to manage the scheme successfully, made him an unsafe counsellor respecting it. Within a week from this time the reading for the Charity was to be given. 'They have let,' Dickens wrote on the 9th of April, 'five 'hundred stalls for the Hospital night; and as people come 'every day for more, and it is out of the question to make 'more, they cannot be restrained at St. Martin's Hall from 'taking down names for other Readings.' This closed the attempt at further objection. Exactly a fortnight after the reading for the children's hospital, on Thursday the 29th April, came the first public reading for his own benefit; and before the next month was over, this launch into a new life had been followed by a change in his old home. Thenceforward he and his wife lived apart. The eldest son went with his mother, Dickens at once giving effect to her expressed wish in this respect; and the other children remained with himself, their intercourse with Mrs. Dickens being left entirely to themselves. It was thus far an arrangement of a strictly private nature, and no decent person could have had excuse for regarding it in any other light, if public attention had not been unexpectedly invited to it by a printed statement in *Household Words*. Dickens was stung into this by some miserable gossip at which in ordinary circumstances no man would more determinedly have been silent; but he had now publicly to show himself, at stated times, as a public en-

Child's Hospital reading.

Change in home.

Unwise printed statement.

LONDON: 1858.

tertainer, and this, with his name even so aspersed, he found to be impossible. All he would concede to my strenuous resistance against such a publication, was an offer to suppress it, if, upon reference to the opinion of a certain distinguished man (still living), that opinion should prove to be in agreement with mine. Unhappily it fell in with his own, and the publication went on. It was followed by another statement, a letter subscribed with his name, which got into print without his sanction; nothing publicly being known of it (I was not among those who had read it privately) until it appeared in the *New York Tribune.* It had been addressed and given to Mr. Arthur Smith as an authority for correction of false rumours and scandals, and Mr. Smith had given a copy of it, with like intention, to the *Tribune* correspondent in London. Its writer referred to it always afterwards as his 'violated letter.'

A 'violated 'letter.'

The course taken by the author of this book at the time of these occurrences, will not be departed from here. Such illustration of grave defects in Dickens's character as the passage in his life affords, I have not shrunk from placing side by side with such excuses in regard to it as he had unquestionable right to claim should be put forward also. How far what remained of his story took tone or colour from it, and especially from the altered career on which at the same time he entered, will thus be sufficiently explained; and with anything else the public have nothing to do.

What alone concerned the public.

# CHAPTER VIII.

## GADSHILL PLACE.

### 1856—1870.

'I WAS better pleased with Gadshill Place last Saturday,' he wrote to me from Paris on the 13th of February 1856, 'on going down there, even than I had prepared 'myself to be. The country, against every disadvantage 'of season, is beautiful; and the house is so old fashioned, 'cheerful, and comfortable, that it is really pleasant to look 'at. The good old Rector now there, has lived in it six and 'twenty years, so I have not the heart to turn him out. 'He is to remain till Lady-Day next year, when I shall go 'in, please God; make my alterations; furnish the house; 'and keep it for myself that summer.' Returning to England through the Kentish country with Mr. Wilkie Collins in July, other advantages occurred to him. 'A railroad 'opened from Rochester to Maidstone, which connects 'Gadshill at once with the whole sea coast, is certainly an 'addition to the place, and an enhancement of its value. 'Bye and bye we shall have the London, Chatham and 'Dover, too; and that will bring it within an hour of Canterbury and an hour and a half of Dover. I am glad to 'hear of your having been in the neighbourhood. There

GADSHILL PLACE: 1856-70.

First description of it.

Expected advantages.

Gadshill Place: 1856-70.

'is no healthier (marshes avoided), and none in my eyes 'more beautiful. One of these days I shall show you some 'places up the Medway with which you will be charmed.'

The Porch at Gadshill

The association with his youthful fancy that first made the place attractive to him has been told; and it was with wonder he had heard one day, from his friend and fellow worker at *Household Words*, Mr. W. H. Wills, that not only was the house for sale to which he had so often looked wistfully, but that the lady chiefly interested as its owner had been long known and much esteemed by himself. Such curious chances led Dickens to his saying about the smallness of

Odd chances. i. 4–5.

the world; but the close relation often found thus existing between things and persons far apart, suggests not so much the smallness of the world as the possible importance of the least things done in it, and is better explained by the grander teaching of Carlyle, that causes and effects, connecting every man and thing with every other, extend through all space and time.

i. 65.

It was at the close of 1855 the negociation for its purchase began. 'They wouldn't,' he wrote (25th of November), 'take £1700 for the Gadshill property, but "finally" 'wanted £1800. I have finally offered £1750. It will 'require an expenditure of about £300 more before yielding £100 a year.' The usual discovery of course awaited him that this first estimate would have to be increased threefold. 'The changes absolutely necessary' (9th of February 1856) 'will take a thousand pounds; which sum I 'am always resolving to squeeze out of this, grind out of 'that, and wring out of the other; this, that, and the other 'generally all three declining to come up to the scratch 'for the purpose.' 'This day,'* he wrote on the 14th of March, 'I have paid the purchase money for Gadshill Place. 'After drawing the cheque (£1790) I turned round to give 'it to Wills, and said, "Now isn't it an extraordinary thing '"—look at the Day—Friday! I have been nearly draw-'"ing it half a dozen times when the lawyers have not '"been ready, and here it comes round upon a Friday as '"a matter of course."' He had no thought at this time

Negociations for purchase.

An old superstition.

* On New Year's Day he had written from Paris. 'When in London 'Coutts's advised me not to sell out the money for Gadshill Place (the title of 'my estate sir, my place down in Kent) until the conveyance was settled and 'ready.'

GADSHILL PLACE: 1856-70.

Meant for investment.

of reserving the place wholly for himself, or of making it his own residence except at intervals of summer. He looked upon it as an investment only. 'You will hardly know 'Gadshill again,' he wrote in January 1858, 'I am im-'proving it so much—yet I have no interest in the place.' But continued ownership brought increased liking; he took more and more interest in his own improvements,

Interest in it increased.

which were just the kind of occasional occupation and resource his life most wanted in its next seven or eight years; and any farther idea of letting it he soon abandoned altogether. It only once passed out of his possession thus, for four months in 1859; in the following year, on the sale of Tavistock House, he transferred to it his books and pictures and choicer furniture; and thenceforward, varied only by houses taken from time to time for the London season, he

Becomes his home in 1859.

made it his permanent family abode. Now and then, even during those years, he would talk of selling it; and on his last return from America, when he had sent the last of his sons out into the world, he really might have sold it if he could then have found a house in London suitable to him, and such as he could purchase. But in this he failed; secretly to his own satisfaction, as I believe; and thereupon, in that last autumn of his life, he projected and car-

Improvements and additions.

ried out his most costly addition to Gadshill. Already of course more money had been spent upon it than his first intention in buying it would have justified. He had so enlarged the accommodation, improved the grounds and offices, and added to the land, that, taking also into account this final outlay, the reserved price placed upon the whole after his death more than quadrupled what he had given in 1856 for the house, shrubbery, and twenty years' lease of a meadow field. It was then purchased, and is now inhabited, by his eldest son. GADSHILL PLACE: 1856-70.

Its position has been described, and one of the last-century-histories of Rochester quaintly mentions the principal interest of the locality. 'Near the twenty-seventh 'stone from London is Gadshill, supposed to have been the 'scene of the robbery mentioned by Shakespeare in his 'play of Henry IV; there being reason to think also that 'it was Sir John Falstaff, of truly comic memory, who 'under the name of Oldcastle inhabited Cooling Castle of 'which the ruins are in the neighbourhood. A small dis-'tance to the left appears on an eminence the Hermitage, 'the seat of the late Sir Francis Head, Bart;* and close to 'the road, on a small ascent, is a neat building lately 'erected by Mr. Day. In descending Strood-hill is a fine 'prospect of Strood, Rochester, and Chatham, which three 'towns form a continued street extending above two miles 'in length.' It had been supposed † that 'the neat build-'ing lately erected by Mr. Day' was that which the great novelist made famous; but Gadshill Place had no existence until eight years after the date of the history. The good rector who so long lived in it told me, in 1859, that it had been built eighty years before by a then well-known character in those parts, one Stevens, father-in-law of Henslow

i. 4.

Gadshill a century ago.

Antecedents of Dickens's house.

* Two houses now stand on what was Sir Francis Head's estate, the Great and Little Hermitage, occupied respectively by Mr. Malleson and Mr. Hulkes, who became intimate with Dickens. Perry of the *Morning Chronicle*, whose town house was in that court out of Tavistock-square of which Tavistock House formed part, had occupied the Great Hermitage previously.

† By the obliging correspondent who sent me this *History of Rochester*, 8vo. (Rochester, 1772), p. 302.

GADSHILL PLACE: 1856-70.

the Cambridge professor of botany. Stevens, who could only with much difficulty manage to write his name, had begun life as ostler at an inn; had become husband to the landlord's widow; then a brewer; and finally, as he subscribed himself on one occasion, 'mare' of Rochester.

Its owners and tenants.

Afterwards the house was inhabited by Mr. Lynn (from some of the members of whose family Dickens made his purchase); and, before the Rev. Mr. Hindle became its tenant, it was inhabited by a Macaroni parson named Townshend, whose horses the Prince Regent bought, throwing into the bargain a box of much desired cigars. Altogether the place had notable associations even apart from those which have connected it with the masterpieces of English humour. 'THIS HOUSE, GADSHILL PLACE, stands on 'the summit of Shakespeare's Gadshill, ever memorable for 'its association with Sir John Falstaff in his noble fancy.

Greeting to visitors.

'*But, my lads, my lads, to-morrow morning, by four 'o'clock, early at Gadshill! there are pilgrims going to 'Canterbury with rich offerings, and traders riding to 'London with fat purses: I have vizards for you all; 'you have horses for yourselves.*' Illuminated by Mr. Owen Jones, and placed in a frame on the first-floor landing, these words were the greeting of the new tenant to his visitors. It was his first act of ownership.

All his improvements, it should perhaps be remarked, were not exclusively matters of choice; and to illustrate by his letters what befell at the beginning of his changes, will show what attended them to the close. His earliest difficulty was very grave. There was only one spring of water for gentlefolk and villagers, and from some of the houses or cottages it was two miles away. 'We are still' (6th of July) 'boring for water here, at the rate of two 'pounds per day for wages. The men seem to like it very 'much, and to be perfectly comfortable.' Another of his earliest experiences (5th of September) was thus expressed: 'Hop-picking is going on, and people sleep in the garden, 'and breathe in at the keyhole of the house door. I have 'been amazed, before this year, by the number of miserable 'lean wretches, hardly able to crawl, who go hop-picking. 'I find it is a superstition that the dust of the newly 'picked hop, falling freshly into the throat, is a cure for 'consumption. So the poor creatures drag themselves along 'the roads, and sleep under wet hedges, and get cured 'soon and finally.' Towards the close of the same month (24th of September) he wrote: 'Here are six men per-'petually going up and down the well (I know that some-'body will be killed), in the course of fitting a pump; which 'is quite a railway terminus—it is so iron, and so big. 'The process is much more like putting Oxford-street end-'wise, and laying gas along it, than anything else. By the 'time it is finished, the cost of this water will be something 'absolutely frightful. But of course it proportionately 'increases the value of the property, and that's my only 'comfort. . . The horse has gone lame from a sprain, the 'big dog has run a tenpenny nail into one of his hind feet, 'the bolts have all flown out of the basket-carriage, and 'the gardener says all the fruit trees want replacing with 'new ones.' Another note came in three days. 'I have 'discovered that the seven miles between Maidstone and 'Rochester is one of the most beautiful walks in England.



Deficient water-supply.

Hop-picking.

The well.

Country mishaps: consolation.

GADSHILL PLACE: 1856-70.

'Five men have been looking attentively at the pump for 'a week, and (I should hope) may begin to fit it in the 'course of October.' . .

Exterior and Porch.

With even such varying fortune he effected other changes.* The exterior remained to the last much as it was when he used as a boy to see it first; a plain, old-fashioned, two-story, brick-built country house, with a bell-turret on the roof, and over the front door a quaint neat wooden porch with pillars and seats. But, among his additions and alterations, was a new drawing-room built out from the smaller existing one, both being thrown together ultimately; two good bedrooms built on a third floor at the back; and such re-arrangement of the ground floor as, besides its handsome drawing-room, and its dining-room which he hung with pictures, transformed its bedroom into a study which he lined with books and sometimes wrote in, and changed its breakfast-parlour into a retreat fitted up for smokers into which he put a small billiard-table. These several rooms opened from a hall having in it a series of Hogarth prints, until, after the artist's death, Stanfield's noble scenes were placed there, when the Hogarths were moved to his bedroom; and in this hall, during his last absence in America, a parquet floor was laid down. Nor did he omit such changes as might increase the comfort of his servants. He built entirely new offices and stables, and replaced a very old

Gradual additions.

Later changes.

* 'As to the carpenters,' he wrote to his daughter in September 1860, 'they are absolutely maddening. They are always at work yet never seem to 'do anything. L. was down on Friday, and said (with his eye fixed on Maid-'stone and rubbing his hands to conciliate his moody employer) that "he didn't '"think there would be very much left to do after Saturday the 29th." I 'didn't throw him out of window.

coach-house by a capital servants' hall, transforming the loft above into a commodious school-room or study for his boys. He made at the same time an excellent croquet-ground out of a waste piece of orchard.

GADSHILL PLACE: 1856-70.

Belonging to the house, but unfortunately placed on the other side of the high road, was a shrubbery, well wooded though in desolate condition, in which stood two magnificent cedars; and having obtained, in 1859, the consent of the local authorities for the necessary underground work, Dickens constructed a passage beneath the road* from his front lawn; and in the shrubbery thus rendered accessible, and which he then laid out very prettily, he placed afterwards a Swiss châlet † presented to him by Mr. Fechter, which arrived from Paris in ninety-four pieces fitting like the joints of a puzzle, but which proved to be somewhat costly in setting on its legs by means of a foundation of brickwork. Once up, however, it was a great resource in the summer months, and much of Dickens's work was done there. 'I have put five mirrors in the châlet where I 'write,' ‡ he told an American friend, 'and they reflect and

Connection of shrubbery and lawn.

Gift from Mr. Fechter.

* A passage in his paper on Tramps embodies very amusingly experience recorded in his letters of this brick-work tunnel and the sinking of the well; but I can only borrow one sentence. 'The current of my uncommercial pursuits 'caused me only last summer to want a little body of workmen for a certain 'spell of work in a pleasant part of the country; and I was at one time honoured 'with the attendance of as many as seven-and-twenty, who were looking at 'six. Bits of wonderful observation are in that paper.

Ways of Tramps.

† This was at the beginning of 1865. 'The chalet,' he wrote to me on the 7th of January, 'is going on excellently, though the ornamental part is more 'slowly put together than the substantial. It will really be a very pretty 'thing; and in the summer (supposing it not to be blown away in the spring), 'the upper room will make a charming study. It is much higher than we 'supposed.'

‡ As surely, however, as he did any work there, so surely his indispensable

GADSHILL PLACE: 1856-70.

In the châlet.

'refract, in all kinds of ways, the leaves that are quivering 'at the windows, and the great fields of waving corn, and 'the sail-dotted river. My room is up among the branches 'of the trees; and the birds and the butterflies fly in and 'out, and the green branches shoot in at the open windows, 'and the lights and shadows of the clouds come and go 'with the rest of the company. The scent of the flowers, 'and indeed of everything that is growing for miles and 'miles, is most delicious.' He used to make great boast,

Dickens's writing-table.

little accompaniments of work (ii. 214) were carried along with him; and of these I will quote what was written shortly after his death by his son-in-law, Mr. Charles Collins, to illustrate a very touching sketch by Mr. Fildes of his writing-desk and vacant chair. 'Ranged in front of, and round 'about him, were always a variety of objects for his eye to rest on in the 'intervals of actual writing, and any one of which he would have instantly 'missed had it been removed. There was a French bronze group representing 'a duel with swords, fought by a couple of very fat toads, one of them '(characterised by that particular buoyancy which belongs to corpulence) in the 'act of making a prodigious lunge forward, which the other receives in the 'very middle of his digestive apparatus, and under the influence of which it 'seems likely that he will satisfy the wounded honour of his opponent by 'promptly expiring. There was another bronze figure which always stood near 'the toads, also of French manufacture, and also full of comic suggestion. It 'was a statuette of a dog-fancier, such a one as you used to see on the bridges 'or quays of Paris, with a profusion of little dogs stuck under his arms and 'into his pockets, and everywhere where little dogs could possibly be insinuated, 'all for sale, and all, as even a casual glance at the vendor's exterior would 'convince the most unsuspicious person, with some screw loose in their physical 'constitutions or moral natures, to be discovered immediately after purchase. 'There was the long gilt leaf with the rabbit sitting erect upon its haunches, 'the huge paper-knife often held in his hand during his public readings, and 'the little fresh green cup ornamented with the leaves and blossoms of the 'cowslip, in which a few fresh flowers were always placed every morning—for 'Dickens invariably worked with flowers on his writing-table. There was also 'the register of the day of the week and of the month, which stood always before 'him; and when the room in the châlet in which he wrote his last paragraph 'was opened, some time after his death, the first thing to be noticed by those 'who entered was this register, set at "Wednesday, June 8"—the day of his 'seizure.' It remains to this day as it was found.

GADSHILL PLACE: 1856-70.

too, not only of his crowds of singing birds all day, but of his nightingales at night.

One or two more extracts from letters having reference to these changes may show something of the interest to him with which Gadshill thus grew under his hands. A sun-dial on his back-lawn had a bit of historic interest about it. 'One of the 'balustrades 'of the destroyed old 'Rochester 'Bridge,' he wrote to his daughter in June 1859, 'has been (very nicely) presented to me by the contractors for the works, and has 'been duly stone-masoned and set up on the lawn behind 'the house. I have ordered a sun-dial for the top of it, 'and it will be a very good object indeed.' 'When 'you come down here next month,' he wrote to me, 'we 'have an idea that we shall show you rather a neat 'house. What terrific adventures have been in action;

The Chalêt: presented by Mr. Fechter.

GADSHILL PLACE: 1856-70.

'how many overladen vans were knocked up at Gravesend, 'and had to be dragged out of Chalk-turnpike in the 'dead of the night by the whole equine power of this 'establishment; shall be revealed at another time.' That was in the autumn of 1860, when, on the sale of his London house, its contents were transferred to his country home.

Making Gadshill his home.

'I shall have an alteration or two to show you at 'Gadshill that greatly improve the little property; and 'when I get the workmen out this time, I think I'll leave 'off.' October 1861 had now come, when the new bedrooms were built; but in the same month of 1863 he announced his transformation of the old coach-house. 'I shall have a 'small new improvement to show you at Gads, which I think 'you will accept as the crowning ingenuity of the inimitable.' But of course it was not over yet. 'My small work and 'planting,' he wrote in the spring of 1866, 'really, truly, 'and positively the last, are nearly at an end in these 'regions, and the result will await summer inspection.' No, nor even yet.

A much coveted acquisition.

He afterwards obtained, by exchange of some land with the trustees of Watts's Charity, the much coveted meadow at the back of the house of which heretofore he had the lease only; and he was then able to plant a number of young limes and chesnuts and other quick-growing trees.

Planting trees.

He had already planted a row of limes in front. He had no idea, he would say, of planting only for the benefit of posterity, but would put into the ground what he might himself enjoy the sight and shade of. He put them in two or three clumps in the meadow, and in a belt all round.

Still there were 'more last words,' for the limit was

only to be set by his last year of life. On abandoning his notion, after the American Readings, of exchanging Gadshill for London, a new staircase was put up from the hall; a parquet floor laid on the first landing; and a conservatory built, opening into both drawing-room and dining-room, 'glass and iron,' as he described it, 'brilliant but expensive, 'with foundations as of an ancient Roman work of horrible 'solidity.' This last addition had long been an object of desire with him; though he would hardly even now have given himself the indulgence but for the golden shower from America. He saw it first in a completed state on the Sunday before his death, when his younger daughter was on a visit to him. 'Well, Katey,' he said to her, 'now you 'see POSITIVELY the last improvement at Gadshill;' and every one laughed at the joke against himself. The success of the new conservatory was unquestionable. It was the remark of all around him that he was certainly, from this last of his improvements, drawing more enjoyment than from any of its predecessors, when the scene for ever closed.



**Last great improvement.**

**New conservatory.**

Of the course of his daily life in the country there is not much to be said. Perhaps there was never a man who changed places so much and habits so little. He was always methodical and regular; and passed his life from day to day, divided for the most part between working and walking, the same wherever he was. The only exception was when special or infrequent visitors were with him. When such friends as Longfellow and his daughters, or Charles Eliot Norton and his wife, came, or when Mr. Fields brought his wife and Professor Lowell's daughter, or when

**Course of daily life.**

GADSHILL PLACE: 1856-70.

he received other Americans to whom he owed special courtesy, he would compress into infinitely few days an enormous amount of sight seeing and country enjoyment, castles, cathedrals, and fortified lines, lunches and picnics among cherry orchards and hop-gardens, excursions to Canterbury or Maidstone and their beautiful neighbourhoods,

House and conservatory: from the meadow.

Druid-stone and Blue Bell Hill. 'All the neighbouring 'country that could be shown in so short a time,' he wrote of the Longfellow visit, 'they saw. I turned out a couple 'of postilions in the old red jackets of the old red royal 'Dover road for our ride, and it was like a holiday ride in 'England fifty years ago.' For Lord Lytton he did the same, for the Emerson Tennents, for Mr. Layard and Mr. Helps, for Lady Molesworth and the Higginses (Jacob Omnium), and such other less frequent visitors.

Visits of friends.

Excepting on such particular occasions however, and not always even then, his mornings were reserved wholly to himself; and he would generally preface his morning work (such was his love of order in everything around him) by seeing that all was in its place in the several rooms, visiting also the dogs, stables, and kitchen garden, and closing, unless the weather was very bad indeed, with a turn or two round the meadow before settling to his desk. His dogs were a great enjoyment to him;* and, with his high road traversed as frequently as any in England by tramps and wayfarers of a singularly undesirable description, they were also a necessity. There were always two, of the mastiff kind, but latterly the number increased. His own favourite was Turk, a noble animal, full of affection and intelligence, whose death by a railway-accident, shortly after the Staplehurst catastrophe, caused him great grief. Turk's sole companion up to that date was Linda, puppy of a great St.

GADSHILL PLACE: 1856-70.

Morning work.

The dogs.

Turk and Linda.

* Dickens's interest in dogs (as in the habits and ways of all animals) was inexhaustible, and he welcomed with delight any new trait. The subjoined, told him by a lady friend, was a great acquisition. 'I must close' (14th of May 1867) 'with an odd story of a Newfoundland dog. An immense black good-'humoured Newfoundland dog. He came from Oxford and had lived all his 'life at a brewery. Instructions were given with him that if he were let out 'every morning alone, he would immediately find out the river; regularly take 'a swim; and gravely come home again. This he did with the greatest punc-'tuality, but after a little while was observed to smell of beer. She was so 'sure that he smelt of beer that she resolved to watch him. Accordingly, he 'was seen to come back from his swim, round the usual corner, and to go up a 'flight of steps into a beer-shop. Being instantly followed, the beer-shop-'keeper is seen to take down a pot (pewter pot), and is heard to say: "Well, '"old chap! Come for your beer as usual, have you?" Upon which he 'draws a pint and puts it down, and the dog drinks it. Being required to ex-'plain how this comes to pass, the man says, "Yes ma'am. I know he's '"your dog ma'am, but I didn't when he first come. He looked in ma'am '"—as a Brickmaker might—and then he come in—as a Brickmaker might—'"and he wagged his tail at the pots, and he giv' a sniff round, and conveyed '"to me as he was used to beer. So I draw'd him a drop, and he drunk it '"up. Next morning he come agen by the clock and I drawed him a pint, '"and ever since he has took his pint reglar."'

A dog with a taste.

GADSHILL PLACE: 1856-70.

Bernard brought over by Mr. Albert Smith, and grown into a superbly beautiful creature. After Turk there was an interval of an Irish dog, Sultan, given by Mr. Percy Fitzgerald; a cross between a St. Bernard and a bloodhound, built and coloured like a lioness and of splendid proportions, but of such indomitably aggressive propensities, that, after breaking his kennel-chain and nearly devouring a luckless little sister of one of the servants, he had to be killed. Dickens always protested that Sultan was a Fenian, for that no dog, not a secretly sworn member of that body, would ever have made such a point, muzzled as he was, of rushing at and bearing down with fury anything in scarlet with the remotest resemblance to a British uniform. Sultan's successor was Don, presented by Mr. Frederic Lehmann, a grand Newfoundland brought over very young, who with Linda became parent to a couple of Newfoundlands, that were still gambolling about their master, huge, though hardly out of puppydom, when they lost him. He had given to one of them the name of Bumble, from having observed, as he described it, 'a peculiarly pompous and 'overbearing manner he had of appearing to mount guard 'over the yard when he was an absolute infant.' Bumble was often in scrapes. Describing to Mr. Fields a drought in the summer of 1868, when their poor supply of ponds and surface wells had become waterless, he wrote: 'I do 'not let the great dogs swim in the canal, because the 'people have to drink of it. But when they get into the 'Medway, it is hard to get them out again. The other 'day Bumble (the son, Newfoundland dog) got into diffi-'culties among some floating timber, and became frightened.

Sultan.

A Fenian.

Linda and Don.

Don and Bumble.

GADSHILL PLACE: 1856–70.

'Don (the father) was standing by me, shaking off the wet 'and looking on carelessly, when all of a sudden he per'ceived something amiss, and went in with a bound and 'brought Bumble out by the ear. The scientific way in 'which he towed him along was charming.' The description of his own reception, on his reappearance after America, by Bumble and his brother, by the big and beautiful Linda, and by his daughter Mary's handsome little Pomeranian, may be added from his letters to the same correspondent. 'The two Newfoundland dogs coming to meet me, with 'the usual carriage and the usual driver, and beholding me 'coming in my usual dress out at the usual door, it struck 'me that their recollection of my having been absent for 'any unusual time was at once cancelled. They behaved '(they are both young dogs) exactly in their usual manner; 'coming behind the basket phaeton as we trotted along, 'and lifting their heads to have their ears pulled, a special 'attention which they receive from no one else. But when 'I drove into the stable-yard, Linda (the St. Bernard) was 'greatly excited; weeping profusely, and throwing herself 'on her back that she might caress my foot with her great 'fore-paws. Mary's little dog too, Mrs. Bouncer, barked 'in the greatest agitation on being called down and asked 'by Mary, "Who is this?" and tore round and round me 'like the dog in the Faust outlines.' The father and mother and their two sons, four formidable-looking companions, were with him generally in his later walks.

Welcome home.

Reception by friends.

Mrs. Bouncer.

Round Cobham, skirting the park and village, and passing the Leather Bottle famous in the page of *Pickwick*, was a favourite walk with Dickens. By Rochester and the

GADSHILL PLACE: 1856-70.

Medway, to the Chatham Lines, was another. He would turn out of Rochester High-street through The Vines (where some old buildings, from one of which called Restoration-house he took Satis-house for *Great Expectations*, had a curious attraction for him), would pass round by Fort Pitt, and coming back by Frindsbury would bring himself by some cross fields again into the high road.

Favourite walks.

Or, taking the other side, he would walk through the marshes to Gravesend, return by Chalk church, and stop always to have greeting with a comical old monk who for some incomprehensible reason sits carved in stone, cross-legged with a jovial pot, over the porch of that sacred edifice. To another drearier churchyard, itself forming part of the marshes beyond the Medway, he often took friends to show them the dozen small tombstones of various sizes adapted to the respective ages of a dozen small children of one family which he made part of his story of *Great Expectations*, though, with the reserves always necessary in copying nature not to overstep her modesty by copying too closely, he makes

Cooling churchyard.

the number that appalled little Pip not more than half the reality. About the whole of this Cooling churchyard, indeed, and the neighbouring castle ruins, there was a weird strangeness that made it one of his attractive walks in the late year or winter, when from Higham he could get to it across country over the stubble fields; and, for a shorter summer walk, he was not less fond of going round the village of Shorne, and sitting on a hot afternoon in its pretty shaded churchyard. But on the whole, though Maidstone had also much that attracted him to its neighbourhood, the Cobham neighbourhood was certainly that which he had greatest pleasure in; and he would have taken oftener than he did the walk through Cobham park and woods, which was the last he enjoyed before life suddenly closed upon him, but that here he did not like his dogs to follow.

Dickens's last walk.

Don now has his home there with Lord Darnley, and Linda lies under one of the cedars at Gadshill.

The Study at Gadshill.

# CHAPTER IX.

## FIRST PAID READINGS.

1858—1859.

London: 1858–9.

Dickens gave his paid public Readings successively, with not long intervals, at four several dates; in 1858–9, in 1861–63, in 1866–67, and in 1868–70; the first series under Mr. Arthur Smith's management, the second under Mr. Headland's, and the third and fourth, in America as well as before and after it, under that of Mr. George Dolby, who, excepting in America, acted for the Messrs. Chappell. The references in the present chapter are to the first series only.

Various managements.

It began with sixteen nights at St. Martin's Hall, the first on the 29th of April, the last on the 22nd of July, 1858; and there was afterwards a provincial tour of 87 readings, beginning at Clifton on the 2nd of August, ending at Brighton on the 13th of November, and taking in Ireland and Scotland as well as the principal English cities: to which were added, in London, three Christmas readings, three in January, with two in the following month; and, in the provinces in the month of October, fourteen, beginning at Ipswich and Norwich, taking in Cambridge and Oxford, and closing with Birmingham and Cheltenham. The series

First series.

had comprised altogether 125 Readings when it ended on the 27th of October, 1859; and without the touches of character and interest afforded by his letters written while thus employed, the picture of the man would not be complete.

PROVINCES: 1858.

One day's work.

Here was one day's work at the opening which will show something of the fatigue they involved even at their outset. 'On Friday we came from Shrewsbury to Chester; 'saw all right for the evening; and then went to Liverpool. 'Came back from Liverpool and read at Chester. Left 'Chester at 11 at night, after the reading, and went to 'London. Got to Tavistock House at 5 A.M. on Saturday, 'left it at a quarter past 10 that morning, and came down 'here' (Gadshill: 15th of August 1858).

Exeter audience.

The 'greatest personal affection and respect' had greeted him everywhere. Nothing could have been 'more strongly 'marked or warmly expressed;' and the readings had 'gone' quite wonderfully. What in this respect had most impressed him, at the outset of his adventures, was Exeter. 'I think they were the finest audience I ever read to; I 'don't think I ever read in some respects so well; and I 'never beheld anything like the personal affection which 'they poured out upon me at the end. I shall always 'look back upon it with pleasure.' He often lost his voice in these early days, having still to acquire the art of husbanding it; and in the trial to recover it would again waste its power. 'I think I sang half the Irish melodies 'to myself as I walked about, to test it.'

Liverpool.

An audience of two thousand three hundred people (the largest he had had) greeted him at Liverpool on his way to Dublin, and, besides the tickets sold, more than two

IRELAND: 1858.

hundred pounds in money was taken at the doors. This taxed his business staff a little. 'They turned away hun-'dreds, sold all the books, rolled on the ground of my room 'knee-deep in checks, and made a perfect pantomime of the 'whole thing.' (20th of August.) He had to repeat the reading thrice.*

Impressions of Dublin.

It was the first time he had seen Ireland, and Dublin greatly surprised him by appearing to be so much larger and more populous than he had supposed. He found it to have altogether an unexpectedly thriving look, being pretty nigh as big, he first thought, as Paris; of which some places in it, such as the quays on the river, reminded him. Half the first day he was there, he took to explore it; walking till tired, and then taking a car. 'Power, dressed for 'the character of Teddy the Tiler, drove me: in a suit of 'patches, and with his hat unbrushed for twenty years. 'Wonderfully pleasant, light, intelligent, and careless.'† The

* This was the *Carol* and *Pickwick*. 'We are reduced sometimes,' he adds, 'to a ludicrous state of distress by the quantity of silver we have to carry 'about. Arthur Smith is always accompanied by an immense black leather-'bag full.' Mr. Smith had an illness a couple of days later, and Dickens whimsically describes his rapid recovery on discovering the state of their balances. 'He is now sitting opposite to me on a bag of £40 of silver. It must be 'dreadfully hard.'

Irish car-driver.

† A letter to his eldest daughter (23rd of Aug.) makes humorous addition. 'The man who drove our jaunting car yesterday hadn't a piece in his coat as 'big as a penny roll, and had had his hat on (apparently without brushing it) 'ever since he was grown-up. But he was remarkably intelligent and agree-'able, with something to say about everything. For instance, when I asked 'him what a certain building was, he didn't say "Courts of Law" and nothing 'else, but "Av yer plase Sir, its the foor Coorts o' looyers, where Misther '"O'Connell stood his trial wunst, as ye'll remimbir sir, afore I till ye ov '"it." When we got into the Phœnix Park, he looked round him as if it 'were his own, and said "THAT's a Park sir, av ye plase!" I complimented 'it, and he said "Gintlemen tills me as they iv bin, sir, over Europe and

number of common people he saw in his drive, 'also riding 'about in cars as hard as they could split,' brought to his recollection a more distant scene, and but for the dresses he could have thought himself on the Toledo at Naples. IRELAND: 1858.

In respect of the number of his audience, and their reception of him, Dublin was one of his marked successes. He came to have some doubt of their capacity of receiving the pathetic, but of their quickness as to the humorous there could be no question, any more than of their heartiness. He got on wonderfully well with the Dublin people.* The Boots at Morrison's expressed the general feeling in a patriotic point of view. 'He was waiting for me at the hotel 'door last night. "Whaat sart of a hoose sur?" he asked 'me. "Capital." "The Lard be praised fur the 'onor o' 'Dooblin!"' Within the hotel, on getting up next morning, he had a dialogue with a smaller resident, landlord's son he supposed, a little boy of the ripe age of six, which he presented, in his letter to his sister-in-law, as a colloquy between

The audience.

Boots at Morrison's.

' "never see a Park aqualling ov it. Yander's the Vice-regal Lodge, sir; in ' "thim two corners lives the two Sicretaries, wishing I was thim sir. There's ' "air here sir, av yer plase! There's scenery here sir! There's mountains ' "thim sir! Yer coonsider it a Park sir? It is that sir!" '

* The Irish girls outdid the American (i. 365) in one particular. He wrote to his sister-in-law: 'Every night, by the bye, since I have been in Ireland, 'the ladies have beguiled John out of the bouquet from my coat; and yesterday 'morning, as I had showered the leaves from my geranium in reading *Little 'Dombey*, they mounted the platform after I was gone, and picked them all 'up as a keepsake.' A few days earlier he had written to the same correspondent: 'The papers are full of remarks upon my white tie, and describe it 'as being of enormous size, which is a wonderful delusion; because, as you 'very well know, it is a small tie. Generally, I am happy to report, the 'Emerald press is in favour of my appearance, and likes my eyes. But one 'gentleman comes out with a letter at Cork, wherein he says that although 'only 46, I look like an old man.'

Irish girls.

IRELAND: 1858.

Old England and Young Ireland inadequately reported for want of the 'imitation' it required for its full effect. 'I am 'sitting on the sofa, writing, and find him sitting beside me.

'*Old England.* Halloa old chap.

'*Young Ireland.* Hal—loo!

'*Old England* (in his delightful way). What a nice old 'fellow you are. I am very fond of little boys.

'*Young Ireland.* Air yes? Ye'r right.

'*Old England.* What do you learn, old fellow?

'*Young Ireland* (very intent on Old England, and 'always childish except in his brogue). I lairn wureds of 'three sillibils—and wureds of two sillibils—and wureds of 'one sillibil.

Young Ireland and Old England.

'*Old England* (cheerfully). Get out, you humbug! You 'learn only words of one syllable.

'*Young Ireland* (laughs heartily). You may say that it 'is mostly wureds of one sillibil.

'*Old England.* Can you write?

'*Young Ireland.* Not yet. Things comes by deegrays.

'*Old England.* Can you cipher?

'*Young Ireland* (very quickly). Whaat's that?

'*Old England.* Can you make figures?

'*Young Ireland.* I can make a nought, which is not 'asy, being roond.

'*Old England.* I say, old boy! Wasn't it you I saw on 'Sunday morning in the Hall, in a soldier's cap? You 'know!—In a soldier's cap?

'*Young Ireland* (cogitating deeply). Was it a very good 'cap?

'*Old England.* Yes.

IRELAND: 1858.

'*Young Ireland.* Did it fit ankommon?

'*Old England.* Yes.

'*Young Ireland.* Dat was me!'

Extra-ordinary scene.

The last night in Dublin was an extraordinary scene. 'You can hardly imagine it. All the way from the hotel 'to the Rotunda (a mile), I had to contend against the 'stream of people who were turned away. When I got 'there, they had broken the glass in the pay-boxes, and 'were offering £5 freely for a stall. Half of my platform 'had to be taken down, and people heaped in among the 'ruins. You never saw such a scene.'* But he would not return after his other Irish engagements. 'I have posi-'tively said No. The work is too hard. It is not like 'doing it in one easy room, and always the same room. 'With a different place every night, and a different audience 'with its own peculiarity every night, it is a tremendous 'strain . . . I seem to be always either in a railway carriage 'or reading, or going to bed; and I get so knocked up 'whenever I have a minute to remember it, that then I 'go to bed as a matter of course.'

Strain of work.

Belfast he liked quite as much as Dublin in another way. 'A fine place with a rough people; everything looking 'prosperous; the railway ride from Dublin quite amazing 'in the order, neatness, and cleanness of all you see; every 'cottage looking as if it had been whitewashed the day 'before; and many with charming gardens, prettily kept

A railway ride.

* 'They had offered frantic prices for stalls. Eleven bank-notes were thrust 'into a paybox at one time for eleven stalls. Our men were flattened against 'walls and squeezed against beams. Ladies stood all night with their chins 'against my platform. Other ladies sat all night upon my steps. We turned 'away people enough to make immense houses for a week.' Letter to his eldest daughter.

IRELAND: 1858.

'with bright flowers.' The success, too, was quite as great. 'Enormous audiences. We turn away half the town.* I 'think them a better audience on the whole than Dublin; 'and the personal affection is something overwhelming. I 'wish you and the dear girls' (he is writing to his sister-in-law) 'could have seen the people look at me in the street; 'or heard them ask me, as I hurried to the hotel after the 'reading last night, to "do me the honor to shake hands '"Misther Dickens and God bless you sir; not ounly for '"the light you've been to me this night, but for the light '"you've been in mee house sir (and God love your face!) '"this many a year!"'† He had never seen men 'go in 'to cry so undisguisedly,' as they did at the Belfast *Dombey* reading; and as to the *Boots* and *Mrs. Gamp* 'it was just 'one roar with me and them. For they made me laugh 'so, that sometimes I *could not* compose my face to go on.'

Reception in Belfast.

HARROGATE.

His greatest trial in this way however was a little later at Harrogate—'the queerest place, with the strangest people 'in it, leading the oddest lives of dancing, newspaper-read-'ing, and tables d'hôte'—where he noticed, at the same reading, embodiments respectively of the tears and laughter to which he has moved his fellow creatures so largely. 'There was one gentleman at the *Little Dombey* yesterday 'morning' (he is still writing to his sister-in-law) 'who 'exhibited—or rather concealed—the profoundest grief.

Paul Dombey.

* 'Shillings get into stalls, and half-crowns get into shillings, and stalls 'get nowhere, and there is immense confusion.' Letter to his daughter.

Brought near his Fame.

† 'I was brought very near to what I sometimes dream may be my Fame,' he says in a letter of later date to myself from York, 'when a lady whose face 'I had never seen stopped me yesterday in the street, and said to me, *Mr. 'Dickens, will you let me touch the hand that has filled my house with many 'friends.*' October 1858.

'After crying a good deal without hiding it, he covered his 'face with both his hands, and laid it down on the back of 'the seat before him, and really shook with emotion. He 'was not in mourning, but I supposed him to have lost 'some child in old time... There was a remarkably good 'fellow too, of thirty or so, who found something so very 'ludicrous in Toots that he *could not* compose himself at 'all, but laughed until he sat wiping his eyes with his 'handkerchief; and whenever he felt Toots coming again, 'he began to laugh and wipe his eyes afresh; and when 'Toots came once more, he gave a kind of cry, as if it were 'too much for him. It was uncommonly droll, and made 'me laugh heartily.'

HARROGATE: 1858.

Mr. Toots.

At Harrogate he read twice on one day (a Saturday), and had to engage a special engine to take him back that night to York, which, having reached at one o'clock in the morning, he had to leave, because of Sunday restrictions on travel, the same morning at half-past four, to enable him to fulfil a Monday's reading at Scarborough. Such fatigues became matters of course; but their effect, not noted at the time, was grave. 'At York I had a most 'magnificent audience, and might have filled the place for 'a week. . . . I think the audience possessed of a better 'knowledge of character than any I have seen. But I 'recollect Doctor Belcombe to have told me long ago that 'they first found out Charles Mathews's father, and to the 'last understood him (he used to say) better than any 'other people. . . The let is enormous for next Saturday 'at Manchester, stalls alone four hundred! I shall soon 'be able to send you the list of places to the 15th of

YORK.

A knowing audience.

YORK: 1858.

Cheering prospect.

'November, the end. I shall be, O most heartily glad, 'when that time comes! But I must say that the intelli-'gence and warmth of the audiences are an immense sus-'tainment, and one that always sets me up. Sometimes 'before I go down to read (especially when it is in the 'day), I am so oppressed by having to do it that I feel 'perfectly unequal to the task. But the people lift me 'out of this directly; and I find that I have quite forgotten 'everything but them and the book, in a quarter of an 'hour.'

MANCHESTER.

The reception that awaited him at Manchester had very special warmth in it, occasioned by an adverse tone taken in the comment of one of the Manchester daily papers on the letter which by a breach of confidence had been then recently printed. 'My violated letter' Dickens always called it. 'When I came to Manchester on 'Saturday I found seven hundred stalls taken! When I 'went into the room at night 2500 people had paid, and 'more were being turned away from every door. The 'welcome they gave me was astounding in its affectionate 'recognition of the late trouble, and fairly for once un-'manned me. I never saw such a sight or heard such a 'sound. When they had thoroughly done it, they settled 'down to enjoy themselves; and certainly did enjoy them-'selves most heartily to the last minute.' Nor, for the rest of his English tour, in any of the towns that remained, had he reason to complain of any want of hearty greeting. At Sheffield great crowds came in excess of the places. At Leeds the hall overflowed in half an hour. At Hull the vast concourse had to be addressed by Mr. Smith on

'Violated 'letter.' *Ante*, 176.

Affectionate greeting.

Continued successes.

the gallery stairs, and additional Readings had to be given, day and night, 'for the people out of town and for the 'people in town.'

SCOTLAND: 1858.

The net profit to himself, thus far, had been upwards of three hundred pounds a week; * but this was nothing to the success in Scotland, where his profit in a week, with all expenses paid, was five hundred pounds. The pleasure was enhanced, too, by the presence of his two daughters, who had joined him over the Border. At first the look of Edinburgh was not promising. 'We began with, for us, a poor 'room. . . But the effect of that reading (it was the *Chimes*) 'was immense; and on the next night, for *Little Dombey*, 'we had a full room. It is our greatest triumph every-'where. Next night (*Poor Traveller, Boots,* and *Gamp*) 'we turned away hundreds upon hundreds of people; and 'last night, for the *Carol,* in spite of advertisements in 'the morning that the tickets were gone, the people had 'to be got in through such a crowd as rendered it a work 'of the utmost difficulty to keep an alley into the room.

Joined by his daughters.

Scene at Edinburgh.

* 'That is no doubt immense, our expenses being necessarily large, and the 'travelling party being always five.' Another source of profit was the sale of the copies of the several Readings prepared by himself. 'Our people alone 'sell eight, ten, and twelve dozen a night.' A later letter says: 'The men with 'the reading books were sold out, for about the twentieth time, at Manchester. 'Eleven dozen of the *Poor Traveller, Boots,* and *Gamp* being sold in about ten 'minutes, they had no more left; and Manchester became green with the 'little tracts, in every bookshop, outside every omnibus, and passing along 'every street. The sale of them, apart from us, must be very great.' 'Did I 'tell you,' he writes in another letter, 'that the agents for our tickets who 'are also booksellers, say very generally that the readings decidedly increase 'the sale of the books they are taken from? We were first told of this by a 'Mr. Parke, a wealthy old gentleman in a very large way at Wolverhampton, 'who did all the business for love, and would not take a farthing. Since then, 'we have constantly come upon it; and M'Glashin and Gill at Dublin were 'very strong about it indeed.'

Books of Readings.

Mr. Parke of Wolverhampton.

SCOTLAND: 1858.

'They were seated about me on the platform, put into the 'doorway of the waiting-room, squeezed into every con-'ceivable place, and a multitude turned away once more. 'I think I am better pleased with what was done in Edin-'burgh than with what has been done anywhere, almost. 'It was so completely taken by storm, and carried in spite 'of itself. Mary and Katey have been infinitely pleased and 'interested with Edinburgh. We are just going to sit down 'to dinner and therefore I cut my missive short. Travel-'ling, dinner, reading, and everything else, come crowding 'together into this strange life.'

Strange life.

Then came Dundee: 'An odd place,' he wrote, 'like 'Wapping with high rugged hills behind it. We had the 'strangest journey here—bits of sea, and bits of railroad, 'alternately; which carried my mind back to travelling in 'America. The room is an immense new one, belonging 'to Lord Kinnaird, and Lord Panmure, and some others 'of that sort. It looks something between the Crystal-'palace and Westminster-hall (I can't imagine who 'wants it in this place), and has never been tried yet for 'speaking in. Quite disinterestedly of course, I hope it 'will succeed.' The people he thought, in respect of taste and intelligence, below any other of his Scotch audiences; but they woke up surprisingly, and the rest of his Cale-donian tour was a succession of triumphs. 'At Aberdeen 'we were crammed to the street, twice in one day. At 'Perth (where I thought when I arrived, there literally 'could be nobody to come) the gentlefolk came posting in 'from thirty miles round, and the whole town came besides, 'and filled an immense hall. They were as full of percep-

At Dundee.

At Aberdeen and Perth.

'tion, fire, and enthusiasm as any people I have seen. At 'Glasgow, where I read three evenings and one morning, 'we took the prodigiously large sum of six hundred 'pounds! And this at the Manchester prices, which are 'lower than St. Martin's Hall. As to the effect—I wish 'you could have seen them after Lilian died in the '*Chimes*, or when Scrooge woke in the *Carol* and talked to 'the boy outside the window. And at the end of *Dombey* 'yesterday afternoon, in the cold light of day, they all got 'up, after a short pause, gentle and simple, and thundered 'and waved their hats with such astonishing heartiness 'and fondness that, for the first time in all my public 'career, they took me completely off my legs, and I saw the 'whole eighteen hundred of them reel to one side as if a 'shock from without had shaken the hall. Notwithstand-'ing which, I must confess to you, I am very anxious to 'get to the end of my Readings, and to be at home again, 'and able to sit down and think in my own study. There 'has been only one thing quite without alloy. The dear 'girls have enjoyed themselves immensely, and their trip 'with me has been a great success.'

SCOTLAND: 1858.

At Glasgow.

Glasgow audience.

Anxious for home.

The subjects of his readings during this first circuit were the *Carol*, the *Chimes*, the *Trial in Pickwick*, the chapters containing *Paul Dombey, Boots at the Holly Tree Inn*, the *Poor Traveller* (Captain Doubledick), and *Mrs. Gamp:* to which he continued to restrict himself through the supplementary nights that closed in the autumn of 1859.* Of these the most successful in their uniform

Subjects of first readings.

* The last of them were given immediately after his completion of the *Tale of Two Cities*: 'I am a little tired; but as little, I suspect, as any man could be with the work of the last four days, and perhaps the change of work

LONDON: 1858-9.

effect upon his audiences were undoubtedly the *Carol*, the *Pickwick* scene, *Mrs. Gamp*, and the *Dombey*—the quickness, variety, and completeness of his assumption of character, having greatest scope in these. Here, I think, more than in the pathos or graver level passages, his strength lay; but this is entitled to no weight other than as an individual opinion, and his audiences gave him many reasons for thinking differently.*

The incidents of the period covered by this chapter that had any general interest in them, claim to be mentioned briefly. At the close of 1857 he presided at the fourth anniversary of the Warehousemen and Clerks' Schools, describing and discriminating, with keenest wit and kindliest fun, the sort of schools he liked and he disliked. To the spring and summer of 1858 belongs the first collection of his writings into a succinct library form, each of the larger novels occupying two volumes. In March he paid warm public tribute to Thackeray (who had been induced to take the chair at the General Theatrical Fund) as one for whose genius he entertained the warmest admiration, who did honour to literature, and in whom literature was honoured. In May he presided at the Artists' Benevolent Fund dinner, and made striking appeal for that excellent charity. In July he took earnest part in the opening efforts on behalf

First Library edition of his books.

Tribute to Thackeray.

At public meetings.

'was better than subsiding into rest and rust. The Norwich people were a 'noble audience. There, and at Ipswich and Bury, we had the demonstra-'tiveness of the great working-towns, and a much finer perception.'—14th of October 1859.

* Two pleasing little volumes may here be named as devoted to special descriptions of the several Readings; by his friend Mr. Charles Kent in England (*Charles Dickens as a Reader*), and by Miss Kate Field in America (*Pen Photographs*).

of the Royal Dramatic College, which he supplemented later by a speech for the establishment of schools for actors' children; in which he took occasion to declare his belief that there were no institutions in England so socially liberal as its public schools, and that there was nowhere in the country so complete an absence of servility to mere rank, position, or riches. 'A boy, there, is always what his 'abilities or his personal qualities make him. We may 'differ about the curriculum and other matters, but of the 'frank, free, manly, independent spirit preserved in our 'public schools, I apprehend there can be no kind of ques-'tion.' In December* he was entertained at a public dinner in Coventry on the occasion of receiving, by way of thanks for help rendered to their Institute, a gold repeater of special construction by the watchmakers of the town; as to which he kept faithfully his pledge to the givers, that it

LONDON: 1858-9.

Dramatic College.

On public schools.

At Coventry.

* Let me subjoin his own note of a less important incident of that month which will show his quick and sure eye for any bit of acting out of the common. The lady has since justified its closing prediction. Describing an early dinner with Chauncy Townshend, he adds (17th of December 1858): 'I escaped at half-'past seven, and went to the Strand Theatre: having taken a stall beforehand, 'for it is always crammed. I really wish you would go, between this and next 'Thursday, to see the *Maid and the Magpie* burlesque there. There is the 'strangest thing in it that ever I have seen on the stage. The boy, Pippo, by 'Miss Wilton. While it is astonishingly impudent (must be, or it couldn't be 'done at all), it is so stupendously like a boy, and unlike a woman, that it is 'perfectly free from offence. I never have seen such a thing. Priscilla Horton, 'as a boy, not to be thought of beside it. She does an imitation of the dancing 'of the Christy Minstrels—wonderfully clever—which, in the audacity of its 'thorough-going, is surprising. A thing that you *can not* imagine a woman's 'doing at all; and yet the manner, the appearance, the levity, impulse, and 'spirits of it, are so exactly like a boy that you cannot think of anything like 'her sex in association with it. It begins at 8, and is over by a quarter-past '9. I never have seen such a curious thing, and the girl's talent is un-'challengeable. I call her the cleverest girl I have ever seen on the stage 'in my time, and the most singularly original.'

Miss Marie Wilton as 'Pippo.'

LONDON: 1858–9.

should be thenceforward the inseparable companion of his workings and wanderings, and reckon off the future labours of his days until he should have done with the measurement of time. Within a day from this celebration, he presided at the Institutional Association of Lancashire and Cheshire in Manchester Free Trade Hall; gave prizes to candidates from a hundred and fourteen local mechanics' institutes affiliated to the Association; described in his most attractive language the gallant toiling fellows by whom the prizes had been won; and ended with the monition he never failed to couple with his eulogies of Knowledge, that it should follow the teaching of the Saviour, and not satisfy the understanding merely. 'Knowledge 'has a very limited power when it informs the head only; 'but when it informs the heart as well, it has a power over 'life and death, the body and the soul, and dominates the 'universe.'

At Manchester.

Frith's portrait of Dickens.

This too was the year when Mr. Frith completed Dickens's portrait, and it appeared upon the walls of the Academy in the following spring. 'I wish,' said Edwin Landseer as he stood before it, 'he looked less eager and 'busy, and not so much out of himself, or beyond himself. I 'should like to catch him asleep and quiet now and then.' There is something in the objection, and he also would be envious at times of what he too surely knew could never be his lot. On the other hand who would willingly have lost the fruits of an activity on the whole so healthy and beneficent?

# CHAPTER X.

## ALL THE YEAR ROUND AND THE UNCOMMERCIAL TRAVELLER.

### 1859—1861.

LONDON: 1859-61.

IN the interval before the close of the first circuit of readings, painful personal disputes arising out of the occurrences of the previous year were settled by the discontinuance of *Household Words*, and the establishment in its place of *All the Year Round.* The disputes turned upon matters of feeling exclusively, and involved no charge on either side that would render any detailed reference here other than gravely out of place. The question into which the difference ultimately resolved itself was that of the respective rights of the parties as proprietors of *Household Words;* and this, upon a bill filed in Chancery, was settled by a winding-up order, under which the property was sold. It was bought by Dickens, who, even before the sale, exactly fulfilling a previous announcement of the proposed discontinuance of the existing periodical and establishment of another in its place, precisely similar but under a different title, had started *All the Year Round.* It was to be regretted perhaps that he should have thought it necessary to move at all, but he moved strictly within his rights.

*All the Year Round* started.

*Household Words* discontinued.

*Ante,* 36.

P 2

LONDON: 1859-61.

To the publishers first associated with his great success in literature, Messrs. Chapman and Hall, he now returned for the issue of the remainder of his books; of which he always in future reserved the copyrights, making each the subject of such arrangement as for the time might seem to him desirable. In this he was met by no difficulty; and indeed it will be only proper to add, that, in any points affecting his relations with those concerned in the production of his books, though his resentments were easily and quickly roused, they were never very lasting. The only fair rule therefore was, in a memoir of his life, to confine the mention of such things to what was strictly necessary to explain its narrative. This accordingly has been done; and, in the several disagreements it has been necessary to advert to, I cannot charge myself with having in a single instance overstepped the rule. Objection has been made to my revival of the early differences with Mr. Bentley. But silence respecting them was incompatible with what absolutely required to be said, if the picture of Dickens in his most interesting time, at the outset of his career in letters, was not to be omitted altogether; and, suppressing everything of mere temper that gathered round the dispute, use was made of those letters only containing the young writer's urgent appeal to be absolved, rightly or wrongly, from engagements he had too precipitately entered into. Wrongly, some might say, because the law was undoubtedly on Mr. Bentley's side; but all subsequent reflection has confirmed the view I was led strongly to take at the time, that in the facts there had come to be involved what the law could not afford to overlook, and that the sale of brain-

Earliest and latest publishers.

Differences with Mr. Bentley.

Literary agreements.

work can never be adjusted by agreement with the same exactness and certainty as that of ordinary goods and chattels. Quitting the subject once for all with this remark, it is not less incumbent on me to say that there was no stage of the dispute in which Mr. Bentley, holding as strongly the other view, might not think it to have sufficient justification; and certainly in later years there was no absence of friendly feeling on the part of Dickens to his old publisher. This already has been mentioned; and on the occasion of Hans Andersen's recent visit to Gadshill, Mr. Bentley was invited to meet the celebrated Dane. Nor should I omit to say, that, in the year to which this narrative has now arrived, his prompt compliance with an intercession made to him for a common friend pleased Dickens greatly.

Friendly relations of Dickens and Mr. Bentley. ii. 450.

At the opening of 1859, bent upon such a successor to *Household Words* as should carry on the associations connected with its name, Dickens was deep in search of a title to give expression to them. 'My determination to 'settle the title arises out of my knowledge that I shall 'never be able to do anything for the work until it has a 'fixed name; also out of my observation that the same 'odd feeling affects everybody else.' He had proposed to himself a title that, as in *Household Words*, might be capable of illustration by a line from Shakespeare; and alighting upon that wherein poor Henry the Sixth is fain to solace his captivity by the fancy, that, like birds encaged he might soothe himself for loss of liberty 'at last 'by notes of household harmony,' he for the time forgot that this might hardly be accepted as a happy comment

In search of a name for new periodical.

LONDON: 1859–61.

on the occurrences out of which the supposed necessity had arisen of replacing the old by a new household friend. Don't you think,' he wrote on the 24th of January, 'this is 'a good name and quotation? I have been quite delighted 'to get hold of it for our title.

First title chosen.

'HOUSEHOLD HARMONY.

' "At last by notes of Household Harmony."—*Shakespeare.*'

Reply to a doubt.

He was at first reluctant even to admit the objection when stated to him. 'I am afraid we must not be too 'particular about the possibility of personal references and 'applications: otherwise it is manifest that I never can 'write another book. I could not invent a story of any 'sort, it is quite plain, incapable of being twisted into 'some such nonsensical shape. It would be wholly impos-'sible to turn one through half a dozen chapters.' Of course he yielded, nevertheless; and much consideration followed over sundry other titles submitted. Reviving none of those formerly rejected, here were a few of these now rejected in their turn. THE HEARTH. THE FORGE. THE CRUCIBLE. THE ANVIL OF THE TIME. CHARLES DICKENS'S OWN. SEASONABLE LEAVES. EVERGREEN LEAVES. HOME. HOME-MUSIC. CHANGE. TIME AND TIDE. TWOPENCE. ENGLISH BELLS. WEEKLY BELLS. THE ROCKET. GOOD HUMOUR. Still the great want was the line adaptable from Shakespeare, which at last exultingly he sent on the 28th of January. 'I am dining early, before reading, 'and write literally with my mouth full. But I have just 'hit upon a name that I think really an admirable one—

Other titles suggested.

'especially with the quotation *before* it, in the place where 'our present *H. W.* quotation stands. LONDON: 1859–61.

'"The story of our lives, from year to year."—*Shakespeare.*'

'ALL THE YEAR ROUND. Title found.

'A weekly journal conducted by Charles Dickens.'

With the same resolution and energy other things necessary to the adventure were as promptly done. 'I 'have taken the new office,' he wrote from Tavistock House on the 21st of February; 'have got workmen in; 'have ordered the paper; settled with the printer; and 'am getting an immense system of advertising ready. 'Blow to be struck on the 12th of March. . . Meantime I 'cannot please myself with the opening of my story' (the *Tale of Two Cities,* which *All the Year Round* was to start with), 'and cannot in the least settle at it or take to 'it. . . I wish you would come and look at what I flatter 'myself is a rather ingenious account to which I have 'turned the Stanfield scenery here.' He had placed the *Lighthouse* scene in a single frame; had divided the scene of the *Frozen Deep* into two subjects, a British man-of-war and an Arctic sea, which he had also framed; and the school-room that had been the theatre was now hung with sea-pieces by a great painter of the sea. To believe them to have been but the amusement of a few mornings was difficult indeed. Seen from the due distance there was nothing wanting to the most masterly and elaborate art.

Opening a story.

*Ante*, 50, 141.

Stanfield scenes at Tavistock House.

The first number of *All the Year Round* appeared on the 30th of April, and the result of the first quarter's accounts of the sale will tell everything that needs to be said

LONDON: 1859–61.

of a success that went on without intermission to the close. 'A word before I go back to Gadshill,' he wrote from Tavistock House in July, 'which I know you will be glad to 'receive. So well has *All the Year Round* gone that it 'was yesterday able to repay me, with five per cent interest, 'all the money I advanced for its establishment (paper, 'print &c. all paid, down to the last number), and yet to 'leave a good £500 balance at the banker's!' Beside the opening of his *Tale of Two Cities* its first number had contained another piece of his writing, the 'Poor Man and his 'Beer;' as to which an interesting note has been sent me. The Rev. T. B. Lawes, of Rothamsted, St. Alban's, had been associated upon a sanitary commission with Mr. Henry Austin, Dickens's brother-in-law and counsellor in regard to all such matters in his own houses, or in the houses of the poor; and this connection led to Dickens's knowledge of a club that Mr. Lawes had established at Rothamsted, which he became eager to recommend as an example to other country neighbourhoods. The club had been set on foot* to enable the agricultural labourers of the parish to have their beer and pipes independent of the public-house; and the description of it, says Mr. Lawes, 'was the occupation of a drive between this place (Rotham-'sted) and London, 25 miles, Mr. Dickens refusing the 'offer of a bed, and saying that he could arrange his ideas 'on the journey. In the course of our conversation I 'mentioned that the labourers were very jealous of the 'small tradesmen, blacksmiths and others, holding allot-

Success of new periodical.

Beer without the public-house.

* It is pleasant to have to state that it was still flourishing when I received Mr. Lawes's letter, on the 18th of December 1871.

'ment-gardens; but that the latter did so indirectly by pay-
'ing higher rents to the labourers for a share. This circum-
'stance is not forgotten in the verses on the Blacksmith in
'the same number, composed by Mr. Dickens and repeated
'to me while he was walking about, and which close the
'mention of his gains with allusion to

LONDON: 1859–61.

Verses in first number.

'A share (concealed) in the poor man's field,
'Which adds to the poor man's store.'

The periodical thus established was in all respects, save one, so exactly the counterpart of what it replaced, that a mention of this point of difference is the only description of it called for. Besides his own three-volume stories of *The Tale of Two Cities* and *Great Expectations,* Dickens admitted into it other stories of the same length by writers of character and name, of which the authorship was avowed. It published tales of varied merit and success by Mr. Edmund Yates, Mr. Percy Fitzgerald, and Mr. Charles Lever. Mr. Wilkie Collins contributed to it his *Woman in White, No Name,* and *Moonstone,* the first of which had a pre-eminent success; Mr. Reade his *Hard Cash;* and Lord Lytton his *Strange Story.* Conferring about the latter Dickens passed a week at Knebworth, accompanied by his daughter and sister-in-law, in the summer of 1861, as soon as he had closed *Great Expectations;* and there met Mr. Arthur Helps, with whom and Lord Orford he visited the so-called 'Hermit' near Stevenage, whom he described as Mr. Mopes in *Tom Tiddler's Ground.* With his great brother-artist he thoroughly enjoyed himself, as he invariably did; and reported him as in better health and spirits 'than I have seen him in, in all these years,—a little weird

Difference between *Household Words* and *All the Year Round.*

LONDON: 1859–61.

At Knebworth with Bulwer Lytton.

'occasionally regarding magic and spirits, but always fair 'and frank under opposition. He was brilliantly talkative, 'anecdotical, and droll; looked young and well; laughed 'heartily; and enjoyed with great zest some games we 'played. In his artist-character and talk, he was full of 'interest and matter, saying the subtlest and finest things '—but that he never fails in. I enjoyed myself immensely, 'as we all did.'*

Sale of Christmas numbers.

In *All the Year Round*, as in its predecessor, the tales for Christmas were of course continued, but with a surprisingly increased popularity; and Dickens never had such sale for any of his writings as for his Christmas pieces in the later periodical. It had reached, before he died, to nearly three hundred thousand. The first was called the *Haunted House*, and had a small mention of a true occurrence in his boyhood which is not included in the bitter record on a former page. i. 25. 'I was taken home, and there was debt 'at home as well as death, and we had a sale there. My 'own little bed was so superciliously looked upon by a 'power unknown to me hazily called The Trade, that a 'brass coal-scuttle, a roasting jack, and a bird cage were 'obliged to be put into it to make a lot of it, and then it 'went for a song. So I heard mentioned, and I wondered

True incident.

Famous men going off.

* From the same letter, dated 1st of July 1861, I take what follows. 'Poor 'Lord Campbell's seems to me as easy and good a death as one could desire. 'There must be a sweep of these men very soon, and one feels as if it must 'fall out like the breaking of an arch—one stone goes from a prominent place, 'and then the rest begin to drop. So, one looks, not without satisfaction (in 'our sadness) at lives so rounded and complete, towards Brougham, and Lyndhurst, and Pollock' . . . Yet, of Dickens's own death, Pollock lived to write to me as the death of 'one of the most distinguished and honoured men 'England has ever produced; in whose loss every man among us feels that he 'has lost a friend and an instructor.' Temple-Hatton, 10th of June 1870.

'what song, and thought what a dismal song it must have 'been to sing!' The other subjects will have mention in another chapter.

Detached papers.

His tales were not his only important work in *All the Year Round.* The detached papers written by him there had a character and completeness derived from their plan, and from the personal tone, as well as frequent individual confessions, by which their interest is enhanced, and which will always make them specially attractive. Their title expressed a personal liking. Of all the societies, charitable or self-assisting, which his tact and eloquence in the 'chair' so often helped, none had interested him by the character of its service to its members, and the perfection of its management, so much as that of the Commercial Travellers. His admiration of their schools introduced him to one who then acted as their treasurer, and whom, of all the men he had known, I think he rated highest for the union of business qualities in an incomparable measure to a nature comprehensive enough to deal with masses of men, however differing in creed or opinion, humanely and justly. He never afterwards wanted support for any good work that he did not think first of Mr. George Moore,* and

Commercial Travellers' schools.

Children and Bishop.

* If space were available here, his letters would supply many proofs of his interest in Mr. George Moore's admirable projects; but I can only make exception for his characteristic allusion to an incident that tickled his fancy very much at the time. 'I hope (20th of Aug. 1863) 'you have been as much 'amused as I am by the account of the Bishop of Carlisle at (my very par- 'ticular friend's) Mr. George Moore's schools? It strikes me as the funniest 'piece of weakness I ever saw, his addressing those unfortunate children con- 'cerning Colenso. I cannot get over the ridiculous image I have erected in 'my mind, of the shovel-hat and apron holding forth, at that safe distance, to 'that safe audience. There is nothing so extravagant in Rabelais, or so sati- 'rically humorous in Swift or Voltaire.'

LONDON: 1859–61.

Mr. George Moore.

appeal was never made to him in vain. 'Integrity, enterprise, public spirit, and benevolence,' he told the Commercial Travellers on one occasion, 'had their synonym in 'Mr. Moore's name;' and it was another form of the same liking when he took to himself the character and title of a Traveller *Un*commercial. 'I am both a town traveller 'and a country traveller, and am always on the road. 'Figuratively speaking, I travel for the great house of 'Human-interest Brothers, and have rather a large connec'tion in the fancy goods way. Literally speaking, I am 'always wandering here and there from my rooms in 'Covent-garden, London: now about the city streets; 'now about the country by-roads: seeing many little 'things, and some great things, which, because they in'terest me, I think may interest others.' In a few words that was the plan and drift of the papers which he began in 1860, and continued to write from time to time until the last autumn of his life.

A traveller for Human-interest Brothers.

Personal references.

Many of them, such as 'Travelling Abroad,' 'City 'Churches,' 'Dullborough,' 'Nurses' Stories,' and 'Birthday 'Celebrations,' have supplied traits, chiefly of his younger days, to portions of this memoir; and parts of his later life receive illustration from others, such as 'Tramps,' 'Night 'Walks,' 'Shy Neighbourhoods,' 'The Italian Prisoner,' and 'Chatham Dockyard.' Indeed hardly any is without its personal interest or illustration. One may learn from them, among other things, what kind of treatment he resorted to for the disorder of sleeplessness from which he had often suffered amid his late anxieties. Experimenting upon it in bed, he found to be too slow and doubtful a process for him;

LONDON: 1859–61.

but he very soon defeated his enemy by the brisker treatment, of getting up directly after lying down, going out, and coming home tired at sunrise. 'My last special feat was 'turning out of bed at two, after a hard day pedestrian 'and otherwise, and walking thirty miles into the country 'to breakfast.' One description he did not give in his paper, but I recollect his saying that he had seldom seen anything so striking as the way in which the wonders of an equinoctial dawn (it was the 15th of October 1857) presented themselves during that walk. He had never before happened to see night so completely at odds with morning, 'which was which.' Another experience of his night ramblings used to be given in vivid sketches of the restlessness of a great city, and the manner in which *it* also tumbles and tosses before it can get to sleep. Nor should anyone curious about his habits and ways omit to accompany him with his Tramps into Gadshill lanes; or to follow him into his Shy Neighbourhoods of the Hackney-road, Waterloo-road, Spitalfields, or Bethnal-green. For delightful observation both of country and town, for the wit that finds analogies between remote and familiar things, and for humorous personal sketches and experience, these are perfect of their kind.

Remedy for sleeplessness.

A great city getting to sleep.

'I have my eye upon a piece of Kentish road, bordered 'on either side by a wood, and having on one hand, be'tween the road-dust and the trees, a skirting patch of 'grass. Wild flowers grow in abundance on this spot, and 'it lies high and airy, with a distant river stealing steadily 'away to the ocean, like a man's life. To gain the mile'stone here, which the moss, primroses, violets, blue-bells, 'and wild roses, would soon render illegible but for peer-

'Tramp' experiences

LONDON: 1859–61.

Gipsy tracks.

'ing travellers pushing them aside with their sticks, you 'must come up a steep hill, come which way you may. 'So, all the tramps with carts or caravans—the Gipsy-'tramp, the Show-tramp, the Cheap Jack—find it impos-'sible to resist the temptations of the place; and all turn 'the horse loose when they come to it, and boil the pot. 'Bless the place, I love the ashes of the vagabond fires 'that have scorched its grass!' It was there he found Dr. Marigold, and Chops the Dwarf, and the White-haired Lady with the pink eyes eating meat-pie with the Giant. So, too, in his Shy Neighbourhoods, when he relates his experiences of the bad company that birds are fond of, and of the effect upon domestic fowls of living in low districts, his method of handling the subject has all the charm of a discovery. 'That anything born of an egg and invested 'with wings should have got to the pass that it hops con-'tentedly down a ladder into a cellar, and calls *that* going 'home, is a circumstance so amazing as to leave one nothing 'more in this connexion to wonder at.' One of his illustrations is a reduced Bantam family in the Hackney-road deriving their sole enjoyment from crowding together in a pawnbroker's side-entry; but seeming as if only newly come down in the world, and always in a feeble flutter of fear that they may be found out. He contrasts them with others. 'I know a low fellow, originally of a good 'family from Dorking, who takes his whole establishment 'of wives, in single file, in at the door of the Jug Depart-'ment of a disorderly tavern near the Haymarket, man-'œuvres them among the company's legs, emerges with 'them at the Bottle Entrance, and so passes his life: sel-

Birds and low company.

Reduced Bantams.

'dom, in the season, going to bed before two in the morning. '. . . But, the family I am best acquainted with, reside in 'the densest part of Bethnal-green. Their abstraction 'from the objects among which they live, or rather their 'conviction that those objects have all come into existence 'in express subservience to fowls, has so enchanted me, 'that I have made them the subject of many journeys at 'divers hours. After careful observation of the two lords 'and the ten ladies of whom this family consists, I have 'come to the conclusion that their opinions are represented 'by the leading lord and leading lady: the latter, as I 'judge, an aged personage, afflicted with a paucity of fea- 'ther and visibility of quill that gives her the appearance 'of a bundle of office pens. When a railway goods-van 'that would crush an elephant comes round the corner, 'tearing over these fowls, they emerge unharmed from 'under the horses, perfectly satisfied that the whole rush 'was a passing property in the air, which may have left 'something to eat behind it. They look upon old shoes, 'wrecks of kettles and saucepans, and fragments of bon- 'nets, as a kind of meteoric discharge, for fowls to peck at. '. . . Gaslight comes quite as natural to them as any other 'light; and I have more than a suspicion that, in the 'minds of the two lords, the early public-house at the 'corner has superseded the sun. They always begin to 'crow when the public-house shutters begin to be taken 'down, and they salute the Potboy, the instant he appears 'to perform that duty, as if he were Phœbus in person.' For the truth of the personal adventure in the same essay, which he tells in proof of a propensity to bad company in more

LONDON: 1859–61.

Bethnal-green fowls.

Aged hen.

Potboy Phœbus.

refined members of the feathered race, I am myself in a position to vouch. Walking by a dirty court in Spitalfields one day, the quick little busy intelligence of a goldfinch, drawing water for himself in his cage, so attracted him that he bought the bird, which had other accomplishments; but not one of them would the little creature show off in his new abode in Doughty-street, and he drew no water but by stealth or under the cloak of night. 'After an interval of 'futile and at length hopeless expectation, the merchant 'who had educated him was appealed to. The merchant was 'a bow-legged character, with a flat and cushiony nose, like 'the last new strawberry. He wore a fur cap, and shorts, and 'was of the velveteen race, velveteeny. He sent word 'that he would "look round." He looked round, appeared 'in the doorway of the room, and slightly cocked up his 'evil eye at the goldfinch. Instantly a raging thirst 'beset that bird; and when it was appeased, he still drew 'several unnecessary buckets of water, leaping about his 'perch and sharpening his bill with irrepressible satis'faction.'

An incident of Doughty-street.

The goldfinch and his friend.

The Uncommercial Traveller papers, his two serial stories, and his Christmas tales, were all the contributions of any importance made by Dickens to *All the Year Round;* but he reprinted in it, on the completion of his first story, a short tale called 'Hunted Down,' written for a newspaper in America called the *New York Ledger*. Its subject had been taken from the life of a notorious criminal already named, and its principal claim to notice was the price paid for it. For a story not longer than half of one of the numbers of *Chuzzlewit* or *Copperfield*, he had received

'Hunted 'Down.'

i. 160.
ii. 307.

LONDON: 1859–61.

a thousand pounds.* It was one of the indications of the eager desire which his entry on the career of a public reader had aroused in America to induce him again to visit that continent; and at the very time he had this magnificent offer from the New York journal, Mr. Fields of Boston, who was then on a visit to Europe, was pressing him so much to go that his resolution was almost shaken. 'I am now,' he wrote to me from Gadshill on the 9th of July 1859, 'getting the *Tale of Two Cities* into that 'state that IF I should decide to go to America late in 'September, I could turn to, at any time, and write on 'with great vigour. Mr. Fields has been down here for a 'day, and with the strongest intensity urges that there is 'no drawback, no commercial excitement or crisis, no po- 'litical agitation; and that so favourable an opportunity, 'in all respects, might not occur again for years and years. 'I should be one of the most unhappy of men if I were to 'go, and yet I cannot help being much stirred and influ- 'enced by the golden prospect held before me.'

Offers from America.

Visit of Mr. Fields.

He yielded nevertheless to other persuasion, and for that time the visit was not to be. In six months more the Civil War began, and America was closed to any such enterprise for nearly five years.

Not yet to be.

* Eight years later he wrote 'Holiday Romance' for a Child's Magazine published by Mr. Fields, and 'George Silverman's Explanation'—of the same length, and for the same price. There are no other such instances, I suppose, in the history of literature.

## CHAPTER XI.

### SECOND SERIES OF READINGS.

### 1861—1863.

GADSHILL: 1860.

AT the end of the first year of residence at Gadshill it was the remark of Dickens that nothing had gratified him so much as the confidence with which his poorer neighbours treated him. He had tested generally their worth and good conduct, and they had been encouraged in illness or trouble to resort to him for help. There was pleasant indication of the feeling thus awakened, when, in the summer of 1860, his younger daughter Kate was married to Charles Alston Collins, brother of the novelist, and younger son of the painter and academician, who might have found, if spared to witness that summer-morning scene, subjects not unworthy of his delightful pencil in many a rustic group near Gadshill. All the villagers had turned out in honour of Dickens, and the carriages could hardly get to and from the little church for the succession of triumphal arches they had to pass through. It was quite unexpected by him; and when the feu de joie of the blacksmith in the lane, whose enthusiasm had smuggled a couple of small cannon into his forge, exploded upon him at the return, I doubt if the shyest of men was ever so taken aback at an ovation.

Daughter Kate's marriage.

GADSHILL: 1860.

To name the principal persons present that day will indicate the faces that (with addition of Miss Mary Boyle, Miss Marguerite Power, Mr. Fechter, Mr. Charles Kent, Mr. Edmund Yates, Mr. Percy Fitzgerald, and members of the family of Mr. Frank Stone, whose sudden death* in the preceding year had been a great grief to Dickens) were most familiar at Gadshill in these later years. Mr. Frederic Lehmann was there with his wife, whose sister, Miss Chambers, was one of the bridesmaids; Mr. and Mrs. Wills were there, and Dickens's old fast friend Mr. Thomas Beard; the two nearest country neighbours with whom the family had become very intimate, Mr. Hulkes and Mr. Malleson, with their wives, joined the party; among the others were Henry Chorley, Chauncy Townshend, and Wilkie Collins; and, for friend special to the occasion, the bridegroom had brought his old fellow-student in art, Mr. Holman Hunt. Mr. Charles Collins had himself been bred as a painter, for success in which line he had some rare gifts; but inclination and capacity led him also to literature, and, after much indecision between the two callings, he took finally to letters. His contributions to *All the Year Round* were among the most charming of its detached papers, and two stories published independently showed strength of wing for higher flights. But his health

Wedding party.

*Ante*, 181.

Charles Alston Collins.

* 'You will be grieved,' he wrote (Saturday 19th of Nov. 1859) 'to hear of 'poor Stone. On Sunday he was not well. On Monday, went to Dr. Todd, 'who told him he had aneurism of the heart. On Tuesday, went to Dr. Walsh, 'who told him he hadn't. On Wednesday I met him in a cab in the Square 'here, and he got out to talk to me. I walked about with him ittle while 'at a snail's pace, cheering him up; but when I came home, I told them that 'I thought him much changed, and in danger. Yesterday at 2 o'clock he died 'of spasm of the heart. I am going up to Highgate to look for a grave for him.'

Death of Frank Stone, A.R.A.

GADSHILL: 1860.

broke down, and his taste was too fastidious for his failing power. It is possible however that he may live by two small books of description, the *New Sentimental Journey* and the *Cruize on Wheels,* which have in them unusual delicacy and refinement of humour; and if those volumes should make any readers in another generation curious about the writer, they will learn, if correct reply is given to their inquiries, that no man disappointed so many reasonable hopes with so little fault or failure of his own, that his difficulty always was to please himself, and that an inferior mind would have been more successful in both the arts he followed. He died in 1873 in his forty-fifth year; and until then it was not known, even by those nearest to him, how great must have been the suffering which he had borne, through many trying years, with uncomplaining patience.

Sale of Tavistock House.

His daughter's marriage was the chief event that had crossed the even tenor of Dickens's life since his first paid readings closed; and it was followed by the sale of Tavistock House, with the resolve to make his future home at Gadshill. In the brief interval (29th of July) he wrote to me of his brother Alfred's death. 'I was telegraphed for 'to Manchester on Friday night. Arrived there at a 'quarter past ten, but he had been dead three hours, poor 'fellow! He is to be buried at Highgate on Wednesday. 'I brought the poor young widow back with me yesterday.' All that this death involved,* the troubles of his change of

Brother Alfred's death.

Conditions of literary work.

* He was now hard at work on his story; and a note written from Gadshill after the funeral shows, what so frequently was incident to his pursuits, the hard conditions under which sorrow, and its claim on his exertion, often came to him. 'To-morrow I have to work against time and tide and every- 'thing else, to fill up a No. keeping open for me, and the stereotype plates

home, and some difficulties in working out his story, gave him more than sufficient occupation till the following spring; and as the time arrived for the new Readings, the change was a not unwelcome one.

LONDON: 1861.

The first portion of this second series was planned by Mr. Arthur Smith, but he only superintended the six readings in London which opened it. These were the first at St. James's Hall (St. Martin's Hall having been burnt since the last readings there) and were given in March and April 1861. 'We are all well here and flourish-'ing,' he wrote to me from Gadshill on the 28th of April. 'On the 18th I finished the readings as I purposed. We 'had between seventy and eighty pounds *in the stalls*, 'which, at four shillings apiece, is something quite un-'precedented in these times. . . The result of the six was, 'that, after paying a large staff of men and all other 'charges, and Arthur Smith's ten per cent. on the receipts, 'and replacing everything destroyed in the fire at St. 'Martin's Hall (including all our tickets, country-baggage, 'cheque-boxes, books, and a quantity of gas-fittings and 'what not), I got upwards of £500. A very great result. 'We certainly might have gone on through the season, but 'I am heartily glad to be concentrated on my story.'

Metropolitan readings.

Result.

It had been part of his plan that the Provincial Readings should not begin until a certain interval after the close of his story of *Great Expectations*. They were delayed accordingly

Proposed Provincial Readings.

'of which must go to America on Friday. But indeed the enquiry into 'poor Alfred's affairs; the necessity of putting the widow and children some-'where; the difficulty of knowing what to do for the best; and the need 'I feel under of being as composed and deliberate as I can be, and yet of not 'shirking or putting off the occasion that there is for doing a duty; would 'have brought me back here to be quiet, under any circumstances.

LONDON: 1861.

until the 28th of October, from which date, when they opened at Norwich, they went on with the Christmas intervals to be presently named to the 30th of January 1862, when they closed at Chester. Kept within England and Scotland, they took in the border town of Berwick, and, besides the Scotch cities, comprised the contrasts and varieties of Norwich and Lancaster, Bury St. Edmunds and Cheltenham, Carlisle and Hastings, Plymouth and Birmingham, Canterbury and Torquay, Preston and Ipswich, Manchester and Brighton, Colchester and Dover, Newcastle and Chester.

What the second series comprised.

They were followed by ten readings at the St. James's Hall, between the 13th of March and the 27th of June 1862; and by four at Paris in January 1863, given at the Embassy in aid of the British Charitable Fund. The second series had thus in the number of the readings nearly equalled the first, when it closed at London in June 1863 with thirteen readings in the Hanover Square Rooms; and it is exclusively the subject of such illustrations or references as this chapter will supply.

On *Great Expectations* closing in June 1861, Bulwer Lytton, at Dickens's earnest wish, took his place in *All the Year Round* with the 'Strange Story;' and he then in-

Good of doing nothing.

dulged himself in idleness for a little while. 'The subsi-'dence of those distressing pains in my face the moment I 'had done my work, made me resolve to do nothing in that 'way for some time if I could help it.' * But his 'doing 'nothing' was seldom more than a figure of speech, and what it meant in this case was soon told. 'Every day for two or

* The same letter adds: 'The fourth edition of *Great Expectations* is now 'going to press; the third being nearly out. Bulwer's story keeps us up 'bravely. As well as we can make out, we have even risen fifteen hundred.'

'three hours, I practise my new readings, and (except in 'my office work) do nothing else. With great pains I have 'made a continuous narrative out of *Copperfield*, that I 'think will reward the exertion it is likely to cost me. Unless I am much mistaken, it will be very valuable in London. 'I have also done *Nicholas Nickleby* at the Yorkshire school, 'and hope I have got something droll out of Squeers, John 'Browdie, & Co. Also, the Bastille prisoner from the *Tale* '*of Two Cities*. Also, the Dwarf from one of our Christ'mas numbers.' Only the first two were added to the list for the present circuit.

Preparing readings.

New subjects for readings.

It was in the midst of these active preparations that painful news reached him. An illness under which Mr. Arthur Smith had been some time suffering took unexpectedly a dangerous turn, and there came to be but small chance of his recovery. A distressing interview on the 28th of September gave Dickens little hope. 'And yet his 'wakings and wanderings so perpetually turn on his arrange'ments for the Readings, and he is so desperately unwill'ing to relinquish the idea of "going on with the business" 'to-morrow and to-morrow and to-morrow, that I had not 'the heart to press him for the papers. He told me that 'he believed he had by him "70 or 80 letters unanswered." 'You may imagine how anxious it makes me, and at what 'a deadstop I stand.' Another week passed, and with it the time fixed at the places where his work was to have opened; but he could not bring himself to act as if all hope had gone. 'With a sick man who has been so zealous and 'faithful, I feel bound to be very tender and patient. 'When I told him the other day about my having engaged

Illness of manager.

LONDON: 1861.

Mr. Arthur Smith's death.

'Headland—"to do all the personally bustling and fatiguing '"part of your work," I said—he nodded his heavy head 'with great satisfaction, and faintly got out of himself 'the words, "Of course I pay him, and not you."' The poor fellow died in October; and on the day after attending the funeral,* Dickens heard of the death of his brother-in-law and friend, Mr. Henry Austin, whose abilities and character he respected as much as he liked the man. He lost much in losing the judicious and safe counsel which had guided him on many public questions in which he took lively interest, and it was with a heavy heart he set out at last upon his second circuit. 'With what difficulty I get 'myself back to the readings after all this loss and trouble, 'or with what unwillingness I work myself up to the mark 'of looking them in the face, I can hardly say. As for poor 'Arthur Smith at this time, it is as if my right arm were 'gone. It is only just now that I am able to open one of 'the books, and screw the text out of myself in a flat dull 'way. Enclosed is the list of what I have to do. You will 'see that I have left ten days in November for the Christ-'mas number, and also a good Christmas margin for our 'meeting at Gadshill. I shall be very glad to have the

Brother-in-law's death. *Ante*, 216.

Interruption to Readings.

Funeral of Mr. Arthur Smith.

* 'There was a very touching thing in the Chapel' (at Brompton). 'When 'the body was to be taken up and carried to the grave, there stepped out, 'instead of the undertaker's men with their hideous paraphernalia, the men 'who had always been with the two brothers at the Egyptian Hall; and they, 'in their plain, decent, own mourning clothes, carried the poor fellow away. 'Also, standing about among the gravestones, dressed in black, I noticed every 'kind of person who had ever had to do with him—from our own gas man and 'doorkeepers and billstickers, up to Johnson the printer and that class of man. 'The father and Albert and he now lie together, and the grave, I suppose, will 'be no more disturbed. I wrote a little inscription for the stone, and it is 'quite full.'

'money that I expect to get; but it will be earned.' That November interval was also the date of the marriage of his eldest son to the daughter of Mr. Evans, so long, in connection with Mr. Bradbury, his publisher and printer.

Eldest son's marriage.

The start of the readings at Norwich was not good, so many changes of vexation having been incident to the opening announcements as to leave some doubt of their fulfilment. But the second night, when trial was made of the *Nickleby* scenes, 'wé had a splendid hall, and I think '*Nickleby* will top all the readings. Somehow it seems 'to have got in it, by accident, exactly the qualities best 'suited to the purpose; and it went last night, not only 'with roars, but with a general hilarity and pleasure that 'I have never seen surpassed.'* From this night onward, the success was uninterrupted, and here was his report to me from Brighton on the 8th of November. 'We turned 'away half Dover and half Hastings and half Colchester; 'and, if you can believe such a thing, I may tell you that 'in round numbers we find 1000 stalls already taken here 'in Brighton! I left Colchester in a heavy snow-storm. 'To-day it is so warm here that I can hardly bear the fire, 'and am writing with the window open down to the ground. 'Last night I had a most charming audience for *Copper-'field*, with a delicacy of perception that really made the 'work delightful. It is very pretty to see the girls and

Effect of *Nickleby*.

Audience at Brighton.

* Of his former manager he writes in the same letter: 'I miss him dread-'fully. The sense I used to have of compactness and comfort about me while 'I was reading, is quite gone; and on my coming out for the ten minutes, 'when I used to find him always ready for me with something cheerful to say, 'it is forlorn. . . Besides which, H. and all the rest of them are always 'somewhere, and he was always everywhere.

DOVER: 1861.

'women generally, in the matter of Dora; and everywhere 'I have found that peculiar personal relation between my 'audience and myself on which I counted most when I 'entered on this enterprise. *Nickleby* continues to go in 'the wildest manner.'

A storm.

A storm was at this time sweeping round the coast, and while at Dover he had written of it to his sister-in-law (7th of November): 'The bad weather has not in the least 'touched us, and the storm was most magnificent at Dover. 'All the great side of the Lord Warden next the sea had 'to be emptied, the break of the waves was so prodigious, 'and the noise so utterly confounding. The sea came in 'like a great sky of immense clouds, for ever breaking sud-'denly into furious rain; all kinds of wreck were washed 'in; among other things, a very pretty brass-bound chest 'being thrown about like a feather ... The unhappy Ostend 'packet, unable to get in or go back, beat about the Channel 'all Tuesday night, and until noon yesterday; when I saw 'her come in, with five men at the wheel, a picture of 'misery inconceivable ... The effect of the readings at 'Hastings and Dover really seems to have outdone the 'best usual impression; and at Dover they wouldn't go, 'but sat applauding like mad. The most delicate audience 'I have seen in any provincial place, is Canterbury' ('an in-'telligent and delightful response in them,' he wrote to his daughter, 'like the touch of a beautiful instrument'); 'but 'the audience with the greatest sense of humour certainly 'is Dover. The people in the stalls set the example of 'laughing, in the most curiously unreserved way; and they 'laughed with such really cordial enjoyment, when Squeers

Audiences at Canterbury and Dover.

'read the boys' letters, that the contagion extended to me. 'For, one couldn't hear them without laughing too . . . So, 'I am thankful to say, all goes well, and the recompense 'for the trouble is in every way Great.'

NEW-CASTLE: 1861.

From the opposite quarter of Berwick-on-Tweed he wrote again in the midst of storm. But first his mention of Newcastle, which he had also taken on his way to Edinburgh, reading two nights there, should be given. 'At New-'castle, against the very heavy expenses, I made more 'than a hundred guineas profit. A finer audience there is 'not in England, and I suppose them to be a specially 'earnest people; for, while they can laugh till they shake 'the roof, they have a very unusual sympathy with what is 'pathetic or passionate. An extraordinary thing occurred 'on the second night. The room was tremendously crowded 'and my gas-apparatus fell down. There was a terrible 'wave among the people for an instant, and God knows 'what destruction of life a rush to the stairs would have 'caused. Fortunately a lady in the front of the stalls ran 'out towards me, exactly in a place where I knew that the 'whole hall could see her. So I addressed her, laughing, 'and half-asked and half-ordered her to sit down again; 'and, in a moment, it was all over. But the men in 'attendance had such a fearful sense of what might have 'happened (besides the real danger of Fire) that they 'positively shook the boards I stood on, with their trem-'bling, when they came up to put things right. I am 'proud to record that the gas-man's sentiment, as delivered 'afterwards, was, "The more you want of the master, the '"more you'll find in him." With which complimentary

Alarming scene.

Gas-man's compliment to his master.

BERWICK-ON-TWEED: 1861.

'homage, and with the wind blowing so that I can hardly 'hear myself write, I conclude.'*

It was still blowing, in shape of a gale from the sea, when, an hour before the reading, he wrote from the King's Arms at Berwick-on-Tweed. 'As odd and out of 'the way a place to be at, it appears to me, as ever was 'seen! And such a ridiculous room designed for me to 'read in! An immense Corn Exchange, made of glass 'and iron, round, dome-topp'd, lofty, utterly absurd for 'any such purpose, and full of thundering echoes; with a 'little lofty crow's nest of a stone gallery, breast high, 'deep in the wall, into which it was designed to put—— '*me!* I instantly struck, of course; and said I would 'either read in a room attached to this house (a very snug 'one, capable of holding 500 people), or not at all. Terri-'fied local agents glowered, but fell prostrate, and my 'men took the primitive accommodation in hand. Ever

Impromptu reading-hall.

* The more detailed account of the scene which he wrote to his daughter is also well worth giving. 'A most tremendous hall here last night. Something 'almost terrible in the cram. A fearful thing might have happened. Sud-'denly when they were all very still over Smike, my Gas Batten came down, and 'it looked as if the room were falling. There were three great galleries crammed 'to the roof, and a high steep flight of stairs; and a panic must have destroyed 'numbers of people. A lady in the front row of stalls screamed, and ran out 'wildly towards me, and for one instant there was a terrible wave in the crowd. 'I addressed that lady, laughing (for I knew she was in sight of everybody 'there), and called out as if it happened every night—"There's nothing the '"matter I assure you; don't be alarmed; pray sit down——" and she sat 'down directly, and there was a thunder of applause. It took some five 'minutes to mend, and I looked on with my hands in my pockets; for I think if 'I had turned my back for a moment, there might still have been a move. My 'people were dreadfully alarmed—Boycott' (the gas-man) 'in particular, who I 'suppose had some notion that the whole place might have taken fire—"but there '"stood the master," he did me the honour to say afterwards, in addressing the 'rest, "as cool as ever I see him a lounging at a Railway Station."'

More of the alarm at Newcastle.

'since, I am alarmed to add, the people (who besought the 'honour of the visit) have been coming in numbers quite 'irreconcileable with the appearance of the place, and 'what is to be the end I do not know. It was poor Arthur 'Smith's principle that a town on the way paid the expenses 'of a long through-journey, and therefore I came.' The Reading paid more than those expenses.

BERWICK-ON-TWEED: 1861.

SCOTLAND.

Enthusiastic greeting awaited him in Edinburgh. 'We had in the hall exactly double what we had on the 'first night last time. The success of *Copperfield* was per- 'fectly unexampled. Four great rounds of applause with 'a burst of cheering at the end, and every point taken in 'the finest manner.' But this was nothing to what befell on the second night, when, by some mistake of the local agents, the tickets issued were out of proportion to the space available. Writing from Glasgow next day (3rd of December) he described the scene. 'Such a pouring of 'hundreds into a place already full to the throat, such in- 'describable confusion, such a rending and tearing of dresses, 'and yet such a scene of good humour on the whole, I 'never saw the faintest approach to. While I addressed the 'crowd in the room, G addressed the crowd in the street. 'Fifty frantic men got up in all parts of the hall and ad- 'dressed me all at once. Other frantic men made speeches 'to the walls. The whole B family were borne in on the top 'of a wave, and landed with their faces against the front of 'the platform. I read with the platform crammed with 'people. I got them to lie down upon it, and it was like 'some impossible tableau or gigantic pic-nic—one pretty 'girl in full dress, lying on her side all night, holding on

*Ante*, 205.

Over-issue of tickets.

Confusion and good-humour.

EDINBURGH: 1861.

'to one of the legs of my table! It was the most extraordinary sight. And yet, from the moment I began to 'the moment of my leaving off, they never missed a point, 'and they ended with a burst of cheers. . . . The expenditure of lungs and spirits was (as you may suppose) rather

Results of excitement.

'great; and to sleep well was out of the question. I am 'therefore rather fagged to-day; and as the hall in which 'I read to-night is a large one, I must make my letter a 'short one. . . . My people were torn to ribbons last 'night. They have not a hat among them—and scarcely 'a coat.' He came home for his Christmas rest by way of Manchester, and thus spoke of the reading there on the 14th of December. '*Copperfield* in the Free Trade 'Hall last Saturday was really a grand scene.'

PROVINCES: 1862.

He was in southern latitudes after Christmas, and on the 8th of January wrote from Torquay: 'We are now in 'the region of small rooms, and therefore this trip will not 'be as profitable as the long one. I imagine the room 'here to be very small. Exeter I know, and that is small 'too. I am very much used up on the whole, for I cannot 'bear this moist warm climate. It would kill me very soon. 'And I have now got to the point of taking so much out 'of myself with *Copperfield* that I might as well do Richard

Torquay.

'Wardour . . . This is a very pretty place—a compound 'of Hastings, Tunbridge Wells, and little bits of the hills 'about Naples; but I met four respirators as I came up 'from the station, and three pale curates without them who 'seemed in a bad way.' They had been not bad omens, however. The success was good, at both Torquay and Exeter; and he closed the month, and this series of the country readings, at the great towns of Liverpool and Chester. 'The beautiful St. George's Hall crowded to excess last 'night' (28th of January 1862) 'and numbers turned 'away. Brilliant to see when lighted up, and for a reading 'simply perfect. You remember that a Liverpool audience 'is usually dull; but they put me on my mettle last night, 'for I never saw such an audience—no, not even in Edin-'burgh! The agents (alone, and of course without any 'reference to ready money at the doors) had taken for the 'two readings two hundred pounds.' But as the end approached the fatigues had told severely on him. He described himself sleeping horribly, and with head dazed and worn by gas and heat. Rest, before he could resume at the St. James's Hall in March, was become an absolute necessity.

PROVINCES: 1862.

Liverpool.

Two brief extracts from letters of the dates respectively of the 8th of April * and the 28th of June will sufficiently describe the London readings. 'The money returns have 'been quite astounding. Think of £190 a night! The 'effect of *Copperfield* exceeds all the expectations which 'its success in the country led me to form. It seems to 'take people entirely by surprise. If this is not new to

Metropolitan success.

* The letter referred also to the death of his American friend Professor Felton. 'Your mention of poor Felton's death is a shock of surprise as 'well as grief to me, for I had not heard a word about it. Mr. Fields told me 'when he was here that the effect of that hotel disaster of bad drinking 'water had not passed away; so I suppose, as you do, that he sank under it. 'Poor dear Felton! It is 20 years since I told you of the delight my first 'knowledge of him gave me, and it is as strongly upon me to this hour. I wish 'our ways had crossed a little oftener, but that would not have made it better 'for us now. Alas! alas! all ways have the same finger-post at the head of 'them, and at every turning in them.'

Death of C. C. Felton, i. 295, 301.

LONDON: 1862.

'you, I have not a word of news. The rain that raineth 'every day seems to have washed news away or got it under 'water.' That was in April. In June he wrote: 'I finished 'my readings on Friday night to an enormous hall—nearly '£200. The success has been throughout complete. It 'seems almost suicidal to leave off with the town so full, 'but I don't like to depart from my public pledge. A man 'from Australia is in London ready to pay £10,000 for eight 'months there. If——' It was an If that troubled him for some time, and led to agitating discussion. The civil war having closed America, an increase made upon the just-named offer tempted him to Australia. He tried to familiarize himself with the fancy that he should thus also get new material for observation, and he went so far as to plan an Uncommercial Traveller Upside Down.* It is

Offer from Australia.

An Australian scheme.

Case for and against Australia.

* I give the letter in which he put the scheme formally before me, after the renewed and larger offers had been submitted. 'If there were reasonable 'hope and promise, I could make up my mind to go to Australia and get 'money. I would not accept the Australian people's offer. I would take no 'money from them; would bind myself to nothing with them; but would 'merely make them my agents at such and such a per centage, and go and 'read there. I would take some man of literary pretensions as a secretary '(Charles Collins? What think you?) and with his aid' (he afterwards made the proposal to his old friend Mr. Thomas Beard) 'would do, for *All the Year 'Round* while I was away, The Uncommercial Traveller Upside Down. If 'the notion of these speculators be anything like accurate, I should come 'back rich. I should have seen a great deal of novelty to boot. I should 'have been very miserable too. . . Of course one cannot possibly count upon 'the money to be realized by a six months' absence, but £12,000 is supposed 'to be a low estimate. Mr. S. brought me letters from members of the legislature, newspaper editors, and the like, exhorting me to come, saying how much 'the people talk of me, and dwelling on the kind of reception that would 'await me. No doubt this is so, and of course a great deal of curious experi'ence for after use would be gained over and above the money. Being my 'own master too, I could "work" myself more delicately than if I bound 'myself for money beforehand. A few years hence, if all other circumstances

however very doubtful if such a scheme would have been entertained for a moment, but for the unwonted difficulties of invention that were now found to beset a twenty-number story. Such a story had lately been in his mind, and he had just chosen the title for it (*Our Mutual Friend*); but still he halted and hesitated sorely. 'If it was not' (he wrote on the 5th of October 1862) 'for the hope of a gain 'that would make me more independent of the worst, I 'could not look the travel and absence and exertion in the 'face. I know perfectly well beforehand how unspeakably 'wretched I should be. But these renewed and larger 'offers tempt me. I can force myself to go aboard a ship, 'and I can force myself to do at that reading-desk what I 'have done a hundred times; but whether, with all this 'unsettled fluctuating distress in my mind, I could force an 'original book out of it, is another question.' On the 22nd, still striving hard to find reasons to cope with the all but irresistible arguments against any such adventure, which indeed, with everything that then surrounded him, would have been little short of madness, he thus stated his experience of his two circuits of public reading. 'Remember 'that at home here the thing has never missed fire, but invariably does more the second time than it did the first; 'and also that I have got so used to it, and have worked

Writing not always possible.

Reading always possible.

Experiences.

'were the same, I might not be so well fitted for the excessive wear and tear. 'This is about the whole case. But pray do not suppose that I am in my own 'mind favourable to going, or that I have any fancy for going.' That was late in October. From Paris in November (1862), he wrote: 'I mentioned 'the question to Bulwer when he dined with us here last Sunday, and he was 'all for going. He said that not only did he think the whole population 'would go to the Readings, but that the country would strike me in some 'quite new aspect for a Book; and that wonders might be done with such 'book in the way of profit, over there as well as here.'

LONDON: 1862.

'so hard at it, as to get out of it more than I ever thought 'was in it for that purpose. I think all the probabilities 'for such a country as Australia are immense.' The terrible difficulty was that the home argument struck both ways. 'If I were to go it would be a penance and a misery, 'and I dread the thought more than I can possibly express. 'The domestic life of the Readings is all but intolerable to 'me when I am away for a few weeks at a time merely, 'and what would it be——.' On the other hand it was also a thought of home, far beyond the mere personal loss or gain of it, that made him willing still to risk even so much misery and penance; and he had a fancy that it might be possible to take his eldest daughter with him. 'It is useless and needless for me to say what the conflict 'in my own mind is. How painfully unwilling I am to 'go, and yet how painfully sensible that perhaps I ought 'to go—with all the hands upon my skirts that I cannot 'fail to feel and see there, whenever I look round. It is a 'struggle of no common sort, as you will suppose, you who 'know the circumstances of the struggler.' It closed at once when he clearly saw that to take any of his family with him, and make satisfactory arrangement for the rest during such an absence, would be impossible. By this time also he began to find his way to the new story, and better hopes and spirits had returned.

Home argument Against.

Home argument For.

FRANCE: 1863.

Readings in Paris.

In January 1863 he had taken his daughter and his sister-in-law to Paris, and he read twice at the Embassy in behalf of the British Charitable Fund, the success being such that he consented to read twice again.* He passed his

* A person present thus described (1st of February 1863) the second night

birthday of that year (the 7th of the following month) at Arras. 'You will remember me to-day, I know. Thanks for it. 'An odd birthday, but I am as little out of heart as you 'would have me be—floored now and then, but coming up 'again at the call of Time. I wanted to see this town, 'birthplace of our amiable Sea Green' (Robespierre); 'and 'I find a Grande Place so very remarkable and picturesque 'that it is astonishing how people miss it. Here too I 'found, in a bye-country place just near, a Fair going on, 'with a Religious Richardson's in it—THÉÂTRE RELIGIEUX '—"donnant six fois par jour, l'histoire de la Croix en '"tableaux vivants, depuis la naissance de notre Seigneur '"jusqu'à son sepulture. Aussi l'immolation d'Isaac, par '"son père Abraham." It was just before nightfall when 'I came upon it; and one of the three wise men was up to 'his eyes in lamp oil, hanging the moderators. A woman 'in blue and fleshings (whether an angel or Joseph's wife 'I don't know) was addressing the crowd through an 'enormous speaking-trumpet; and a very small boy with 'a property lamb (I leave you to judge who *he* was) was 'standing on his head on a barrel-organ.' Returning to England by Boulogne in the same year, as he stepped into the Folkestone boat he encountered a friend, Mr. Charles Manby (for, in recording a trait of character so pleasing and honourable, it is not necessary that I should suppress the name), also passing over to England. 'Taking leave of 'Manby was a shabby man of whom I had some remem-

FRANCE: 1863.

Birthday at Arras.

A religious Richardson's show.

to Miss Dickens. 'No one can imagine the scene of last Friday night at the 'Embassy . . a two hours' storm of excitement and pleasure. They actually 'murmured and applauded right away into their carriages and down the 'street.'

At British Embassy.

FRANCE: 1863.

On the Boulogne pier.

'brance, but whom I could not get into his place in my 'mind. Noticing when we stood out of the harbour that 'he was on the brink of the pier, waving his hat in a deso- 'late manner, I said to Manby, "Surely I know that man." '——"I should think you did," said he; "Hudson!" He 'is living—just living—at Paris, and Manby had brought 'him on. He said to Manby at parting, "I shall not have '"a good dinner again, till you come back." I asked 'Manby why he stuck to him? He said, Because he '(Hudson) had so many people in his power, and had held 'his peace; and because he (Manby) saw so many Nota- 'bilities grand with him now, who were always grovelling 'for "shares" in the days of his grandeur.'

Exiled ex-potentate.

Upon Dickens's arrival in London the second series of his readings was brought to a close; and opportunity may be taken, before describing the third, to speak of the manuscript volume found among his papers, containing Memoranda for use in his writings.

# CHAPTER XII.

## HINTS FOR BOOKS WRITTEN AND UNWRITTEN.

1855—1865.

LONDON: 1855–65.

DICKENS began the Book of Memoranda for possible use in his work, to which occasional reference has been made, in January 1855, six months before the first page of *Little Dorrit* was written; and I find no allusion leading me to suppose, except in one very doubtful instance, that he had made addition to its entries, or been in the habit of resorting to them, after the date of *Our Mutual Friend.* It seems to comprise that interval of ten years in his life.

Book of MS. Memoranda.

In it were put down any hints or suggestions that occurred to him. A mere piece of imagery or fancy, it might be at one time; at another the outline of a subject or a character; then a bit of description or dialogue; no order or sequence being observed in any. Titles for stories were set down too, and groups of names for the actors in them; not the least curious of the memoranda belonging to this class. More rarely, entry is made of some oddity of speech; and he has thus preserved in it, *verbatim et literatim,* what he declared to have been as startling a message as he ever received. A confidential servant at Tavistock House, having conferred on some proposed changes

LONDON: 1855–65.

in his bed-room with the party that was to do the work, delivered this ultimatum to her master. 'The gas-fitter 'says, sir, that he can't alter the fitting of your gas in your 'bed-room without taking up almost the ole of your bed-'room floor, and pulling your room to pieces. He says, of 'course you can have it done if you wish, and he'll do it 'for you and make a good job of it, but he would have to 'destroy your room first, and go entirely under the jistes.'*

Startling message.

It is very interesting in this book, last legacy as it is of the literary remains of such a writer, to compare the way in which fancies were worked out with their beginnings entered in its pages. Those therefore will first be taken that in some form or other appeared afterwards in his writings, with such reference to the latter as may enable the reader to make comparison for himself.

Home of the Barnacles.

'Our House. Whatever it is, it is in a first-rate situation, 'and a fashionable neighbourhood. (Auctioneer called it '"a gentlemanly residence.") A series of little closets 'squeezed up into the corner of a dark street—but a Duke's 'Mansion round the corner. The whole house just large 'enough to hold a vile smell. The air breathed in it, at 'the best of times, a kind of Distillation of Mews.' He made it the home of the Barnacles in *Little Dorrit.*

Original of Mrs. Clennam.

What originally he meant to express by Mrs. Clennam in the same story has narrower limits, and a character less repellent, in the Memoranda than it assumed in the book. 'Bed-ridden (or room-ridden) twenty—five-and-twenty—

* From the same authority proceeded, in answer to a casual question one day, a description of the condition of his wardrobe of which he has also made note in the Memoranda. 'Well, sir, your clothes is all shabby, and your boots 'is all burst.'

'years; any length of time. As to most things, kept at a 'standstill all the while. Thinking of altered streets as 'the old streets—changed things as the unchanged things '—the youth or girl I quarrelled with all those years ago, 'as the same youth or girl now. Brought out of doors by 'an unexpected exercise of my latent strength of character, 'and then how strange!'

LONDON: 1855–65.

Fancies used.

One of the people of the same story who becomes a prominent actor in it, Henry Gowan, a creation on which he prided himself as forcible and new, seems to have risen to his mind in this way. 'I affect to believe that I would 'do anything myself for a ten-pound note, and that any-'body else would. I affect to be always book-keeping in 'every man's case, and posting up a little account of good 'and evil with every one. Thus the greatest rascal becomes '"the dearest old fellow," and there is much less difference 'than you would be inclined to suppose between an honest 'man and a scoundrel. While I affect to be finding good 'in most men, I am in reality decrying it where it really 'is, and setting it up where it is not. Might not a pre-'sentation of this far from uncommon class of character, 'if I could put it strongly enough, be likely to lead some 'men to reflect, and change a little? I think it has never 'been done.'

Too much impartiality between evil and good.

In *Little Dorrit* also will be found a picture which seems to live with a more touching effect in his first pleasing fancy of it. 'The ferryman on a peaceful river, 'who has been there from youth, who lives, who grows old, 'who does well, who does ill, who changes, who dies—the 'river runs six hours up and six hours down, the current

River and ferryman.

LONDON: 1855–65.

'sets off that point, the same allowance must be made for 'the drifting of the boat, the same tune is always played 'by the rippling water against the prow.'

Notions for *Little Dorrit.*

Here was an entry made when the thought occurred to him of the close of old Dorrit's life. 'First sign of the 'father failing and breaking down. Cancels long interval. 'Begins to talk about the turnkey who first called him the 'Father of the Marshalsea—as if he were still living. "Tell '"Bob I want to speak to him. See if he is on the Lock, '"my dear."' And here was the first notion of Clennam's reverse of fortune. 'His falling into difficulty, and himself 'imprisoned in the Marshalsea. Then she, out of all her 'wealth and changed station, comes back in her old dress, 'and devotes herself in the old way.'

My lord and his followers.

He seems to have designed, for the sketches of society in the same tale, a 'Full-length portrait of his lordship, 'surrounded by worshippers;' of which, beside that brief memorandum, only his first draft of the general outline was worked at. 'Sensible men enough, agreeable men 'enough, independent men enough in a certain way;—but 'the moment they begin to circle round my lord, and to 'shine with a borrowed light from his lordship, heaven 'and earth how mean and subservient! What a competi'tion and outbidding of each other in servility.'

The last of the Memoranda hints which were used in the story whose difficulties at its opening seem first to have suggested them, ran thus: 'The unwieldy ship taken 'in tow by the snorting little steam tug'—by which was prefigured the patriarch Casby and his agent Panks.

In a few lines are the germ of the tale called *Hunted*

*Down:* 'Devoted to the Destruction of a man. Revenge 'built up on love. The secretary in the Wainewright 'case, who had fallen in love (or supposed he had) with 'the murdered girl.'—The hint on which he worked in his description of the villain of that story, is also in the Memoranda. 'The man with his hair parted straight up the 'front of his head, like an aggravating gravel-walk. Always 'presenting it to you. "Up here, if you please. Neither '"to the right nor left. Take me exactly in this direction. '"Straight up here. Come off the grass—"'

LONDON: 1855–65.

Original of *Hunted Down.*

His first intention as to the *Tale of Two Cities* was to write it upon a plan proposed in this manuscript book. 'How as to a story in two periods—with a lapse of time 'between, like a French Drama? Titles for such a notion. 'TIME! THE LEAVES OF THE FOREST. SCATTERED LEAVES. 'THE GREAT WHEEL. ROUND AND ROUND. OLD LEAVES. 'LONG AGO. FAR APART. FALLEN LEAVES. FIVE AND 'TWENTY YEARS. YEARS AND YEARS. ROLLING YEARS. 'DAY AFTER DAY. FELLED TREES. MEMORY CARTON. 'ROLLING STONES. TWO GENERATIONS.' That special title of *Memory Carton* shows that what led to the greatest success of the book as written was always in his mind; and another of the memoranda is this rough hint of the character itself. 'The drunken?—dissipated?—What?— 'LION—and his JACKALL and Primer, stealing down to 'him at unwonted hours.'

Titles for *Tale of Two Cities.*

First germ of *Carton.*

The studies of Silas Wegg and his patron as they exist in *Our Mutual Friend,* are hardly such good comedy as in the form which the first notion of them seems to have intended. 'Gibbon's Decline and Fall. The two cha-

Hints for *Mutual Friend.*

LONDON: 1855–65.

Wegg and Boffin.

'racters. One reporting to the other as he reads. Both 'getting confused as to whether it is not all going on now.' In the same story may be traced, more or less clearly, other fancies which had found their first expression in the Memoranda. A touch for Bella Wilfer is here. 'Buying 'poor shabby—FATHER?—a new hat. So incongruous 'that it makes him like African King Boy, or King George; 'who is usually full dressed when he has nothing upon 'him but a cocked hat or a waistcoat.' Here undoubtedly is the voice of Podsnap. 'I stand by my friends and ac-'quaintances;—not for their sakes, but because they are '*my* friends and acquaintances. *I* know them, *I* have 'licensed them, they have taken out *my* certificate. Ergo, 'I champion them as myself.' To the same redoubtable person another trait clearly belongs. 'And by denying a 'thing, supposes that he altogether puts it out of exist-'ence.' A third very perfectly expresses the boy, ready for mischief, who does all the work there is to be done in Eugene Wrayburn's place of business. 'The office boy for 'ever looking out of window, who never has anything to do.'

Bella Wilfer.

Podsnap.

Office boy.

The poor wayward purposeless good-hearted master of the boy, Eugene himself, is as evidently in this: 'If they 'were great things, I, the untrustworthy man in little 'things, would do them earnestly——But O No, I wouldn't!' What follows has a more direct reference; being indeed almost literally copied in the story. 'As to the question 'whether I, Eugene, lying ill and sick even unto death, 'may be consoled by the representation that coming 'through this illness, I shall begin a new life, and have 'energy and purpose and all I have yet wanted: "*I*

Eugene.

'"*hope* I should, but *I know* I shouldn't. Let me die, my '"dear."' LONDON: 1855–65.

In connection with the same book, the last in that form which he lived to complete, another fancy may be copied from which, though not otherwise worked out in the tale, the relation of Lizzie Hexam to her brother was taken. 'A man, and his wife—or daughter—or niece. The man, 'a reprobate and ruffian; the woman (or girl) with good 'in her, and with compunctions. He believes nothing, and 'defies everything; yet has suspicions always, that she is '"praying against" his evil schemes, and making them go 'wrong. He is very much opposed to this, and is always 'angrily harping on it. "If she *must* pray, why can't she '"pray in their favour, instead of going against 'em? She's '"always ruining me—she always is—and calls that, Duty! '"There's a religious person! Calls it Duty to fly in my '"face! Calls it Duty to go sneaking against me!"'

Reprobate's notion of Duty.

Other fancies preserved in his Memoranda were left wholly unemployed, receiving from him no more permanent form of any kind than that which they have in this touching record; and what most people would probably think the most attractive and original of all the thoughts he had thus set down for future use, are those that were never used.

Fancies never used.

Here were his first rough notes for the opening of a story. 'Beginning with the breaking up of a large party of guests 'at a country house: house left lonely with the shrunken 'family in it: guests spoken of, and introduced to the 'reader that way.—OR, beginning with a house abandoned 'by a family fallen into reduced circumstances. Their old

Proposed opening for a story.

LONDON: 1855–65.

House abandoned by fallen family.

'furniture there, and numberless tokens of their old com-'forts. Inscriptions under the bells downstairs—"Mr. '"John's Room," "Miss Caroline's Room." Great gardens 'trimly kept to attract a tenant: but no one in them. A 'landscape without figures. Billiard room: table covered 'up, like a body. Great stables without horses, and great 'coach-houses without carriages. Grass growing in the 'chinks of the stone-paving, this bright cold winter day. '*Downhills*.' Another opening had also suggested itself to him. 'Open a story by bringing two strongly con-'trasted places and strongly contrasted sets of people, into 'the connexion necessary for the story, by means of an 'electric message. Describe the message—*be* the message '—flashing along through space, over the earth, and under 'the sea.'* Connected with which in some way would seem to be this other notion, following it in the Memoranda. 'Representing London—or Paris, or any other great place '—in the new light of being actually unknown to all the 'people in the story, and only taking the colour of their 'fears and fancies and opinions. So getting a new aspect, 'and being unlike itself. An *odd* unlikeness of itself.'

Uses for an electric message.

Great cities under new aspects.

The subjects for stories are various, and some are striking. There was one he clung to much, and thought of frequently as in a special degree available for a series of papers in

Idea for a book.

* The date when this fancy dropped into his Memoranda is fixed by the following passage in a letter to me of the 25th of August 1862. 'I am trying 'to coerce my thoughts into hammering out the Christmas number. And I 'have an idea of opening a book (not the Christmas number—a book) by 'bringing together two strongly contrasted places and two strongly contrasted 'sets of people, with which and with whom the story is to rest, through the 'agency of an electric message. I think a fine thing might be made of the 'message itself shooting over the land and under the sea, and it would be a 'curious way of sounding the key note.'

his periodical; but when he came to close quarters with it the difficulties were found to be too great. 'English land-'scape. The beautiful prospect, trim fields, clipped hedges, 'everything so neat and orderly—gardens, houses, roads. 'Where are the people who do all this? There must be a 'great many of them, to do it. Where are they all? And 'are *they*, too, so well kept and so fair to see? Suppose 'the foregoing to be wrought out by an Englishman: say, 'from China: who knows nothing about his native country.' To which may be added a fancy that savours of the same mood of discontent, political and social. 'How do I know 'that I, a man, am to learn from insects—unless it is to 'learn how little my littlenesses are? All that bothera-'tion in the hive about the queen bee, may be, in little, 'me and the court circular.'

England first seen by an Englishman.

Insects and men.

A domestic story he had met with in the State Trials struck him greatly by its capabilities, and I may preface it by mentioning another subject, not entered in the Memoranda, which for a long time impressed him as capable of attractive treatment. It was after reading one of the witch-trials that this occurred to him; and the heroine was to be a girl who for a special purpose had taken a witch's disguise, and whose trick was not discovered until she was actually at the stake. Here is the State Trials story as told by Dickens. 'There is a case in the State 'Trials, where a certain officer made love to a (supposed) 'miser's daughter, and ultimately induced her to give her 'father slow poison, while nursing him in sickness. Her 'father discovered it, told her so, forgave her, and said '"Be patient my dear—I shall not live long, even if I re-

Touching fancy.

Miser's daughter.

LONDON: 1855–65.

Story from State Trials.

'" cover: and then you shall have all my wealth." Though 'penitent then, she afterwards poisoned him again (under 'the same influence), and successfully. Whereupon it ap-'peared that the old man had no money at all, and had 'lived on a small annuity which died with him, though 'always feigning to be rich. He had loved this daughter 'with great affection.'

Father and son's wife.

A theme touching closely on ground that some might think dangerous, is sketched in the following fancy. 'The 'father (married young) who, in perfect innocence, venerates 'his son's young wife, as the realization of his ideal of 'woman. (He not happy in his own choice.) The son 'slights her, and knows nothing of her worth. The father 'watches her, protects her, labours for her, endures for her, '—is for ever divided between his strong natural affection 'for his son as his son, and his resentment against him as 'this young creature's husband.' Here is another, less dangerous, which he took from an actual occurrence made known to him when he was at Bonchurch. 'The idea of 'my being brought up by my mother (me the narrator), 'my father being dead; and growing up in this belief until 'I find that my father is the gentleman I have sometimes 'seen, and oftener heard of, who has the handsome young 'wife, and the dog I once took notice of when I was a 'little child, and who lives in the great house and drives 'about.'

Daughter and unknown father.

Very admirable is this. 'The girl separating herself 'from the lover who has shewn himself unworthy—loving 'him still—living single for his sake—but never more re-'newing their old relations. Coming to him when they are 'both grown old, and nursing him in his last illness.' Nor is the following less so. 'Two girls *mis-marrying* two 'men. The man who has evil in him, dragging the superior 'woman down. The man who has good in him, raising the 'inferior woman up.' Dickens would have been at his best in working out both fancies.

Girls mis-marrying.

In some of the most amusing of his sketches of character, women also take the lead. 'The lady un peu passée, who 'is determined to be interesting. No matter how much I 'love that person—nay, the more so for that very reason— 'I MUST flatter, and bother, and be weak and apprehensive 'and nervous, and what not. If I were well and strong, 'agreeable and self-denying, my friend might forget me.' Another not remotely belonging to the same family is as neatly hit off. 'The sentimental woman feels that the 'comic, undesigning, unconscious man, is "Her Fate."—I 'her fate? God bless my soul, it puts me into a cold per-'spiration to think of it. *I* her fate? How can *I* be her 'fate? I don't mean to be. I don't want to have anything 'to do with her.—Sentimental woman perceives neverthe-'less that Destiny must be accomplished.'

Over-interesting.

Sentimentalist and her Fate.

Other portions of a female group are as humorously sketched and hardly less entertaining. 'The enthusias-'tically complimentary person, who forgets you in her own 'flowery prosiness: as—"I have no need to say to a '"person of your genius and feeling, and wide range of '"experience"—and then, being shortsighted, puts up her 'glass to remember who you are.'—'Two sisters' (these were real people known to him). 'One going in for 'being generally beloved (which she is not by any means);

Complimentary.

Female groups.

'and the other for being generally hated (which she needn't 'be).'—'The bequeathed maid-servant, or friend. Left as 'a legacy. And a devil of a legacy too.'—'The woman 'who is never on any account to hear of anything shocking. 'For whom the world is to be of barley-sugar.'—'The lady 'who lives on her enthusiasm; and hasn't a jot.'—'Bright-'eyed creature selling jewels. The stones and the eyes.' Much significance is in the last few words. One may see to what uses Dickens would have turned them.

Fallen women.

A more troubled note is sounded in another of these female characters. 'I am a common woman—fallen. Is 'it devilry in me—is it a wicked comfort—what is it—that 'induces me to be always tempting other women down, 'while I hate myself!' This next, with as much truth in it, goes deeper than the last. 'The prostitute who will 'not let one certain youth approach her. "O let there '"be some one in the world, who having an inclination '"towards me has not gratified it, and has not known me '"in my degradation!" She almost loving him.—Suppose, 'too, this touch in her could not be believed in by his 'mother or mistress: by some handsome and proudly vir-'tuous woman, always revolting from her.' A more agreeable sketch than either follows, though it would not please

Baby-wife.

M. Taine so well. 'The little baby-like married woman—'so strange in her new dignity, and talking with tears in 'her eyes, of her sisters "and all of them" at home. Never 'from home before, and never going back again.' Another from the same manuscript volume not less attractive, which was sketched in his own home, I gave upon a former page

ii. 27.

The female character in its relations with the opposite

sex has lively illustration in the Memoranda. 'The man 'who is governed by his wife, and is heartily despised in 'consequence by all other wives; who still want to govern '*their* husbands, notwithstanding.' An alarming family pair follows that. 'The playful—and scratching—family. 'Father and daughter.' And here is another. 'The agree- 'able (and wicked) young-mature man, and his devoted 'sister.' What next was set down he had himself partly seen; and, by enquiry at the hospital named, had ascertained the truth of the rest. 'The two people in the 'Incurable Hospital.—The poor incurable girl lying on a 'water-bed, and the incurable man who has a strange flir- 'tation with her; comes and makes confidences to her; 'snips and arranges her plants; and rehearses to her the 'comic songs (!) by writing which he materially helps out 'his living.'*

Unpleasant though agreeable.

Two incurables.

Two lighter figures are very pleasantly touched. 'Set of 'circumstances which suddenly bring an easy, airy fellow 'into near relations with people he knows nothing about, 'and has never even seen. This, through his being thrown 'in the way of the innocent young personage of the story. '"Then there is Uncle Sam to be considered," says she. '"Aye to be sure," says he, "so there is! By Jupiter, I

Uncle Sam.

* Following this in the 'Memoranda' is an advertisement cut from the *Times*: of a kind that always expressed to Dickens a child-farming that deserved the gallows quite as much as the worst kind of starving, by way of farming, babies. The fourteen guineas a-year, 'tender' age of the 'dear' ones, maternal care, and no vacations or extras, to him had only one meaning.

Children-farming.

EDUCATION FOR LITTLE CHILDREN.—Terms 14 to 18 guineas per annum; no extras or vacations. The system of education embraces the wide range of each useful and ornamental study suited to the tender age of the dear children. Maternal care and kindness may be relied on.—X., Heald's Library, Fulham-road.

LONDON: 1855-65.

'"forgot Uncle Sam. He's a rock ahead, is Uncle Sam. '"He must be considered, of course; he must be smoothed '"down; he must be cleared out of the way. To be sure. '"I never thought of Uncle Sam.—By the bye, who *is* '"Uncle Sam?"'

There are several such sketches as that, to set against the groups of women; and some have Dickens's favourite vein of satire in them. 'The man whose vista is always 'stopped up by the image of Himself. Looks down a long 'walk, and can't see round himself, or over himself, or 'beyond himself. Is always blocking up his own way. 'Would be such a good thing for him, if he could knock 'himself down.' Another picture of selfishness is touched with greater delicacy. '"Too good" to be grateful to, or 'dutiful to, or anything else that ought to be. "I won't '"thank you: you are too good."—"Don't ask me to '"marry you: you are too good."—In short, I don't par-'ticularly mind ill-using you, and being selfish with you: 'for you are *so* good. Virtue its own reward!' A third, which seems to reverse the dial, is but another face of it: frankly avowing faults, which are virtues. 'In effect—I 'admit I am generous, amiable, gentle, magnanimous. 'Reproach me—I deserve it—I know my faults—I have 'striven in vain to get the better of them.' Dickens would have made much, too, of the working out of the next. 'The knowing man in distress, who borrows a round sum 'of a generous friend. Comes, in depression and tears, 'dines, gets the money, and gradually cheers up over his 'wine, as he obviously entertains himself with the reflec-'tion that his friend is an egregious fool to have lent it to

'Himself' in the way.

Generous selfishness.

Selfish generosity.

Self-knowledge.

'him, and that *he* would have known better.' And so of this other. 'The man who invariably says apposite things '(in the way of reproof or sarcasm) THAT HE DON'T MEAN. 'Astonished when they are explained to him.'

Here is a fancy that I remember him to have been more than once bent upon making use of: but the opportunity never came. 'The two men to be guarded against, 'as to their revenge. One, whom I openly hold in some 'serious animosity, whom I am at the pains to wound and 'defy, and whom I estimate as worth wounding and defy-'ing;—the other, whom I treat as a sort of insect, and 'contemptuously and pleasantly flick aside with my glove. 'But, it turns out to be the latter who is the really dan-'gerous man; and, when I expect the blow from the other, 'it comes from *him*.'

Danger not on the surface.

We have the master hand in the following bit of dialogue, which takes wider application than that for which it appears to have been intended.

'"There is some virtue in him too."

'"Virtue! Yes. So there is in any grain of seed in a '"seedsman's shop—but you must put it in the ground, '"before you can get any good out of it."

How to get good out of a man.

'"Do you mean that *he* must be put in the ground '"before any good comes of *him?*"

'"Indeed I do. You may call it burying him, or you '"may call it sowing him, as you like. You must set him '"in the earth, before you get any good of him."'

One of the entries is a list of persons and places meant to have been made subjects for special description, and it will awaken regret that only as to one of them (the Mugby

Subjects for description.

LONDON: 1855-65.

Unused subjects.

Refreshments) his intention was fulfilled. 'A Vestryman. 'A Briber. A Station Waiting-Room. Refreshments at 'Mugby. A Physician's Waiting-Room. The Royal Aca-'demy. An Antiquary's house. A Sale Room. A Picture 'Gallery (for sale). A Waste-paper Shop. A Post-Office. 'A Theatre.'

All will have been given that have particular interest or value, from this remarkable volume, when the thoughts and fancies I proceed to transcribe have been put before the reader.

---

Fancies not worked upon.

'The man who is incapable of his own happiness. Or 'who is always in pursuit of happiness. Result, Where is 'happiness to be found then? Surely not Everywhere? 'Can that be so, after all? Is *this* my experience?'

---

'The people who persist in defining and analysing their '(and everybody else's) moral qualities, motives and what 'not, at once in the narrowest spirit and the most lumber-'ing manner;—as if one should put up an enormous scaf-'folding for the building of a pigstye.'

---

'The house-full of Toadies and Humbugs. They all 'know and despise one another; but—partly to keep 'their hands in, and partly to make out their own indivi-'dual cases—pretend not to detect one another.'

---

'People realising immense sums of money, imaginatively '—speculatively—counting their chickens before hatched. 'Inflaming each other's imaginations about great gains of 'money, and entering into a sort of intangible, impossible, 'competition as to who is the richer.'

Unused characters.

'The advertising sage, philosopher, and friend: who 'educates "for the bar, the pulpit, or the stage."'

---

'The character of the real refugee—not the conven- 'tional; the real.'

---

'The mysterious character, or characters, interchanging 'confidences. "Necessary to be very careful in that direc- '"tion."—"In what direction?"—"B"—"You don't say '"so. What, do you mean that C——?"—"Is aware of D. '"Exactly."'

---

'The father and boy, as I dramatically see them. Open- 'ing with the wild dance I have in my mind.'

---

Old children.

'The old child. That is to say, born of parents advanced 'in life, and observing the parents of other children to be 'young. Taking an old tone accordingly.'

---

'A thoroughly sulky character—perverting everything. 'Making the good, bad—and the bad, good.'

---

'The people who lay all their sins negligences and ignor- 'ances, on Providence.'

---

'The man who marries his cook at last, after being so 'desperately knowing about the sex.'

---

Showy and mean.

'The swell establishment, frightfully mean and miserable 'in all but the "reception rooms." Those very showy.'

---

'B. tells M. what my opinion is of his work, &c. Quoting 'the man you have once spoken to, as if he had talked a 'life's talk in two minutes.'

LONDON: 1855-65.

Hide and seek.

'A misplaced and mis-married man; always, as it were, 'playing hide and seek with the world; and never finding 'what Fortune seems to have hidden when he was born.'

---

Dead children.

'Certain women in Africa who have lost children, carry 'little wooden images of children on their heads, and always 'put their food to the lips of those images, before tasting it 'themselves. This is in a part of Africa where the mor-'tality among children (judging from the number of these 'little memorials) is very great.'

---

Available names.

Two more entries are the last which he made. 'AVAIL-'ABLE NAMES' introduces a wonderful list in the exact following classes and order; as to which the reader may be left to his own memory for selection of such as found their way into the several stories from *Little Dorrit* to the end. The rest, not lifted into that higher notice by such favour of their creator, must remain like any other undistinguished crowd. But among them may perhaps be detected, by those who have special insight for the physiognomy of a name, some few with so great promise in them of fun and character as will make the 'mute inglorious' fate which has befallen them a subject for special regret; and much ingenious speculation will probably wait upon all. Dickens has generally been thought, by the curious, to display not a few of his most characteristic traits in this particular field of invention.

First there are titles for books; and from the list subjoined were taken two for Christmas numbers and two for stories, though *Nobody's Fault* had ultimately to give way to *Little Dorrit.*

LONDON: 1855–65.

Titles for books.

'THE LUMBER ROOM.
'SOMEBODY'S LUGGAGE.
'TO BE LEFT TILL CALLED FOR.
'SOMETHING WANTED.
'EXTREMES MEET.
'NOBODY'S FAULT.
'THE GRINDSTONE.
'ROKESMITH'S FORGE.
'OUR MUTUAL FRIEND.
'THE CINDER HEAP.
TWO GENERATIONS.
BROKEN CROCKERY.
DUST.
THE HOME DEPARTMENT.
THE YOUNG PERSON.
NOW OR NEVER.
MY NEIGHBOURS.
THE CHILDREN OF THE FATHERS.
NO THOROUGHFARE.'

Then comes a batch of 'Christian names': Girls and Boys: which stand thus, with mention of the source from which he obtained them. These therefore can hardly be called pure invention. Some would have been reckoned too extravagant for anything but reality.

'*Girls from Privy Council Education lists.*

Girls' Christian names.

'LELIA.
'MENELLA.
'RUBINA.
'IRIS.
'REBECCA.
ETTY.
REBINAH.
SEBA.
PERSIA.
ARAMANDA.
DORIS.
BALZINA.
PLEASANT.
GENTILLA.

'*Boys from Privy Council Education lists.*

Boys' Christian names.

'DOCTOR.
'HOMER.
'ODEN.
'BRADLEY.
ZERUBBABEL.
MAXIMILIAN.
URBIN.
SAMILIAS.
PICKLES.
ORANGE.
FEATHER.

'*Girls and Boys from Ditto.*

'AMANDA, ETHLYNIDA; BOETIUS, BOLTIUS.'

To which he adds supplementary lists that appear to be his own.

LONDON: 1855–65.

More names for boys.

*'More Boys.*

| | |
|---|---|
| 'ROBERT LADLE. | GEORGE MUZZLE. |
| 'JOLY STICK. | WALTER ASHES. |
| 'BILL MARIGOLD. | ZEPHANIAH FERRY (or FURY). |
| 'STEPHEN MARQUICK. | WILLIAM WHY. |
| 'JONATHAN KNOTWELL. | ROBERT GOSPEL. |
| 'PHILIP BROWNDRESS. | THOMAS FATHERLY. |
| 'HENRY GHOST. | ROBIN SCUBBAM. |

For girls.

*'More Girls.*

| | |
|---|---|
| 'SARAH GOLDSACKS. | ALICE THORNEYWORK. |
| 'ROSETTA DUST. | SALLY GIMBLET. |
| 'SUSAN GOLDRING. | VERITY HAWKYARD. |
| 'CATHERINE TWO. | BIRDIE NASH. |
| 'MATILDA RAINBIRD. | AMBROSINA EVENTS. |
| 'MIRIAM DENIAL. | APAULINA VERNON. |
| 'SOPHIA DOOMSDAY. | NELTIE ASHFORD.' |

And then come the mass of his 'available names,' which stand thus, without other introduction or comment:

Available names.

| | | |
|---|---|---|
| 'TOWNDLING. | SLYANT. | PEDSEY. |
| 'MOOD. | QUEEDY. | DUNCALF. |
| 'GUFF. | BESSELTHUR. | TRICKLEBANK. |
| 'TREBLE. | MUSTY. | SAPSEA. |
| 'CHILBY. | GROUT. | READYHUFF. |
| 'SPESSIFER. | TERTIUS JOBBER. | DUFTY. |
| 'WODDER. | AMON HEADSTON. | FOGGY. |
| 'WHELPFORD. | STRAYSHOTT. | TWINN. |
| 'FENNERCK. | HIGDEN. | BROWNSWORD. |
| 'GANNERSON. | MORFIT. | PEARTREE. |
| 'CHINKERBLE. | GOLDSTRAW. | SUDDS. |
| 'BINTREY. | BARREL. | SILVERMAN. |
| 'FLEDSON. | INGE. | KIMBER. |
| 'HIRLL. | JUMP. | LAUGHLEY. |
| 'BRAYLE. | JIGGINS. | LESSOCK. |
| 'MULLENDER. | BONES. | TIPPINS. |
| 'TRESLINGHAM. | COY. | MINNITT. |
| 'BRANKLE. | DAWN. | RADLOWE. |
| 'SITTERN. | TATKIN. | PRATCHET. |
| 'DOSTONE. | DROWVEY. | MAWDETT. |
| 'CAY-LON. | PUDSEY. | WOZENHAM. |

LONDON: 1855–65.

‘ SNOWELL. WABBLER. STILTWALK.
‘ LOTTRUM. PEEX—SPEEX. STILTINGSTALK.
‘ LAMMLE. GANNAWAY. STILTSTALKING.
‘ FROSER. MRS. FLINKS. RAVENDER.
‘ HOLBLACK. FLINX. PODSNAP.
‘ MULLEY. JEE. CLARRIKER.
‘ REDWORTH. HARDEN. COMPERY.
‘ REDFOOT. MERDLE. STRIVER—STRYVER.
‘ TARBOX (B) MURDEN. PUMBLECHOOK.
‘ TINKLING. TOPWASH. WANGLER.
‘ DUDDLE. PORDAGE. BOFFIN.
‘ JEBUS. DORRET—DORRIT. BANTINCK.
‘ POWDERHILL. CARTON. DIBTON.
‘ GRIMMER. MINIFIE. WILFER.
‘ SKUSE. SLINGO. GLIBBERY.
‘ TITCOOMBE. JOAD. MULVEY.
‘ CRABBLE. KINCH. HORLICK.
‘ SWANNOCK. MAG. DOOLGE.
‘ TUZZEN. CHELLYSON. GANNERY.
‘ TWEMLOW. BLENNAM—CL. GARGERY.
‘ SQUAB. BARDOCK. WILLSHARD.
‘ JACKMAN. SNIGSWORTH. RIDERHOOD.
‘ SUGG. SWENTON. PRATTERSTONE.
‘ BREMMIDGE. CASBY—BEACH. CHINKIBLE.
‘ SILAS BLODGET. LOWLEIGH—LOWELY. WOPSELL.
‘ MELVIN BEAL. PIGRIN. WOPSLE.
‘ BUTTRICK. YERBURY. WHELPINGTON.
‘ EDSON. PLORNISH. WHELPFORD.
‘ SANLORN. MAROON. GAYVERY.
‘ LIGHTWORD. BANDY-NANDY. WEGG.
‘ TITBULL. STONEBURY. HUBBLE.
‘ BANGHAM. MAGWITCH. URRY.
‘ KYLE—NYLE. MEAGLES. KIBBLE.
‘ PEMBLE. PANCKS. SKIFFINS.
‘ MAXEY. HAGGAGE. WODDER.
‘ ROKESMITH. PROVIS. ETSER.
‘ CHIVERY. STILTINGTON. AKERSHEM.’

Available names.

The last of the Memoranda, and the last words written by Dickens in the blank paper book containing them, are these. ‘“Then I’ll give up snuff.” Brobity.—An alarming ‘sacrifice. Mr. Brobity’s snuff-box. The Pawnbroker’s

LONDON: 1855-65.

Mr. Brobity's snuff-box.

'account of it?' What was proposed by this must be left to conjecture; but 'Brobity' is the name of one of the people in his unfinished story, and the suggestion may have been meant for some incident in it. If so, it is the only passage in the volume which can be in any way connected with the piece of writing on which he was last engaged. Some names were taken for it from the lists, but there is otherwise nothing to recall *Edwin Drood.*

# CHAPTER XIII.

## THIRD SERIES OF READINGS.

1864—1867.

LONDON: 1864.

THE sudden death of Thackeray on the Christmas eve of 1863 was a painful shock to Dickens. It would not become me to speak, when he has himself spoken, of his relations with so great a writer and so old a friend.

Death of Thackeray.

'I saw him first, nearly twenty-eight years ago, when he 'proposed to become the illustrator of my earliest book. I 'saw him last,* shortly before Christmas, at the Athenæum 'Club, when he told me that he had been in bed three 'days . . . and that he had it in his mind to try a new 'remedy which he laughingly described. He was cheerful, 'and looked very bright. In the night of that day week, 'he died. The long interval between these two periods is 'marked in my remembrance of him by many occasions 'when he was extremely humorous, when he was irresistibly

Estrangement.

* There had been some estrangement between them since the autumn of 1858, hardly now worth mention even in a note. Thackeray, justly indignant at a published description of himself by the member of a club to which both he and Dickens belonged, referred it to the Committee, who decided to expel the writer. Dickens, thinking expulsion too harsh a penalty for an offence thoughtlessly given, and, as far as might be, manfully atoned for by withdrawal and regret, interposed to avert that extremity. Thackeray resented the interference, and Dickens was justly hurt by the manner in which he did so. Neither was wholly right, nor was either altogether in the wrong.

LONDON: 1864.

'extravagant, when he was softened and serious, when he 'was charming with children. . . No one can be surer than 'I, of the greatness and goodness of his heart. . . In no 'place should I take it upon myself at this time to dis- 'course of his books, of his refined knowledge of character, 'of his subtle acquaintance with the weaknesses of human 'nature, of his delightful playfulness as an essayist, of his 'quaint and touching ballads, of his mastery over the Eng- 'lish language. . . But before me lies all that he had 'written of his latest story . . . and the pain I have felt 'in perusing it has not been deeper than the conviction 'that he was in the healthiest vigour of his powers when 'he worked on this last labour. . . The last words he cor- 'rected in print were "And my heart throbbed with an '"exquisite bliss." God grant that on that Christmas Eve 'when he laid his head back on his pillow and threw up 'his arms as he had been wont to do when very weary, 'some consciousness of duty done, and of Christian hope 'throughout life humbly cherished, may have caused his 'own heart so to throb, when he passed away to his Re- 'deemer's rest. He was found peacefully lying as above 'described, composed, undisturbed, and to all appearance 'asleep.'

Dickens on Thackeray.

*Cornhill Magazine* for February 1864.

Other griefs were with Dickens at this time, and close upon them came the too certain evidence that his own health was yielding to the overstrain which had been placed upon it by the occurrences and anxieties of the few preceding years. His mother, whose infirm health had been tending for more than two years to the close, died in September 1863; and on his own birthday in the follow-

Mother's death.

LONDON: 1864.

Death of his second son.

ing February he had tidings of the death of his second son Walter, on the last day of the old year, in the officers' hospital at Calcutta; to which he had been sent up invalided from his station, on his way home. He was a lieutenant in the 26th Native Infantry regiment, and had been doing duty with the 42nd Highlanders. In 1853 his father had thus written to the youth's godfather, Walter Savage Landor: 'Walter is a very good boy, and comes 'home from school with honorable commendation and a 'prize into the bargain. He never gets into trouble, for he 'is a great favourite with the whole house and one of the 'most amiable boys in the boy-world. He comes out on 'birthdays in a blaze of shirt pin.' The pin was a present from Landor; to whom three years later, when the boy had obtained his cadetship through the kindness of Miss Coutts, Dickens wrote again. 'Walter has done extremely well 'at school; has brought home a prize in triumph; and 'will be eligible to "go up" for his India examination soon 'after next Easter. Having a direct appointment he will 'probably be sent out soon after he has passed, and so will 'fall into that strange life "up the country" before he well 'knows he is alive, or what life is—which indeed seems 'to be rather an advanced state of knowledge.' If he had lived another month he would have reached his twenty-third year, and perhaps not then the advanced state of knowledge his father speaks of. But, never forfeiting his claim to those kindly paternal words, he had the goodness and simplicity of boyhood to the last.

Walter Dickens.

Promise of boyhood.

Dickens had at this time begun his last story in twenty numbers, and my next chapter will show through what

LONDON: 1864.

*Our Mutual Friend.*

unwonted troubles, in this and the following year, he had to fight his way. What otherwise during its progress chiefly interested him, was the enterprise of Mr. Fechter at the Lyceum, of which he had become the lessee; and Dickens was moved to this quite as much by generous sympathy with the difficulties of such a position to an artist who was not an Englishman, as by genuine admiration of Mr. Fechter's acting. He became his helper in disputes, adviser on literary points, referee in matters of management; and for some years no face was more familiar than the French comedian's at Gadshill or in the office of his journal. But theatres and their affairs are things of a season, and even Dickens's whim and humour will not revive for us any interest in these. No bad example, however, of the difficulties in which a French actor may find himself with English playwrights, will appear in a few amusing words from one of his letters about a piece played at the Princess's before the Lyceum management was taken in hand.

Mr. Fechter.

Interest in his management.

Revising a play.

'I have been cautioning Fechter about the play whereof he gave the plot and scenes to B; and out of which I 'have struck some enormities, my account of which will (I 'think) amuse you. It has one of the best first acts I ever 'saw; but if he can do much with the last two, not to say 'three, there are resources in his art that *I* know nothing 'about. When I went over the play this day week, he 'was at least 20 minutes, *in a boat, in the last scene,* dis'cussing with another gentleman (also in the boat) whether 'he should kill him or not; after which the gentleman 'dived overboard and swam for it. Also, in the most im-

Ticklish points.

'portant and dangerous parts of the play, there was a 'young person of the name of Pickles who was constantly 'being mentioned by name, in conjunction with the powers 'of light or darkness; as, "Great Heaven! Pickles?"— '"By Hell, 'tis Pickles!"—"Pickles? a thousand Devils!" '"—"Distraction! Pickles?"' *

Sorrowful New Year.

The old year ended and the new one opened sadly enough. The death of Leech in November affected Dickens very much,† and a severe attack of illness in February put

* As I have thus fallen on theatrical subjects, I may add one or two practical experiences which befell Dickens at theatres in the autumn of 1864, when he sallied forth from his office upon these night wanderings to 'cool' a boiling head. 'I went the other night' (8th of October) 'to see the *Streets of* '*London* at the Princess's. A piece that is really drawing all the town, and 'filling the house with nightly overflows. It is the most depressing instance, 'without exception, of an utterly degraded and debased theatrical taste that 'has ever come under my writhing notice. For not only do the audiences—of 'all classes—go, but they are unquestionably delighted. At Astley's there 'has been much puffing at great cost of a certain Miss Ada Isaacs Menkin, who 'is to be seen bound on the horse in *Mazeppa* "ascending the fearful precipices '"not as hitherto done by a dummy." Last night, having a boiling head, I went 'out from here to cool myself on Waterloo Bridge, and I thought I would go and 'see this heroine. Applied at the box-door for a stall. "None left sir." 'For a box-ticket. "Only standing-room sir." Then the man (busy in count-'ing great heaps of veritable checks) recognizes me and says—"Mr. Smith will '"be very much concerned when he hears that you went away sir"—"Never '"mind; I'll come again." "You never go behind I think sir, or—?" "No '"thank you, I never go behind." "Mr. Smith's box, sir—" "No thank '"you, I'll come again." Now who do you think the lady is? If you don't 'already know, ask that question of the highest Irish mountains that look 'eternal, and they'll never tell you—*Mrs. Heenan!*' This lady, who turned out to be one of Dickens's greatest admirers, addressed him at great length on hearing of this occurrence, and afterwards dedicated a volume of poems to him! There was a pleasanter close to his letter. 'Contrariwise I assisted another 'night at the Adelphi (where I couldn't, with careful calculation, get the house 'up to Nine Pounds), and saw quite an admirable performance of Mr. Toole 'and Mrs. Mellon—she, an old servant, wonderfully like Anne—he, showing 'a power of passion very unusual indeed in a comic actor, as such things go, 'and of a quite remarkable kind.'

*Streets of London* at Princess's.

*Mazeppa* at Astley's.

A poetical admirer.

Mr. Toole. *Ante*, 34.

† Writing to me three months before, he spoke of the death of one whom he

LONDON: 1865.

Lameness. *Post*, 477–8.

a broad mark between his past life and what remained to him of the future. The lameness now began in his left foot which never afterwards wholly left him, which was attended by great suffering, and which baffled experienced physicians. He had persisted in his ordinary exercise during heavy snow-storms, and to the last he had the fancy that his illness was merely local. But that this was an error is now certain; and it is more than probable that if the nervous danger and disturbance it implied had been correctly appreciated at the time, its warning might have been of priceless value to Dickens. Unhappily he never thought of husbanding his strength except for the purpose of making fresh demands upon it, and it was for this he took a brief holiday in France during the summer. 'Before I 'went away,' he wrote to his daughter, 'I had certainly 'worked myself into a damaged state. But the moment I 'got away, I began, thank God, to get well. I hope to profit 'by this experience, and to make future dashes from my desk 'before I want them.' At his return he was in the terrible railway accident at Staplehurst, on a day * which proved

Over-confidence.

Fatal anniversary.

had known from his boyhood (*ante*, i. 27–8) and with whom he had fought unsuccessfully for some years against the management of the Literary Fund. 'Poor Dilke! I am very sorry that the capital old stout-hearted man is dead.' Sorrow may also be expressed that no adequate record should remain of a career which for steadfast purpose, conscientious maintenance of opinion, and pursuit of public objects with disregard of self, was one of very high example. So averse was Mr. Dilke to every kind of display that his name appears to none of the literary investigations which were conducted by him with an acuteness wonderful as his industry, and it was in accordance with his express instructions that the literary journal which his energy and self-denial had established kept silence respecting him at his death.

Charles Wentworth Dilke.

* One day before, the 8th of June 1865, his old friend Sir Joseph Paxton had breathed his last.

LONDON: 1865.

afterwards more fatal to him; and it was with shaken nerves but unsubdued energy he resumed the labour to be presently described. His foot troubled him more or less throughout the autumn;* he was beset by nervous apprehensions which the accident had caused to himself, not lessened by his generous anxiety to assuage the severer sufferings inflicted by it on others; † and that he should nevertheless have determined, on the close of his book, to undertake a series of readings involving greater strain and fatigue than any hitherto, was a startling circumstance. He had perhaps become conscious, without owning it even to himself, that for exertion of this kind the time left him was short; but, whatever pressed him on, his task of the next three years, self-imposed, was to make the most money

Staplehurst sufferers.

New Readings undertaken.

* Here are allusions to it at that time. 'I have got a boot on to-day,—'made on an Otranto scale, but really not very discernible from its ordinary 'sized companion.' After a few days' holiday: 'I began to feel my foot stronger 'the moment I breathed the sea air. Still, during the ten days I have been 'away, I have never been able to wear a boot after four or five in the afternoon, 'but have passed all the evenings with the foot up, and nothing on it. I 'am burnt brown and have walked by the sea perpetually, yet I feel certain 'that if I wore a boot this evening, I should be taken with those torments again 'before the night was out. This last letter ended thus: 'As a relief to my 'late dismal letters, I send you the newest American story. Backwoods 'Doctor is called in to the little boy of a woman-settler. Stares at the child 'some time through a pair of spectacles. Ultimately takes them off, and says 'to the mother: "Wa'al Marm, this is small-pox. 'Tis Marm, small-pox. '"But I am not posted up in Pustuls, and I do not know as I could bring '"him along slick through it. But I'll tell you wa'at I can do Marm:—I can '"send him a draft as will certainly put him into a most etarnal Fit, and I am '"almighty smart at Fits, and we might git round Old Grisly that way."'

Attack in his foot. See *post*, 477–8.

American story.

† I give one such instance: 'The railway people have offered, in the case 'of the young man whom I got out of the carriage just alive, all the expenses 'and a thousand pounds down. The father declines to accept the offer. It 'seems unlikely that the young man, whose destination is India, would ever 'be passed for the Army now by the Medical Board. The question is, how far 'will that contingency tell, under Lord Campbell's Act?'

The accident.

LONDON: 1866.

in the shortest time without any regard to the physical labour to be undergone. The very letter announcing his new engagement shows how entirely unfit he was to enter upon it.

Unfitness for such enterprise.

'For some time,' he wrote at the end of February 1866, 'I have been very unwell. F. B. wrote me word that with 'such a pulse as I described, an examination of the heart 'was absolutely necessary. "Want of muscular power in '"the heart," B said. "Only remarkable irritability of '"the heart," said Doctor Brinton of Brook-street, who had 'been called in to consultation. I was not disconcerted; 'for I knew well beforehand that the effect could not 'possibly be without the one cause at the bottom of it, of 'some degeneration of some function of the heart. Of 'course I am not so foolish as to suppose that all my work 'can have been achieved without *some* penalty, and I have 'noticed for some time a decided change in my buoyancy 'and hopefulness—in other words, in my usual "tone." 'But tonics have already brought me round. So I have 'accepted an offer, from Chappells of Bond-street, of £50 'a night for thirty nights to read "in England, Ireland, '"Scotland, or Paris;" they undertaking all the business, 'paying all personal expenses, travelling and otherwise, of 'myself, John' (his office servant), 'and my gasman; and 'making what they can of it. I begin, I believe, in Liver-'pool on the Thursday in Easter week, and then come to 'London. I am going to read at Cheltenham (on my own 'account) on the 23rd and 24th of this month, staying with 'Macready of course.'

Offer of Messrs. Chappell.

The arrangement of this series of Readings differed from

those of its predecessors in relieving Dickens from every anxiety except of the reading itself; but, by such rapid and repeated change of nights at distant places as kept him almost wholly in a railway carriage when not at the reading-desk or in bed, it added enormously to the physical fatigue. He would read at St. James's Hall in London one night, and at Bradford the next. He would read in Edinburgh, go on to Glasgow and to Aberdeen, then come back to Glasgow, read again in Edinburgh, strike off to Manchester, come back to St. James's Hall once more, and begin the same round again. It was labour that must in time have broken down the strongest man, and what Dickens was when he assumed it we have seen.

LONDON: 1866.

Relieved from management.

Greater fatigues involved.

He did not himself admit a shadow of misgiving. 'As 'to the readings' (11th of March), 'all I have to do is, 'to take in my book and read, at the appointed place and 'hour, and come out again. All the business of every 'kind, is done by Chappells. They take John and my other 'man, merely for my convenience. I have no more to do 'with any detail whatever, than you have. They transact 'all the business at their own cost, and on their own 'responsibility. I think they are disposed to do it in a 'very good spirit, because, whereas the original proposi-'tion was for thirty readings "in England, Ireland, Scot-'"land, or Paris," they wrote out their agreement "in '"London, the Provinces, or elsewhere, *as you and we may* '"*agree*." For this they pay £1500 in three sums: £500 'on beginning, £500 on the fifteenth Reading, £500 at the 'close. Every charge of every kind, they pay besides. I 'rely for mere curiosity on *Doctor Marigold* (I am going

No misgivings.

LONDON: 1866.

Faith in *Marigold.*

'to begin with him in Liverpool, and at St. James's Hall). 'I have got him up with immense pains, and should like 'to give you a notion what I am going to do with him.'

Success beyond hope.

The success everywhere went far beyond even the former successes. A single night at Manchester, when eight hundred stalls were let, two thousand five hundred and sixty-five people admitted, and the receipts amounted to more than three hundred pounds, was followed in nearly the same proportion by all the greater towns; and on the 20th of April the outlay for the entire venture was paid, leaving all that remained, to the middle of the month of June, sheer profit. 'I came back last Sunday,' he wrote on the 30th of May, 'with my last country piece of work for this 'time done. Everywhere the success has been the same. 'St. James's Hall last night was quite a splendid spectacle. 'Two more Tuesdays there, and I shall retire into private 'life. I have only been able to get to Gadshill once since 'I left it, and that was the day before yesterday.'

A memorable evening. 2nd April. i. 91, 129.

One memorable evening he had passed at my house in the interval, when he saw Mrs. Carlyle for the last time. Her sudden death followed shortly after, and near the close of April he had thus written to me from Liverpool. 'It was a terrible shock to me, and poor dear Carlyle has 'been in my mind ever since. How often I have thought 'of the unfinished novel. No one now to finish it. None 'of the writing women come near her at all.' This was an allusion to what had passed at their meeting. It was on the second of April, the day when Mr. Carlyle had delivered his inaugural address as Lord Rector of Edinburgh University, and a couple of ardent words from Professor

Carlyle Lord Rector.

Tyndall had told her of the triumph just before dinner. She came to us flourishing the telegram in her hand, and the radiance of her enjoyment of it was upon her all the night. Among other things she gave Dickens the subject for a novel, from what she had herself observed at the outside of a house in her street; of which the various incidents were drawn from the condition of its blinds and curtains, the costumes visible at its windows, the cabs at its door, its visitors admitted or rejected, its articles of furniture delivered or carried away; and the subtle serious humour of it all, the truth in trifling bits of character, and the gradual progress into a half-romantic interest, had enchanted the skilled novelist. She was well into the second volume of her small romance before she left, being as far as her observation then had taken her; but in a few days exciting incidents were expected, the denouement could not be far off, and Dickens was to have it when they met again. Yet it was to something far other than this amusing little fancy his thoughts had carried him, when he wrote of no one being capable to finish what she might have begun. In greater things this was still more true. No one could doubt it who had come within the fascinating influence of that sweet and noble nature. With some of the highest gifts of intellect, and the charm of a most varied knowledge of books and things, there was something 'beyond, beyond.' No one who knew Mrs. Carlyle could replace her loss when she had passed away.

LONDON: 1866.

Subject for a novel.

Unfinished.

Mrs. Carlyle.

The same letter which told of his uninterrupted success to the last, told me also that he had a heavy cold upon him and was 'very tired and depressed.' Some weeks before

LONDON: 1866.

Offer for more Readings.

the first batch of readings closed, Messrs. Chappell had already tempted him with an offer for fifty more nights to begin at Christmas, for which he meant, as he then said, to ask them seventy pounds a night. 'It would be unrea-'sonable to ask anything now on the ground of the extent 'of the late success, but I am bound to look to myself for 'the future. The Chappells are speculators, though of the 'worthiest and most honourable kind. They make some 'bad speculations, and have made a very good one in this 'case, and will set this against those. I told them when 'we agreed: "I offer these thirty Readings to you at fifty '"pounds a night, because I know perfectly well before-'"hand that no one in your business has the least idea '"of their real worth, and I wish to prove it." The sum 'taken is £4720.' The result of the fresh negotiation, though not completed until the beginning of August, may be at once described. 'Chappell instantly accepts my proposal of forty 'nights at sixty pounds a night, and every conceivable and 'inconceivable expense paid. To make an even sum, I 'have made it forty-two nights for £2500. So I shall now 'try to discover a Christmas number' (he means the subject for one), 'and shall, please Heaven, be quit of the 'whole series of readings so as to get to work on a new 'story for the new series of *All the Year Round* early in 'the spring. The readings begin probably with the New 'Year.' These were fair designs, but the fairest are the sport of circumstance, and though the subject for Christmas was found, the new series of *All the Year Round* never had a new story from its founder. With whatever consequence to himself, the strong tide of the Readings was to

Result of the last.

What was designed to be done. *Post*, 425.

What was done.

sweep on to its full. The American war had ceased, and the first renewed offers from the States had been made and rejected. Hovering over all, too, were other sterner dispositions. 'I think,' he wrote in September, 'there is 'some strange influence in the atmosphere. Twice last 'week I was seized in a most distressing manner—apparently in the heart; but, I am persuaded, only in the 'nervous system.'

PROVINCES: 1866.

Grave warnings.

In the midst of his ovations such checks had not been wanting. 'The police reported officially,' he wrote to his daughter from Liverpool on the 14th of April, 'that three 'thousand people were turned away from the hall last 'night. . . Except that I can *not* sleep, I really think 'myself in very much better training than I had anticipated. A dozen oysters and a little champagne be'tween the parts every night, seem to constitute the best 'restorative I have ever yet tried.' 'Such a prodigi'ous demonstration last night at Manchester,' he wrote to the same correspondent twelve days later, 'that I was 'obliged (contrary to my principle in such cases) to go 'back. I am very tired to-day; for it would be of itself 'very hard work in that immense place, if there were not 'to be added eighty miles of railway and late hours to 'boot.' 'It has been very heavy work,' he wrote to his sister-in-law on the 11th of May from Clifton, 'getting up 'at 6·30 each morning after a heavy night, and I am not 'at all well to-day. We had a tremendous hall at Bir'mingham last night, £230 odd, 2100 people; and I made 'a most ridiculous mistake. Had *Nickleby* on my list to 'finish with, instead of *Trial*. Read *Nickleby* with great

At Liverpool.

At Manchester.

At Birmingham.

PROVINCES: 1866.

More than he intended.

'go, *and the people remained.* Went back again at '10 o'clock, and explained the accident: but said if they 'liked I would give them the *Trial.* They *did* like;—and 'I had another half hour of it, in that enormous place. . . 'I have so severe a pain in the ball of my left eye that it 'makes it hard for me to do anything after 100 miles 'shaking since breakfast. My cold is no better, nor my 'hand either.' It was his left eye, it will be noted, as it was his left foot and hand; the irritability or faintness of heart was also of course on the left side; and it was on the same left side he felt most of the effect of the railway accident.

See *Post*, 343.

SCOTLAND.

At Aberdeen.

Everything was done to make easier the labour of travel, but nothing could materially abate either the absolute physical exhaustion, or the nervous strain. 'We arrived 'here,' he wrote from Aberdeen (16th of May), 'safe and 'sound between 3 and 4 this morning. There was a com- 'partment for the men, and a charming room for ourselves 'furnished with sofas and easy chairs. We had also a 'pantry and washing-stand. This carriage is to go about 'with us.' Two days later he wrote from Glasgow: 'We 'halted at Perth yesterday, and got a lovely walk there. 'Until then I had been in a condition the reverse of 'flourishing; half strangled with my cold, and dyspeptically 'gloomy and dull; but, as I feel much more like myself 'this morning, we are going to get some fresh air aboard 'a steamer on the Clyde.' The last letter during his country travel was from Portsmouth on the 24th of May, and contained these words: 'You need have no fear about 'America.' The readings closed in June.

At Perth.

On the Clyde.

PROVINCES: 1867.

The readings of the new year began with even increased enthusiasm, but not otherwise with happier omen. Here was his first outline of plan: 'I start on Wednesday after-'noon (the 15th of January) for Liverpool, and then go on 'to Chester, Derby, Leicester, and Wolverhampton. On 'Tuesday the 29th I read in London again, and in Feb-'ruary I read at Manchester and then go on into Scotland.' From Liverpool he wrote on the 21st: 'The enthusiasm 'has been unbounded. On Friday night I quite astonished 'myself; but I was taken so faint afterwards that they 'laid me on a sofa at the hall for half an hour. I attri-'bute it to my distressing inability to sleep at night, and 'to nothing worse. Everything is made as easy to me as 'it possibly can be. Dolby would do anything to lighten 'the work, and *does* everything.' The weather was sorely against him. 'At Chester,' he wrote on the 24th from Birmingham, 'we read in a snow-storm and a fall of ice. 'I think it was the worst weather I ever saw . . . At 'Wolverhampton last night the thaw had thoroughly 'set in, and it rained furiously, and I was again heavily 'beaten. We came on here after the reading (it is only 'a ride of forty miles), and it was as much as I could do to 'hold out the journey. But I was not faint, as at Liver-'pool. I was only exhausted.' Five days later he had returned for his Reading in London, and thus replied to a summons to dine with Macready at my house: 'I am 'very tired; cannot sleep; have been severely shaken on 'an atrocious railway; read to-night, and have to read at 'Leeds on Thursday. But I have settled with Dolby to 'put off our going to Leeds on Wednesday, in the hope of

Exertion and its result.

Heavily beaten.

PROVINCES: 1867.

'coming to dine with you, and seeing our dear old friend. I 'say "in the hope," because if I should be a little more used-'up to-morrow than I am to-day, I should be constrained, 'in spite of myself, to take to the sofa and stick there.'

On the 15th of February he wrote to his sister-in-law from Liverpool that they had had 'an enormous turn-'away' the previous night. 'The day has been very fine, 'and I have turned it to the wholesomest account by walk-'ing on the sands at New Brighton all the morning. I 'am not quite right within, but believe it to be an effect 'of the railway shaking. There is no doubt of the fact 'that, after the Staplehurst experience, it tells more and 'more (railway shaking, that is) instead of, as one might 'have expected, less and less.' The last remark is a strange one, from a man of his sagacity; but it was part of the too-willing self-deception which he practised, to justify him in his professed belief that these continued excesses of labour and excitement were really doing him no harm. The day after that last letter he pushed on to Scotland, and on the 17th wrote to his daughter from Glasgow. The closing night at Manchester had been enormous. 'They cheered to that 'extent after it was over that I was obliged to huddle on 'my clothes (for I was undressing to prepare for the 'journey) and go back again. After so heavy a week, it '*was* rather stiff to start on this long journey at a quarter 'to two in the morning; but I got more sleep than I ever 'got in a railway-carriage before . . . I have, as I had in 'the last series of readings, a curious feeling of soreness 'all round the body—which I suppose to arise from the 'great exertion of voice . . .' Two days later he wrote to

Self-deception.

SCOTLAND.

1.45 a.m.

his sister-in-law from the Bridge of Allan, which he had reached from Glasgow that morning. 'Yesterday I was so 'unwell with an internal malady that occasionally at long 'intervals troubles me a little, and it was attended with 'the sudden loss of so much blood, that I wrote to F. B. 'from whom I shall doubtless hear to-morrow . . . I felt it 'a little more exertion to read, afterwards, and I passed a 'sleepless night after that again; but otherwise I am in 'good force and spirits to-day: I may say, in the best 'force . . . The quiet of this little place is sure to do me 'good.' He rallied again from this attack, and, though he still complained of sleeplessness, wrote cheerfully from Glasgow on the 21st, describing himself indeed as confined to his room, but only because 'in close hiding from a local 'poet who has christened his infant son in my name, and 'consequently haunts the building.' On getting back to Edinburgh he wrote to me, with intimation that many troubles had beset him; but that the pleasure of his audiences, and the providence and forethought of Messrs. Chappell, had borne him through. 'Everything is done for 'me with the utmost liberality and consideration. Every 'want I can have on these journeys is anticipated, and not 'the faintest spark of the tradesman spirit ever peeps out. 'I have three men in constant attendance on me; besides 'Dolby, who is an agreeable companion, an excellent 'manager, and a good fellow.'

SCOTLAND: 1867.

An old malady, i. 263.

In close 'hiding.'

What bore him through.

On the 4th of March he wrote from Newcastle: 'The 'readings have made an immense effect in this place, and 'it is remarkable that although the people are individually 'rough, collectively they are an unusually tender and

Audiences at Newcastle.

NEW-CASTLE: 1867.

'sympathetic audience; while their comic perception is 'quite up to the high London standard. The atmosphere 'is so very heavy that yesterday we escaped to Tynemouth 'for a two hours' sea walk. There was a high north wind 'blowing, and a magnificent sea running. Large vessels 'were being towed in and out over the stormy bar, with 'prodigious waves breaking on it; and, spanning the rest-'less uproar of the waters, was a quiet rainbow of trans-'cendent beauty. The scene was quite wonderful. We 'were in the full enjoyment of it when a heavy sea caught 'us, knocked us over, and in a moment drenched us and 'filled even our pockets. We had nothing for it but to 'shake ourselves together (like Doctor Marigold), and dry 'ourselves as well as we could by hard walking in the wind 'and sunshine. But we were wet through for all that, 'when we came back here to dinner after half-an-hour's 'railway drive. I am wonderfully well, and quite fresh 'and strong.' Three days later he was at Leeds; from which he was to work himself round through the most important neighbouring places to another reading in London, before again visiting Ireland.

Scene at Tynemouth.

Fenian excitements.

This was the time of the Fenian excitements; it was with great reluctance he consented to go;* and he told

Reluctance to go to Ireland.

* He wrote to me on the 15th of March from Dublin: 'So profoundly dis-'couraging were the accounts from here in London last Tuesday that I held 'several councils with Chappell about coming at all; had actually drawn up a bill 'announcing (indefinitely) the postponement of the readings; and had meant 'to give him a reading to cover the charges incurred—but yielded at last to 'his representations the other way. We ran through a snow storm nearly the 'whole way, and in Wales got snowed up, came to a stoppage, and had to dig 'the engine out. . . We got to Dublin at last, found it snowing and raining, 'and heard that it had been snowing and raining since the first day of the 'year . . . As to outward signs of trouble or preparation, they are very few.

us all at his first arrival that he should have a complete breakdown. More than 300 stalls were gone at Belfast two days before the reading, but on the afternoon of the reading in Dublin not 50 were taken. Strange to say however a great crowd pressed in at night, he had a tumultuous greeting, and on the 22nd of March I had this announcement from him: 'You will be surprised to be 'told that we have done WONDERS! Enthusiastic crowds 'have filled the halls to the roof each night, and hundreds 'have been turned away. At Belfast the night before last 'we had £246 5*s.* In Dublin to-night everything is sold 'out, and people are besieging Dolby to put chairs any-'where, in doorways, on my platform, in any sort of hole 'or corner. In short the Readings are a perfect rage at 'a time when everything else is beaten down.' He took the Eastern Counties at his return, and this brought the series to a close. 'The reception at Cambridge was some-'thing to be proud of in such a place. The colleges mus-'tered in full force, from the biggest guns to the smallest; 'and went beyond even Manchester in the roars of wel-'come and rounds of cheers. The place was crammed, and

IRELAND: 1867.

In Dublin.

Unexpected crowds.

EASTERN COUNTIES.

Cambridge.

'At Kingstown our boat was waited for by four armed policemen, and some 'stragglers in various dresses who were clearly detectives. But there was no 'show of soldiery. My people carry a long heavy box containing gas-fittings. 'This was immediately laid hold of; but one of the stragglers instantly inter-'posed on seeing my name, and came to me in the carriage and apologised . . . 'The worst looking young fellow I ever saw, turned up at Holyhead before we 'went to bed there, and sat glooming and glowering by the coffee-room fire while 'we warmed ourselves. He said he had been snowed up with us (which we didn't 'believe), and was horribly disconcerted by some box of his having gone to 'Dublin without him. We said to one another "Fenian:" and certainly he 'disappeared in the morning, and let his box go where it would.' What Dickens heard and saw in Dublin, during this visit, convinced him that Fenianism and disaffection had found their way into several regiments.

Attentions of police.

'Fenian.'

EASTERN COUNTIES: 1867.

'all through the reading everything was taken with the 'utmost heartiness of enjoyment.' The temptation of offers from America had meanwhile again been presented to him so strongly, and in such unlucky connection with immediate family claims threatening excess of expenditure even beyond the income he was making, that he was fain to write to his sister-in-law: "I begin to feel myself drawn 'towards America as Darnay in the *Tale of Two Cities* 'was attracted to Paris. It is my Loadstone Rock.' Too surely it was to be so; and Dickens was not to be saved from the consequence of yielding to the tempation, by any such sacrifice as had rescued Darnay.

Yielding to temptation.

The letter which told me of the close of his English readings had in it no word of the farther enterprise, yet it seemed to be in some sort a preparation for it. 'Last 'Monday evening' (14th May) 'I finished the 50 Read-'ings with great success. You have no idea how I have 'worked at them. Feeling it necessary, as their reputa-'tion widened, that they should be better than at first, I 'have *learnt them all*, so as to have no mechanical draw-'back in looking after the words. I have tested all the 'serious passion in them by everything I know; made 'the humorous points much more humorous; corrected 'my utterance of certain words; cultivated a self-pos-'session not to be disturbed; and made myself master 'of the situation. Finishing with *Dombey* (which I had 'not read for a long time) I learnt that, like the rest; and 'did it to myself, often twice a day, with exactly the 'same pains as at night, over and over and over again.'. . Six days later brought his reply to a remark that no degree

Close of the third series.

Study given to the readings.

LONDON: 1867.

of excellence to which he might have brought his readings could reconcile me to what there was little doubt would soon be pressed upon him. 'It is curious' (20th May) 'that you should touch the American subject, because I must confess that my mind is in a most disturbed 'state about it. That the people there have set themselves 'on having the readings, there is no question. Every 'mail brings me proposals, and the number of Americans at 'St. James's Hall has been surprising. A certain Mr. Grau, 'who took Ristori out, and is highly responsible, wrote to 'me by the last mail (for the second time) saying that if 'I would give him a word of encouragement he would come 'over immediately and arrange on the boldest terms for 'any number I chose, and would deposit a large sum of 'money at Coutts's. Mr. Fields writes to me on behalf of a 'committee of private gentlemen at Boston who wished 'for the credit of getting me out, who desired to hear the 'readings and did not want profit, and would put down 'as a guarantee £10,000—also to be banked here. Every 'American speculator who comes to London repairs straight 'to Dolby, with similar proposals. And, thus excited, 'Chappells, the moment this last series was over, proposed 'to treat for America!' Upon the mere question of these various offers he had little difficulty in making up his mind. If he went at all, he would go on his own account, making no compact with any one. Whether he should go at all, was what he had to determine.

Desire in America to hear Dickens read.

Offers.

Will go on his own account only.

One thing with his usual sagacity he saw clearly enough. He must make up his mind quickly. 'The Presidential 'election would be in the autumn of next year. They are

LONDON: 1867.

'a people whom a fancy does not hold long. They are bent 'upon my reading there, and they believe (on no foundation whatever) that I am going to read there. If I ever 'go, the time would be when the Christmas number goes 'to press. Early in this next November.' Every sort of enquiry he accordingly set on foot; and so far came to the immediate decision, that, if the answers left him no room to doubt that a certain sum might be realized, he would go. 'Have no fear that anything will induce me to make the 'experiment, if I do not see the most forcible reasons for 'believing that what I could get by it, added to what I 'have got, would leave me with a sufficient fortune. I 'should be wretched beyond expression there. My small 'powers of description cannot describe the state of mind 'in which I should drag on from day to day.' At the end of May he wrote: 'Poor dear Stanfield!' (our excellent friend had passed away the week before). 'I cannot think 'even of him, and of our great loss, for this spectre of doubt 'and indecision that sits at the board with me and stands 'at the bedside. I am in a tempest-tossed condition, and can 'hardly believe that I stand at bay at last on the American 'question. The difficulty of determining amid the variety 'of statements made to me is enormous, and you have no 'idea how heavily the anxiety of it sits upon my soul. But 'the prize looks so large!' One way at last seemed to open by which it was possible to get at some settled opinion. 'Dolby sails for America' (2nd of July) 'on Saturday 'the 3rd of August. It is impossible to come to any reasonable conclusion, without sending eyes and ears on the 'actual ground. He will take out my MS. for the *Chil-*

Will go quickly if at all.

Sole motive in going.

At bay at last.

Sends agent to America.

'*dren's Magazine.* I hope it is droll, and very child-like; 'though the joke is a grown-up one besides. You must 'try to like the pirate story, for I am very fond of it.' The allusion is to his pleasant *Holiday Romance* which he had written for Mr. Fields.

LONDON: 1867.

*Post*, 346.

Hardly had Mr. Dolby gone when there came that which should have availed to dissuade, far more than any of the arguments which continued to express my objection to the enterprise. 'I am laid up,' he wrote on the 6th of August, 'with another attack in my foot, and was on the sofa all 'last night in tortures. I cannot bear to have the fomenta- 'tions taken off for a moment. I was so ill with it on 'Sunday, and it looked so fierce, that I came up to Henry 'Thompson. He has gone into the case heartily, and says 'that there is no doubt the complaint originates in the 'action of the shoe, in walking, on an enlargement in the 'nature of a bunion. Erysipelas has supervened upon the 'injury; and the object is to avoid a gathering, and to stay 'the erysipelas where it is. Meantime I am on my back, 'and chafing. . . I didn't improve my foot by going down 'to Liverpool to see Dolby off, but I have little doubt of 'its yielding to treatment, and repose.' A few days later he was chafing still; the accomplished physician he consulted having dropped other hints that somewhat troubled him. 'I could not walk a quarter of a mile to-night for '£500. I make out so many reasons against supposing it 'to be gouty that I really do not think it is.'

Warning unheeded.

Chafing.

Sir Henry Thompson's opinion.

So momentous in my judgment were the consequences of the American journey to him that it seemed right to preface thus much of the inducements and temptations that led to it.

LONDON: 1867.

Discussion useless.

My own part in the discussion was that of steady dissuasion throughout: though this might perhaps have been less persistent if I could have reconciled myself to the belief, which I never at any time did, that Public Readings were a worthy employment for a man of his genius. But it had by this time become clear to me that nothing could stay the enterprise. The result of Mr. Dolby's visit to America—drawn up by Dickens himself in a paper possessing still the interest of having given to the Readings when he crossed the Atlantic much of the form they then assumed *—reached me when I was staying at Ross; and

* This renders it worth preservation in a note. He called it

'THE CASE IN A NUTSHELL.

The case in a nutshell.

'1. I think it may be taken as proved, that general enthusiasm and excitement are awakened in America on the subject of the Readings, and 'that the people are prepared to give me a great reception. *The New 'York Herald*, indeed, is of opinion that "Dickens must apologise '"first"; and where a *New York Herald* is possible, any thing is possible. But the prevailing tone, both of the press and of people of all 'conditions, is highly favourable. I have an opinion myself that the 'Irish element in New York is dangerous; for the reason that the 'Fenians would be glad to damage a conspicuous Englishman. This is 'merely an opinion of my own.

'2. All our original calculations were based on 100 Readings. But an unexpected result of careful enquiry on the spot, is the discovery that 'the month of May is generally considered (in the large cities) bad for 'such a purpose. Admitting that what governs an ordinary case in 'this wise, governs mine, this reduces the Readings to 80, and consequently at a blow makes a reduction of 20 per cent. in the means of 'making money within the half year—unless the objection should not 'apply in my exceptional instance.

'3. I dismiss the consideration that the great towns of America could not 'possibly be exhausted—or even visited—within 6 months, and that a 'large harvest would be left unreaped. Because I hold a second series 'of Readings in America is to be set down as out of the question: 'whether regarded as involving two more voyages across the Atlantic, 'or a vacation of five months in Canada.

LONDON: 1867.

upon it was founded my last argument against the scheme. This he received in London on the 28th of September, on which day he thus wrote to his eldest daughter: 'As I 'telegraphed after I saw you, I am off to Ross to consult 'with Mr. Forster and Dolby together. You shall hear, 'either on Monday, or by Monday's post from London, how 'I decide finally.' The result he wrote to her three days later: 'You will have had my telegram that I go to 'America. After a long discussion with Forster, and con-'sideration of what is to be said on both sides, I have

Final consultation.

'4. The narrowed calculation we have made, is this: What is the largest 'amount of clear profit derivable, under the most advantageous circum-'stances possible, as to their public reception, fron 80 Readings and no 'more? In making this calculation, the expenses have been throughout 'taken on the New York scale—which is the dearest; as much as '20 per cent. has been deducted for management, including Mr. Dolby's 'commission; and no credit has been taken for any extra payment on 'reserved seats, though a good deal of money is confidently expected 'from this source. But on the other hand it is to be observed that 'four Readings (and a fraction over) are supposed to take place every 'week, and that the estimate of receipts is based on the assumption 'that the audiences are, on all occasions, as large as the rooms will 'reasonably hold.

For and against reading in America.

'5. So considering 80 Readings, we bring out the nett profit of that number, 'remaining to me after payment of all charges whatever, as £15,500.

'6. But it yet remains to be noted that the calculation assumes New York 'City, and the State of New York, to be good for a very large propor-'tion of the 80 Readings; and that the calculation also assumes the 'necessary travelling not to extend beyond Boston and adjacent places, 'New York City and adjacent places, Philadelphia, Washington, and 'Baltimore. But, if the calculation should prove too sanguine on this 'head, and if these places should *not* be good for so many Readings, 'then it may prove impracticable to get through 80 within the time: 'by reason of other places that would come into the list, lying wide 'asunder, and necessitating long and fatiguing journeys.

'7. The loss consequent on the conversion of paper money into gold (with 'gold at the present ruling premium) is allowed for in the calculation. 'It counts seven dollars to the pound.'

LONDON: 1867.

Decision to go.

'decided to go through with it. We have telegraphed '"Yes" to Boston.' Seven days later he wrote to me: 'The Scotia being full, I do not sail until lord mayor's 'day; for which glorious anniversary I have engaged an 'officer's cabin on deck in the Cuba. I am not in very 'brilliant spirits at the prospect before me, and am deeply 'sensible of your motive and reasons for the line you have 'taken; but I am not in the least shaken in the convic- 'tion that I could never quite have given up the idea.'

Departure.

The remaining time was given to preparations; on the 2nd of November there was a Farewell Banquet in the Freemasons' Hall over which Lord Lytton presided; and on the 9th Dickens sailed for Boston. Before he left he had contributed his part to the last of his Christmas Numbers; all the writings he lived to complete were done; and the interval of his voyage may be occupied by a general review of the literary labour of his life.

# CHAPTER XIV.

## DICKENS AS A NOVELIST.

1836—1870.

THE TALE OF TWO CITIES.
GREAT EXPECTATIONS.
CHRISTMAS SKETCHES.
OUR MUTUAL FRIEND.
DR. MARIGOLD AND TALES FOR AMERICA.

LONDON: 1836–70.

WHAT I have to say generally of Dickens's genius as a writer may be made part of the notice, which still remains to be given, of his writings from *The Tale of Two Cities* to the time at which we have arrived, leaving *Edwin Drood* for mention in its place; and this will be accompanied, as in former notices of individual stories, by illustrations drawn from his letters and life. His literary work was so intensely one with his nature that he is not separable from it, and the man and the method throw a singular light on each other. But some allusion to what has been said of these books, by writers assuming to speak with authority, will properly precede what has to be offered by me; and I shall preface this part of my task with the hint of Carlyle, that in looking at a man out of the common it is good for common men to make sure that they 'see' before they attempt to 'oversee' him.

See before you oversee.

Of the French writer, M. Henri Taine, it has before been

LONDON: 1836–70.

remarked that his inability to appreciate humour is fatal to his pretensions as a critic of the English novel. But there is much that is noteworthy in his criticism notwithstanding, as well as remarkable in his knowledge of our language; his position entitles him to be heard without a suspicion of partizanship or intentional unfairness; whatever the value of his opinion, the elaboration of its form and expression is itself no common tribute; and what is said in it of Dickens's handling in regard to style and character, embodies temperately objections which have since been taken by some English critics without his impartiality and with less than his ability. As to style M. Taine does not find that the natural or simple prevails sufficiently. The tone is too passionate. The imaginative or poetic side of allusion is so uniformly dwelt on, that the descriptions cease to be subsidiary, and the minute details of pain or pleasure wrought out by them become active agencies in the tale. So vivid and eager is the display of fancy that everything is borne along with it; imaginary objects take the precision of real ones; living thoughts are controlled by inanimate things; the chimes console the poor old ticket-porter; the cricket steadies the rough carrier's doubts; the sea waves soothe the dying boy; clouds, flowers, leaves, play their several parts; hardly a form of matter without a living quality; no silent thing without its voice. Fondling and exaggerating thus what is occasional in the subject of his criticism, into what he has evidently at last persuaded himself is a fixed and universal practice with Dickens, M. Taine proceeds to explain the exuberance by comparing such imagination in its vividness to

M. Taine's criticism.

Too much passion and fancy.

that of a monomaniac. He fails altogether to apprehend that property in Humour which involves the feeling of subtlest and most affecting analogies, and from which is drawn the rare insight into sympathies between the nature of things and their attributes or opposites, in which Dickens's fancy revelled with such delight. Taking the famous lines which express the lunatic, the lover, and the poet as 'of Imagina-'tion all compact,' in a sense that would have startled not a little the great poet who wrote them, M. Taine places on the same level of creative fancy the phantoms of the lunatic and the personages of the artist. He exhibits Dickens as from time to time, in the several stages of his successive works of fiction, given up to one idea, possessed by it, seeing nothing else, treating it in a hundred forms, exaggerating it, and so dazzling and overpowering his readers with it that escape is impossible. This he maintains to be equally the effect as Mr. Mell the usher plays the flute, as Tom Pinch enjoys or exposes his Pecksniff, as the guard blows his bugle while Tom rides to London, as Ruth Pinch crosses Fountain Court or makes the beefsteak pudding, as Jonas Chuzzlewit commits and returns from the murder, and as the storm which is Steerforth's death-knell beats on the Yarmouth shore. To the same kind of power he attributes the extraordinary clearness with which the commonest objects in all his books, the most ordinary interiors, any old house, a parlour, a boat, a school, fifty things that in the ordinary tale-teller would pass unmarked, are made vividly present and indelible; are brought out with a strength of relief, precision, and force, unapproached in any other writer of prose fiction; with everything minute yet nothing cold,

What M. Taine overlooks.

'Lunatic 'and poet.'

Examples of monomania.

LONDON: 1836–70.

Too exciting.

'with all the passion and the patience of the painters of 'his country.' And while excitement in the reader is thus maintained to an extent incompatible with a natural style or simple narrative, M. Taine yet thinks he has discovered, in this very power of awakening a feverish sensibility and moving laughter or tears at the commonest things, the source of Dickens's astonishing popularity. Ordinary people, he says, are so tired of what is always around them, and take in so little of the detail that makes up their lives, that when, all of a sudden, there comes a man to make these things interesting, and turn them into objects of admiration, tenderness, or terror, the effect is enchantment. Without leaving their arm-chairs or their firesides, they find themselves trembling with emotion, their eyes are filled with tears, their cheeks are broad with laughter, and, in the discovery they have thus made that they too can suffer, love, and feel, their very existence seems doubled to them. It had not occurred to M. Taine that to effect so much might seem to leave little not achieved.

Why so popular.

Doubling the sensations of ordinary people.

So far from it, the critic had satisfied himself that such a power of style must be adverse to a just delineation of character. Dickens is not calm enough, he says, to penetrate to the bottom of what he is dealing with. He takes sides with it as friend or enemy, laughs or cries over it, makes it odious or touching, repulsive or attractive, and is too vehement and not enough inquisitive to paint a likeness. His imagination is at once too vivid and not sufficiently large. Its tenacious quality, and the force and concentration with which his thoughts penetrate into the details he desires to apprehend, form limits to his knowledge, confine

Excesses and defects.

him to single traits, and prevent his sounding all the depths of a soul. He seizes on one attitude, trick, expression, or grimace; sees nothing else; and keeps it always unchanged. Mercy Pecksniff laughs at every word, Mark Tapley is nothing but jolly, Mrs. Gamp talks incessantly of Mrs. Harris, Mr. Chillip is invariably timid, and Mr. Micawber is never tired of emphasizing his phrases or passing with ludicrous brusqueness from joy to grief. Each is the incarnation of some one vice, virtue, or absurdity; whereof the display is frequent, invariable, and exclusive. The language I am using condenses with strict accuracy what is said by M. Taine, and has been repeated *ad nauseam* by others, professing admirers as well as open detractors. Mrs. Gamp and Mr. Micawber, who belong to the first rank of humorous creation, are thus without another word dismissed by the French critic; and he shows no consciousness whatever in doing it, of that very fault in himself for which Dickens is condemned, of mistaking lively observation for real insight.

Types not people.

Our own fault condemned in another.

He has however much concession in reserve, being satisfied, by his observation of England, that it is to the people for whom Dickens wrote his deficiencies in art are mainly due. The taste of his nation had prohibited him from representing character in a grand style. The English require too much morality and religion for genuine art. They made him treat love, not as holy and sublime in itself, but as subordinate to marriage; forced him to uphold society and the laws, against nature and enthusiasm; and compelled him to display, in painting such a seduction as in *Copperfield*, not the progress, ardour, and intoxication of passion, but only the misery, remorse, and despair. The

Excuse for Dickens.

LONDON: 1836–70.

Morality too popular in England.

result of such surface religion and morality, combined with the trading spirit, M. Taine continues, leads to so many national forms of hypocrisy, and of greed as well as worship for money, as to justify this great writer of the nation in his frequent choice of those vices for illustration in his tales. But his defect of method again comes into play. He does not deal with vices in the manner of a physiologist, feeling a sort of love for them, and delighting in their finer traits as if they were virtues. He gets angry over them. (I do not interrupt M. Taine, but surely, to take one instance illustrative of many, Dickens's enjoyment in dealing with Pecksniff is as manifest as that he never ceases all the time to make him very hateful.) He cannot, like Balzac, leave morality out of account, and treat a passion, however loathsome, as that great tale-teller did, from the only safe ground of belief, that it is a force, and that force of whatever kind is good. It is essential to an artist of that superior grade, M. Taine holds, no matter how vile his subject, to show its education and temptations, the form of brain or habits of mind that have reinforced the natural tendency, to deduce it from its cause, to place its circumstances around it, and to develop its effects to their extremes. In handling such and such a capital miser, hypocrite, debauchee, or what not, he should never trouble himself about the evil consequences of the vices. He should be too much of a philosopher and artist to remember that he is a respectable citizen. But this is what Dickens never forgets, and he renounces all beauties requiring so corrupt a soil. M. Taine's conclusion upon the whole nevertheless is, that though those triumphs of art which become the property

Dickens over-angry with vice.

Balzac's better method.

LONDON: 1836–70.

of all the earth have not been his, much has yet been achieved by him. Out of his unequalled observation, his satire, and his sensibility, has proceeded a series of original characters existing nowhere but in England, which will exhibit to future generations not the record of his own genius only, but that of his country and his times.

What Dickens achieved.

Between the judgment thus passed by the distinguished French lecturer, and the later comment to be now given from an English critic, certainly not in arrest of that judgment, may fitly come a passage from one of Dickens's letters saying something of the limitations placed upon the artist in England. It may read like a quasi-confession of one of M. Taine's charges, though it was not written with reference to his own but to one of Scott's later novels. 'Similarly' (15th of August 1856) 'I have always a fine 'feeling of the honest state into which we have got, when 'some smooth gentleman says to me or to some one else 'when I am by, how odd it is that the hero of an English 'book is always uninteresting—too good—not natural, &c. 'I am continually hearing this of Scott from English people here, who pass their lives with Balzac and Sand. But 'O my smooth friend, what a shining impostor you must 'think yourself and what an ass you must think me, when 'you suppose that by putting a brazen face upon it you 'can blot out of my knowledge the fact that this same unnatural young gentleman (if to be decent is to be necessarily unnatural), whom you meet in those other books 'and in mine, *must be* presented to you in that unnatural 'aspect by reason of your morality, and is not to have, I 'will not say any of the indecencies you like, but not even

Limitations of art in England.

From Paris.

Anticipatory reply to M. Taine.

LONDON: 1836-70.

'any of the experiences, trials, perplexities, and confusions 'inseparable from the making or unmaking of all men!'

Praise and blame in England.

M. Taine's criticism was written three or four years before Dickens's death, and to the same date belong some notices in England which adopted more or less the tone of depreciation; conceding the great effects achieved by the writer, but disputing the quality and value of his art. For it is incident to all such criticism of Dickens to be of necessity accompanied by the admission, that no writer has so completely impressed himself on the time in which he lived, that he has made his characters a part of literature, and that his readers are the world.

Blame and praise to be reconciled.

But, a little more than a year after his death, a paper was published of which the object was to reconcile such seeming inconsistency, to expound the inner meanings of 'Dickens in relation to Criticism,' and to show that, though he had a splendid genius and a wonderful imagination, yet the objectors were to be excused who called him only a stagy sentimentalist and a clever caricaturist. This critical essay appeared in the *Fortnightly Review* for February 1872, with the signature of Mr. George Henry Lewes; and the pretentious airs of the performance, with its prodigious professions of candour, force upon me the painful task of stating what it really is. During Dickens's life, especially when any fresh novelist could be found available for strained comparison with him, there were plenty of attempts to write him down: but the trick of studied depreciation was never carried so far or made so odious as in this case, by intolerable assumptions of an indulgent superiority; and to repel it in such a form once for all is due to Dickens's memory.

Paper by Mr. Lewes.

The paper begins by the usual concessions—that he was a writer of vast popularity, that he delighted no end of people, that his admirers were in all classes and all countries, that he stirred the sympathy of masses not easily reached through literature and always to healthy emotion, that he impressed a new direction on popular writing, and modified the literature of his age in its spirit no less than its form. The very splendour of these successes, on the other hand, so deepened the shadow of his failures, that to many there was nothing but darkness. Was it unnatural? Could greatness be properly ascribed, by the fastidious, to a writer whose defects were so glaring, exaggerated, untrue, fantastic, and melodramatic? Might they not fairly insist on such defects as outweighing all positive qualities, and speak of him with condescending patronage or sneering irritation? Why, very often such men, though their talk would be seasoned with quotations from, and allusions to, his writings, and though they would lay aside their most favourite books to bury themselves in his new 'number,' had been observed by this critic to be as niggardly in their praise of him as they were lavish in their scorn. He actually heard '*a very distinguished man*,' on one occasion, express measureless contempt for Dickens, and a few minutes afterwards admit that Dickens had 'entered into 'his life.' And so the critic betook himself to the task of reconciling this immense popularity and this critical contempt, which he does after the following manner.

'Dickens 'in relation to 'Criticism.'

Plea for objectors to Dickens.

A 'distinguished' man's contempt.

He says that Dickens was so great in 'fun' (humour he does not concede to him anywhere) that Fielding and Smollett are small in comparison, but that this would only

'Fun.'

LONDON: 1836–70.

have been a passing amusement for the world if he had not been 'gifted with an imagination of marvellous vivid-'ness, and an emotional sympathetic nature capable of 'furnishing that imagination with elements of universal 'power.' To people who think that words should carry some meaning it might seem, that, if only a man could be 'gifted' with all this, nothing more need be said. With marvellous imagination, and a nature to endow it with elements of universal power, what secrets of creative art could possibly be closed to him? But this is reckoning without your philosophical critic. The vividness of Dickens's imagination M. Taine found to be simply monomaniacal, and his follower finds it to be merely hallucinative. Not the less he heaps upon it epithet after epithet. He talks of its irradiating splendour; calls it glorious as well as imperial and marvellous; and, to make us quite sure he is not with these fine phrases puffing-off an inferior article, he interposes that such imagination is 'common 'to all great writers.' Luckily for great writers in general, however, their creations are of the old, immortal, commonplace sort; whereas Dickens in his creative processes, according to this philosophy of criticism, is tied up hard and fast within hallucinative limits.

Alleged 'gifts.'

Again the mono-maniac.

'Hallu-'cinative' imagination.

Dickens a 'seer of 'visions.'

'He was,' we are told, 'a seer of visions.' Amid silence and darkness, we are assured, he heard voices and saw objects; of which the revived impressions to him had the vividness of sensations, and the images his mind created in explanation of them had the coercive force of realities;* so that what he brought into existence in this

* I hope my readers will find themselves able to understand that, as well as

way, no matter how fantastic and unreal, was (whatever this may mean) universally intelligible. 'His types esta-'blished themselves in the public mind like personal ex-'periences. Their falsity was unnoticed in the blaze of 'their illumination. Every humbug seemed a Pecksniff, 'every jovial improvident a Micawber, every stinted serving-'wench a Marchioness.' The critic, indeed, saw through it all, but he gave his warnings in vain. 'In vain 'critical reflection showed these figures to be merely 'masks; not characters, but personified characteristics; 'caricatures and distortions of human nature. The vivid-'ness of their presentation triumphed over reflection; their 'creator managed to communicate to the public his own 'unhesitating belief.' What, however, is the public? Mr. Lewes goes on to relate. 'Give a child a wooden horse, 'with hair for mane and tail, and wafer-spots for colouring, 'he will never be disturbed by the fact that this horse 'does not move its legs but runs on wheels; and this 'wooden horse, which he can handle and draw, is believed 'in more than a pictured horse by a Wouvermanns or an 'Ansdell (!!) It may be said of Dickens's human figures 'that they too are wooden, and run on wheels; but these 'are details which scarcely disturb the belief of admirers.

Vain critical warnings.

Intelligence of 'the 'public.'

'Wooden figures of Dickens.

this which follows: 'What seems preposterous, impossible to us, seemed to 'him simple fact of observation. When he imagined a street, a house, a room, 'a figure, he saw it not in the vague schematic way of ordinary imagination, 'but in the sharp definition of actual perception, all the salient details obtrud-'ing themselves on his attention. He, seeing it thus vividly, made us also see 'it; and believing in its reality however fantastic, he communicated something 'of his belief to us. He presented it in such relief that we ceased to think of 'it as a picture. So definite and insistent was the image, that even while 'knowing it was false we could not help, for a moment, being affected, as it 'were, by his hallucination.'

The preposterous and impossible made facts of observation.

LONDON: 1836–70.

'Just as the wooden horse is brought within the range of 'the child's emotions, and dramatizing tendencies, when he 'can handle and draw it, so Dickens's figures are brought 'within the range of the reader's interests, and receive from 'these interests a sudden illumination, when they are the 'puppets of a drama every incident of which appeals to 'the sympathies.'

Criticised and critic.

*Risum teneatis?* But the smile is grim that rises to the face of one to whom the relations of the writer and his critic, while both writer and critic lived, are known; and who sees the drift of now scattering such rubbish as this over an established fame. As it fares with the imagination that is imperial, so with the drama every incident of which appeals to the sympathies. The one being explained by hallucination, and the other by the wooden horse, plenty of fine words are to spare by which contempt may receive the show of candour. When the characters in a play are puppets, and the audiences of the theatre fools or children, no wise man forfeits his wisdom by proceeding to admit that the successful playwright, 'with a fine felicity 'of instinct,' seized upon situations, for his wooden figures, having 'irresistible hold over the domestic affections;' that, through his puppets, he spoke 'in the mother-'tongue of the heart;' that, with his spotted horses and so forth, he 'painted the life he knew and everyone 'knew;' that he painted, of course, nothing ideal or heroic, and that the world of thought and passion lay beyond his horizon; but that, with his artificial performers and his feeble-witted audiences, 'all the resources 'of the bourgeois epic were in his grasp; the joys and pains

Contempt under show of candour.

What puppets and spotted horses may do.

LONDON: 1836–70.

'of childhood, the petty tyrannies of ignoble natures, the 'genial pleasantries of happy natures, the life of the poor, 'the struggles of the street and back parlour, the insolence 'of office, the sharp social contrasts, east wind and Christ-'mas jollity, hunger, misery, and hot punch'—'so that 'even critical spectators who complained that these broadly 'painted pictures were artistic daubs could not wholly re-'sist their effective suggestiveness.' Since Trinculo and Caliban were under one cloak, there has surely been no such delicate monster with two voices. 'His forward voice, 'now, is to speak well of his friend; his backward voice 'is to utter foul speeches and to detract.' One other of the foul speeches I may not overlook, since it contains what is alleged to be a personal revelation of Dickens made to the critic himself.

Effective suggestiveness of daubs.

'When one thinks of Micawber always presenting him-'self in the same situation, moved with the same springs 'and uttering the same sounds, always confident of some-'thing turning up, always crushed and rebounding, always 'making punch—and his wife always declaring she will 'never part from him, always referring to his talents and 'her family—when one thinks of the "catchwords" per-'sonified as characters, one is reminded of the frogs whose 'brains have been taken out for physiological purposes, 'and whose actions henceforth want the distinctive pecu-'liarity of organic action, that of fluctuating spontaneity.' Such was that sheer inability of Dickens, indeed, to comprehend this complexity of the organism, that it quite accounted, in the view of this philosopher, for all his unnaturalness, for the whole of his fantastic people, and for

An opinion on Mr. and Mrs. Micawber.

Inability to comprehend complex organisms.

LONDON: 1836–70.

the strained dialogues of which his books are made up, painfully resembling in their incongruity 'the absurd and 'eager expositions which insane patients pour into the lis- 'tener's ear when detailing their wrongs, or their schemes. 'Dickens once declared to me,' Mr. Lewes continues, 'that 'every word said by his characters was distinctly *heard* 'by him; I was at first not a little puzzled to account for 'the fact that he could hear language so utterly unlike 'the language of real feeling, and not be aware of its pre- 'posterousness; but the surprise vanished when I thought 'of the phenomena of hallucination.' Wonderful sagacity! to unravel easily such a bewildering 'puzzle'! And so to the close. Between the uncultivated whom Dickens moved, and the cultivated he failed to move; between the power that so worked in delf as to stir the universal heart, and the commonness that could not meddle with porcelain or aspire to any noble clay; the pitiful see-saw is continued up to the final sentence, where, in the impartial critic's eagerness to discredit even the value of the emotion awakened in such men as Jeffrey by such creations as Little Nell, he reverses all he has been saying about the cultivated and uncultivated, and presents to us a cultivated philosopher, in his ignorance of the stage, applauding an actor whom every uncultivated playgoing apprentice despises as stagey. But the bold stroke just exhibited, of bringing forward Dickens himself in the actual crisis of one of his fits of hallucination, requires an additional word.

Hallucinative phenomena.

Common delf and finer clay.

Dickens in a fit of hallucination.

To establish the hallucinative theory, he is said on one occasion to have declared to the critic that every word uttered by his characters was distinctly *heard* by him before

LONDON: 1836–70.

it was written down. Such an averment, not credible for a moment as thus made, indeed simply untrue to the extent described, may yet be accepted in the limited and quite different sense which a passage in one of Dickens's letters gives to it. All writers of genius to whom their art has become as a second nature, will be found capable of doing upon occasion what the vulgar may think to be 'halluci-'nation,' but hallucination will never account for. After Scott began the *Bride of Lammermoor* he had one of his terrible seizures of cramp, yet during his torment he dictated* that fine novel; and when he rose from his bed, and the published book was placed in his hands, 'he did not,' James Ballantyne explicitly assured Lockhart, 'recollect 'one single incident, character, or conversation it con-'tained.' When Dickens was under the greatest trial of his life, and illness and sorrow were contending for the mastery over him, he thus wrote to me. 'Of my distress 'I will say no more than that it has borne a terrible, 'frightful, horrible proportion to the quickness of the gifts 'you remind me of. But may I not be forgiven for think-'ing it a wonderful testimony to my being made for my art, 'that when, in the midst of this trouble and pain, I sit 'down to my book, some beneficent power shows it all

Composition of the *Bride of Lammermoor*.

Not inventing but seeing what is written.

* 'Though,' John Ballantyne told Lockhart, 'he often turned himself on 'his pillow with a groan of torment, he usually continued the sentence in the 'same breath. But when dialogue of peculiar animation was in progress, 'spirit seemed to triumph altogether over matter—he arose from his couch and 'walked up and down the room, raising and lowering his voice, and as it were 'acting the parts.' *Lockhart*, vi. 67-8. The statement of James Ballantyne is at p. 89 of the same volume. The original incidents on which Scott had founded the tale he remembered, but 'not a single character woven by the romancer, 'not one of the many scenes and points of humour, nor anything with which he 'was connected as the writer of the work.'

LONDON: 1836–70.

'to me, and tempts me to be interested, and I don't invent 'it—really do not—*but see it*, and write it down. . . It 'is only when it all fades away and is gone, that I begin 'to suspect that its momentary relief has cost me some-'thing.'

Whatever view may be taken of the man who wrote those words, he had the claim to be judged by reference to the highest models in the art which he studied. In the literature of his time, from 1836 to 1870, he held the most conspicuous place, and his claim to the most popular one in the literature of fiction was by common consent admitted. He obtained this rank by the sheer force of his genius, unhelped in any way, and he held it without dispute. As he began he closed. After he had written for only four months, and after he had written incessantly for four and thirty years, he was of all living writers the most widely read. It is of course quite possible that such popularity might imply rather littleness in his contemporaries than greatness in him: but his books are the test to judge by. Each thus far, as it appeared, has had notice in these pages for its illustration of his life, or of his method of work, or of the variety and versatility in the manifestations of his power. But his latest books remain still for notice, and will properly suggest what is farther to be said of his general place in literature.

A claim to be fairly judged.

His leading quality was Humour. It has no mention in either of the criticisms cited, but it was his highest faculty; and it accounts for his magnificent successes, as well as for his not infrequent failures, in characteristic delineation. He was conscious of this himself. Five years before he

Dickens's leading quality.

LONDON: 1836–70.

died, a great and generous brother artist, Lord Lytton, amid much ungrudging praise of a work he was then publishing, asked him to consider, as to one part of it, if the modesties of art were not a little overpassed. 'I cannot tell you,' he replied, 'how highly I prize your letter, or with what 'pride and pleasure it inspires me. Nor do I for a moment 'question its criticism (if objection so generous and easy 'may be called by that hard name) otherwise than on this 'ground—that I work slowly and with great care, and 'never give way to my invention recklessly, but constantly 'restrain it; and that I think it is my infirmity to fancy 'or perceive relations in things which are not apparent 'generally. Also, I have such an inexpressible enjoyment 'of what I see in a droll light, that I dare say I pet it as 'if it were a spoilt child. This is all I have to offer in 'arrest of judgment.' To perceive relations in things which are not apparent generally, is one of those exquisite properties of humour by which are discovered the affinities between the high and the low, the attractive and the repulsive, the rarest things and things of every day, which bring us all upon the level of a common humanity. It is this which gives humour an immortal touch that does not belong of necessity to pictures, even the most exquisite, of mere character or manners; the property which in its highest aspects Carlyle so subtly described as a sort of inverse sublimity, exalting into our affections what is below us as the other draws down into our affections what is above us. But it has a danger which Dickens also hints at, and into which he often fell. All humour has in it, is indeed identical with, what ordinary people are apt to call

Reply to a remonstrance from Bulwer Lytton.

Apology for occasional excess.

Humour at its highest.

Its dangers.

LONDON: 1836–70.

exaggeration; but there is an excess beyond the allowable even here, and to 'pet' or magnify out of proper bounds its sense of what is droll, is to put the merely grotesque in its place. What might have been overlooked in a writer with no uncommon powers of invention, was thrown into overpowering prominence by Dickens's wealth of fancy; and a splendid excess of his genius came to be objected to as its integral and essential quality.

Dickens's earlier books.

It cannot be said to have had any place in his earlier books. His powers were not at their highest and the humour was less fine and subtle, but there was no such objection to be taken. No misgiving interrupted the enjoyment of the wonderful freshness of animal spirits in *Pickwick;* but beneath its fun, laughter, and light-heartedness were indications of power of the first rank in the delineation of character. Some caricature was in the plan; but as the circle of people widened beyond the cockney club, and the delightful oddity of Mr. Pickwick took more of an independent existence, a different method revealed itself, nothing appeared beyond the exaggerations permissible to humorous comedy, and the art was seen which can combine traits vividly true to particular men or women with propensities common to all mankind. This has its highest expression in Fielding: but even the first of Dickens's books showed the same kind of mastery; and, by the side of its life-like middle-class people universally familiar, there was one figure before seen by none but at once knowable by all, delightful for the surprise it gave by its singularity and the pleasure it gave by its truth; and, though short of the highest in this form of art, taking

*Pickwick Papers.*

Sam Weller.

rank with the class in which live everlastingly the dozen unique inventions that have immortalized the English novel. The groups in *Oliver Twist*, Fagin and his pupils, Sikes and Nancy, Mr. Bumble and his parish-boy, belong to the same period; when Dickens also began those pathetic delineations that opened to the neglected, the poor, and the fallen, a world of compassion and tenderness. Yet I think it was not until the third book, *Nickleby*, that he began to have his place as a writer conceded to him; and that he ceased to be regarded as a mere phenomenon or marvel of fortune, who had achieved success by any other means than that of deserving it, and who challenged no criticism better worth the name than such as he has received from the Fortnightly reviewer. It is to be added to what before was said of *Nickleby*, that it established beyond dispute his mastery of dialogue, or that power of making characters real existences, not by describing them but by letting them describe themselves, which belongs only to story-tellers of the first rank. Dickens never excelled the easy handling of the subordinate groups in this novel, and he never repeated its mistakes in the direction of aristocratic or merely polite and dissipated life. It displayed more than before of his humour on the tragic side; and, in close connection with its affecting scenes of starved and deserted childhood, were placed those contrasts of miser and spendthrift, of greed and generosity, of hypocrisy and simple-heartedness, which he handled in later books with greater power and fullness, but of which the first formal expression was here. It was his first general picture, so to speak, of the character and manners of his time, which

Character-drawing in *Oliver Twist*.

Effect of *Nicholas Nickleby*.

Mastery of dialogue.

Contrasts taken from the time.

LONDON: 1836-70.

*Nicholas Nickleby.*

it was the design more or less of all his books to exhibit; and it suffers by comparison with his later productions, because the humour is not to the same degree enriched by imagination; but it is free from the not infrequent excess into which that supreme gift also tempted its possessor. None of the tales is more attractive throughout, and on the whole it was a step in advance even of the stride previously taken. Nor was the gain lost in the succeeding story of the *Old Curiosity Shop*. The humorous traits of Mrs. Nickleby could hardly be surpassed: but, in Dick Swiveller and the Marchioness, there was a subtlety and lightness of touch that led to finer issues; and around Little Nell* and her fortunes, surpassingly touching and beautiful, let criticism object what it will, were gathered some small characters that had a deeper intention and more imaginative insight, than anything yet done. Strokes of this kind were also observable in the hunted life of the murderer in *Barnaby Rudge;* and his next book, *Chuzzlewit,* was, as it still remains, one of his greatest achievements. Even so brief a retrospect of the six opening years of Dickens's literary labour will help to a clearer judgment of the work of the twenty-eight more years that remained to him.

People in the *Curiosity Shop.*

*Barnaby Rudge.*

To the special observations already made on the series

Sara Coleridge on Little Nell.

* 'Do you know *Master Humphrey's Clock?* I admire Nell in the *Old* '*Curiosity Shop* exceedingly. The whole thing is a good deal borrowed from '*Wilhelm Meister*. But Little Nell is a far purer, lovelier, more *English* 'conception than Mignon, treasonable as the saying would seem to some. No 'doubt it was suggested by Mignon.'—Sara Coleridge to Aubrey de Vere (*Memoirs and Letters,* ii. 269-70). Expressing no opinion on this comparison, I may state it as within my knowledge that the book referred to was not then known to Dickens.

of stories which followed the return from America, *Chuzzlewit*, *Dombey*, *Copperfield*, and *Bleak House*, in which attention has been directed to the higher purpose and more imaginative treatment that distinguished them,* a general remark is to be added. Though the range of character they traverse is not wide, it is surrounded by a fertility of invention and illustration without example in any previous novelist; and it is represented in these books, so to speak, by a number and variety of existences sufficiently real to have taken places as among the actual people of the world. Could half as many known and universally recognisable men and women be selected out of one story, by any other prose writer of the first rank, as at once rise to the mind from one of the masterpieces of Dickens? So difficult of dispute is this, that as much perhaps will be admitted; but then it will be added, if the reply is by a critic of the school burlesqued by Mr. Lewes, that after all they are not individual or special men and women so much as general impersonations of men and women, abstract types made up of telling catchwords or surface traits, though with such accumulation upon them of a wonderful wealth of humorous illustration, itself filled with minute and accurate knowledge of life, that the real nakedness of

LONDON: 1836–70.

Books after first American visit.

Realities of fiction.

* The distinction I then pointed out was remarked by Sara Coleridge (*Memoirs and Letters*, ii. 169) in writing of her children. 'They like to talk 'to me . . . above all about the productions of Dickens, the never-to-be-'exhausted fun of *Pickwick*, and the capital new strokes of *Martin Chuzzlewit*. 'This last work contains, besides all the fun, some very marked and available 'morals. I scarce know any book in which the evil and odiousness of selfish-'ness are more forcibly brought out, or in a greater variety of exhibitions. In 'the midst of the merry quotations, or at least on any fair opportunity, I draw 'the boys' attention to these points.'

Sara Coleridge on *Chuzzlewit*.

LONDON: 1836–70.

the land of character is hidden. Well, what can be rejoined to this, but that the poverty or richness of any territory worth survey will for the most part lie in the kind of observation brought to it. There was no finer observer than Johnson of the manners of his time, and he protested of their greatest delineator that he knew only the shell of life. Another of his remarks, after a fashion followed by the criticizers of Dickens, places Fielding below one of his famous contemporaries; but who will not now be eager to reverse such a comparison, as that Fielding tells you correctly enough what o'clock it is by looking at the face of the dial, but that Richardson shows you how the watch is made? There never was a subtler or a more sagacious observer than Fielding, or who better deserved what is generously said of him by Smollett, that he painted the characters and ridiculed the follies of life with equal strength, humour, and propriety. But might it not be said of him, as of Dickens, that his range of character was limited; and that his method of proceeding from a central idea in all his leading people, exposed him equally to the charge of now and then putting human nature itself in place of the individual who should only be a small section of it? This is in fact but another shape of what I have expressed on a former page, that what a character, drawn by a master, will roughly present upon its surface, is frequently such as also to satisfy its more subtle requirements; and that when only the salient points or sharper prominences are thus displayed, the great novelist is using his undoubted privilege of showing the large degree to which human intercourse is carried on, not by men's habits

Johnson and his contemporaries.

Richardson preferred to Fielding.

Fielding and Dickens.

*Ante*, 26.

or ways at their commonest, but by the touching of their extremes. A definition of Fielding's genius has been made with some accuracy in the saying, that he shows common propensities in connection with the identical unvarnished adjuncts which are peculiar to the individual, nor could a more exquisite felicity of handling than this be any man's aim or desire; but it would be just as easy, by employment of the critical rules applied to Dickens, to transform it into matter of censure. Partridge, Adams, Trulliber, Squire Western, and the rest, present themselves often enough under the same aspects, and use with sufficient uniformity the same catchwords, to be brought within the charge of mannerism; and though M. Taine cannot fairly say of Fielding as of Dickens, that he suffers from too much morality, he brings against him precisely the charge so strongly put against the later novelist of 'looking upon 'the passions not as simple forces but as objects of appro-'bation or blame.' We must keep in mind all this to understand the worth of the starved fancy, that can find in such a delineation as that of Micawber only the man described by Mr. Lewes as always in the same situation, moved with the same springs and uttering the same sounds, always confident of something turning up, always crushed and rebounding, always making punch, and his wife always declaring she will never part from him. It is not thus that such creations are to be viewed; but by the light which enables us to see why the country squires, village schoolmasters, and hedge parsons of Fielding became immortal. The later ones will live, as the earlier do, by the subtle quality of genius that makes their doings and say-

Touching of extremes.

Definition of Fielding's method.

M. Taine's criticism Fielding.

Why the creations of fiction live.

LONDON: 1836-70.

ings part of those general incentives which pervade mankind. Who has not had occasion, however priding himself on his unlikeness to Micawber, to think of Micawber as he reviewed his own experiences? Who has not himself waited, like Micawber, for something to turn up? Who has not at times discovered, in one or other acquaintance or friend, some one or other of that cluster of sagacious hints and fragments of human life and conduct which the kindly fancy of Dickens embodied in this delightful form? If the irrepressible New Zealander ever comes over to achieve his long promised sketch of St. Paul's, who can doubt that it will be no other than our undying Micawber, who had taken to colonisation the last time we saw him, and who will thus again have turned up? There are not many conditions of life or society to which his and his wife's experiences are not applicable; and when, the year after the immortal couple made their first appearance on earth, Protection was in one of its then frequent difficulties, declaring it could not live without something widely different from existing circumstances shortly turning up, and imploring its friends to throw down the gauntlet and boldly challenge society to turn up a majority and rescue it from its embarrassments, a distinguished wit seized upon the likeness to Micawber, showed how closely it was borne out by the jollity and gin-punch of the banquets at which the bewailings were heard, and asked whether Dickens had stolen from the farmer's friends or the farmer's friends had stolen from Dickens. 'Corn, 'said Mr. Micawber, may be gentlemanly, but it is not 'remunerative. . . I ask myself this question: if corn is

Universality of Micawber experiences.

Protectionist Micawbers.

Micawber on corn.

'not to be relied on, what is? We must live. . .' Loud as the general laughter was, I think the laughter of Dickens himself was loudest, at this discovery of so exact and unexpected a likeness.*

LONDON: 1836-70.

A readiness in all forms thus to enjoy his own pleasantry was indeed always observable (it is common to great humourists, nor would it be easier to carry it farther than Sterne did), and his own confession on the point may receive additional illustration before proceeding to the later books. He accounted by it, as we have seen, for occasional even grotesque extravagances. In another of his letters there is this passage: 'I can report that I have finished 'the job I set myself, and that it has in it something— 'to me at all events—so extraordinarily droll, that though

Dickens's enjoyment of his own humour.

* All the remarks in my text had been some time in type when Lord Lytton sent me what follows, from one of his father's manuscript (and unpublished) note-books. Substantially it agrees with what I have said; and such unconscious testimony of a brother novelist of so high a rank, careful in the study of his art, is of special value. 'The greatest masters of the novel of modern 'manners have generally availed themselves of Humour for the illustration of 'manners; and have, with a deep and true, but perhaps unconscious, know- 'ledge of art, pushed the humour almost to the verge of caricature. For, as 'the serious ideal requires a certain exaggeration in the proportions of the 'natural, so also does the ludicrous. Thus Aristophanes, in painting the 'humours of his time, resorts to the most poetical extravagance of machinery, 'and calls the Clouds in aid of his ridicule of philosophy, or summons Frogs 'and Gods to unite in his satire on Euripides. The Don Quixote of Cervantes 'never lived, nor, despite the vulgar belief, ever could have lived, in Spain; 'but the art of the portrait is in the admirable exaltation of the humorous by 'means of the exaggerated. With more or less qualification, the same may 'be said of Parson Adams, of Sir Roger de Coverley, and even of the Vicar of 'Wakefield. . . It follows therefore that art and correctness are far from 'identical, and that the one is sometimes proved by the disdain of the other. 'For the ideal, whether humorous or serious, does not consist in the imitation 'but in the exaltation of nature. And we must accordingly enquire of art, not 'how far it resembles what we have seen, so much as how far it embodies what 'we can imagine.'

Unpublished note by the late Lord Lytton.

Defence of humourists from charges of exaggeration.

LONDON: 1836-70.

An example from Mrs. Lirriper.

'I have been reading it some hundred times in the course 'of the working, I have never been able to look at it with 'the least composure, but have always roared in the most 'unblushing manner. I leave you to find out what it was.' It was the encounter of the major and the tax-collector in the second Mrs. Lirriper. Writing previously of the papers in *Household Words* called The Lazy Tour of Two Idle Apprentices, after saying that he and Mr. Wilkie Collins had written together a story in the second part, 'in which 'I think you would find it very difficult to say where I 'leave off and he comes in,' he had said of the preceding descriptions: 'Some of my own tickle me very much; but 'that may be in great part because I know the originals, 'and delight in their fantastic fidelity.' 'I have been at 'work with such a will' he writes later of a piece of humour for the holidays, that I have done the opening 'and conclusion of the Christmas number. They are done 'in the character of a waiter, and I think are exceedingly 'droll. The thread on which the stories are to hang, is 'spun by this waiter, and is, purposely, very slight; but 'has, I fancy, a ridiculously comical and unexpected end. 'The waiter's account of himself includes (I hope) every-'thing you know about waiters, presented humorously.' In this last we have a hint of the 'fantastic fidelity' with which, when a fancy 'tickled' him, he would bring out what Corporal Nym calls the humour of it under so astonishing a variety of conceivable and inconceivable aspects of subtle exaggeration, that nothing was left to the subject but that special individual illustration of it. In this, however, humour was not his servant but his master; because

Another from 'Lazy 'Tour,' *ante*, 146.

The waiter in *Somebody's Luggage*.

'The 'Humour 'of it.'

it reproduced too readily, and carried too far, the grotesque imaginings to which great humourists are prone; which lie indeed deep in their nature; and from which they derive their genial sympathy with eccentric characters that enables them to find motives for what to other men is hopelessly obscure, to exalt into types of humanity what the world turns impatiently aside at, and to enshrine in a form for eternal homage and love such whimsical absurdity as Captain Toby Shandy's. But Dickens was too conscious of these excesses from time to time, not zealously to endeavour to keep the leading characters in his more important stories under some strictness of discipline. To confine exaggeration within legitimate limits was an art he laboriously studied; and, in whatever proportions of failure or success, during the vicissitudes of both that attended his later years, he continued to endeavour to practise it. In regard to mere description, it is true, he let himself loose more frequently, and would sometimes defend it even on the ground of art; nor would it be fair to omit his reply, on one occasion, to some such remonstrance as M. Taine has embodied in his adverse criticism, against the too great imaginative wealth thrown by him into mere narrative.* 'It does not seem to me to be enough to

Temptations of all great humourists.

Excesses in descriptive writing.

* I cannot refuse myself the satisfaction of quoting, from the best criticism of Dickens I have seen since his death, remarks very pertinent to what is said in my text. 'Dickens possessed an imagination unsurpassed, not only in 'vividness, but in swiftness. I have intentionally avoided all needless com'parisons of his works with those of other writers of his time, some of whom 'have gone before him to their rest, while others survive to gladden the dark'ness and relieve the monotony of our daily life. But in the power of his 'imagination—of this I am convinced—he surpassed them, one and all. That 'imagination could call up at will those associations which, could we but 'summon them in their full number, would bind together the human family,

Professor Ward on Dickens.

LONDON: 1836–70.

'say of any description that it is the exact truth. The 'exact truth must be there; but the merit or art in the 'narrator, is the manner of stating the truth. As to which 'thing in literature, it always seems to me that there is a 'world to be done. And in these times, when the tendency 'is to be frightfully literal and catalogue-like—to make 'the thing, in short, a sort of sum in reduction that any 'miserable creature can do in that way—I have an idea '(really founded on the love of what I profess), that the very 'holding of popular literature through a kind of popular 'dark age, may depend on such fanciful treatment.'

A word for the fanciful in description.

---

THE TALE OF TWO CITIES.

Origin of *Tale of Two Cities.* 1857–8.

Dickens's next story to *Little Dorrit* was the *Tale of Two Cities,* of which the first notion occurred to him while acting with his friends and his children in the summer of 1857 in Mr. Wilkie Collins's drama of *The Frozen Deep.*

'and make that expression no longer a name, but a living reality. . . Such 'associations sympathy alone can warm into life, and imagination alone can 'at times discern. The great humourist reveals them to every one of us; and 'his genius is indeed an inspiration from no human source, in that it enables 'him to render this service to the brotherhood of mankind. But more than 'this. So marvellously has this earth become the inheritance of mankind, 'that there is not a thing upon it, animate or inanimate, with which, or with 'the likeness of which, man's mind has not come into contact; . . . with 'which human feelings, aspirations, thoughts, have not acquired an endless 'variety of single or subtle associations. . . These also, which we imperfectly 'divine or carelessly pass by, the imagination of genius distinctly reveals to 'us, and powerfully impresses upon us. When they appeal directly to the 'emotions of the heart, it is the power of Pathos which has awakened them; 'and when the suddenness, the unexpectedness, the apparent oddity of the 'one by the side of the other, strike the mind with irresistible force, it is the 'equally divine gift of Humour which has touched the spring of laughter by 'the side of the spring of tears.'—*Charles Dickens. A Lecture by Professor Ward. Delivered in Manchester,* 30*th November,* 1870.

But it was only a vague fancy, and the sadness and trouble of the winter of that year were not favourable to it. Towards the close (27th) of January 1858, talking of improvements at Gadshill in which he took little interest, it was again in his thoughts. 'Growing inclinations of a 'fitful and undefined sort are upon me sometimes to fall 'to work on a new book. Then I think I had better not 'worry my worried mind yet awhile. Then I think it 'would be of no use if I did, for I couldn't settle to one 'occupation.—And that's all!' 'If I can discipline my 'thoughts,' he wrote three days later, 'into the channel of 'a story, I have made up my mind to get to work on one: 'always supposing that I find myself, on the trial, able to 'do well. Nothing whatever will do me the least "good" 'in the way of shaking the one strong possession of change 'impending over us that every day makes stronger; but 'if I could work on with some approach to steadiness, 'through the summer, the anxious toil of a new book 'would have its neck well broken before beginning to 'publish, next October or November. Sometimes, I think 'I may continue to work; sometimes, I think not. What 'do you say to the title, ONE OF THESE DAYS?' That title held its ground very briefly. 'What do you think,' he wrote after six weeks, 'of *this* name for my story—BURIED 'ALIVE? Does it seem too grim? Or, THE THREAD OF 'GOLD? Or, THE DOCTOR OF BEAUVAIS?' But not until twelve months later did he fairly buckle himself to the task he had contemplated so long. *All the Year Round* had taken the place of *Household Words* in the interval; and the tale was then started to give strength

LONDON: 1857–8.

Untoward time.

Title-hunting.

LONDON: 1859.

to the new weekly periodical for whose pages it was designed.

Name found.

'This is merely to certify,' he wrote on the 11th of March 1859, 'that I have got exactly the name for the story that 'is wanted; exactly what will fit the opening to a T. A 'TALE OF TWO CITIES. Also, that I have struck out a 'rather original and bold idea. That is, at the end of each 'month to publish the monthly part in the green cover, 'with the two illustrations, at the old shilling. This will 'give *All the Year Round* always the interest and prece- 'dence of a fresh weekly portion during the month; and 'will give me my old standing with my old public, and the 'advantage (very necessary in this story) of having num- 'bers of people who read it in no portions smaller than a 'monthly part. . . My American ambassador pays a thou- 'sand pounds for the first year, for the privilege of repub- 'lishing in America one day after we publish here. Not 'bad?' . . He had to struggle at the opening through a sharp attack of illness, and on the 9th of July progress was thus reported. 'I have been getting on in health very 'slowly and through irksome botheration enough. But I 'think I am round the corner. This cause—and the heat— 'has tended to my doing no more than hold my ground, 'my old month's advance, with the *Tale of Two Cities*. 'The small portions thereof, drive me frantic; but I think 'the tale must have taken a strong hold. The run upon 'our monthly parts is surprising, and last month we sold '35,000 back numbers. A note I have had from Carlyle 'about it has given me especial pleasure.' A letter of the following month expresses the intention he had when

Monthly numbers as well as weekly parts.

Success.

LONDON: 1859.

he began the story, and in what respect it differs as to method from all his other books. Sending in proof four numbers ahead of the current publication, he adds: 'I hope 'you will like them. Nothing but the interest of the sub-'ject, and the pleasure of striving with the difficulty of the 'form of treatment,—nothing in the way of mere money, 'I mean,—could else repay the time and trouble of the 'incessant condensation. But I set myself the little task 'of making *a picturesque story*, rising in every chapter, 'with characters true to nature, but whom the story should 'express more than they should express themselves by 'dialogue. I mean in other words, that I fancied a story 'of incident might be written (in place of the odious 'stuff that *is* written under that pretence), pounding the 'characters in its own mortar, and beating their interest 'out of them. If you could have read the story all at 'once, I hope you wouldn't have stopped halfway.'* Another of his letters supplies the last illustration I need to give of the design and meanings in regard to this tale

Method different from his other books.

Speciality in the treatment.

Not dialogue but incident.

* The opening of this letter (25th of August 1859), referring to a conviction for murder, afterwards reversed by a Home Office pardon against the continued and steadily expressed opinion of the judge who tried the case, is much too characteristic of the writer to be lost. 'I cannot easily tell you how much in-'terested I am by what you tell me of our brave and excellent friend. . . I 'have often had more than half a mind to write and thank that upright judge. 'I declare to heaven that I believe such a service one of the greatest that a 'man of intellect and courage can render to society. . . Of course I have 'been driving the girls out of their wits here, by incessantly proclaiming that 'there needed no medical evidence either way, and that the case was plain 'without it. . . Lastly of course (though a merciful man—because a merciful 'man, I mean), I would hang any Home Secretary, Whig, Tory, Radical, or 'otherwise, who should step in between so black a scoundrel and the gallows. . . 'I am reminded of Tennyson by thinking that King Arthur would have made 'short work of the amiable man! How fine the Idylls are! Lord! what a

Conviction reversed by pardon.

Tennyson's Idylls.

LONDON: 1859.

expressed by himself. It was a reply to some objections of which the principal were, a doubt if the feudal cruelties came sufficiently within the date of the action to justify his use of them, and some question as to the manner of disposing of the chief revolutionary agent in the plot. 'I 'had of course full knowledge of the formal surrender of 'the feudal privileges, but these had been bitterly felt 'quite as near to the time of the Revolution as the Doctor's 'narrative, which you will remember dates long before the 'Terror. With the slang of the new philosophy on the 'one side, it was surely not unreasonable or unallowable, 'on the other, to suppose a nobleman wedded to the old 'cruel ideas, and representing the time going out as his 'nephew represents the time coming in. If there be any-'thing certain on earth, I take it that the condition of the 'French peasant generally at that day was intolerable. No 'later enquiries or provings by figures will hold water 'against the tremendous testimony of men living at the 'time. There is a curious book printed at Amsterdam, 'written to make out no case whatever, and tiresome 'enough in its literal dictionary-like minuteness; scattered 'up and down the pages of which is full authority for my 'marquis. This is Mercier's *Tableau de Paris*. Rousseau 'is the authority for the peasant's shutting up his house 'when he had a bit of meat. The tax-tables are the autho-'rity for the wretched creature's impoverishment. . . I am

Reply to an objection.

Authorities.

'blessed thing it is to read a man who really can write. I thought nothing 'could be finer than the first poem, till I came to the third; but when I 'had read the last, it seemed to me to be absolutely unapproachable.' Other literary likings rose and fell with him, but he never faltered in his allegiance to Tennyson.

LONDON: 1859.

'not clear, and I never have been clear, respecting the 'canon of fiction which forbids the interposition of acci- 'dent in such a case as Madame Defarge's death. Where 'the accident is inseparable from the passion and action 'of the character; where it is strictly consistent with the 'entire design, and arises out of some culminating pro- 'ceeding on the part of the individual which the whole 'story has led up to; it seems to me to become, as it were, 'an act of divine justice. And when I use Miss Pross '(though this is quite another question) to bring about 'such a catastrophe, I have the positive intention of 'making that half-comic intervention a part of the despe- 'rate woman's failure; and of opposing that mean death, 'instead of a desperate one in the streets which she 'wouldn't have minded, to the dignity of Carton's. Wrong 'or right, this was all design, and seemed to me to be in 'the fitness of things.'

Madame Defarge's death.

Intended contrast of Carton's.

These are interesting intimations of the care with which Dickens worked; and there is no instance in his novels, excepting this, of a deliberate and planned departure from the method of treatment which had been pre-eminently the source of his popularity as a novelist. To rely less upon character than upon incident, and to resolve that his actors should be expressed by the story more than they should express themselves by dialogue, was for him a hazardous, and can hardly be called an entirely successful, experiment. With singular dramatic vivacity, much constructive art, and with descriptive passages of a high order everywhere (the dawn of the terrible outbreak in the journey of the marquis from Paris to his country seat, and the

Care with which Dickens worked.

LONDON: 1859.

*Tale of Two Cities* characterized.

London crowd at the funeral of the spy, may be instanced for their power), there was probably never a book by a great humourist, and an artist so prolific in the conception of character, with so little humour and so few rememberable figures. Its merits lie elsewhere. Though there are excellent traits and touches all through the revolutionary scenes, the only full-length that stands out prominently is the picture of the wasted life saved at last by heroic sacrifice. Dickens speaks of his design to make impressive the dignity of Carton's death, and in this he succeeded perhaps even beyond his expectation. Carton suffers him-

Conception of Carton's self-sacrifice.

self to be mistaken for another, and gives his life that the girl he loves may be happy with that other; the secret being known only to a poor little girl in the tumbril that takes them to the scaffold, who at the moment has discovered it, and whom it strengthens also to die. The incident is beautifully told; and it is at least only fair to set against verdicts not very favourable as to this effort of his invention, what was said of the particular character and scene, and of the book generally, by an American critic whose literary studies had most familiarized him with the rarest forms of imagi-

Opinion of an American critic.

native writing.* 'Its pourtrayal of the noble-natured cast-'away makes it almost a peerless book in modern litera-'ture, and gives it a place among the highest examples of 'literary art. . . The conception of this character shows in 'its author an ideal of magnanimity and of charity unsur-'passed. There is not a grander, lovelier figure than the 'self-wrecked, self-devoted Sydney Carton, in literature or

* Mr. Grant White, whose edition of Shakespeare has been received with much respect in England.

'history; and the story itself is so noble in its spirit, so 'grand and graphic in its style, and filled with a pathos 'so profound and simple, that it deserves and will surely 'take a place among the great serious works of imagina-'tion.' I should myself prefer to say that its distinctive merit is less in any of its conceptions of character, even Carton's, than as a specimen of Dickens's power in imaginative story-telling. There is no piece of fiction known to me, in which the domestic life of a few simple private people is in such a manner knitted and interwoven with the outbreak of a terrible public event, that the one seems but part of the other. When made conscious of the first sultry drops of a thunderstorm that fall upon a little group sitting in an obscure English lodging, we are witness to the actual beginning of a tempest which is preparing to sweep away everything in France. And, to the end, the book in this respect is really remarkable.

LONDON: 1859.

Mr. Grant White on Sydney Carton.

Public and private incidents interwoven.

---

## GREAT EXPECTATIONS.

1860.

The *Tale of Two Cities* was published in 1859; the series of papers collected as the *Uncommercial Traveller* were occupying Dickens in 1860; and it was while engaged in these, and throwing off in the course of them capital 'samples' of fun and enjoyment, he thus replied to a suggestion that he should let himself loose upon some single humorous conception, in the vein of his youthful achievements in that way. 'For a little piece I have been 'writing—or am writing; for I hope to finish it to-day—'such a very fine, new, and grotesque idea has opened upon 'me, that I begin to doubt whether I had not better cancel

Germ of new tale.

LONDON: 1860.

'the little paper, and reserve the notion for a new book. 'You shall judge as soon as I get it printed. But it so 'opens out before *me* that I can see the whole of a serial 'revolving on it, in a most singular and comic manner.' This was the germ of Pip and Magwitch, which at first he intended to make the groundwork of a tale in the old twenty-number form, but for reasons perhaps fortunate brought afterwards within the limits of a less elaborate novel. 'Last week,' he wrote on the 4th of October 1860, 'I got to work on the new story. I had previously very care-'fully considered the state and prospects of *All the Year* '*Round*, and, the more I considered them, the less hope 'I saw of being able to get back, *now*, to the profit of a 'separate publication in the old 20 numbers.' (A tale, which at the time was appearing in his serial, had disappointed expectation.) 'However I worked on, knowing that what 'I was doing would run into another groove; and I called 'a council of war at the office on Tuesday. It was perfectly 'clear that the one thing to be done was, for me to strike 'in. I have therefore decided to begin the story as of the 'length of the *Tale of Two Cities* on the first of December '—begin publishing, that is. I must make the most I can 'out of the book. You shall have the first two or three 'weekly parts to-morrow. The name is GREAT EXPECTA-'TIONS. I think a good name?' Two days later he wrote: 'The sacrifice of *Great Expectations* is really and truly 'made for myself. The property of *All the Year Round* 'is far too valuable, in every way, to be much endangered. 'Our fall is not large, but we have a considerable advance 'in hand of the story we are now publishing, and there is

Pip and Magwitch.

Intended for 20 numbers.

Judicious change.

Published in *All the Year Round.*

'no vitality in it, and no chance whatever of stopping the 'fall; which on the contrary would be certain to increase. 'Now, if I went into a twenty-number serial, I should cut 'off my power of doing anything serial here for two good 'years—and that would be a most perilous thing. On the 'other hand, by dashing in now, I come in when most 'wanted; and if Reade and Wilkie follow me, our course 'will be shaped out handsomely and hopefully for between 'two and three years. A thousand pounds are to be paid 'for early proofs of the story to America.' A few more days brought the first instalment of the tale, and explanatory mention of it. 'The book will be written in the first 'person throughout, and during these first three weekly 'numbers you will find the hero to be a boy-child, like 'David. Then he will be an apprentice. You will not have 'to complain of the want of humour as in the *Tale of Two* '*Cities*. I have made the opening, I hope, in its general 'effect exceedingly droll. I have put a child and a good-'natured foolish man, in relations that seem to me very 'funny. Of course I have got in the pivot on which the 'story will turn too—and which indeed, as you remember, 'was the grotesque tragi-comic conception that first encou-'raged me. To be quite sure I had fallen into no uncon-'scious repetitions, I read *David Copperfield* again the 'other day, and was affected by it to a degree you would 'hardly believe.'

LONDON: 1860.

Stopping a fall.

Another boy-child for hero.

Reading *Copperfield* again.

It may be doubted if Dickens could better have established his right to the front rank among novelists claimed for him, than by the ease and mastery with which, in these two books of *Copperfield* and *Great Expectations*, he kept

LONDON: 1861.

Unlikeness in likeness: David and Pip.

Gargery and Peggotty.

Fiction and Fact.

perfectly distinct the two stories of a boy's childhood, both told in the form of autobiography. A subtle penetration into character marks the unlikeness in the likeness; there is enough at once of resemblance and of difference in the position and surroundings of each to account for the divergences of character that arise; both children are good-hearted, and both have the advantage of association with models of tender simplicity and oddity, perfect in their truth and quite distinct from each other; but a sudden tumble into distress steadies Peggotty's little friend, and as unexpected a stroke of good fortune turns the head of the small protégé of Joe Gargery. What a deal of spoiling nevertheless, a nature that is really good at the bottom of it will stand without permanent damage, is nicely shown in Pip; and the way he reconciles his determination to act very shabbily to his early friends, with a conceited notion that he is setting them a moral example, is part of the shading of a character drawn with extraordinary skill. His greatest trial comes out of his good luck; and the foundations of both are laid at the opening of the tale, in a churchyard down by the Thames, as it winds past desolate marshes twenty miles to the sea, of which a masterly picture in half a dozen lines will give only average example of the descriptive writing that is everywhere one of the charms of the book. It is strange, as I transcribe the words, with what wonderful vividness they bring back the very spot on which we stood when he said he meant to make it the scene of the opening of his story—Cooling Castle ruins and the desolate Church, lying out among the marshes seven miles from Gadshill! 'My first most vivid 'and broad impression . . on a memorable raw afternoon 'towards evening . . was . . that this bleak place, overgrown 'with nettles, was the churchyard, and that the dark flat 'wilderness beyond the churchyard, intersected with dykes 'and mounds and gates, with scattered cattle feeding on it, 'was the marshes; and that the low leaden line beyond, 'was the river; and that the distant savage lair from which 'the wind was rushing, was the sea . . . On the edge of the 'river . . only two black things in all the prospect seemed 'to be standing upright . . one, the beacon by which the 'sailors steered, like an unhooped cask upon a pole, an ugly 'thing when you were near it; the other, a gibbet with 'some chains hanging to it which had once held a pirate.' Here Magwitch, an escaped convict from Chatham, terrifies the child Pip into stealing for him food and a file; and though recaptured and transported, he carries with him to Australia such a grateful heart for the small creature's service, that on making a fortune there he resolves to make his little friend a gentleman. This requires circumspection; and is so done, through the Old-Bailey attorney who has defended Magwitch at his trial (a character of surprising novelty and truth), that Pip imagines his present gifts and 'great expectations' to have come from the supposed rich lady of the story (whose eccentricities are the unattractive part of it, and have yet a weird character that somehow fits in with the kind of wrong she has suffered). When therefore the closing scenes bring back Magwitch himself, who risks his life to gratify his longing to see the gentleman he has made, it is an unspeakable horror to the youth to discover his benefactor in the convicted felon. If any

Vivid descriptive writing.

Groundwork of the story.

The great expectations.

What they end in.

LONDON: 1861.

one doubts Dickens's power of so drawing a character as to get to the heart of it, seeing beyond surface peculiarities into the moving springs of the human being himself, let him narrowly examine those scenes. There is not a grain of substitution of mere sentiment, or circumstance, for the inner and absolute reality of the position in which these two creatures find themselves. Pip's loathing of what had built up his fortune, and his horror of the uncouth architect, are apparent in even his most generous efforts to protect him from exposure and sentence. Magwitch's convict habits strangely blend themselves with his wild pride in, and love for, the youth whom his money has turned into a gentleman. He has a craving for his good opinion; dreads to offend him by his 'heavy grubbing,' or by the oaths he lets fall now and then; and pathetically hopes his Pip, his dear boy, won't think him 'low': but, upon a chum of Pip's appearing unexpectedly while they are together, he pulls out a jack-knife by way of hint he can defend himself, and produces afterwards a greasy little clasped black Testament on which the startled new-comer, being found to have no hostile intention, is sworn to secrecy. At the opening of the story there had been an exciting scene of the wretched man's chase and recapture among the marshes, and this has its parallel at the close in his chase and recapture on the river while poor Pip is helping to get him off. To make himself sure of the actual course of a boat in such circumstances, and what possible incidents the adventure might have, Dickens hired a steamer for the day from Blackwall to Southend. Eight or nine friends and three or four members of his family were on board,

Masterly drawing of character.

A chase and recapture.

Preliminary survey of the Thames.

and he seemed to have no care, the whole of that summer day (22nd of May 1861), except to enjoy their enjoyment and entertain them with his own in shape of a thousand whims and fancies; but his sleepless observation was at work all the time, and nothing had escaped his keen vision on either side of the river. The fifteenth chapter of the third volume is a masterpiece.

LONDON: 1861.

Jaggers and Wemmick.

The characters generally afford the same evidence as those two that Dickens's humour, not less than his creative power, was at its best in this book. The Old-Bailey attorney Jaggers, and his clerk Wemmick (both excellent, and the last one of the oddities that live in everybody's liking for the goodheartedness of its humorous surprises), are as good as his earliest efforts in that line; the Pumblechooks and Wopsles are perfect as bits of *Nickleby* fresh from the mint; and the scene in which Pip, and Pip's chum Herbert, make up their accounts and schedule their debts and obligations, is original and delightful as Micawber himself.

Minor people.

Living on nothing and making the best of it.

It is the art of living upon nothing and making the best of it, in the most pleasing form. Herbert's intentions to trade east and west, and get himself into business transactions of a magnificent extent and variety, are as perfectly warranted to us, in his way of putting them, by merely 'being in a counting-house and looking about you,' as Pip's means of paying his debts are lightened and made easy by his method of simply adding them up with a margin. 'The time comes,' says Herbert, 'when you 'see your opening. And you go in, and you swoop upon 'it, and you make your capital, and then there you are! 'When you have once made your capital you have nothing

Margins and openings.

LONDON: 1861.

'to do but employ it.' In like manner Pip tells us 'Suppose your debts to be one hundred and sixty four pounds 'four and twopence, I would say, leave a margin and put 'them down at two hundred; or suppose them to be four 'times as much, leave a margin and put them down at 'seven hundred.' He is sufficiently candid to add, that, while he has the highest opinion of the wisdom and prudence of the margin, its dangers are that in the sense of freedom and solvency it imparts there is a tendency to run into new debt. But the satire that thus enforces the old warning against living upon vague hopes, and paying ancient debts by contracting new ones, never presented itself in more amusing or kindly shape. A word should be added of the father of the girl that Herbert marries, Bill Barley, ex-ship's purser, a gouty, bed-ridden, drunken old rascal, who lies on his back in an upper floor on Mill Pond Bank by Chinks's Basin, where he keeps, weighs, and serves out the family stores or provisions, according to old professional practice, with one eye at a telescope which is fitted on his bed for the convenience of sweeping the river. This is one of those sketches, slight in itself but made rich with a wealth of comic observation, in which Dickens's humour took especial delight; and to all this part of the story, there is a quaint riverside flavour that gives it amusing reality and relish.

Homely and shrewd satire.

Bill Barley.

Sending the chapters that contain it, which open the third division of the tale, he wrote thus: 'It is a pity that 'the third portion cannot be read all at once, because its 'purpose would be much more apparent; and the pity 'is the greater, because the general turn and tone of the

Dickens on progress of the tale.

'working out and winding up, will be away from all such 'things as they conventionally go. But what must be, 'must be. As to the planning out from week to week, 'nobody can imagine what the difficulty is, without trying. 'But, as in all such cases, when it is overcome the pleasure 'is proportionate. Two months more will see me through 'it, I trust. All the iron is in the fire, and I have "only" 'to beat it out.' One other letter throws light upon an objection taken not unfairly to the too great speed with which the heroine, after being married, reclaimed, and widowed, is in a page or two again made love to, and remarried by the hero. This summary proceeding was not originally intended. But, over and above its popular acceptance, the book had interested some whose opinions Dickens specially valued (Carlyle among them, I remember);* and upon Bulwer Lytton objecting to a close that should leave Pip a solitary man, Dickens substituted what now stands. 'You will be surprised' he wrote 'to hear that 'I have changed the end of *Great Expectations* from and 'after Pip's return to Joe's, and finding his little likeness 'there. Bulwer, who has been, as I think you know, ex-'traordinarily taken by the book, so strongly urged it upon 'me, after reading the proofs, and supported his view with 'such good reasons, that I resolved to make the change. 'You shall have it when you come back to town. I have 'put in as pretty a little piece of writing as I could, and I 'have no doubt the story will be more acceptable through

LONDON: 1861.

Incident at close objected to.

Not as first written.

Changed at Bulwer Lytton's suggestion.

* A dear friend now gone, used laughingly to relate what outcry there used to be, on the night of the week when a number was due, for 'that Pip nonsense!' and what roars of laughter followed, though at first it was entirely put aside as not on any account to have time wasted over it.

At Chelsea.

LONDON: 1861.

'the alteration.' This turned out to be the case; but the first ending nevertheless seems to be more consistent with the drift, as well as natural working out, of the tale, and for this reason it is preserved in a note.*

---

CHRISTMAS SKETCHES.

Between that fine novel, which was issued in three volumes in the autumn of 1861, and the completion of his next serial story, were interposed three sketches in his happiest vein at which everyone laughed and cried in the

1862–3–4.

Christmas times of 1862, '3, and '4. Of the waiter in *Some-*

Close of *Great Expectations* as originally written.

* There was no Chapter XX. as now; but the sentence which opens it ('For eleven years' in the original, altered to 'eight years') followed the paragraph about his business partnership with Herbert, and led to Biddy's question whether he is sure he does not fret for Estella ('I am sure and certain, 'Biddy' as originally written, altered to 'O no—I think not, Biddy'): from which point here was the close. 'It was two years more, before I saw herself. 'I had heard of her as leading a most unhappy life, and as being separated from 'her husband who had used her with great cruelty, and who had become quite 'renowned as a compound of pride, brutality, and meanness. I had heard of 'the death of her husband (from an accident consequent on ill-treating a horse), 'and of her being married again to a Shropshire doctor, who, against his 'interest, had once very manfully interposed, on an occasion when he was in 'professional attendance on Mr. Drummle, and had witnessed some outrageous 'treatment of her. I had heard that the Shropshire doctor was not rich, and 'that they lived on her own personal fortune. I was in England again—in 'London, and walking along Piccadilly with little Pip—when a servant came 'running after me to ask would I step back to a lady in a carriage who 'wished to speak to me. It was a little pony carriage, which the lady was 'driving; and the lady and I looked sadly enough on one another. "I am '"greatly changed, I know; but I thought you would like to shake hands '"with Estella too, Pip. Lift up that pretty child and let me kiss it!" '(She supposed the child, I think, to be my child.) I was very glad afterwards to have had the interview; for, in her face and in her voice, and in her 'touch, she gave me the assurance, that suffering had been stronger than Miss 'Havisham's teaching, and had given her a heart to understand what my heart 'used to be.'

*body's Luggage* Dickens has himself spoken; and if any theme is well treated, when, from the point of view taken, nothing more is left to say about it, that bit of fun is perfect. Call it exaggeration, grotesqueness, or by what hard name you will, laughter will always intercept any graver criticism. Writing from Paris of what he was himself responsible for in the articles left by Somebody with his wonderful Waiter, he said that in one of them he had made the story a camera obscura of certain French places and styles of people; having founded it on something he had noticed in a French soldier. This was the tale of Little Bebelle, which had a small French corporal for its hero, and became highly popular. But the triumph of the Christmas achievements in these days was Mrs. Lirriper. She took her place at once among people known to everybody; and all the world talked of Major Jemmy Jackman, and his friend the poor elderly lodging-house keeper of the Strand, with her miserable cares and rivalries and worries, as if they had both been as long in London and as well known as Norfolk-street itself. A dozen volumes could not have told more than those dozen pages did. The *Legacy* followed the *Lodgings* in 1864, and there was no falling off in the fun and laughter.

LONDON: 1862–4.

*Somebody's Luggage.*

Little Bebelle.

*Mrs. Lirriper's Lodgings* and *Legacy.*

---

### OUR MUTUAL FRIEND.

The publication of *Our Mutual Friend,* in the form of the earliest stories, extended from May 1864 to November 1865. Four years earlier he had chosen this title as a good one, and he held to it through much objection. Between that time and his actual commencement there is

New book in 20 numbers.

LONDON: 1864-5.

mention, in his letters, of the three leading notions on which he founded the story. In his waterside wanderings during his last book, the many handbills he saw posted up, with dreary description of persons drowned in the river, suggested the 'long shore men and their ghastly calling whom he sketched in Hexam and Riderhood. 'I think,' he had written, 'a man, young and perhaps eccentric, feigning 'to be dead, and *being* dead to all intents and purposes 'external to himself, and for years retaining the singular 'view of life and character so imparted, would be a good 'leading incident for a story;' and this he partly did in Rokesmith. For other actors in the tale, he had thought of 'a poor impostor of a man marrying a woman for her 'money; she marrying *him* for *his* money; after marriage 'both finding out their mistake, and entering into a league 'and covenant against folks in general:' with whom he had proposed to connect some Perfectly New people. 'Every-'thing new about them. If they presented a father and 'mother, it seemed as if THEY must be bran new, like the 'furniture and the carriages—shining with varnish, and just 'home from the manufacturers.' These groups took shape in the Lammles and the Veneerings. 'I must use somehow,' is the remark of another letter, 'the uneducated father in 'fustian and the educated boy in spectacles whom Leech and 'I saw at Chatham;' of which a hint is in Charley Hexam and his father. The benevolent old Jew whom he makes the unconscious agent of a rascal, was meant to wipe out a reproach against his Jew in *Oliver Twist* as bringing dislike upon the religion of the race he belonged to.*

First notion for it.

Germ of characters for it.

Fustian-clad father and spectacled son.

* On this reproach, from a Jewish lady whom he esteemed, he had written

Having got his title in '61 it was his hope to have begun in '62. 'Alas!' he wrote in the April of that year, 'I 'have hit upon nothing for a story. Again and again I 'have tried. But this odious little house' (he had at this time for a few weeks exchanged Gadshill for a friend's house near Kensington) 'seems to have stifled and darkened 'my invention.' It was not until the autumn of the following year he saw his way to a beginning. 'The Christmas 'number has come round again' (30th of August 1863) '—it seems only yesterday that I did the last—but I am 'full of notions besides for the new twenty numbers. When 'I can clear the Christmas stone out of the road, I think I 'can dash into it on the grander journey.' He persevered through much difficulty; which he described six weeks later, with characteristic glance at his own ways when writing, in a letter from the office of his journal. 'I came here 'last night, to evade my usual day in the week—in fact 'to shirk it—and get back to Gad's for five or six con'secutive days. My reason is, that I am exceedingly 'anxious to begin my book. I am bent upon getting to 'work at it. I want to prepare it for the spring; but I 'am determined not to begin to publish with less than 'five numbers done. I see my opening perfectly, with 'the one main line on which the story is to turn; and if 'I don't strike while the iron (meaning myself) is hot, I

LONDON: 1864–5.

Delays in beginning. 1862.

Writing numbers in advance.

two years before. 'Fagin, in *Oliver Twist*, is a Jew, because it unfortunately 'was true, of the time to which that story refers, that that class of criminal 'almost invariably *was* a Jew. But surely no sensible man or woman of your 'persuasion can fail to observe—firstly, that all the rest of the wicked *dramatis* '*personæ* are Christians; and, secondly, that he is called "The Jew," not 'because of his religion, but because of his race.'

LONDON: 1864–5.

'shall drift off again, and have to go through all this un-'easiness once more.'

Autumn of 1863.

He had written, after four months, very nearly three numbers, when upon a necessary rearrangement of his chapters he had to hit upon a new subject for one of them. 'While 'I was considering' (25th of February) 'what it should

New illustrator.

'be, Marcus,* who has done an excellent cover, came to tell 'me of an extraordinary trade he had found out, through 'one of his painting requirements. I immediately went 'with him to Saint Giles's to look at the place, and found '—what you will see.' It was the establishment of Mr.

Original of Mr. Venus. 1864.

Venus, preserver of animals and birds, and articulator of human bones; and it took the place of the last chapter of No. 2, which was then transferred to the end of No. 3. But a start with three full numbers done, though more than enough to satisfy the hardest self-conditions formerly, did not satisfy him now. With his previous thought given to the story, with his Memoranda to help him, with the people he had in hand to work it with, and ready as he still was to turn his untiring observation to instant use

Working slowly.

on its behalf, he now moved, with the old large canvas before him, somewhat slowly and painfully. 'If I were 'to lose' (29th of March) 'a page of the five numbers I 'have proposed to myself to be ready by the publication 'day, I should feel that I had fallen short. I have grown

So much (not fiction) in his thoughts.

'hard to satisfy, and write very slowly. And I have so 'much—not fiction—that *will* be thought of, when I don't

* Mr. Marcus Stone had, upon the separate issue of the *Tale of Two Cities*, taken the place of Mr. Hablot Browne as his illustrator. *Hard Times* and the first edition of *Great Expectations* were not illustrated; but when Pip's story appeared in one volume, Mr. Stone contributed designs for it.

'want to think of it, that I am forced to take more care 'than I once took.'

LONDON: 1864–5.

Sale of first and drop of second number.

The first number was launched at last, on the first of May; and after two days he wrote: 'Nothing can be better 'than *Our Friend*, now in his thirtieth thousand, and 'orders flowing in fast.' But between the first and second number there was a drop of five thousand, strange to say, for the larger number was again reached, and much exceeded, before the book closed. 'This leaves me' (10th of June) 'going round and round like a carrier-pigeon before 'swooping on number seven.' Thus far he had held his ground; but illness came, with some other anxieties, and on the 29th of July he wrote sadly enough. 'Although I 'have not been wanting in industry, I have been wanting 'in invention, and have fallen back with the book. Loom-'ing large before me is the Christmas work, and I can 'hardly hope to do it without losing a number of *Our 'Friend*. I have very nearly lost one already, and two 'would take one half of my whole advance. This week I 'have been very unwell; am still out of sorts; and, as I 'know from two days' slow experience, have a very 'mountain to climb before I shall see the open country 'of my work.' The three following months brought hardly more favourable report. 'I have not done my number. 'This death of poor Leech (I suppose) has put me out 'woefully. Yesterday and the day before I could do 'nothing; seemed for the time to have quite lost the 'power; and am only by slow degrees getting back into 'the track to-day.' He rallied after this, and satisfied himself for a while; but in February 1865 that formidable

Falling back.

Impdiments.

Death of Leech.

LONDON: 1864–5.

Suffering from lameness. *Ante*, 272. *Post*, 477–8.

illness in his foot broke out which, at certain times for the rest of his life, deprived him more or less of his inestimable solace of bodily exercise. In April and May he suffered severely; and after trying the sea went abroad for more complete change. 'Work and worry, without exercise, 'would soon make an end of me. If I were not going

Holiday in France.

'away now, I should break down. No one knows as I 'know to-day how near to it I have been.'

That was the day of his leaving for France, and the day of his return brought these few hurried words. 'Saturday,

In the Staplehurst accident.

'tenth of June, 1865. I was in the terrific Staplehurst acci'dent yesterday, and worked for hours among the dying 'and dead. I was in the carriage that did not go over, but 'went off the line, and hung over the bridge in an inex'plicable manner. No words can describe the scene.* I 'am away to Gads.' Though with characteristic energy he resisted the effects upon himself of that terrible ninth of June, they were for some time evident; and, up to the day

A fatal anniversary.

of his death on its fatal fifth anniversary, were perhaps never wholly absent. But very few complaints fell from

A MS. number of his book: 9th of June, 1865.

* He thus spoke of it in his 'Postscript in lieu of Preface' (dated 2nd of September 1865), which accompanied the last number of the story under notice. 'On Friday the ninth of June in the present year, Mr. and Mrs. 'Boffin (in their manuscript dress of receiving Mr. and Mrs. Lammle at break'fast) were on the South-Eastern Railway with me, in a terribly destructive 'accident. When I had done what I could to help others, I climbed back into 'my carriage—nearly turned over a viaduct, and caught aslant upon the turn '—to extricate the worthy couple. They were much soiled, but otherwise 'unhurt. The same happy result attended Miss Bella Wilfer on her wedding'day, and Mr. Riderhood inspecting Bradley Headstone's red neckerchief as 'he lay asleep. I remember with devout thankfulness that I can never be 'much nearer parting company with my readers for ever, than I was then, 'until there shall be written against my life the two words with which I have 'this day closed this book—THE END.'

him. 'I am curiously weak—weak as if I were recovering 'from a long illness.' 'I begin to feel it more in my head. 'I sleep well and eat well; but I write half a dozen notes, 'and turn faint and sick.' 'I am getting right, though 'still low in pulse and very nervous. Driving into Roches- 'ter yesterday I felt more shaken than I have since the 'accident.' 'I cannot bear railway travelling yet. A 'perfect conviction, against the senses, that the carriage is 'down on one side (and generally that is the left, and *not* 'the side on which the carriage in the accident really went 'over), comes upon me with anything like speed, and is 'inexpressibly distressing.' These are passages from his letters up to the close of June. Upon his book the immediate result was that another lost number was added to the losses of the preceding months, and 'alas!' he wrote at the opening of July, 'for the two numbers you write of! 'There is only one in existence. I have but just begun 'the other.' 'Fancy!' he added next day, 'fancy my having 'under-written number sixteen by two and a half pages— 'a thing I have not done since *Pickwick!*' He did it once with *Dombey*, and was to do it yet again.

LONDON: 1864–5.

Effects of accident on himself:

on his novel.

ii. 307.

The book thus begun and continued under adverse influences, though with fancy in it, descriptive power, and characters well designed, will never rank with his higher efforts. It has some pictures of a rare veracity of soul amid the lowest forms of social degradation, placed beside others of sheer falsehood and pretence amid unimpeachable social correctness, which lifted the writer to his old place; but the judgment of it on the whole must be, that it wants freshness and natural development. This indeed will be

*Our Mutual Friend.*

LONDON: 1864–5.

most freely admitted by those who feel most strongly that all the old cunning of the master hand is yet in the wayward loving Bella Wilfer, in the vulgar canting Podsnap, and in the dolls' dressmaker Jenny Wren, whose keen little quaint weird ways, and precocious wit sharpened by trouble, are fitted into a character as original and delightfully conceived as it is vividly carried through to the last. A dull coarse web her small life seems made of; but even from its taskwork, which is undertaken for childhood itself, there are glittering threads cast across its woof and warp of care. The unconscious philosophy of her tricks and manners has in it more of the subtler vein of the satire aimed at in the book, than even the voices of society which the tale begins and ends with. In her very kindliness there is the touch of malice that shows a childish playfulness familiar with unnatural privations; this gives a depth as well as tenderness to her humours which entitles them to rank with the writer's happiest things; and though the odd little creature's talk is incessant when she is on the scene, it has the individuality that so seldom tires. It is veritably her own small 'trick' and 'manner,' and is never mistakeable for any one else's. 'I have been reading,' Dickens wrote to me from France while he was writing the book, 'a 'capital little story by Edmond About—*The Notary's Nose.* 'I have been trying other books; but so infernally con-'versational, that I forget who the people are before they 'have done talking, and don't in the least remember what 'they talked about before when they begin talking again!' The extreme contrast to his own art could not be defined more exactly; and other examples from this tale will be

The dolls' dress-maker.

One of Dickens's master-pieces.

On a tale by Edmond About.

found in the differing members of the Wilfer family, in the riverside people at the Fellowship Porters, in such marvellous serio-comic scenes as that of Rogue Riderhood's restoration from drowning, and in those short and simple annals of Betty Higden's life and death which might have given saving virtue to a book more likely than this to perish prematurely. It has not the creative power which crowded his earlier page, and transformed into popular realities the shadows of his fancy; but the observation and humour he excelled in are not wanting to it, nor had there been, in his first completed work, more eloquent or generous pleading for the poor and neglected, than this last completed work contains. Betty Higden finishes what Oliver Twist began.

LONDON: 1864–5.

Betty Higden.

First and last.

---

DR. MARIGOLD AND TALES FOR AMERICA.

He had scarcely closed that book in September, wearied somewhat with a labour of invention which had not been so free or self-sustaining as in the old facile and fertile days, when his customary contribution to Christmas became due from him; and his fancy, let loose in a narrower field, resumed its old luxury of enjoyment. Here are notices of it from his letters. 'If people at large understand a 'Cheap Jack, my part of the Christmas number will do 'well. It is wonderfully like the real thing, of course a 'little refined and humoured.' 'I do hope that in the be'ginning and end of this Christmas number you will find 'something that will strike you as being fresh, forcible, 'and full of spirits.' He described its mode of composition afterwards. 'Tired with *Our Mutual*, I sat down to cast

1865.

A Cheap Jack.

LONDON: 1865.

How *Doctor Marigold* was written.

'about for an idea, with a depressing notion that I was, 'for the moment, overworked. Suddenly, the little cha-'racter that you will see, and all belonging to it, came 'flashing up in the most cheerful manner, and I had only 'to look on and leisurely describe it.' This was *Dr. Marigold's Prescriptions*, one of the most popular of all the pieces selected for his readings, and a splendid example of his humour, pathos, and character. There were three more Christmas pieces before he made his last visit to America: *Barbox Brothers*, *The Boy at Mugby Station*, and *No Thoroughfare:* the last a joint piece of work with Mr. Wilkie Collins, who during Dickens's absence in the States transformed it into a play for Mr. Fechter, with a view to which it had been planned originally. There were also two papers written for first publication in America, *George Silverman's Explanation*, and *Holiday Romance*, containing about the quantity of half a shilling number of his ordinary serials, and paid for at a rate unexampled in literature. They occupied him not many days in the writing, and he received a thousand pounds for them.

Minor stories. i. 119.

How remunerated. *Ante*, 224-5.

---

*Edwin Drood.*

The year after his return, as the reader knows, saw the commencement of the work which death interrupted. The fragment will hereafter be described; and here meanwhile may close my criticism—itself a fragment left for worthier completion by a stronger hand than mine.

But at least I may hope that the ground has been cleared by it from those distinctions and comparisons never safely to be applied to an original writer, and which always more or less intercept his fair appreciation. It was long the fashion to set up wide divergences between novels of incident and manners, and novels of character; the narrower range being left to Fielding and Smollett, and the larger to Richardson; yet there are not many now who will accept such classification. Nor is there more truth in other like distinctions alleged between novelists who are assumed to be real, or ideal, in their methods of treatment. To any original novelist of the higher grade there is no meaning in these contrasted phrases. Neither mode can exist at all perfectly without the other. No matter how sensitive the mind to external impressions, or how keen the observation to whatever can be seen, without the rarer seeing of imagination nothing will be arrived at that is real in any genuine artist-sense. Reverse the proposition, and the result is expressed in an excellent remark of Lord Lytton's, that the happiest effort of imagination, however lofty it may be, is that which enables it to be cheerfully at home with the real. I have said that Dickens felt criticism, of whatever kind, with too sharp a relish for the indifference he assumed to it; but the secret was that he believed himself to be entitled to higher tribute than he was always in the habit of receiving. It was the feeling which suggested a memorable saying of Wordsworth. 'I am not at all desirous that any one should 'write a critique on my poems. If they be from above, 'they will do their own work in course of time; if not, 'they will perish as they ought.'

Needless classifications.

'Real' worthless without 'ideal.'

Failing common to men of genius.

The something 'from above' never seems to me absent from Dickens, even at his worst. When the strain upon his invention became apparent, and he could only work freely in a more confined space than of old, it was still able

'Something 'from 'above.'

London: 1836–70.

Purity of Dickens's writings.

to assert itself triumphantly; and his influence over his readers was continued by it to the last day of his life. Looking back over the series of his writings, the first reflection that rises to the mind of any thoughtful person, is one of thankfulness that the most popular of writers, who had carried into the lowest scenes and conditions an amount of observation, fun, and humour not approached by any of his contemporaries, should never have sullied that world-wide influence by a hint of impurity or a possibility of harm. Nor is there anything more surprising than the freshness and variety of character which those writings include, within the range of the not numerous types of character that were the limit of their author's genius. For, this also appears, upon any review of them collectively, that the teeming life which is in them is that of the time in which his own life was passed; and that with the purpose of showing vividly its form and pressure, was joined the hope and design to leave it better than he found it.

Life of the time reproduced and bettered.

It has been objected that humanity receives from him no addition to its best types; that the burlesque humourist is always stronger in him than the reflective moralist; that the light thrown by his genius into out of the way corners of life never steadily shines in its higher beaten ways; and that beside his pictures of what man is or does, there is no attempt to show, by delineation of an exalted purpose or a great career, what man is able to be or to do. In the charge abstractedly there is truth; but the fair remark upon it is that whatever can be regarded as essential in the want implied by it will be found in other forms in his writings, that the perfect innocence of their laughter and

An alleged deficiency.

tears has been itself a prodigious blessing, and that it is otherwise incident to so great a humourist to work after the fashion most natural to the genius of humour. What kind of work it has been in his case, the attempt is made in preceding pages to show; and on the whole it can be said with some certainty that the best ideals in this sense are obtained, not by presenting with added comeliness or grace the figures which life is ever eager to present as of its best, but by connecting the singularities and eccentricities, which ordinary life is apt to reject or overlook, with the apprecia-tion that is deepest and the laws of insight that are most universal. It is thus that all things human are happily brought within human sympathy. It was at the heart of everything Dickens wrote. It was the secret of the hope he had that his books might help to make people better; and it so guarded them from evil, that there is scarcely a page of the thousands he has written which might not be put into the hands of a little child.* It made him the intimate of every English household, and a familiar friend wherever the language is spoken whose stores of harmless pleasure he has so largely increased.

A sufficient substitute.

True province of Humour.

'The loss of no single man during the present generation, 'if we except Abraham Lincoln alone,' said Mr. Horace Greeley, describing the profound and universal grief of America at his death, 'has carried mourning into so many

9th June, 1870. Effect in America.

* I borrow this language from the Bishop of Manchester, who, on the third day after Dickens's death, in the Abbey where he was so soon to be laid, closed a plea for the toleration of differences of opinion where the foundations of religious truth are accepted, with these words. 'It will not be out of harmony with the 'line of thought we have been pursuing—certainly it will be in keeping with the 'associations of this place, dear to Englishmen, not only as one of the proudest 'Christian temples, but as containing the memorials of so many who by their

LONDON: 1836–70.

H. W. Longfellow.

'families, and been so unaffectedly lamented through all the 'ranks of society.' 'The terrible news from England,' wrote Longfellow to me (Cambridge, Mass. 12th of June 1870), 'fills us all with inexpressible sadness. Dickens was so full 'of life that it did not seem possible he could die, and yet he 'has gone before us, and we are sorrowing for him .... I never 'knew an author's death cause such general mourning. It 'is no exaggeration to say that this whole country is stricken 'with grief . . .' Nor was evidence then wanting, that far beyond the limits of society on that vast continent the English writer's influence had penetrated. Of this, very touching illustration was given in my first volume; and proof even more striking has since been afforded to me,

i. 192–3.

The Bishop of Manchester on Dickens's writings.

'genius in arts, or arms, or statesmanship, or literature, have made England 'what she is—if in the simplest and briefest words I allude to that sad and 'unexpected death which has robbed English literature of one of its highest 'living ornaments, and the news of which, two mornings ago, must have made 'every household in England feel as though they had lost a personal friend. 'He has been called in one notice an apostle of the people. I suppose it is 'meant that he had a mission, but in a style and fashion of his own; a gospel, 'a cheery, joyous, gladsome message, which the people understood, and by 'which they could hardly help being bettered; for it was the gospel of kindliness, 'of brotherly love, of sympathy in the widest sense of the word. I am sure 'I have felt in myself the healthful spirit of his teaching. Possibly we might 'not have been able to subscribe to the same creed in relation to God, but I 'think we should have subscribed to the same creed in relation to man. He 'who has taught us our duty to our fellow men better than we knew it before, 'who knew so well to weep with them that wept, and to rejoice with them that 'rejoiced, who has shown forth in all his knowledge of the dark corners of the 'earth how much sunshine may rest upon the lowliest lot, who had such evi- 'dent sympathy with suffering, and such a natural instinct of purity that there is 'scarcely a page of the thousands he has written which might not be put into 'the hands of a little child, must be regarded by those who recognise the 'diversity of the gifts of the spirit as a teacher sent from God. He would 'have been welcomed as a fellow-labourer in the common interests of humanity 'by Him who asked the question "If a man love not his brother whom he '"hath seen, how can he love God whom he hath not seen?"'

Praise worth having.

that not merely in wild or rude communities, but in life the most savage and solitary, his genius had helped to while time away.

LONDON: 1836–70.

'Like all Americans who read,' writes an American gentleman, 'and that takes in nearly all our people, I am an 'admirer and student of Dickens. . . . Its perusal' (that of my second volume) 'has recalled an incident which may 'interest you. Twelve or thirteen years ago I crossed the 'Sierra Nevada mountains as a Government surveyor under 'a famous frontiersman and civil engineer—Colonel Lander. 'We were too early by a month, and became snow-bound 'just on the very summit. Under these circumstances it 'was necessary to abandon the wagons for a time, and drive 'the stock (mules) down the mountains to the valleys 'where there was pasturage and running water. This was 'a long and difficult task, occupying several days. On the 'second day, in a spot where we expected to find nothing 'more human than a grizzly bear or an elk, we found a 'little hut, built of pine boughs and a few rough boards 'clumsily hewn out of small trees with an axe. The hut 'was covered with snow many feet deep, excepting only 'the hole in the roof which served for a chimney, and a 'small pit-like place in front to permit egress. The occu'pant came forth to hail us and solicit whisky and tobacco. 'He was dressed in a suit made entirely of flour-sacks, and 'was curiously labelled on various parts of his person *Best 'Family Flour. Extra.* His head was covered by a wolf's 'skin drawn from the brute's head—with the ears stand'ing erect in a fierce alert manner. He was a most extra'ordinary object, and told us he had not seen a human

Letter from an American to the author of this book.

On the Nevada Mountains.

Strange encounter.

LONDON: 1836–70.

'being in four months. He lived on bear and elk meat 'and flour laid in during his short summer. Emigrants in 'the season paid him a kind of ferry-toll. I asked him 'how he passed his time, and he went to a barrel and pro-'duced *Nicholas Nickleby* and *Pickwick*. I found he knew 'them almost by heart. He did not know, or seem to care, 'about the author; but he gloried in Sam Weller, despised 'Squeers, and would probably have taken the latter's scalp 'with great skill and cheerfulness. For Mr. Winkle he 'had no feeling but contempt, and in fact regarded a fowl-'ing-piece as only a toy for a squaw. He had no Bible; 'and perhaps if he practised in his rude savage way all 'Dickens taught, he might less have felt the want even of 'that companion.'

Companions in solitude.

## CHAPTER XV.

### AMERICA REVISITED: NOVEMBER AND DECEMBER 1867.

1867.

It is the intention of this and the following chapter to narrate the incidents of the visit to America in Dickens's own language, and in that only. They will consist almost exclusively of extracts from his letters written home, to members of his family and to myself.

AMERICA: 1867.

On the night of Tuesday the 19th of November he arrived at Boston, where he took up his residence at the Parker House hotel; and his first letter (21st) stated that the tickets for the first four Readings, all to that time issued, had been sold immediately on their becoming saleable. 'An immense train of people waited in the freezing 'street for twelve hours, and passed into the office in their 'turns, as at a French theatre. The receipts already taken 'for these nights exceed our calculation by more than £250.' Up to the last moment, he had not been able to clear off wholly a shade of misgiving that some of the old grudges might make themselves felt; but from the instant of his setting foot in Boston not a vestige of such fear remained. The greeting was to the full as extraordinary as that of twenty-five years before, and was given now, as then, to

At Parker House: Boston.

Warmth of the greeting.

AMERICA: 1867.

the man who had made himself the most popular writer in the country. His novels and tales were crowding the shelves of all the dealers in books in all the cities of the Union. In every house, in every car, on every steam-boat, in every theatre of America, the characters, the fancies, the phraseology of Dickens were become familiar beyond those of any other writer of books. 'Even in England,' said one of the New York journals, 'Dickens is less known than 'here; and of the millions here who treasure every word he 'has written, there are tens of thousands who would make 'a large sacrifice to see and hear the man who has made 'happy so many hours. Whatever sensitiveness there once 'was to adverse or sneering criticism, the lapse of a 'quarter of a century, and the profound significance of a 'great war, have modified or removed.' The point was more pithily, and as truly, put by Mr. Horace Greeley in the *Tribune*. 'The fame as a novelist which Mr. Dickens 'had already created in America, and which, at the best, 'has never yielded him anything particularly munificent 'or substantial, is become his capital stock in the present 'enterprise.'

Same cause for greeting as in 1842. i. 282.

Capital stock of the enterprise.

The first Reading was appointed for the second of December, and in the interval he saw some old friends and made some new ones.* Boston he was fond of com-

Agassiz.

* Among these I think he was most delighted with the great naturalist and philosopher, Agassiz, whose death is unhappily announced while I write, and as to whom it will no longer be unbecoming to quote his allusion. 'Agassiz, 'who married the last Mrs. Felton's sister, is not only one of the most accom-'plished but the most natural and jovial of men.' Again he says: 'I cannot 'tell you how pleased I was by Agassiz, a most charming fellow, or how I have 'regretted his seclusion for a while by reason of his mother's death.' A valued correspondent, Mr. Grant Wilson, sends me a list of famous Americans who

AMERICA: 1867.

Old and new friends.

paring to Edinburgh as Edinburgh was in the days when several dear friends of his own still lived there. Twenty-five years had changed much in the American city; some genial faces were gone, and on ground which he had left a swamp he found now the most princely streets; but there was no abatement of the old warmth of kindness, and, with every attention and consideration shown to him, there was no intrusion. He was not at first completely conscious of the change in this respect, or of the prodigious increase in the size of Boston. But the latter grew upon him from day to day, and then there was impressed along with it a contrast to which it was difficult to reconcile himself. Nothing enchanted him so much as what he again saw of the delightful domestic life of Cambridge, simple, self-respectful, cordial, and affectionate; and it seemed impossible to believe that within half an hour's distance of it should be found what might at any time be witnessed in such hotels as that which he was staying at: crowds of swaggerers, loafers, bar-loungers, and dram-drinkers, that seemed to be making up, from day to day, not the least important part of the human life of the city. But

Cambridge and Boston.

A contrast.

greeted Dickens at his first visit, and in the interval had passed away. 'It 'is melancholy to contemplate the large number of American authors who 'had, between the first and second visits of Mr. Dickens, "gone hence, to '"be no more seen." The sturdy Cooper, the gentle Irving, his friend and 'kinsman Paulding, Prescott the historian and Percival the poet, the eloquent 'Everett, Nathaniel Hawthorne, Edgar A. Poe, N. P. Willis, the genial Hal-'leck, and many lesser lights, including Prof. Felton and Geo. P. Morris, had 'died during the quarter of a century that elapsed between Dickens's visits to 'this country, leaving a new generation of writers to extend the hand of 'friendship to him on his second coming.'—Let me add to this that Dickens was pleased, at this second visit, to see his old secretary who had travelled so agreeably with him through his first tour of triumph. 'He would have 273
'known him anywhere.'

Famous writers dead since 1842.

AMERICA: 1867.

no great mercantile resort in the States, such as Boston had now become, could be without that drawback; and fortunate should we account any place to be, though even so plague-afflicted, that has yet so near it the healthier influence of the other life which our older world has well-nigh lost altogether.

Changes since 1842.

'The city has increased prodigiously in twenty-five 'years,' he wrote to his daughter Mary. 'It has grown 'more mercantile. It is like Leeds mixed with Preston, 'and flavoured with New Brighton. Only, instead of 'smoke and fog, there is an exquisitely bright light air.' 'Cambridge is exactly as I left it,' he wrote to me. 'Boston more mercantile, and much larger. The hotel I 'formerly stayed at, and thought a very big one, is now 'regarded as a very small affair. I do not yet notice—'but a day, you know, is not a long time for observation! '—any marked change in character or habits. In this

i. 279.

'immense hotel I live very high up, and have a hot and 'cold bath in my bed room, with other comforts not in 'existence in my former day. The cost of living is 'enormous.' 'Two of the staff are at New York,' he wrote to his sister-in-law on the 25th of November, 'where we

Speculators.

'are at our wits' end how to keep tickets out of the hands 'of speculators. We have communications from all parts 'of the country, but we take no offer whatever. The young

Cambridge under-graduates.

'under-graduates of Cambridge have made a representa'tion to Longfellow that they are 500 strong and cannot 'get one ticket. I don't know what is to be done, but I 'suppose I must read there, somehow. We are all in the 'clouds until I shall have broken ground in New York.'

The sale of tickets, there, had begun two days before the first reading in Boston. 'At the New York barriers,' he wrote to his daughter on the first of December, 'where 'the tickets were on sale and the people ranged as at the 'Paris theatres, speculators went up and down offering 'twenty dollars for any body's place. The money was in 'no case accepted. But one man sold two tickets for the 'second, third, and fourth nights; his payment in exchange 'being one ticket for the first night, fifty dollars (about '£7 10*s.*), and a "brandy cock-tail."'

Sale of tickets in New York.

On Monday the second of December he read for the first time in Boston, his subjects being the *Carol* and the *Trial from Pickwick;* and his reception, from an audience than which perhaps none more remarkable could have been brought together, went beyond all expectations formed. 'It is really impossible,' he wrote to me next morning, 'to 'exaggerate the magnificence of the reception or the effect 'of the reading. The whole city will talk of nothing else 'and hear of nothing else to-day. Every ticket for those 'announced here, and in New York, is sold. All are sold 'at the highest price, for which in our calculation we made 'no allowance; and it is impossible to keep out speculators 'who immediately sell at a premium. At the decreased 'rate of money even, we had above £450 English in the 'house last night; and the New York hall holds 500 people 'more. Everything looks brilliant beyond the most san-'guine hopes, and I was quite as cool last night as though I 'were reading at Chatham.' The next night he read again; and also on Thursday and Friday; on Wednesday he had rested; and on Saturday he travelled to New York.

First Boston Reading: effect of it.

AMERICA: 1867.

Profits.

He had written, the day before he left, that he was making a clear profit of thirteen hundred pounds English a week, even allowing seven dollars to the pound; but words were added having no good omen in them, that the weather was taking a turn of even unusual severity, and that he found the climate, in the suddenness of its changes, 'and the wide 'leaps they take,' excessively trying. 'The work is of course 'rather trying too; but the sound position that everything 'must be subservient to it enables me to keep aloof from 'invitations. To-morrow,' ran the close of the letter, we 'move to New York. We cannot beat the speculators in 'our tickets. We sell no more than six to any one person 'for the course of four readings; but these speculators, 'who sell at greatly increased prices and make large profits, 'will employ any number of men to buy. One of the chief 'of them—now living in this house, in order that he may 'move as we move!—can put on 50 people in any place we 'go to; and thus he gets 300 tickets into his own hands.' Almost while Dickens was writing these words an eye-witness was describing to a Philadelphia paper the sale of the New York tickets. The pay-place was to open at nine on a Wednesday morning, and at midnight of Tuesday a long line of speculators were assembled in *queue;* at two in the morning a few honest buyers had begun to arrive; at five there were, of all classes, two lines of not less than 800 each; at eight there were at least 5000 persons in the two lines; at nine each line was more than three-quarters of a mile in length, and neither became sensibly shorter during the whole morning. 'The tickets for the 'course were all sold before noon. Members of families

Drawbacks

Troubles from speculators.

Scene at first New York sales.

'relieved each other in the *queues;* waiters flew across 'the streets and squares from the neighbouring restaurant, 'to serve parties who were taking their breakfast in the 'open December air; while excited men offered five and 'ten dollars for the mere permission to exchange places 'with other persons standing nearer the head of the line!'

AMERICA: 1867.

Strange picture.

The effect of the reading in New York corresponded with this marvellous preparation, and Dickens characterised his audience as an unexpected support to him; in its appreciation quick and unfailing, and highly demonstrative in its satisfactions. On the 11th of December he wrote to his daughter: 'Amazing success. A very fine audience, 'far better than at Boston. *Carol* and *Trial* on first 'night, great: still greater, *Copperfield* and *Bob Sawyer* 'on second. For the tickets of the four readings of next 'week there were, at nine o'clock this morning, 3000 'people in waiting, and they had begun to assemble in the 'bitter cold as early as two o'clock in the morning.' To myself he wrote on the 15th, adding touches to the curious picture. 'Dolby has got into trouble about the manner 'of issuing the tickets for next week's series. He cannot 'get four thousand people into a room holding only two 'thousand, he cannot induce people to pay at the ordinary 'price for themselves instead of giving thrice as much to 'speculators, and he is attacked in all directions. . . I don't 'much like my hall, for it has two large balconies far 'removed from the platform; but no one ever waylays me 'as I go into it or come out of it, and it is kept as 'rigidly quiet as the Français at a rehearsal. We have 'not yet had in it less than £430 per night, allowing for

First New York reading.

Enthusiasm!

Manager's troubles.

AMERICA: 1867.

the depreciated currency! I send £3000 to England by this packet. From all parts of the States, applications 'and offers continually come in. We go to Boston next 'Saturday for two more readings, and come back here on 'Christmas Day for four more. I am not yet bound to go 'elsewhere, except three times (each time for two nights) 'to Philadelphia; thinking it wisest to keep free for the 'largest places. I have had an action brought against 'me by a man who considered himself injured (and really 'may have been) in the matter of his tickets. Personal 'service being necessary, I was politely waited on by a 'marshal for that purpose; whom I received with the 'greatest courtesy, apparently very much to his amaze-'ment. The action was handsomely withdrawn next day, 'and the plaintiff paid his own costs. . . Dolby hopes 'you are satisfied with the figures so far; the profit each 'night exceeding the estimated profit by £130 odd. He 'is anxious I should also tell you that he is the most un-'popular and best-abused man in America.' Next day a letter to his sister-in-law related an incident too common in American cities to disconcert any but strangers. He had lodged himself, I should have said, at the Westminster Hotel in Irving Place. 'Last night I was getting into bed just at 12 o'clock, when Dolby came to my door to inform 'me that the house was on fire. I got Scott up directly; 'told him first to pack the books and clothes for the 'Readings; dressed, and pocketed my jewels and papers; 'while the manager stuffed himself out with money. Mean-'while the police and firemen were in the house tracing the mischief to its source in a certain fire-grate. By

An action against Dickens: handsomely withdrawn.

The most 'unpopular 'man in 'America.'

At Westminster Hotel: Irving Place.

'this time the hose was laid all through from a great tank 'on the roof, and everybody turned out to help. It was 'the oddest sight, and people had put the strangest things 'on! After chopping and cutting with axes through stairs, 'and much handing about of water, the fire was confined 'to a dining-room in which it had originated; and then 'everybody talked to everybody else, the ladies being 'particularly loquacious and cheerful. I may remark that 'the second landlord (from both, but especially the first, 'I have had untiring attention) no sooner saw me on 'this agitating occasion, than, with his property blazing, 'he insisted on taking me down into a room full of hot 'smoke, to drink brandy and water with him! And so 'we got to bed again about 2.'

A fire at the hotel.

Dickens had been a week in New York before he was able to identify the great city which a lapse of twenty-five years had so prodigiously increased. 'The only portion 'that has even now come back to me,' he wrote, 'is the 'part of Broadway in which the Carlton Hotel (long since 'destroyed) used to stand. There is a very fine new park 'in the outskirts, and the number of grand houses and 'splendid equipages is quite surprising. There are hotels 'close here with 500 bedrooms and I don't know how 'many boarders; but this hotel is quite as quiet as, and 'not much larger than, Mivart's in Brook Street. My 'rooms are all en suite, and I come and go by a private 'door and private staircase communicating with my bed-'room. The waiters are French, and one might be living 'in Paris. One of the two proprietors is also proprietor 'of Niblo's Theatre, and the greatest care is taken of me.

Increase of New York city.

i. 296.

Quiet of the hotel.

AMERICA: 1867.

Niblo's theatre.

'Niblo's great attraction, the *Black Crook*, has now been 'played every night for 16 months (!), and is the most pre-'posterous peg to hang ballets on that was ever seen. The 'people who act in it have not the slightest idea of what it 'is about, and never had; but, after taxing my intellectual 'powers to the utmost, I fancy that I have discovered Black 'Crook to be a malignant hunchback leagued with the Powers 'of Darkness to separate two lovers; and that the Powers 'of Lightness coming (in no skirts whatever) to the rescue, 'he is defeated. I am quite serious in saying that I do 'not suppose there are two pages of *All the Year Round* 'in the whole piece (which acts all night); the whole of the 'rest of it being ballets of all sorts, perfectly unaccountable 'processions, and the Donkey out of last year's Covent 'Garden pantomime! At the other theatres, comic operas, melodramas, and domestic dramas prevail all over the 'city, and my stories play no inconsiderable part in them. 'I go nowhere, having laid down the rule that to combine 'visiting with my work would be absolutely impossible. . . 'The Fenian explosion at Clerkenwell was telegraphed here in a few hours. I do not think there is any sympathy 'whatever with the Fenians on the part of the American 'people, though political adventurers may make capital 'out of a show of it. But no doubt large sections of the 'Irish population of this State are themselves Fenian; 'and the local politics of the place are in a most depraved 'condition, if half of what is said to me be true. I prefer 'not to talk of these things, but at odd intervals I look 'round for myself. Great social improvements in respect 'of manners and forbearance have come to pass since I

Story of *Black Crook!*

Fenianism.

Local and general politics.

'was here before, but in public life I see as yet but little 'change.'

He had got through half of his first New York readings when a winter storm came on, and from this time until very near his return the severity of the weather was exceptional even for America. When the first snow fell, the railways were closed for some days; and he described New York crowded with sleighs, and the snow piled up in enormous walls the whole length of the streets. 'I 'turned out in a rather gorgeous sleigh yesterday with 'any quantity of buffalo robes, and made an imposing 'appearance.' 'If you were to behold me driving out,' he wrote to his daughter, 'furred up to the moustache, with 'an immense white red-and-yellow-striped rug for a cover-'ing, you would suppose me to be of Hungarian or Polish 'nationality.' These protections nevertheless availed him little; and when the time came for getting back to Boston, he found himself at the close of his journey with a cold and cough that never again left him until he had quitted the country, and of which the effects became more and more disastrous. For the present there was little allusion to this, his belief at the first being strong that he should overmaster it; but it soon forced itself into all his letters.

Snow storm.

Imposing sight.

Struck with cold.

His railway journey otherwise had not been agreeable. 'The railways are truly alarming. Much worse (because 'more worn I suppose) than when I was here before. We 'were beaten about yesterday, as if we had been aboard the 'Cuba. Two rivers have to be crossed, and each time the 'whole train is banged aboard a big steamer. The steamer 'rises and falls with the river, which the railroad don't do;

Railway travelling. i. 317, 349.

AMERICA: 1867.

'and the train is either banged up hill or banged down 'hill. In coming off the steamer at one of these crossings 'yesterday, we were banged up such a height that the rope 'broke, and one carriage rushed back with a run down-hill 'into the boat again. I whisked out in a moment, and 'two or three others after me; but nobody else seemed to 'care about it. The treatment of the luggage is perfectly 'outrageous. Nearly every case I have is already broken. 'When we started from Boston yesterday, I beheld, to my 'unspeakable amazement, Scott, my dresser, leaning a 'flushed countenance against the wall of the car, and *weep-'ing bitterly*. It was over my smashed writing-desk. Yet 'the arrangements for luggage are excellent, if the porters 'would not be beyond description reckless.' The same excellence of provision, and flinging away of its advantages, are observed in connection with another subject in the same letter. 'The halls are excellent. Imagine one hold-'ing two thousand people, seated with exact equality for 'every one of them, and every one seated separately. I 'have nowhere, at home or abroad, seen so fine a police 'as the police of New York; and their bearing in the 'streets is above all praise. On the other hand, the laws 'for regulation of public vehicles, clearing of streets, and 'removal of obstructions, are wildly outraged by the people 'for whose benefit they are intended. Yet there is un-'doubtedly improvement in every direction, and I am 'taking time to make up my mind on things in general. 'Let me add that I have been tempted out at three in the 'morning to visit one of the large police station-houses, 'and was so fascinated by the study of a horrible pho-

Treatment of luggage.

Police of New York.

'tograph-book of thieves' portraits that I couldn't shut 'it up.'

Again in Boston.

A letter of the same date (22nd) to his sister-in-law told of personal attentions awaiting him on his return to Boston by which he was greatly touched. He found his rooms garnished with flowers and holly, with real red berries, and with festoons of moss; and the homely Christmas look of the place quite affected him. 'There is a certain Captain 'Dolliver belonging to the Boston custom-house, who came 'off in the little steamer that brought me ashore from the 'Cuba; and he took it into his head that he would have a 'piece of English mistletoe brought out in this week's 'Cunard, which should be laid upon my breakfast-table. 'And there it was this morning. In such affectionate 'touches as this, these New England people are especially 'amiable. . . As a general rule you may lay it down that 'whatever you see about me in the papers is not true; 'but you may generally lend a more believing ear to the 'Philadelphia correspondent of the *Times*, a well-informed 'gentleman. Our hotel in New York was on fire again 'the other night. But fires in this country are quite 'matters of course. There was a large one in Boston at 'four this morning; and I don't think a single night has 'passed, since I have been under the protection of the 'Eagle, that I have not heard the Fire Bells dolefully 'clanging all over both cities.' The violent abuse of his manager by portions of the press is the subject of the rest of the letter, and receives farther illustration in one of the same date to me. 'A good specimen of the sort of news- 'paper you and I know something of, came out in Boston

Remembrance of Christmas.

Mistletoe from England.

More fires.

AMERICA: 1867.

A nuisance in all countries.

'here this morning. The editor had applied for our advertisements, saying that "it was at Mr. D's disposal for "paragraphs." The advertisements were not sent; Dolby 'did not enrich its columns paragraphically; and among 'its news to-day is the item that "this chap calling him-"self Dolby got drunk down town last night, and was "taken to the police station for fighting an Irishman!" I 'am sorry to say that I don't find anybody to be much 'shocked by this liveliness.' It is right to add what was said to me a few days later. 'The *Tribune* is an excellent 'paper. Horace Greeley is editor in chief, and a consider-'able shareholder too. All the people connected with it 'whom I have seen are of the best class. It is also a very 'fine property—but here the *New York Herald* beats it 'hollow, hollow, hollow! Another able and well edited 'paper is the *New York Times*. A most respectable journal 'too is Bryant's *Evening Post*, excellently written. There 'is generally a much more responsible and respectable tone 'than prevailed formerly, however small may be the lite-'rary merit, among papers pointed out to me as of large 'circulation. In much of the writing there is certainly 'improvement, but it might be more widely spread.'

As to newspapers generally.

Settling the Readings for other cities.

The time had now come when the course his Readings were to take independently of the two leading cities must be settled, and the general tour made out. His agent's original plan was that they should be in New York every week. 'But I say No. By the 10th of January I shall 'have read to 35,000 people in that city alone. Put the 'readings out of the reach of all the people behind them, 'for the time. It is that one of the popular peculiarities 'which I most particularly notice, that they must not have 'a thing too easily. Nothing in the country lasts long; and 'a thing is prized the more, the less easy it is made. Re'flecting therefore that I shall want to close, in April, with 'farewell readings here and in New York, I am convinced 'that the crush and pressure upon these necessary to their 'adequate success is only to be got by absence; and that 'the best thing I can do is not to give either city as much 'reading as it wants now, but to be independent of both 'while both are most enthusiastic. I have therefore re'solved presently to announce in New York so many read'ings (I mean a certain number) as the last that can be 'given there, before I travel to promised places; and that 'we select the best places, with the largest halls, on our 'list. This will include, East here—the two or three best 'New England towns; South—Baltimore and Washington; 'West—Cincinnati, Pittsburgh, Chicago, and St. Louis; and 'towards Niagara—Cleveland and Buffalo. Philadelphia 'we are already pledged to, for six nights; and the scheme 'will pretty easily bring us here again twice before the 'farewells. I feel convinced that this is the sound policy.' (It was afterwards a little modified, as will be seen, by public occurrences and his own condition of health; the West, as well as a promise to Canada, having to be abandoned; but otherwise it was carried out.) 'I read here to'morrow and Tuesday; all tickets being sold to the end of the 'series, even for subjects not announced. I have not read 'a single time at a lower clear profit per night (all deduc'tions made) than £315. But rely upon it I shall take 'great care not to read oftener than four times a week—

Nothing lasts long.

Cities chosen for Readings.

Plan as carried out.

AMERICA: 1867.

'after this next week, when I stand committed to five. 'The inevitable tendency of the staff, when these great 'houses excite them, is, in the words of an old friend of 'ours, to "hurge the hartist hon;" and a night or two ago 'I had to cut away five readings from *their* list.'

Resisting temptation.

An incident at Boston should have mention before he resumes his readings in New York. In the interval since he was first in America, the Harvard professor of chemistry, Dr. Webster, whom he had at that visit met among the honoured men who held chairs in their Cambridge University, had been hanged for the murder, committed in his laboratory in the college, of a friend who had lent him money, portions of whose body lay concealed under the lid of the lecture-room table where the murderer continued to meet his students. 'Being in Cambridge,' Dickens wrote to Lord Lytton, 'I thought I would go over the 'Medical School, and see the exact localities where Professor 'Webster did that amazing murder, and worked so hard to 'rid himself of the body of the murdered man. (I find 'there is of course no rational doubt that the Professor was 'always a secretly cruel man). They were horribly grim, 'private, cold, and quiet; the identical furnace smelling fear-'fully (some anatomical broth in it I suppose) as if the body 'were still there; jars of pieces of sour mortality standing 'about, like the forty robbers in *Ali Baba* after being 'scalded to death; and bodies near us ready to be carried 'in to next morning's lecture. At the house where I 'afterwards dined I heard an amazing and fearful story; 'told by one who had been at a dinner-party of ten or a 'dozen, at Webster's, less than a year before the murder.

The Webster murder in 1849.

Letter to Lord Lytton.

Going over scenes of a murder.

'They began rather uncomfortably, in consequence of one 'of the guests (the victim of an instinctive antipathy) 'starting up with the sweat pouring down his face, and 'crying out, "O Heaven! There's a cat somewhere in the '"room!" The cat was found and ejected, but they didn't 'get on very well. Left with their wine, they were getting 'on a little better; when Webster suddenly told the servants 'to turn the gas off and bring in that bowl of burning 'minerals which he had prepared, in order that the com-'pany might see how ghastly they looked by its weird 'light. All this was done, and every man was looking, 'horror-stricken, at his neighbour; when Webster was seen 'bending over the bowl with a rope round his neck, hold-'ing up the end of the rope, with his head on one side and 'his tongue lolled out, to represent a hanged man!'

AMERICA: 1867.

Dinner at the murderer's in 1848.

Disagreeable but appropriate.

Dickens read at Boston on the 23rd and the 24th of December, and on Christmas day travelled back to New York where he was to read on the 26th. The last words written before he left were of illness. 'The low action of the 'heart, or whatever it is, has inconvenienced me greatly 'this last week. On Monday night, after the reading, I 'was laid upon a bed, in a very faint and shady state; and 'on the Tuesday I did not get up till the afternoon.' But what in reality was less grave took outwardly the form of a greater distress; and the effects of the cold which had struck him in travelling to Boston, as yet not known to his English friends, appear most to have alarmed those about him. I depart from my rule in this narrative, otherwise strictly observed, in singling out one of those friends for mention by name: but a business connection with the

Again at New York.

*Ante*, 274, 280.

Illness.

AMERICA: 1867.

Mr. James T. Fields.

Readings, as well as untiring offices of personal kindness and sympathy, threw Mr. Fields into closer relations with Dickens from arrival to departure than any other person had; and his description of the condition of health in which Dickens now quitted Boston and went through the rest of the labour he had undertaken, will be a sad though fit prelude to what the following chapter has to tell. 'He went 'from Boston to New York carrying with him a severe 'catarrh contracted in our climate. He was quite ill from 'the effects of the disease; but he fought courageously 'against them. . . His spirit was wonderful, and, although 'he lost all appetite and could partake of very little food, he 'was always cheerful and ready for his work when the even-'ing came round. A dinner was tendered to him by some of his literary friends in Boston; but he was so ill the day 'before that the banquet had to be given up. The strain 'upon his strength and nerves was very great during all the 'months he remained, and only a man of iron will could 'have accomplished what he did. He was accustomed to 'talk and write a good deal about eating and drinking, but 'I have rarely seen a man eat and drink less. He liked to 'dilate in imagination over the brewing of a bowl of punch, 'but when the punch was ready he drank less of it than any 'one who might be present. It was the sentiment of the 'thing and not the thing itself that engaged his attention. 'I scarcely saw him eat a hearty meal during his whole stay. 'Both at Parker's hotel in Boston, and at the Westminster 'in New York, everything was arranged by the proprietors 'for his comfort, and tempting dishes to pique his invalid 'appetite were sent up at different hours of the day; but

Account of Dickens while in America.

Illness and abstinence.

'the influenza had seized him with masterful power, and 'held the strong man down till he left the country.'

AMERICA: 1867.

Christmas Day.

When he arrived in New York on the evening of Christmas Day he found a letter from his daughter. Answering her next day he told her: 'I wanted it much, for I had a 'frightful cold (English colds are nothing to those of this 'country) and was very miserable . . . It is a bad country 'to be unwell and travelling in. You are one of, say, a hun-'dred people in a heated car with a great stove in it, all the 'little windows being closed; and the bumping and bang-'ing about are indescribable, the atmosphere detestable, the 'ordinary motion all but intolerable.' The following day this addition was made to the letter. 'I managed to read 'last night, but it was as much as I could do. To-day I am 'so very unwell that I have sent for a doctor. He has just 'been, and is in doubt whether I shall not have to stop 'reading for a while.'

Miseries of American travel.

His stronger will prevailed, and he went on without stopping. On the last day of the year he announced to us that though he had been very low he was getting right again; that in a couple of days he should have accomplished a fourth of the entire Readings; and that the first month of the new year would see him through Philadelphia and Baltimore, as well as through two more nights in Boston. He also prepared his English friends for the startling intelligence they might shortly expect, of four readings coming off in a church, before an audience of two thousand people accommodated in pews, and with himself emerging from a vestry.

Startling prospect.

## CHAPTER XVI.

### AMERICA REVISITED: JANUARY TO APRIL 1868.

1868.

AMERICA: 1868.

THE Reading on the third of January closed a fourth of the entire series, and on that day Dickens wrote of the trouble brought on them by the 'speculators,' which to some extent had affected unfavourably the three previous nights in New York. When adventurers buy up the best places, the public resent it by refusing the worst; to prevent it by first helping themselves, being the last thing they ever think of doing. 'We try to withhold the best seats from the speculators, but the unaccountable thing 'is that the great mass of the public buy of them (prefer 'it), and the rest of the public are injured if we have not 'got those very seats to sell them. We have now a travel-'ling staff of six men, in spite of which Dolby, who is leav-'ing me to-day to sell tickets in Philadelphia to-morrow 'morning, will no doubt get into a tempest of difficulties. 'Of course also, in such a matter, as many obstacles as pos-'sible are thrown in an Englishman's way; and he may 'himself be a little injudicious into the bargain. Last 'night, for instance, he met one of the "ushers" (who show 'people to their seats) coming in with one of our men. It

Speculators and the public.

An Englishman's disadvantage and mistakes.

'is against orders that any one employed in front should 'go out during the reading, and he took this man to task 'in the British manner. Instantly, the free and independent usher put on his hat and walked off. Seeing which, 'all the other free and independent ushers (some 20 in 'number) put on *their* hats and walked off; leaving us 'absolutely devoid and destitute of a staff for to-night. 'One has since been improvised: but it was a small matter 'to raise a stir and ill-will about, especially as one of our 'men was equally in fault; and really there is little to be 'done at night. American people are so accustomed to 'take care of themselves, that one of these immense audiences will fall into their places with an ease amazing to 'a frequenter of St. James's Hall; and the certainty with 'which they are all in, before I go on, is a very acceptable 'mark of respect. Our great labour is outside; and we 'have been obliged to bring our staff up to six, besides a 'boy or two, by employment of a regular additional clerk, 'a Bostonian. The speculators buying the front-seats (we 'have found instances of this being done by merchants in 'good position), the public won't have the back seats; 'return their tickets; write and print volumes on the 'subject; and deter others from coming. You are not to 'suppose that this prevails to any great extent, as our 'lowest house here has been £300; but it does hit us. 'There is no doubt about it. Fortunately I saw the 'danger when the trouble began, and changed the list 'at the right time. . . You may get an idea of the staff's 'work, by what is in hand now. They are preparing, 'numbering, and stamping, 6000 tickets for Philadelphia,

'Freedom 'and independence.'

Republican self-help.

Receipts affected by speculators.

AMERICA: 1868.

Work of the staff.

'and 8000 tickets for Brooklyn. The moment those are 'done, another 8000 tickets will be wanted for Baltimore, 'and probably another 6000 for Washington; and all this in 'addition to the correspondence, advertisements, accounts, 'travelling, and the nightly business of the Readings four 'times a week . . . I cannot get rid of this intolerable cold! 'My landlord invented for me a drink of brandy, rum, and 'snow, called it a "Rocky Mountain Sneezer," and said it 'was to put down all less effectual sneezing; but it has 'not yet had the effect. Did I tell you that the favourite 'drink before you get up is an Eye-Opener? There has 'been another fall of snow, succeeded by a heavy thaw.'

Rocky Mountain Sneezers and Eye-openers.

Again at Boston: 5th Jan.

The day after (the 4th) he went back to Boston, and next day wrote to me: 'I am to read here on Monday 'and Tuesday, return to New York on Wednesday, and 'finish there (except the farewells in April) on Thursday 'and Friday. The New York reading of *Doctor Marigold* 'made really a tremendous hit. The people doubted at 'first, having evidently not the least idea what could be 'done with it, and broke out at last into a perfect chorus 'of delight. At the end they made a great shout, and 'gave a rush towards the platform as if they were going to 'carry me off. It puts a strong additional arrow into my 'quiver. Another extraordinary success has been *Nickleby* 'and *Boots at the Holly Tree* (appreciated here in Boston, 'by the bye, even more than *Copperfield*); and think of 'our last New York night bringing £500 English into the 'house, after making more than the necessary deduction 'for the present price of gold! The manager is always going about with an immense bundle that looks like a

Hit of *Marigold*:

and of *Boots at Holly Tree*.

'sofa-cushion, but is in reality paper-money, and it had risen 'to the proportions of a sofa on the morning he left for 'Philadelphia. Well, the work is hard, the climate is hard, 'the life is hard: but so far the gain is enormous. My 'cold steadily refuses to stir an inch. It distresses me 'greatly at times, though it is always good enough to leave 'me for the needful two hours. I have tried allopathy, 'homœopathy, cold things, warm things, sweet things, 'bitter things, stimulants, narcotics, all with the same 'result. Nothing will touch it.'

The work and the gain.

In the same letter, light was thrown on the ecclesiastical mystery. 'At Brooklyn I am going to read in Mr. Ward 'Beecher's chapel: the only building there available for the 'purpose. You must understand that Brooklyn is a kind 'of sleeping-place for New York, and is supposed to be a 'great place in the money way. We let the seats pew 'by pew! the pulpit is taken down for my screen and gas! 'and I appear out of the vestry in canonical form! These 'ecclesiastical entertainments come off on the evenings of 'the 16th, 17th, 20th, and 21st, of the present month.' His first letter after returning to New York (9th of January) made additions to the Brooklyn picture. 'Each evening an 'enormous ferry-boat will convey me and my state-carriage '(not to mention half a dozen wagons and any number of 'people and a few score of horses) across the river to Brooklyn, 'and will bring me back again. The sale of tickets there 'was an amazing scene. The noble army of speculators 'are now furnished (this is literally true, and I am quite 'serious) each man with a straw mattress, a little bag of bread 'and meat, two blankets, and a bottle of whiskey. With

Chapel readings.

To and from Brooklyn.

Equipment of speculators.

AMERICA: 1868.

'this outfit, *they lie down in line on the pavement* the 'whole of the night before the tickets are sold: generally 'taking up their position at about 10. It being severely 'cold at Brooklyn, they made an immense bonfire in the 'street—a narrow street of wooden houses—which the 'police turned out to extinguish. A general fight then took 'place; from which the people farthest off in the line 'rushed bleeding when they saw any chance of ousting 'others nearer the door, put their mattresses in the spots so 'gained, and held on by the iron rails. At 8 in the morning 'Dolby appeared with the tickets in a portmanteau. He 'was immediately saluted with a roar of Halloa! Dolby! 'So Charley has let you have the carriage, has he, Dolby? 'How is he, Dolby? Don't drop the tickets, Dolby! Look 'alive, Dolby! &c. &c. &c. in the midst of which he proceeded 'to business, and concluded (as usual) by giving universal 'dissatisfaction. He is now going off upon a little journey 'to look over the ground and cut back again. This little 'journey (to Chicago) is twelve hundred miles on end, by 'railway, besides the back again!' It might tax the Englishman, but was nothing to the native American. It was part of his New York landlord's ordinary life in a week, Dickens told me, to go to Chicago and look at his theatre there on a Monday; to pelt back to Boston and look at his theatre there on a Thursday; and to come rushing to New York on a Friday, to apostrophize his enormous ballet.

Bonfire in a street of wood.

Salutations to manager

A small journey!

Nothing to a native American.

12th Jan.

Three days later, still at New York, he wrote to his sister-in-law. 'I am off to Philadelphia this evening for 'the first of three visits of two nights each, tickets for all 'being sold. My cold steadily refuses to leave me, but 'otherwise I am as well as I can hope to be under this 'heavy work. My New York readings are over (except 'the farewell nights), and I look forward to the relief of 'being out of my hardest hall. On Friday I was again 'dead beat at the end, and was once more laid upon a sofa. 'But the faintness went off after a little while. We have 'now cold bright frosty weather, without snow; the best 'weather for me.' Next day from Philadelphia he wrote to his daughter that he was lodged in The Continental, one of the most immense of American hotels, but that he found himself just as quiet as elsewhere. 'Everything is very 'good, my waiter is German, and the greater part of the 'servants seem to be coloured people. The town is very 'clean, and the day as blue and bright as a fine Italian day. 'But it freezes very very hard, and my cold is not im'proved; for the cars were so intolerably hot that I was 'often obliged to stand upon the brake outside, and then 'the frosty air bit me indeed. I find it necessary (so op'pressed am I with this American catarrh as they call it) 'to dine at three o'clock instead of four, that I may have 'more time to get voice; so that the days are cut short and 'letter-writing not easy.'

Faintness.

At Philadelphia.

Sufferings.

He nevertheless found time in this city to write to me (14th of January) the most interesting mention he had yet made of such opinions as he had been able to form during his present visit, apart from the pursuit that absorbed him. Of such of those opinions as were given on a former page, it is only necessary to repeat that while the tone of party politics still impressed him unfavourably, he had thus far seen everywhere great changes for the better

ii. 18.

AMERICA: 1868.

Changes for the better.

Irish element in New York.

Looking up the judges.

ii. 18.

socially. I will add other points from the same letter. That he was unfortunate in his time of visiting New York, as far as its politics were concerned, what has since happened conclusively shows. 'The Irish element is acquiring 'such enormous influence in New York city, that when I 'think of it, and see the large Roman Catholic cathedral 'rising there, it seems unfair to stigmatise as "American" 'other monstrous things that one also sees. But the general 'corruption in respect of the local funds appears to be stu-'pendous, and there is an alarming thing as to some of 'the courts of law which I am afraid is native-born. A 'case came under my notice the other day in which it was 'perfectly plain, from what was said to me by a person inter-'ested in resisting an injunction, that his first proceeding 'had been to "look up the Judge."' Of such occasional provincial oddity, harmless in itself but strange in large cities, as he noticed in the sort of half disappointment at the small fuss made by himself about the Readings, and in the newspaper references to 'Mr. Dickens's extraordinary 'composure' on the platform, he gives an illustration. 'Last night here in Philadelphia (my first night), a very 'impressible and responsive audience were so astounded 'by my simply walking in and opening my book that I 'wondered what was the matter. They evidently thought 'that there ought to have been a flourish, and Dolby sent 'in to prepare for me. With them it is the simplicity of 'the operation that raises wonder. With the newspapers '"Mr. Dickens's extraordinary composure" is not reasoned 'out as being necessary to the art of the thing, but is sen-'sitively watched with a lurking doubt whether it may not 'imply disparagement of the audience. Both these things 'strike me as drolly expressive.'. .

Improved social ways.

His testimony as to improved social habits and ways was expressed very decidedly. 'I think it reasonable to expect 'that as I go westward, I shall find the old manners going 'on before me, and may tread upon their skirts mayhap. 'But so far, I have had no more intrusion or boredom than 'I have when I lead the same life in England. I write 'this in an immense hotel, but I am as much at peace in my 'own rooms, and am left as wholly undisturbed, as if I were 'at the Station Hotel in York. I have now read in New 'York city to 40,000 people, and am quite as well known 'in the streets there as I am in London. People will turn 'back, turn again and face me, and have a look at me, or 'will say to one another "Look here! Dickens coming!" 'But no one ever stops me or addresses me. Sitting read-'ing in the carriage outside the New York post-office while 'one of the staff was stamping the letters inside, I be-'came conscious that a few people who had been looking 'at the turn-out had discovered me within. On my peep-'ing out good-humouredly, one of them (I should say a 'merchant's book-keeper) stepped up to the door, took off 'his hat, and said in a frank way: "Mr. Dickens, I should '"very much like to have the honour of shaking hands with '"you"—and, that done, presented two others. Nothing 'could be more quiet or less intrusive. In the railway 'cars, if I see anybody who clearly wants to speak to me, 'I usually anticipate the wish by speaking myself. If I 'am standing on the brake outside (to avoid the intoler-'able stove), people getting down will say with a smile:

No intrusiveness.

In railway cars.

AMERICA: 1868.

'"As I am taking my departure, Mr. Dickens, and can't '"trouble you for more than a moment, I should like to '"take you by the hand sir." And so we shake hands 'and go our ways. . . Of course many of my impressions 'come through the readings. Thus I find the people lighter 'and more humorous than formerly; and there must be 'a great deal of innocent imagination among every class, or 'they never could pet with such extraordinary pleasure as 'they do, the Boots' story of the elopement of the two little 'children. They seem to see the children; and the women 'set up a shrill undercurrent of half-pity and half-pleasure 'that is quite affecting. To-night's reading is my 26th; 'but as all the Philadelphia tickets for four more are sold, 'as well as four at Brooklyn, you must assume that I am 'at—say—my 35th reading. I have remitted to Coutts's 'in English gold £10,000 odd; and I roughly calculate 'that on this number Dolby will have another thousand 'pounds profit to pay me. These figures are of course 'between ourselves, at present; but are they not magnifi-'cent? The expenses, always recollect, are enormous. 'On the other hand we never have occasion to print a 'bill of any sort (bill-printing and posting are great charges 'at home); and have just now sold off £90 worth of bill-'paper, provided beforehand, as a wholly useless incum-'brance.'

In the halls.

Result of 34 Readings.

Indisputable evidence!

Then came, as ever, the constant shadow that still attended him, the slave in the chariot of his triumph. 'The 'work is very severe. There is now no chance of my being 'rid of this American catarrh until I embark for England. 'It is very distressing. It likewise happens, not seldom, that

Shadow to the sunshine.

'I am so dead beat when I come off that they lay me down 'on a sofa after I have been washed and dressed, and I lie 'there, extremely faint, for a quarter of an hour. In that 'time I rally and come right.' One week later from New York, where he had become due on the 16th for the first of his four Brooklyn readings, he wrote to his sister-in-law. 'My cold sticks to me, and I can scarcely exaggerate what 'I undergo from sleeplessness. I rarely take any break-'fast but an egg and a cup of tea—not even toast or bread 'and butter. My small dinner at 3, and a little quail or 'some such light thing when I come home at night, is my 'daily fare; and at the hall I have established the custom 'of taking an egg beaten up in sherry before going in, and 'another between the parts, which I think pulls me up. . . 'It is snowing hard now, and I begin to move to-morrow. 'There is so much floating ice in the river, that we are 'obliged to have a pretty wide margin of time for getting 'over the ferry to read.' The last of the readings over the ferry was on the day when this letter was written. 'I 'finished at my church to-night. It is Mrs. Stowe's bro-'ther's, and a most wonderful place to speak in. We had 'it enormously full last night (*Marigold* and *Trial*), but it 'scarcely required an effort. Mr. Ward Beecher being pre-'sent in his pew, I sent to invite him to come round before 'he left. I found him to be an unostentatious, evidently 'able, straightforward, and agreeable man; extremely well-'informed, and with a good knowledge of art.'

AMERICA: 1868.

Faintness.

Sleeplessness.

Daily fare.

Church readings.

Mr. Ward Beecher.

Baltimore and Washington were the cities in which he was now, on quitting New York, to read for the first time; and as to the latter some doubts arose. The exceptional

AMERICA: 1868.

Arrangements for Washington.

course had been taken in regard to it, of selecting a hall with space for not more than 700 and charging everybody five dollars; to which Dickens, at first greatly opposed, had yielded upon use of the argument, you have more people 'at New York, thanks to the speculators, paying more than 'five dollars every night.' But now other suggestions came. 'Horace Greeley dined with me last Saturday,' he wrote on the 20th, 'and didn't like my going to Washington,

A suggestion from Horace Greeley.

'now full of the greatest rowdies and worst kind of people 'in the States. Last night at eleven came B. expressing 'like doubts; and though they may be absurd I thought 'them worth attention, B. coming so close on Greeley.' Mr. Dolby was in consequence sent express to Washington with power to withdraw or go on, as enquiry on the spot might dictate; and Dickens took the additional resolve so far to modify the last arrangements of his tour as to avoid the

Change of plan.

distances of Chicago, St. Louis, and Cincinnati, to content himself with smaller places and profits, and thereby to get home nearly a month earlier. He was at Philadelphia on the 23rd of January, when he announced this intention. 'The worst of it is, that everybody one advises with

Chicago dropped.

'has a monomania respecting Chicago. "Good heavens '"sir," the great Philadelphia authority said to me this 'morning, "if you don't read in Chicago the people will '"go into fits!" Well, I answered, I would rather they 'went into fits than I did. But he didn't seem to see it 'at all.'

At Baltimore.

From Baltimore he wrote to his sister-in-law on the 29th, in the hour's interval he had to spare before going back to Philadelphia. 'It has been snowing hard for four and 'twenty hours—though this place is as far south as Valentia in Spain; and my manager, being on his way to New 'York, has a good chance of being snowed up somewhere. 'This is one of the places where Butler carried it with a 'high hand during the war, and where the ladies used to 'spit when they passed a Northern soldier. They are very 'handsome women, with an Eastern touch in them, and 'dress brilliantly. I have rarely seen so many fine faces 'in an audience. They are a bright responsive people 'likewise, and very pleasant to read to. My hall is a charming little opera house built by a society of Germans: 'quite a delightful place for the purpose. I stand on the 'stage, with the drop curtain down, and my screen before 'it. The whole scene is very pretty and complete, and the 'audience have a "ring" in them that sounds deeper than 'the ear. I go from here to Philadelphia, to read to-morrow 'night and Friday; come through here again on Saturday 'on my way back to Washington; come back here on 'Saturday week for two finishing nights; then go to Philadelphia for two farewells—and so turn my back on the 'southern part of the country. Our new plan will give 82 'readings in all.' (The real number was 76, six having been dropped on subsequent political excitements.) 'Of 'course I afterwards discovered that we had finally settled 'the list on a Friday. I shall be halfway through it at 'Washington; of course on a Friday also, and my birthday.' To myself he wrote on the following day from Philadelphia, beginning with a thank Heaven that he had struck off Canada and the West, for he found the wear and tear 'enormous.' 'Dolby decided that the croakers were wrong about Wash-

Baltimore women.

Reading at Baltimore.

Movements to and fro.

End of doubt as to Washington.

AMERICA: 1868.

'ington, and went on; the rather as his raised prices, which 'he put finally at three dollars each, gave satisfaction. 'Fields is so confident about Boston, that my remaining list 'includes, in all, 14 more readings there. I don't know 'how many more we might not have had here (where I 'have had attentions otherwise that have been very grate- 'ful to me), if we had chosen. Tickets are now being re- 'sold at ten dollars each. At Baltimore I had a charming 'little theatre, and a very apprehensive impulsive audience. 'It is remarkable to see how the Ghost of Slavery haunts 'the town; and how the shambling, untidy, evasive, and 'postponing Irrepressible proceeds about his free work, going 'round and round it, instead of at it. The melancholy ab- 'surdity of giving these people votes, at any rate at present, 'would glare at one out of every roll of their eyes, chuckle 'in their mouths, and bump in their heads, if one did not see '(as one cannot help seeing in the country) that their en- 'franchisement is a mere party trick to get votes. Being 'at the Penitentiary the other day (this, while we mention 'votes), and looking over the books, I noticed that almost 'every man had been "pardoned" a day or two before 'his time was up. Why? Because, if he had served his 'time out, he would have been *ipso facto* disfranchised. 'So, this form of pardon is gone through to save his vote; 'and as every officer of the prison holds his place only in 'right of his party, of course his hopeful clients vote for 'the party that has let them out! . When I read in Mr. 'Beecher's church at Brooklyn, we found the trustees had 'suppressed the fact that a certain upper gallery holding '150 was "the Coloured Gallery." On the first night

Success in Philadelphia.

Ghost of Slavery.

Alleged party devices.

Value vote.

'not a soul could be induced to enter it; and it was not 'until it became known next day that I was certainly 'not going to read there more than four times, that we 'managed to fill it. One night at New York, on our second 'or third row, there were two well-dressed women with a 'tinge of colour—I should say, not even quadroons. But the 'holder of one ticket who found his seat to be next them, 'demanded of Dolby "what he meant by fixing him next '"to those two Gord darmed cusses of niggers?" and in- 'sisted on being supplied with another good place. Dolby 'firmly replied that he was perfectly certain Mr. Dickens 'would not recognize such an objection on any account, but 'he could have his money back, if he chose. Which, after 'some squabbling, he had. In a comic scene in the New 'York Circus one night, when I was looking on, four white people sat down upon a form in a barber's shop to be 'shaved. A coloured man came as the fifth customer, and 'the four immediately ran away. This was much laughed 'at and applauded. In the Baltimore Penitentiary, the 'white prisoners dine on one side of the room, the coloured 'prisoners on the other; and no one has the slightest 'idea of mixing them. But it is indubitably the fact that 'exhalations not the most agreeable arise from a number of 'coloured people got together, and I was obliged to beat a 'quick retreat from their dormitory. I strongly believe that 'they will die out of this country fast. It seems, looking 'at them, so manifestly absurd to suppose it possible that 'they can ever hold their own against a restless, shifty, 'striving, stronger race.'

Objections to coloured people.

Ground for getting your money back.

Successful joke!

But in white dormitories is it not the same?

On the fourth of February he wrote from Washington.

At Washington.

AMERICA: 1868.

Washington.

'You may like to have a line to let you know that it is all 'right here, and that the croakers were simply ridiculous. I 'began last night. A charming audience, no dissatisfaction 'whatever at the raised prices, nothing missed or lost, cheers 'at the end of the *Carol,* and rounds upon rounds of applause 'all through. All the foremost men and their families had 'taken tickets for the series of four. A small place to read 'in. £300 in it.' It will be no violation of the rule of avoiding private detail if the very interesting close of this letter is given. Its anecdote of President Lincoln was repeatedly told by Dickens after his return, and I am under no necessity to withhold from it the authority of Mr. Sumner's name. 'I am going to-morrow to see the President, who 'has sent to me twice. I dined with Charles Sumner last 'Sunday, against my rule; and as I had stipulated for no 'party, Mr. Secretary Stanton was the only other guest, 'besides his own secretary. Stanton is a man with a very 'remarkable memory, and extraordinarily familiar with my 'books . . He and Sumner having been the first two public 'men at the dying President's bedside, and having remained 'with him until he breathed his last, we fell into a very 'interesting conversation after dinner, when, each of them 'giving his own narrative separately, the usual discre'pancies about details of time were observable. Then Mr. 'Stanton told me a curious little story which will form the 'remainder of this short letter.

A great success.

With Sumner and Stanton.

President Lincoln's death.

Lincoln's last cabinet council.

'On the afternoon of the day on which the President 'was shot, there was a cabinet council at which he pre'sided. Mr. Stanton, being at the time commander-in-chief 'of the Northern troops that were concentrated about 'here, arrived rather late. Indeed they were waiting for 'him, and on his entering the room, the President broke off 'in something he was saying, and remarked : "Let us pro- '"ceed to business, gentlemen." Mr. Stanton then noticed, 'with great surprise, that the President sat with an air of 'dignity in his chair instead of lolling about it in the most 'ungainly attitudes, as his invariable custom was; and that 'instead of telling irrelevant or questionable stories, he was 'grave and calm, and quite a different man. Mr. Stanton, 'on leaving the council with the Attorney-General, said 'to him, "That is the most satisfactory cabinet meeting '"I have attended for many a long day! What an extra- '"ordinary change in Mr. Lincoln!" The Attorney-Gene- 'ral replied, "We all saw it, before you came in. While we '"were waiting for you, he said, with his chin down on '"his breast, 'Gentlemen, something very extraordinary '"'is going to happen, and that very soon.'" To which 'the Attorney-General had observed, "Something good, "'sir, I hope?" when the President answered very gravely: '"I don't know; I don't know. But it will happen, and '"shortly too!" As they were all impressed by his man- 'ner, the Attorney-General took him up again: "Have you '"received any information, sir, not yet disclosed to us?" '"No," answered the President: "but I have had a dream. '"And I have now had the same dream three times. Once, '"on the night preceding the Battle of Bull Run. Once, '"on the night preceding" such another (naming a battle 'also not favourable to the North). His chin sank on 'his breast again, and he sat reflecting. "Might one ask '"the nature of this dream, sir?" said the Attorney-

Day of President Lincoln's death.

Altered bearing of the President.

Lincoln's dream.

AMERICA: 1868.

President Lincoln.

'General. "Well," replied the President, without lifting 'his head or changing his attitude, "I am on a great broad '"rolling river—and I am in a boat—and I drift—and I '"drift!—But this is not business—" suddenly raising his 'face and looking round the table as Mr. Stanton entered, '"let us proceed to business, gentlemen." Mr. Stanton and 'the Attorney-General said, as they walked on together, it 'would be curious to notice whether anything ensued on 'this; and they agreed to notice. He was shot that night.'

Interview with President Johnson.

On his birthday, the seventh of February, Dickens had his interview with President Andrew Johnson. 'This 'scrambling scribblement is resumed this morning, because 'I have just seen the President: who had sent to me very 'courteously asking me to make my own appointment. He 'is a man with a remarkable face, indicating courage, 'watchfulness, and certainly strength of purpose. It is a 'face of the Webster type, but without the "bounce" of 'Webster's face. I would have picked him out anywhere as 'a character of mark. Figure, rather stoutish for an Ameri-'can; a trifle under the middle size; hands clasped in front 'of him; manner, suppressed, guarded, anxious. Each of 'us looked at the other very hard. . . . It was in his own

English minister.

'cabinet that I saw him. As I came away, Thornton drove 'up in a sleigh—turned out for a state occasion—to deliver 'his credentials. There was to be a cabinet council at 12. 'The room was very like a London club's ante-drawing 'room. On the walls, two engravings only: one, of his own

An old acquaintance.

'portrait; one, of Lincoln's. . . In the outer room was sitting 'a certain sunburnt General Blair, with many evidences of 'the war upon him. He got up to shake hands with me, and

AMERICA: 1868.

i. 374–5.

'then I found that he had been out on the Prairie with me 'five-and-twenty years ago. . . The papers having referred 'to my birthday's falling to-day, my room is filled with most 'exquisite flowers.* They came pouring in from all sorts 'of people at breakfast time. The audiences here are really 'very fine. So ready to laugh or cry, and doing both so 'freely, that you would suppose them to be Manchester 'shillings rather than Washington half-sovereigns. Alas! 'alas! my cold worse than ever.' So he had written too at the opening of his letter.

Washington audiences.

The first reading had been four days earlier, and was described to his daughter in a letter on the 4th, with a comical incident that occurred in the course of it. 'The 'gas was very defective indeed last night, and I began 'with a small speech to the effect that I must trust to the 'brightness of their faces for the illumination of mine. 'This was taken greatly. In the *Carol* a most ridiculous 'incident occurred. All of a sudden, I saw a dog leap out 'from among the seats in the centre aisle, and look very 'intently at me. The general attention being fixed on 'me, I don't think anybody saw this dog; but I felt so 'sure of his turning up again and barking, that I kept my 'eye wandering about in search of him. He was a very

Incident at first reading.

One of the audience.

* A few days later he described it to his daughter. 'I couldn't help 'laughing at myself on my birthday at Washington; it was observed so much 'as though I were a little boy. Flowers and garlands of the most exquisite 'kind, arranged in all manner of green baskets, bloomed over the room; 'letters radiant with good wishes poured in; a shirt pin, a handsome silver 'travelling bottle, a set of gold shirt studs, and a set of gold sleeve links, were 'on the dinner table. Also, by hands unknown, the hall at night was 'decorated; and after *Boots at the Holly Tree*, the whole audience rose and 'remained, great people and all, standing and cheering, until I went back to 'the table and made them a little speech.'

Birthday at Washington.

Presents.

AMERICA: 1868.

Comical dog:

'comic dog, and it was well for me that I was reading a 'comic part of the book. But when he bounced out into 'the centre aisle again, in an entirely new place, and (still 'looking intently at me) tried the effect of a bark upon my 'proceedings, I was seized with such a paroxysm of laugh- 'ter that it communicated itself to the audience, and we 'roared at one another, loud and long.' Three days later the sequel came, in a letter to his sister-in-law. 'I men- 'tioned the dog on the first night here? Next night, I 'thought I heard (in *Copperfield*) a suddenly-suppressed 'bark. It happened in this wise:—One of our people, 'standing just within the door, felt his leg touched, and 'looking down beheld the dog, staring intently at me, and 'evidently just about to bark. In a transport of presence 'of mind and fury, he instantly caught him up in both 'hands, and threw him over his own head, out into the 'entry, where the check-takers received him like a game at 'ball. Last night he came again, *with another dog;* but 'our people were so sharply on the look-out for him that 'he didn't get in. He had evidently promised to pass the 'other dog, free.'

Comes to second reading.

Brings a friend to third.

What is expressed in these letters, of a still active, hopeful, enjoying, energetic spirit, able to assert itself against illness of the body and in some sort to overmaster it, was also so strongly impressed upon those who were with him, that, seeing his sufferings as they did, they yet found it difficult to understand the extent of them. The sadness thus ever underlying his triumph makes it all very tragical. 'That afternoon of my birthday,' he wrote from Baltimore on the 11th, 'my catarrh was in such a state that Charles

AMERICA: 1868.

'Sumner, coming in at five o'clock, and finding me covered 'with mustard poultice, and apparently voiceless, turned to 'Dolby and said : "Surely, Mr. Dolby, it is impossible that '"he can read to-night!" Says Dolby: "Sir, I have told '"Mr. Dickens so, four times to-day, and I have been very '"anxious. But you have no idea how he will change, '"when he gets to the little table." After five minutes of 'the little table I was not (for the time) even hoarse. The 'frequent experience of this return of force when it is 'wanted, saves me a vast amount of anxiety; but I am not 'at times without the nervous dread that I may some day 'sink altogether.' To the same effect in another letter he adds: 'Dolby and Osgood' (the latter represented the publishing firm of Mr. Fields and was one of the travelling staff), 'who do the most ridiculous things to keep me in 'spirits* (I am often very heavy, and rarely sleep much), 'are determined to have a walking match at Boston on the 'last day of February to celebrate the arrival of the day 'when I can say "*next* month!" for home.' The match ended in the Englishman's defeat; which Dickens doubly commemorated, by a narrative of the American victory in sporting-newspaper style, and by a dinner in Boston to a party of dear friends there.

Incident before a Reading.

Virtue of the little table.

Proposed walking-match.

29th of February.

After Baltimore he was reading again at Philadelphia, from which he wrote to his sister-in-law on the 13th as to a characteristic trait observed in both places. 'Nothing

* Mr. Dolby unconsciously contributed at this time to the same happy result by sending out some advertisements in these exact words: 'The Reading will 'be comprised within *two minutes*, and the audience are earnestly entreated to 'be seated *ten hours* before its commencement.' He had transposed the minutes and the hours.

Modest entreaty.

AMERICA: 1868.

No belief in farewells.

'will induce the people to believe in the farewells. At 'Baltimore on Tuesday night (a very brilliant night 'indeed), they asked as they came out: "When will Mr. '"Dickens read here again?" "Never." "Nonsense! '"Not come back, after such houses as these? Come. '"Say when he'll read again." Just the same here. We 'could as soon persuade them that I am the President, as 'that to-morrow night I am going to read here for the last 'time. . . There is a child in this house—a little girl—to 'whom I presented a black doll when I was here last; and as 'I have just seen her eye at the keyhole since I began writ-'ing this, I think she and the doll must be outside still. '"When you sent it up to me by the coloured boy," she 'said after receiving it (coloured boy is the term for black 'waiter), "I gave such a cream that Ma come running in '"and creamed too, 'cos she fort I'd hurt myself. But I '"creamed a cream of joy." She had a friend to play 'with her that day, and brought the friend with her—to 'my infinite confusion. A friend all stockings and much 'too tall, who sat on the sofa very far back with her 'stockings sticking stiffly out in front of her, and glared 'at me, and never spake a word. Dolby found us con-'fronted in a sort of fascination, like serpent and bird.'

In his hotel at Philadelphia.

A scream of joy.

Disconcerting visitor.

On the 15th he was again at New York, in the thick of more troubles with the speculators. They involved even charges of fraud in ticket-sales at Newhaven and Providence; indignation meetings having been held by the Mayors, and unavailing attempts made by his manager to turn the wrath aside. 'I expect him back here presently half 'bereft of his senses, and I should be wholly bereft of mine 'if the situation were not comical as well as disagreeable. 'We can sell at our own box-office to any extent; but we 'cannot buy back of the speculators, because we have in-'formed the public that all the tickets are gone; and 'even if we made the sacrifice of buying at their price and 'selling at ours, we should be accused of treating with 'them and of making money by it.' It ended in Providence by his going himself to the town and making a speech; and in Newhaven it ended by his sending back the money taken, with intimation that he would not read until there had been a new distribution of the tickets approved by all the town. Fresh disturbance broke out upon this; but he stuck to his determination to delay the reading until the heats had cooled down, and what should have been given in the middle of February he did not give until the close of March.

More troubles from speculators.

Providence and Newhaven. i. 294-6.

The Readings he had promised at the smaller outlying places by the Canadian frontier and Niagara district, including Syracuse, Rochester, and Buffalo, were appointed for that same March month which was to be the interval between the close of the ordinary readings and the farewells in the two leading cities. All that had been promised in New York were closed when he returned to Boston on the 23rd of February, ready for the increase he had promised there; but the check of a sudden political excitement came. It was the month when the vote was taken for impeachment of President Johnson. 'It is well' (25th of February) 'that the money has flowed in hitherto 'so fast, for I have a misgiving that the great excitement 'about the President's impeachment will damage our re-

North-west tour.

Return to Boston.

President's impeachment.

AMERICA: 1868.

Political excitement.

'ceipts . . . The vote was taken at 5 last night. At 7 the 'three large theatres here, all in a rush of good business, 'were stricken with paralysis. At 8 our long line of out-'siders waiting for unoccupied places, was nowhere. To-day 'you hear all the people in the streets talking of only one 'thing. I shall suppress my next week's promised readings '(by good fortune, not yet announced), and watch the course 'of events. Nothing in this country, as I before said, lasts 'long; and I think it likely that the public may be heartily 'tired of the President's name by the 9th of March, when 'I read at a considerable distance from here. So behold 'me with a whole week's holiday in view!' Two days later he wrote pleasantly to his sister-in-law of his audiences. 'They have come to regard the Readings and the Reader 'as their peculiar property; and you would be both amused 'and pleased if you could see the curious way in which 'they show this increased interest in both. Whenever they 'laugh or cry, they have taken to applauding as well; and 'the result is very inspiriting. I shall remain here until 'Saturday the 7th; but after to-morrow night shall not read 'here until the 1st of April, when I begin my farewells—'six in number.' On the 28th he wrote: 'To-morrow 'fortnight we purpose being at the Falls of Niagara, and 'then we shall come back and really begin to wind up. I 'have got to know the *Carol* so well that I can't remember 'it, and occasionally go dodging about in the wildest 'manner, to pick up lost pieces. They took it so tremen-'dously last night that I was stopped every five minutes. 'One poor young girl in mourning burst into a passion of 'grief about Tiny Tim, and was taken out. We had a fine

Nothing lasts long.

Boston audiences.

The *Carol* in Boston. 27th Feb.

'house, and, in the interval while I was out, they covered 'the little table with flowers. The cough has taken a fresh 'start as if it were a novelty, and is even worse than 'ever to-day. There is a lull in the excitement about the 'President: but the articles of impeachment are to be 'produced this afternoon, and then it may set in again. 'Osgood came into camp last night from selling in remote 'places, and reports that at Rochester and Buffalo (both 'places near the frontier), tickets were bought by Canada 'people, who had struggled across the frozen river and clambered over all sorts of obstructions to get them. Some of 'those distant halls turn out to be smaller than represented; 'but I have no doubt—to use an American expression—that 'we shall "get along." The second half of the receipts cannot reasonably be expected to come up to the first; political 'circumstances, and all other surroundings, considered.'



Struggle for tickets in remote places.

His old ill luck in travel pursued him. On the day his letter was written a snow-storm began, with a heavy gale of wind; and 'after all the hard weather gone through,' he wrote on the 2nd of March, 'this is the worst day we 'have seen. It is telegraphed that the storm prevails over 'an immense extent of country, and is just the same at 'Chicago as here. I hope it may prove a wind up. We are 'getting sick of the very sound of sleigh-bells even.' The roads were so bad and the trains so much out of time, that he had to start a day earlier; and on the 6th of March his tour north-west began, with the gale still blowing and the snow falling heavily. On the 13th he wrote to me from Buffalo.

Another snow-storm.

'We go to the Falls of Niagara to-morrow for our own

AMERICA: 1868.

At Rochester.

'pleasure; and I take all the men, as a treat. We found 'Rochester last Tuesday in a very curious state. Perhaps 'you know that the Great Falls of the Genessee River '(really very fine, even so near Niagara) are at that place. 'In the height of a sudden thaw, an immense bank of ice 'above the rapids refused to yield; so that the town was 'threatened (for the second time in four years) with sub-'mersion. Boats were ready in the streets, all the people 'were up all night, and none but the children slept. In 'the dead of the night a thundering noise was heard, the 'ice gave way, the swollen river came raging and roaring 'down the Falls, and the town was safe. Very pictu-'resque! but "not very good for business," as the manager 'says. Especially as the hall stands in the centre of 'danger, and had ten feet of water in it on the last occa-'sion of flood. But I think we had above £200 English. 'On the previous night at Syracuse—a most out of the 'way and unintelligible-looking place, with apparently no 'people in it—we had £375 odd. Here, we had last night, 'and shall have to-night, whatever we can cram into the 'hall.

Town threatened: and saved.

At Syracuse: and Buffalo.

'This Buffalo has become a large and important town, 'with numbers of German and Irish in it. But it is very 'curious to notice, as we touch the frontier, that the Ameri-'can female beauty dies out; and a woman's face clumsily 'compounded of German, Irish, Western America, and 'Canadian, not yet fused together, and not yet moulded, 'obtains instead. Our show of Beauty at night is, gene-'rally, remarkable; but we had not a dozen pretty women 'in the whole throng last night, and the faces were all blunt.

American female beauty.

'I have just been walking about, and observing the same 'thing in the streets. . . The winter has been so severe, that 'the hotel on the English side at Niagara (which has the 'best view of the Falls, and is for that reason very prefer- 'able) is not yet open. So we go, perforce, to the American: 'which telegraphs back to our telegram: "all Mr. Dickens's '"requirements perfectly understood." I have not yet 'been in more than two *very bad* inns. I have been in 'some, where a good deal of what is popularly called "slop- '"ping round" has prevailed; but have been able to get on 'very well. "Slopping round," so used, means untidyness 'and disorder. It is a comically expressive phrase, and 'has many meanings. Fields was asking the price of a 'quarter-cask of sherry the other day. "Wa'al Mussr '"Fields," the merchant replies, "that varies according to '"quality, as is but nay'tral. If yer wa'ant a sherry just '"to slop round with it, I can fix you some at a very low '"figger."'

AMERICA: 1868.

Severity of the winter.

'Slopping 'round.'

Sherry to slop round with.

His letter was resumed at Rochester on the 18th. 'After 'two most brilliant days at the Falls of Niagara, we got 'back here last night. To-morrow morning we turn out 'at 6 for a long railway journey back to Albany. But 'it is nearly all "back" now, thank God! I don't know 'how long, though, before turning, we might have gone on 'at Buffalo. . . We went everywhere at the Falls, and saw 'them in every aspect. There is a suspension bridge 'across, now, some two miles or more from the Horse 'Shoe; and another, half a mile nearer, is to be opened in 'July. They are very fine but very ticklish, hanging aloft 'there, in the continual vibration of the thundering water:

Suspension bridge at Niagara.

AMERICA: 1868.

At Niagara.

'nor is one greatly reassured by the printed notice that 'troops must not cross them at step, that bands of 'music must not play in crossing, and the like. I shall 'never forget the last aspect in which we saw Niagara 'yesterday. We had been everywhere, when I thought of 'struggling (in an open carriage) up some very difficult 'ground for a good distance, and getting where we could 'stand above the river, and see it, as it rushes forward to its 'tremendous leap, coming for miles and miles. All away 'to the horizon on our right was a wonderful confusion 'of bright green and white water. As we stood watch-'ing it with our faces to the top of the Falls, our backs 'were towards the sun. The majestic valley below the 'Falls, so seen through the vast cloud of spray, was made 'of rainbow. The high banks, the riven rocks, the forests, 'the bridge, the buildings, the air, the sky, were all made 'of rainbow. Nothing in Turner's finest water-colour 'drawings, done in his greatest day, is so ethereal, so imagi-'native, so gorgeous in colour, as what I then beheld. I 'seemed to be lifted from the earth and to be looking into 'Heaven. What I once said to you, as I witnessed the 'scene five and twenty years ago, all came back at this 'most affecting and sublime sight. The "muddy vesture '"of our clay" falls from us as we look. . . . I chartered a 'separate carriage for our men, so that they might see all 'in their own way, and at their own time.

Final impression of the Falls.

i. 385-6.

Prospects of travel. 18th Feb.

'There is a great deal of water out between Rochester 'and New York, and travelling is very uncertain, as I fear 'we may find to-morrow. There is again some little alarm 'here on account of the river rising too fast. But our to-

'night's house is far ahead of the first. Most charming halls 'in these places; excellent for sight and sound. Almost in'variably built as theatres, with stage, scenery, and good 'dressing-rooms. Audience seated to perfection (every seat 'always separate), excellent doorways and passages, and 'brilliant light. My screen and gas are set up in front of 'the drop-curtain, and the most delicate touches will tell 'anywhere. No creature but my own men ever near me.'

AMERICA: 1868.

At Rochester.

His anticipation of the uncertainty that might beset his travel back had dismal fulfilment. It is described in a letter written on the 21st from Springfield to his valued friend, Mr. Frederic Ouvry, having much interest of its own, and making lively addition to the picture which these chapters give. The unflagging spirit that bears up under all disadvantages is again marvellously shown. 'You 'can hardly imagine what my life is with its present condi'tions—how hard the work is, and how little time I seem 'to have at my disposal. It is necessary to the daily re'covery of my voice that I should dine at 3 when not 'travelling; I begin to prepare for the evening at 6; and I 'get back to my hotel, pretty well knocked up, at half-past '10. Add to all this, perpetual railway travelling in one 'of the severest winters ever known; and you will descry 'a reason or two for my being an indifferent correspondent. 'Last Sunday evening I left the Falls of Niagara for this 'and two intervening places. As there was a great thaw, 'and the melted snow was swelling all the rivers, the whole 'country for three hundred miles was flooded. On the 'Tuesday afternoon (I had read on the Monday) the train 'gave in, as under circumstances utterly hopeless, and

Letter to Mr. Ouvry.

Way of life.

Country flooded.

AMERICA: 1868.

At Utica.

'stopped at a place called Utica; the greater part of which 'was under water, while the high and dry part could 'produce nothing particular to eat. Here, some of the 'wretched passengers passed the night in the train, while 'others stormed the hotel. I was fortunate enough to get 'a bed-room, and garnished it with an enormous jug of gin-'punch; over which I and the manager played a double-'dummy rubber. At six in the morning we were knocked 'up: "to come aboard and try it." At half-past six we 'were knocked up again with the tidings "that it was of '"no use coming aboard or trying it." At eight all the 'bells in the town were set agoing, to summon us to "come '"aboard" instantly. And so we started, through the water, 'at four or five miles an hour; seeing nothing but drowned 'farms, barns adrift like Noah's arks, deserted villages, 'broken bridges, and all manner of ruin. I was to read 'at Albany that night, and all the tickets were sold. A 'very active superintendent of works assured me that if I 'could be "got along," he was the man to get me along: 'and that if I couldn't be got along, I might conclude that 'it couldn't possibly be fixed. He then turned on a 'hundred men in seven-league boots, who went ahead of 'the train, each armed with a long pole and pushing the 'blocks of ice away. Following this cavalcade, we got to 'land at last, and arrived in time for me to read the *Carol* 'and *Trial* triumphantly. My people (I had five of the 'staff with me) turned to at their work with a will, and 'did a day's labour in a couple of hours. If we had not 'come in as we did, I should have lost £350, and Albany 'would have gone distracted. You may conceive what

Through the water.

Getting along!

Reading at Albany.

'the flood was, when I hint at the two most notable incidents of our journey:—1, We took the passengers out of two trains, who had been in the water, immovable all night and all the previous day. 2, We released a large quantity of sheep and cattle from trucks that had been in the water I don't know how long, but so long that the creatures in them had begun to eat each other, and presented a most horrible spectable.' *

AMERICA: 1868.

Incidents of the flood.

Beside Springfield, he had engagements at Portland, New Bedford, and other places in Massachusetts, before the Boston farewells began; and there wanted but two days to bring him to that time, when he thus described to his daughter the labour which was to occupy them. His letter was from Portland on the 29th of March, and it will be observed that he no longer compromises or glozes over what he was and had been suffering. During his terrible travel to Albany his cough had somewhat spared him, but the old illness had broken out in his foot; and, though he persisted in ascribing it to the former supposed origin ('having been lately again wet, from walking in melted 'snow, which I suppose to be the occasion of its swelling in 'the old way'), it troubled him sorely, extended now at intervals to the right foot also, and lamed him for all the time he remained in the States. 'I should have written to you 'by the last mail, but I really was too unwell to do it. The

New England engagements.

Again attacked by lameness. *Ante*, 272. *Post*, 477-8.

* What follows is from the close of the letter. 'On my return, I have 'arranged with Chappell to take my leave of reading for good and all, in a 'hundred autumnal and winter Farewells *for ever*. I return by the Cunard 'steam-ship "Russia." I had the second officer's cabin on deck, when I came out; 'and I am to have the chief steward's going home. Cunard was so considerate 'as to remember that it will be on the sunny side of the vessel.'

'For ever.

AMERICA: 1868.

Reading at New Bedford.

'writing day was last Friday, when I ought to have left 'Boston for New Bedford (55 miles) before eleven in the 'morning. But I was so exhausted that I could not be 'got up, and had to take my chance of an evening train's 'producing me in time to read—which it just did. With 'the return of snow, nine days ago, my cough became as 'bad as ever. I have coughed every morning from two or 'three till five or six, and have been absolutely sleepless.

Illness.

'I have had no appetite besides, and no taste.* Last night 'here, I took some laudanum; and it is the only thing that 'has done me good, though it made me sick this morning. 'But the life, in this climate, is so very hard! When I 'did manage to get to New Bedford, I read with my 'utmost force and vigour. Next morning, well or ill, I must 'turn out at seven, to get back to Boston on my way here.

Exertion.

'I dined at Boston at three, and at five had to come on here '(a hundred and thirty miles or so) for to-morrow night: 'there being no Sunday train. To-morrow night I read here 'in a very large place; and Tuesday morning at six I must 'again start, to get back to Boston once more. But after to-'morrow night I have only the farewells, thank God! Even 'as it is, however, I have had to write to Dolby (who is in 'New York) to see my doctor there, and ask him to send me

Sick diet.

* Here was his account of his mode of living for his last ten weeks in America. 'I cannot eat (to anything like the necessary extent) and have 'established this system. At 7 in the morning, in bed, a tumbler of new 'cream and two tablespoonsful of rum. At 12, a sherry cobbler and a bis-'cuit. At 3 (dinner time) a pint of champagne. At five minutes to 8, an 'egg beaten up with a glass of sherry. Between the parts, the strongest beef 'tea that can be made, drunk hot. At a quarter past 10, soup, and any little 'thing to drink that I can fancy. I do not eat more than half a pound of 'solid food in the whole four-and-twenty hours, if so much.'

'some composing medicine that I can take at night, inas- 'much as without sleep I cannot get through. However 'sympathetic and devoted the people are about one, they 'CAN NOT be got to comprehend, seeing me able to do the 'two hours when the time comes round, that it may also 'involve much misery.' To myself on the 30th he wrote from the same place, making like confession. No comment could deepen the sadness of the story of suffering, revealed in his own simple language. 'I write in a 'town three parts of which were burnt down in a tre- 'mendous fire three years ago. The people lived in tents 'while their city was rebuilding. The charred trunks of 'the trees with which the streets of the old city were 'planted, yet stand here and there in the new thorough- 'fares like black spectres. The rebuilding is still in pro- 'gress everywhere. Yet such is the astonishing energy of 'the people that the large hall in which I am to read to- 'night (its predecessor was burnt) would compare very 'favourably with the Free Trade Hall at Manchester! . . . 'I am nearly used up. Climate, distance, catarrh, travel- 'ling, and hard work, have begun (I may say so, now they 'are nearly all over) to tell heavily upon me. Sleeplessness 'besets me; and if I had engaged to go on into May, I 'think I must have broken down. It was well that I cut 'off the Far West and Canada when I did. There would else 'have been a sad complication. It is impossible to make 'the people about one understand, however zealous and 'devoted (it is impossible even to make Dolby understand 'until the pinch comes), that the power of coming up to 'the mark every night, with spirits and spirit, may coexist

AMERICA: 1868.

Sleeplessness.

Portland burnt and rebuilt.

'Nearly 'used up.'

Seeing prevents believing.

AMERICA: 1868.

'with the nearest approach to sinking under it. When I 'got back to Boston on Thursday, after a very hard three 'weeks, I saw that Fields was very grave about my going 'on to New Bedford (55 miles) next day, and then coming 'on here (180 miles) *next* day. But the stress is over, 'and so I can afford to look back upon it, and think about 'it, and write about it.' On the 31st he closed his letter at Boston, and he was at home when I heard of him again. 'The latest intelligence, my dear old fellow, is, that 'I have arrived here safely, and that I am certainly better.

Work virtually over.

'I consider my work virtually over, now. My impression 'is, that the political crisis will damage the farewells by 'about one half. I cannot yet speak by the card; but my 'predictions here, as to our proceedings, have thus far been 'invariably right. We took last night at Portland, £360 'English; where a costly Italian troupe, using the same hall 'to-night, had not booked £14! It is the same all over 'the country, and the worst is not seen yet. Everything 'is becoming absorbed in the Presidential impeachment,

Political excitements.

'helped by the next Presidential election. Connecticut is 'particularly excited. The night after I read at Hartford 'this last week, there were two political meetings in the 'town; meetings of two parties; and the hotel was full of 'speakers coming in from outlying places. So at Newhaven: 'the moment I had finished, carpenters came in to prepare 'for next night's politics. So at Buffalo. So everywhere 'very soon.'

Farewell readings.

In the same tone he wrote his last letter to his sister-in-law from Boston. 'My notion of the farewells is pretty 'certain now to turn out right. We had £300 English 'here last night. To-day is a Fast Day, and to-night we 'shall probably take much less. Then it is likely that we 'shall pull up again, and strike a good reasonable average; 'but it is not at all probable that we shall do anything 'enormous. Every pulpit in Massachusetts will resound 'with violent politics to-day and to-night.' That was on the second of April, and a postscript was added. 'Friday 'afternoon the 3rd. Catarrh worse than ever! and we 'don't know (at four o clock) whether I can read to-night 'or must stop. Otherwise, all well.'

Last letter from America.

Dickens's last letter from America was written to his daughter Mary from Boston on the 9th of April, the day before his sixth and last farewell night. 'I not only read 'last Friday when I was doubtful of being able to do so, but 'read as I never did before, and astonished the audience 'quite as much as myself. You never saw or heard such 'a scene of excitement. Longfellow and all the Cambridge 'men have urged me to give in. I have been very near 'doing so, but feel stronger to-day. I cannot tell whether 'the catarrh may have done me any lasting injury in the 'lungs or other breathing organs, until I shall have rested 'and got home. I hope and believe not. Consider the 'weather! There have been two snow storms since I wrote 'last, and to-day the town is blotted out in a ceaseless 'whirl of snow and wind. Dolby is as tender as a woman, 'and as watchful as a doctor. He never leaves me during 'the reading, now, but sits at the side of the platform, and 'keeps his eye upon me all the time. Ditto George the 'gasman, steadiest and most reliable man I ever employed. 'I have *Dombey* to do to-night, and must go through it

Last Boston readings.

Care and kindness of Mr. Dolby.

*Ante*, 235-6.

AMERICA: 1868.

'carefully; so here ends my report. The personal affec- 'tion of the people in this place is charming to the last. 'Did I tell you that the New York Press are going to 'give me a public dinner on Saturday the 18th?'

New York farewells.

In New York, where there were five farewell nights, three thousand two hundred and ninety-eight dollars were the receipts of the last, on the 20th of April; those of the last at Boston, on the 8th, having been three thousand four hundred and fifty-six dollars. But on earlier nights in the same cities respectively, these sums also had been reached; and indeed, making allowance for an exceptional night here and there, the receipts varied so wonderfully little, that a mention of the highest average returns from other places will give no exaggerated impression of the ordinary receipts throughout. Excluding fractions of dollars, the lowest were New Bedford ($1640), Rochester ($1906), Springfield ($1970), and Providence ($2140). Albany and Worcester averaged something less than $2400; while Hartford, Buffalo, Baltimore, Syracuse, Newhaven, and Portland rose to $2600. Washington's last night was $2610, no night there having less than $2500. Philadelphia exceeded Washington by $300, and Brooklyn went ahead of Philadelphia by $200. The amount taken at the four Brooklyn readings was 11,128 dollars.

Receipts throughout.

The New York public dinner was given at Delmonico's, the hosts were more than two hundred, and the chair was taken by Mr. Horace Greeley. Dickens attended with great difficulty,* and spoke in pain. But he used

Public dinner to Dickens.

* Here is the newspaper account: 'At about five o'clock on Saturday the 'hosts began to assemble, but at 5.30 news was received that the expected

the occasion to bear his testimony to the changes of twenty-five years; the rise of vast new cities; growth in the graces and amenities of life; much improvement in the press, essential to every other advance; and changes in himself leading to opinions more deliberately formed. He promised his kindly entertainers that no copy of his *Notes*, or his *Chuzzlewit*, should in future be issued by him without accompanying mention of the changes to which he had referred that night; of the politeness, delicacy, sweet temper, hospitality, and consideration in all ways for which he had to thank them; and of his gratitude for the respect shown, during all his visit, to the privacy enforced upon him by the nature of his work and the condition of his health.

A promise which was faithfully redeemed.

He had to leave the room before the proceedings were over. On the following Monday he read to his last American audience, telling them at the close that he hoped often to recall them, equally by his winter fire and in the green summer weather, and never as a mere public audience but as a host of personal friends. He sailed two days later in the 'Russia,' and reached England in the first week of May 1868.

Adieu.

'guest had succumbed to a painful affection of the foot. In a short time, 'however, another bulletin announced Mr. Dickens's intention to attend the 'dinner at all hazards. At a little after six, having been assisted up the 'stairs, he was joined by Mr. Greeley, and the hosts forming in two lines 'silently permitted the distinguished gentlemen to pass through. Mr. Dickens 'limped perceptibly; his right foot was swathed, and he leaned heavily on the 'arm of Mr. Greeley. He evidently suffered great pain.'

# CHAPTER XVII.

## LAST READINGS.

1868—1870.

LONDON: 1868.

FAVOURABLE weather helped him pleasantly home. He had profited greatly by the sea voyage, perhaps greatly more by its repose; and on the 25th of May he described himself to his Boston friends as brown beyond belief, and causing the greatest disappointment in all quarters by looking so well. 'My doctor was quite broken down in 'spirits on seeing me for the first time last Saturday. '*Good Lord! seven years younger!* said the doctor, re- 'coiling.' That he gave all the credit to 'those fine days 'at sea,' and none to the rest from such labours as he had passed through, the close of the letter too sadly showed. 'We are already settling—think of this!—the details of 'my farewell course of readings.'

Health improved.

Project for last readings.

Even on his way out to America that enterprise was in hand. From Halifax he had written to me. 'I told the 'Chappells that when I got back to England, I would 'have a series of farewell readings in town and country; 'and then read No More. They at once offer in writing 'to pay all expenses whatever, to pay the ten per cent. for 'management, and to pay me, for a series of 75, six thou-

'sand pounds.' The terms were raised and settled before the first Boston readings closed. The number was to be a hundred; and the payment, over and above expenses and per centage, eight thousand pounds. Such a temptation undoubtedly was great; and though it was a fatal mistake which Dickens committed in yielding to it, it was not an ignoble one. He did it under no excitement from the American gains, of which he knew nothing when he pledged himself to the enterprise. No man could care essentially less for mere money than he did. But the necessary provision for many sons was a constant anxiety; he was proud of what the Readings had done to abridge this care; and the very strain of them under which it seems certain that his health had first given way, and which he always steadily refused to connect especially with them, had also broken the old confidence of being at all times available for his higher pursuit. What affected his health only he would not regard as part of the question either way. That was to be borne as the lot more or less of all men; and the more thorough he could make his feeling of independence, and of ability to rest, by what was now in hand, the better his final chances of a perfect recovery would be. That was the spirit in which he entered on this last engagement. It was an opportunity offered for making a particular work really complete before he should abandon it for ever. Something of it will not be indiscernible even in the summary of his past acquisitions, which with a pardonable exultation he now sent me.

Yielding to a temptation.

What the Readings did and undid.

The motive for more.

'We had great difficulty in getting our American accounts 'squared to the point of ascertaining what Dolby's com-

LONDON: 1868.

'mission amounted to in English money. After all, we 'were obliged to call in the aid of a money-changer, to 'determine what he should pay as his share of the average 'loss of conversion into gold. With this deduction made, 'I think his commission (I have not the figures at hand) 'was £2,888; Ticknor and Fields had a commission of '£1,000, besides 5 per cent on all Boston receipts. The 'expenses in America to the day of our sailing were 38,948 'dollars;—roughly 39,000 dollars, or £13,000. The prelimi-'nary expenses were £614. The average price of gold was 'nearly 40 per cent, and yet my profit was within a hun-'dred or so of £20,000. Supposing me to have got through 'the present engagement in good health, I shall have made 'by the Readings, *in two years*, £33,000: that is to say, '£13,000 received from the Chappells, and £20,000 from 'America. What I had made by them before, I could only 'ascertain by a long examination of Coutts's books. I should 'say, certainly not less than £10,000: for I remember that 'I made half that money in the first town and country 'compaign with poor Arthur Smith. These figures are of 'course between ourselves; but don't you think them 'rather remarkable? The Chappell bargain began with '£50 a night and everything paid; then became £60; 'and now rises to £80.'

The expenses in America.

The gains.

Profit from all the readings.

The last readings were appointed to begin with October; and at the request of an old friend, Chauncy Hare Townshend, who died during his absence in the States, he had accepted the trust, which occupied him some part of the summer, of examining and selecting for publication a bequest of some papers on matters of religious belief, which

Chauncy Townshend's trust.

were issued in a small volume the following year. There came also in June a visit from Longfellow and his daughters, with later summer visits from the Eliot Nortons; and at the arrival of friends whom he loved and honoured as he did these, from the great country to which he owed so much, infinite were the rejoicings of Gadshill. Nothing could quench his old spirit in this way. But in the intervals of my official work I saw him frequently that summer, and never without the impression that America had told heavily upon him. There was manifest abatement of his natural force, the elasticity of bearing was impaired, and the wonderful brightness of eye was dimmed at times. One day, too, as he walked from his office with Miss Hogarth to dine at our house, he could read only the halves of the letters over the shop doors that were on his right as he looked. He attributed it to medicine. It was an additional unfavourable symptom that his right foot had become affected as well as the left, though not to anything like the same extent, during the journey from the Canada frontier to Boston. But all this disappeared, upon any special cause for exertion; and he was never unprepared to lavish freely for others the reserved strength that should have been kept for himself. This indeed was the great danger, for it dulled the apprehension of us all to the fact that absolute and pressing danger did positively exist.

LONDON: 1868.

*Ante*, 189–90.

Noticeable changes.

Danger in the new scheme.

He had scarcely begun these last readings than he was beset by a misgiving, that, for a success large enough to repay Messrs. Chappell's liberality, the enterprise would require a new excitement to carry him over the old ground; and it was while engaged in Manchester and Liverpool at

LONDON: 1868.

Proposed reading from *Oliver Twist.*

the outset of October that this announcement came. 'I 'have made a short reading of the murder in *Oliver Twist.* 'I cannot make up my mind, however, whether to do it or 'not. I have no doubt that I could perfectly petrify an 'audience by carrying out the notion I have of the way of 'rendering it. But whether the impression would not be 'so horrible as to keep them away another time, is what I 'cannot satisfy myself upon. What do you think? It is 'in three short parts: 1, Where Fagin sets Noah Claypole 'on to watch Nancy. 2, The scene on London Bridge. '3, Where Fagin rouses Claypole from his sleep, to tell 'his perverted story to Sikes. And the Murder, and the 'Murderer's sense of being haunted. I have adapted and 'cut about the text with great care, and it is very power- 'ful. I have to-day referred the book and the question to 'the Chappells as so largely interested.' I had a strong dislike to this proposal, less perhaps on the ground which ought to have been taken of the physical exertion it would involve, than because such a subject seemed to be altogether out of the province of reading; and it was resolved, that, before doing it, trial should be made to a limited private audience in St. James's Hall. The note announcing this, from Liverpool on the 25th of October, is for other reasons worth printing. 'I give you earliest notice that the 'Chappells suggest to me the 18th of November' (the 14th was chosen) 'for trial of the *Oliver Twist* murder, when 'everything in use for the previous day's reading can be 'made available. I hope this may suit you? We have been 'doing well here; and how it was arranged, nobody knows, 'but we had £410 at St. James's Hall last Tuesday, having

Objections to such a reading.

Proposed private trial of it.

'advanced from our previous £360. The expenses are such, 'however, on the princely scale of the Chappells, that we 'never begin at a smaller, often at a larger, cost than £180. '. . I have not been well, and have been heavily tired. 'However, I have little to complain of—nothing, nothing; 'though, like Mariana, I am aweary. But think of this. 'If all go well, and (like Mr. Dennis) I "work off" this 'series triumphantly, I shall have made of these readings '£28,000 in a year and a half.' This did not better reconcile me to what had been too clearly forced upon him by the supposed necessity of some new excitement to ensure a triumphant result; and even the private rehearsal only led to a painful correspondence between us, of which a few words are all that need now be preserved. We might have 'agreed,' he wrote, 'to differ about it very well, because we 'only wanted to find out the truth if we could, and because 'it was quite understood that I wanted to leave behind me 'the recollection of something very passionate and dramatic, 'done with simple means, if the art would justify the 'theme.' Apart from mere personal considerations, the whole question lay in these last words. It was impossible for me to admit that the effect to be produced was legitimate, or such as it was desirable to associate with the recollection of his readings.

LONDON: 1868.

Supposed need for new excitement.

Suggestion for agreement to differ.

Not possible.

Mention should not be omitted of two sorrows which affected him at this time. At the close of the month before the readings began his youngest son went forth from home to join an elder brother in Australia. 'These partings are 'hard hard things' (26th of September), 'but they are the 'lot of us all, and might have to be done without means

Parting from his youngest son. *Post*, 445.

LONDON: 1868.

'or influence, and then would be far harder. God bless 'him!' Hardly a month later, the last of his surviving brothers, Frederick, the next to himself, died at Darlington. 'He had been tended' (24th of October) 'with the 'greatest care and affection by some local friends. It was 'a wasted life, but God forbid that one should be hard 'upon it, or upon anything in this world that is not delibe-'rately and coldly wrong.'

Death of his brother Frederick.

Before October closed the renewal of his labour had begun to tell upon him. He wrote to his sister-in-law on the 29th of sickness and sleepless nights, and of its having become necessary, when he had to read, that he should lie on the sofa all day. After arrival at Edinburgh in December he had been making a calculation that the railway travelling over such a distance involved something more than thirty thousand shocks to the nerves; but he went on to Christmas, alternating these far-off places with nights regularly intervening in London, without much more complaint than of an inability to sleep. Trade reverses at Glasgow had checked the success there,* but Edinburgh made compensation. 'The affectionate regard of the people 'exceeds all bounds and is shown in every way. The audi-'ences do everything but embrace me, and take as much 'pains with the readings as I do... The keeper of the 'Edinburgh hall, a fine old soldier, presented me on Friday

Effect of renewed work and travel.

Old friends.

* 'I think I shall be pretty correct in both places as to the run being on 'the Final readings. We had an immense house here' (Edinburgh, 12th of December) 'last night, and a very large turnaway. But Glasgow being shady 'and the charges very great, it will be the most we can do, I fancy, on these 'first Scotch readings, to bring the Chappells safely home (as to them) with-'out loss.'

'night with the most superb red camellia for my button-'hole that ever was seen. Nobody can imagine how he 'came by it, as the florists had had a considerable demand 'for that colour, from ladies in the stalls, and could get 'no such thing.'

LONDON: 1869.

The red camellia.

The second portion of the enterprise opened with the New Year, and the *Sikes and Nancy* scenes, everywhere his prominent subject, exacted the most terrible physical exertion from him. In January he was at Clifton, where he had given, he told his sister-in-law, 'by far the best Murder yet 'done;' while at the same date he wrote to his daughter: 'At Clifton on Monday night we had a contagion of fainting; 'and yet the place was not hot. I should think we had 'from a dozen to twenty ladies taken out stiff and rigid, at 'various times! It became quite ridiculous.' He was afterwards at Cheltenham. 'Macready is of opinion that the 'Murder is two Macbeths. He declares that he heard every 'word of the reading, but I doubt it. Alas! he is sadly 'infirm.' On the 27th he wrote to his daughter from Torquay that the place into which they had put him to read, and where a pantomime had been played the night before, was something between a Methodist chapel, a theatre, a circus, a riding-school, and a cow-house. That day he wrote to me from Bath: 'Landor's ghost goes along the silent 'streets here before me . . . The place looks to me like a 'cemetery which the Dead have succeeded in rising and 'taking. Having built streets, of their old gravestones, they 'wander about scantly trying to "look alive." A dead failure.'

1869

*Sikes and Nancy* reading.

A fancy about Bath.

In the second week of February he was in London, under engagement to return to Scotland (which he had just left)

LONDON: 1869.

Lameness.

Reading stopped.

Sir Henry Thompson's certificate.

after the usual weekly reading at St. James's Hall, when there was a sudden interruption. 'My foot has turned 'lame again!' was his announcement to me on the 15th, followed next day by this letter. 'Henry Thompson will 'not let me read to-night, and will not let me go to Scotland 'to-morrow. Tremendous house here, and also in Edinburgh. 'Here is the certificate he drew up for himself and Beard to 'sign. "We the undersigned hereby certify that Mr. C. D. '" is suffering from inflammation of the foot (caused by over- '" exertion), and that we have forbidden his appearance on '" the platform this evening, as he must keep his room for '" a day or two." I have sent up to the Great Western 'Hotel for apartments, and, if I can get them, shall move 'there this evening. Heaven knows what engagements 'this may involve in April! It throws us all back, and 'will cost me some five hundred pounds.'

Again travelling to Edinburgh.

A few days' rest again brought so much relief, that, against the urgent entreaties of members of his family as well as other friends, he was in the railway carriage bound for Edinburgh on the morning of the 20th of February, accompanied by Mr. Chappell himself. 'I came down lazily 'on a sofa,' he wrote to me from Edinburgh next day, 'hardly changing my position the whole way. The railway 'authorities had done all sorts of things, and I was more 'comfortable than on the sofa at the hotel. The foot gave 'me no uneasiness, and has been quiet and steady all 'night.'* He was nevertheless under the necessity, two days

* The close of the letter has an amusing picture which I may be excused for printing in a note. 'The only news that will interest you is that the good- 'natured Reverdy Johnson, being at an Art Dinner in Glasgow the other night, 'and falling asleep over the post-prandial speeches (only too naturally), woke

later, of consulting Mr. Syme; and he told his daughter that this great authority had warned him against over-fatigue in the readings, and given him some slight remedies, but otherwise reported him in 'joost pairfactly splendid 'condition.' With care he thought the pain might be got rid of. '"Wa'at mad' Thompson think it was goot?" he 'said often, and seemed to take that opinion extremely ill.' Again before leaving Scotland he saw Mr. Syme, and wrote to me on the second of March of the indignation with which he again treated the gout diagnosis, declaring the disorder to be an affection of the delicate nerves and muscles originating in cold. 'I told him that it had shewn 'itself in America in the other foot as well. "Noo I'll joost '"swear," said he, "that ayond the fatigue o' the readings '"ye'd been tramping i' th' snaw, within twa or three days." 'I certainly had. "Wa'al," said he triumphantly, "and hoo '"did it first begin? I' th' snaw. Goot! Bah!—Thompson '"knew no other name for it, and just ca'd it Goot.—Boh!" 'For which he took two guineas.' Yet the famous pupil, Sir Henry Thompson, went certainly nearer the mark than the distinguished master, Mr. Syme, in giving to it a more than local character.

EDINBURGH: 1869.

Consults a famous surgeon.

Mr. Syme's opinion of the lameness.

A doctors' difference.

The whole of that March month he went on with the

'suddenly on hearing the name of "Johnson" in a list of Scotch painters 'which one of the orators was enumerating; at once plunged up, under 'the impression that somebody was drinking his health; and immediately, and 'with overflowing amiability, began returning thanks. The spectacle was then 'presented to the astonished company, of the American Eagle being restrained 'by the coat tails from swooping at the moon, while the smaller birds endea-'voured to explain to it how the case stood, and the cock robin in possession 'of the chairman's eye twittered away as hard as he could split. I am told 'that it was wonderfully droll.'

American eagle and smaller birds.

LONDON: 1869.

scenes from *Oliver Twist*. 'The foot goes famously,' he wrote to his daughter. 'I feel the fatigue in it (four Murders 'in one week*) but not overmuch. It merely aches at 'night; and so does the other, sympathetically I suppose.' At Hull on the 8th he heard of the death of the old and dear friend, Emerson Tennent, to whom he had inscribed his last book; and on the morning of the 12th I met him at the funeral. He had read the *Oliver Twist* scenes the night before at York; had just been able to get to the express train, after shortening the pauses in the reading, by a violent rush when it was over; and had travelled through the night. He appeared to me 'dazed' and worn. No man could well look more so than he did, that sorrowful morning.

Emerson Tennent's funeral.

The end was near. A public dinner, which will have mention on a later page, had been given him in Liverpool on the 10th of April, with Lord Dufferin in the chair, and a reading was due from him in Preston on the 22nd of that month. But on Sunday the 18th we had ill report of him from Chester, and on the 21st he wrote from Blackpool to his sister-in-law. 'I have come to this Sea-Beach 'Hotel (charming) for a day's rest. I am much better than 'I was on Sunday; but shall want careful looking to, to get 'through the readings. My weakness and deadness are 'all on the left side; and if I don't look at anything I try 'to touch with my left hand, I don't know where it is. I 'am in (secret) consultation with Frank Beard, who says

Public dinner in Liverpool. *Post*, 461–2.

At Blackpool.

Alarming symptoms.

* I take from the letter a mention of the effect on a friend. 'The night 'before last, unable to get in, B. had a seat behind the screen, and was nearly 'frightened off it, by the Murder. Every vestige of colour had left his face when 'I came off, and he sat staring over a glass of champagne in the wildest way.'

PRESTON: 1869.

'that I have given him indisputable evidences of overwork 'which he could wish to treat immediately; and so I have 'telegraphed for him. I have had a delicious walk by the 'sea to-day, and I sleep soundly, and have picked up 'amazingly in appetite. My foot is greatly better too, and 'I wear my own boot.' Next day was appointed for the reading at Preston; and from that place he wrote to me, while waiting the arrival of Mr. Beard. 'Don't say any-'thing about it, but the tremendously severe nature of this 'work is a little shaking me. At Chester last Sunday I 'found myself extremely giddy, and extremely uncertain 'of my sense of touch, both in the left leg and the left hand 'and arms. I had been taking some slight medicine of 'Beard's; and immediately wrote to him describing exactly 'what I felt, and asking him whether those feelings *could* '*be* referable to the medicine? He promptly replied: '"There can be no mistaking them from your exact account. '"The medicine cannot possibly have caused them. I '"recognise indisputable symptoms of overwork, and I wish '"to take you in hand without any loss of time." They 'have greatly modified since, but he is coming down here 'this afternoon. To-morrow night at Warrington I shall 'have but 25 more nights to work through. If he can 'coach me up for them, I do not doubt that I shall get all 'right again—as I did when I became free in America. 'The foot has given me very little trouble. Yet it is remark-'able that it is *the left foot too;* and that I told Henry 'Thompson (before I saw his old master Syme) that I had 'an inward conviction that whatever it was, it was not 'gout. I also told Beard, a year after the Staplehurst acci-

His description of his illness.

Still hoping to go on.

*Ante*, 272. *Post*, 477–8.

LONDON: 1869.

Making the best he can of it.

'dent, that I was certain that my heart had been fluttered, 'and wanted a little helping. This the stethoscope con'firmed; and considering the immense exertion I am under'going, and the constant jarring of express trains, the case 'seems to me quite intelligible. Don't say anything in the 'Gad's direction about my being a little out of sorts. I 'have broached the matter of course; but very lightly. 'Indeed there is no reason for broaching it otherwise.'

Brought to town.

Even to the close of that letter he had buoyed himself up with the hope that he might yet be 'coached' and that the readings need not be discontinued. But Mr. Beard stopped them at once, and brought his patient to London. On Friday morning the 23rd, the same envelope brought me a note from himself to say that he was well enough, but tired; in perfectly good spirits, not at all uneasy, and writing this himself that I should have it under his own hand; with a note from his eldest son to say that his father appeared to him to be very ill, and that a consultation had been appointed with Sir Thomas Watson. The statement of that distinguished physician, sent to myself in June 1872, completes for the present the sorrowful narrative.

Sir Thomas Watson called in.

'It was, I think, on the 23rd of April 1869 that I was 'asked to see Charles Dickens, in consultation with Mr. 'Carr Beard. After I got home I jotted down, from their 'joint account, what follows.

Sir Thomas Watson's note of the case.

'After unusual irritability, C. D. found himself, last 'Saturday or Sunday, giddy, with a tendency to go back'wards, and to turn round. Afterwards, desiring to put 'something on a small table, he pushed it and the table 'forwards, undesignedly. He had some odd feeling of in-'security about his left leg, as if there was something 'unnatural about his heel; but he could lift, and he did 'not drag, his leg. Also he spoke of some strangeness of 'his left hand and arm; missed the spot on which he 'wished to lay that hand, unless he carefully looked at it; 'felt an unreadiness to lift his hands towards his head, 'especially his left hand—when, for instance, he was brush-'ing his hair.

LONDON: 1869.

'He had written thus to Mr. Carr Beard.

'"Is it possible that anything in my medicine can have '"made me extremely giddy, extremely uncertain of my '"footing, especially on the left side, and extremely indis-'"posed to raise my hands to my head. These symptoms '"made me very uncomfortable on Saturday (qy. Sunday?) '"night, and all yesterday, &c."

Sir Thomas Watson's note of Dickens' illness in April 1869.

'The state thus described showed plainly that C. D. had 'been on the brink of an attack of paralysis of his left side, 'and possibly of apoplexy. It was, no doubt, the result of 'extreme hurry, overwork, and excitement, incidental to 'his Readings.

'On hearing from him Mr. Carr Beard had gone at once 'to Preston, or Blackburn (I am not sure which), had for-'bidden his reading that same evening, and had brought 'him to London.

'When I saw him he *appeared* to be well. His mind 'was unclouded, his pulse quiet. His heart was beating 'with some slight excess of the natural impulse. He told 'me he had of late sometimes, but rarely, lost or misused 'a word; that he forgot names, and numbers, but had

LONDON: 1869.

'always done that; and he promised implicit obedience to 'our injunctions.

Certificate of Sir Thomas Watson and Mr. Beard.

'We gave him the following certificate.

'"The undersigned certify that Mr. Charles Dickens '"has been seriously unwell, through great exhaustion and '"fatigue of body and mind consequent upon his public '"Readings and long and frequent railway journeys. In our '"judgment Mr. Dickens will not be able with safety to him- '"self to resume his Readings for several months to come.

'"THOS. WATSON, M.D.
'"F. CARR BEARD."

Appeal to Sir Thomas Watson.

'However, after some weeks, he expressed a wish for 'my sanction to his endeavours to redeem, in a careful 'and moderate way, some of the reading engagements to 'which he had been pledged before those threatenings of 'brain-mischief in the North of England.

'As he had continued uniformly to seem and to feel 'perfectly well, I did not think myself warranted to refuse 'that sanction: and in writing to enforce great caution in 'the trials, I expressed some apprehension that he might 'fancy we had been too peremptory in our injunctions of 'mental and bodily repose in April; and I quoted the 'following remark, which occurs somewhere in one of Cap- 'tain Cook's Voyages. "Preventive measures are always '"invidious, for when most successful, the necessity for '"them is the least apparent."

Guarded sanction to additional Readings.

Sir Thomas Watson to J. F.

'I mention this to explain the letter which I send here- 'with,* and which I must beg you to return to me, as a

* In this letter Dickens wrote: 'I thank you heartily' (23rd of June 1869) 'for your great kindness and interest. It would really pain me if I thought

'precious remembrance of the writer with whom I had 'long enjoyed very friendly and much valued relations.

LONDON: 1869.

'I scarcely need say that if what I have now written 'can, *in any way*, be of use to you, it is entirely at your 'service and disposal—nor need I say with how much 'interest I have read the first volume of your late friend's 'Life. I cannot help regretting that a great pressure of 'professional work at the time, prevented my making a 'fuller record of a case so interesting.'

The twelve readings to which Sir Thomas Watson consented, with the condition that railway travel was not to accompany them, were farther to be delayed until the opening months of 1870. They were an offering from Dickens by way of small compensation to Messrs. Chappell for the breakdown of the enterprise on which they had staked so much. But here practically he finished his career as a public reader, and what remains will come with the end of what is yet to be told. One effort only intervened, by which he hoped to get happily back to his old pursuits; but to this, as to that which preceded it, sterner Fate said also No, and his Last Book, like his Last Readings, prematurely closed.

Close of career as public reader.

'you could seriously doubt my implicit reliance on your professional skill and 'advice. I feel as certain now as I felt when you came to see me on my breaking 'down through over fatigue, that the injunction you laid upon me to stop in 'my course of Readings was necessary and wise. And to its firmness I refer '(humanly speaking) my speedy recovery from that moment. I would on no 'account have resumed, even on the turn of this year, without your sanction. 'Your friendly aid will never be forgotten by me; and again I thank you for 'it with all my heart.'

Dickens to Sir Thomas Watson, June 1869.

# CHAPTER XVIII.

## LAST BOOK.

### 1869—1870.

LONDON: 1869–70.

THE last book undertaken by Dickens was to be published in illustrated monthly numbers, of the old form, but to close with the twelfth.* It closed, unfinished, with

Clause in the agreement for *Edwin Drood.*

Sale of 50,000.

Baron Tauchnitz.

* In drawing the agreement for the publication, Mr. Ouvry had, by Dickens's wish, inserted a clause thought to be altogether needless, but found to be sadly pertinent. It was the first time such a clause had been inserted in one of his agreements. 'That if the said Charles Dickens shall die during the 'composition of the said work of the *Mystery of Edwin Drood*, or shall other-'wise become incapable of completing the said work for publication in twelve 'monthly numbers as agreed, it shall be referred to John Forster, Esq, one 'of Her Majesty's Commissioners in Lunacy, or in the case of his death, inca-'pacity, or refusal to act, then to such person as shall be named by Her 'Majesty's Attorney-General for the time being, to determine the amount 'which shall be repaid by the said Charles Dickens, his executors or adminis-'trators, to the said Frederic Chapman as a fair compensation for so much of 'the said work as shall not have been completed for publication.' The sum to be paid at once for 25,000 copies was £7500; publisher and author sharing equally in the profit of all sales beyond that impression; and the number reached, while the author yet lived, was 50,000. The sum paid for early sheets to America was £1000; and Baron Tauchnitz paid liberally, as he always did, for his Leipzig reprint. 'All Mr. Dickens's works,' M. Tauchnitz writes to me, 'have been published under agreement by me. My intercourse with 'him lasted nearly twenty-seven years. The first of his letters dates in 'October 1843, and his last at the close of March 1870. Our long relations 'were not only never troubled by the least disagreement, but were the occasion 'of most hearty personal feeling; and I shall never lose the sense of his kind 'and friendly nature. On my asking him his terms for *Edwin Drood*, he 'replied "Your terms shall be mine."'

the sixth number, which was itself underwritten by two pages.

First fancy for *Edwin Drood.*

His first fancy for the tale was expressed in a letter in the middle of July. 'What should you think of the idea 'of a story beginning in this way?—Two people, boy and 'girl, or very young, going apart from one another, pledged 'to be married after many years—at the end of the book. 'The interest to arise out of the tracing of their separate 'ways, and the impossibility of telling what will be done 'with that impending fate.' This was laid aside; but it left a marked trace on the story as afterwards designed, in the position of Edwin Drood and his betrothed.

First design.

I first heard of the later design in a letter dated 'Friday 'the 6th of August 1869,' in which after speaking, with the usual unstinted praise he bestowed always on what moved him in others, of a little tale he had received for his journal,* he spoke of the change that had occurred to him for the new tale by himself. 'I laid aside the fancy I told you of, 'and have a very curious and new idea for my new story. 'Not a communicable idea (or the interest of the book 'would be gone), but a very strong one, though difficult 'to work.' The story, I learnt immediately afterward, was to be that of the murder of a nephew by his uncle; the originality of which was to consist in the review of the

*Post*, 454.

Later design.

Story of *Drood* as planned in his mind.

* 'I have a very remarkable story indeed for you to read. It is in only 'two chapters. A thing never to melt into other stories in the mind, but 'always to keep itself apart. The story was published in the 37th number of the new series of *All the Year Round*, with the title of 'An Experience.' The 'new series' had been started to break up the too great length of volumes in sequence, and the only change it announced was the discontinuance of Christmas Numbers. He had tired of them himself; and, observing the extent to which they were now copied in all directions (as usual with other examples set by him), he supposed them likely to become tiresome to the public.

LONDON: 1869–70.

murderer's career by himself at the close, when its temptations were to be dwelt upon as if, not he the culprit, but some other man, were the tempted. The last chapters were to be written in the condemned cell, to which his wickedness, all elaborately elicited from him as if told of another, had brought him. Discovery by the murderer of the utter needlessness of the murder for its object, was to follow hard upon commission of the deed; but all discovery of the murderer was to be baffled till towards the close, when, by means of a gold ring which had resisted the corrosive effects of the lime into which he had thrown the body, not only the person murdered was to be identified but the locality of the crime and the man who committed it.* So much was told to me before any of the book was written; and it will be recollected that the ring, taken by Drood to be given to his betrothed only if their engagement went on, was brought away with him from their last interview. Rosa was to marry Tartar, and Crisparkle the sister of Landless, who was himself, I think, to have perished in assisting Tartar finally to unmask and seize the murderer.

What the end was to be.

Recollections of proposed course of the tale.

Nothing written of his intentions.

Nothing had been written, however, of the main parts of the design excepting what is found in the published numbers; there was no hint or preparation for the sequel in any notes of chapters in advance; and there remained not even what he had himself so sadly written of the book by Thackeray also interrupted by death. The evidence of matured designs never to be accomplished,

* The reader curious in such matters will be helped to the clue for much of this portion of the plot by reference to pp. 90, 103, and 109, in Chapters XII, XIII, and XIV.

intentions planned never to be executed, roads of thought marked out never to be traversed, goals shining in the distance never to be reached, was wanting here. It was all a blank. Enough had been completed nevertheless to give promise of a much greater book than its immediate predecessor. 'I hope his book is finished,' wrote Longfellow when the news of his death was flashed to America. 'It is 'certainly one of his most beautiful works, if not the most 'beautiful of all. It would be too sad to think the pen had 'fallen from his hand, and left it incomplete.' Some of its characters were touched with subtlety, and in its descriptions his imaginative power was at its best. Not a line was wanting to the reality, in the most minute local detail, of places the most widely contrasted; and we saw with equal vividness the lazy cathedral town and the lurid opium-eater's den.* Something like the old lightness and buoyancy of animal spirits gave a new freshness to the humour; the scenes of the child-heroine and her luckless betrothed had both novelty and nicety of character in them; and Mr. Grewgious in chambers with his clerk and the two waiters, the conceited fool Sapsea, and the blustering philanthropist Honeythunder, were first-rate comedy. Miss Twinkleton was of the family of Miss La Creevy; and

Opinion of Longfellow.

Merits of the fragment.

The minor characters.

* I subjoin what has been written to me by an American correspondent. 'I went lately with the same inspector who accompanied Dickens to see the 'room of the opium-smokers, old Eliza and her Lascar or Bengalee friend. 'There a fancy seized me to buy the bedstead which figures so accurately in '*Edwin Drood*, in narrative and picture. I gave the old woman a pound for 'it, and have it now packed and ready for shipment to New York. Another 'American bought a pipe. So you see we have heartily forgiven the novelist his 'pleasantries at our expense. Many military men who came to England from 'America refuse to register their titles, especially if they be Colonels; all the 'result of the basting we got on that score in *Martin Chuzzlewit.*'

Homage to Dickens.

LONDON: 1869–70.

Miss Billickin.

the lodging-house keeper, Miss Billickin, though she gave Miss Twinkleton but a sorry account of her blood, had that of Mrs. Todgers in her veins. 'I was put in life to a 'very genteel boarding-school, the mistress being no less a 'lady than yourself, of about your own age, or it may be, 'some years younger, and a poorness of blood flowed from 'the table which has run through my life.' Was ever anything better said of a school-fare of starved gentility?

Last page of *Edwin Drood*.

The last page of *Edwin Drood* was written in the Châlet in the afternoon of his last day of consciousness; and I have thought there might be some interest in a facsimile of the greater part of this final page of manuscript that ever came from his hand, at which he had worked unusually late in order to finish the chapter. It has very much the character, in its excessive care of correction and interlineation, of all his later manuscripts; and in order that comparison may be made with his earlier and easier method, I place beside it a portion of a page of the original of *Oliver Twist*. His greater pains and elaboration of writing, it may be mentioned, become first very obvious in the later parts of *Martin Chuzzlewit;* but not the least remarkable feature in all his manuscripts, is the accuracy with which the portions of each representing the several numbers are exactly adjusted to the space the printer had to fill. Whether without erasure or so interlined as to be illegible, nothing is wanting, and there is nothing in excess. So assured was the habit, that he has himself remarked upon an instance the other way, in *Our Mutual Friend*, as not having happened to him for thirty years. But *Edwin Drood* more startlingly showed him how

Comparison of his early and his late MSS.

*Ante*, 343.

unsettled the habit he most prized had become, in the clashing of old and new pursuits. 'When I had written' (22nd of December 1869) 'and, as I thought, disposed of 'the first two Numbers of my story, Clowes informed me 'to my horror that they were, together, *twelve printed 'pages too short!!!* Consequently I had to transpose a 'chapter from number two to number one, and remodel 'number two altogether! This was the more unlucky, 'that it came upon me at the time when I was obliged to 'leave the book, in order to get up the Readings' (the additional twelve for which Sir Thomas Watson's consent had been obtained), 'quite gone out of my mind since I 'left them off. However, I turned to it and got it done, 'and both numbers are now in type. Charles Collins has 'designed an excellent cover.' It was his wish that his son-in-law should have illustrated the story; but, this not being practicable, upon an opinion expressed by Mr. Millais which the result thoroughly justified, choice was made of Mr. S. L. Fildes.

LONDON: 1869–70.

*Ante*, 423.

*Ante*, 227.

---

This reference to the last effort of Dickens's genius had been written as it thus stands, when a discovery of some interest was made by the writer. Within the leaves of one of Dickens's other manuscripts were found some detached slips of his writing, on paper only half the size of that used for the tale, so cramped, interlined, and blotted as to be nearly illegible, which on close inspection proved to be a scene in which Sapsea the auctioneer is introduced as the principal figure, among a group of characters new to the story. The explanation of it perhaps is, that, having become a little nervous about the course of the tale, from a fear

Discovery of unpublished scene.

From *Edwin Drood*: the last page written by Dickens. 8th June 1870.

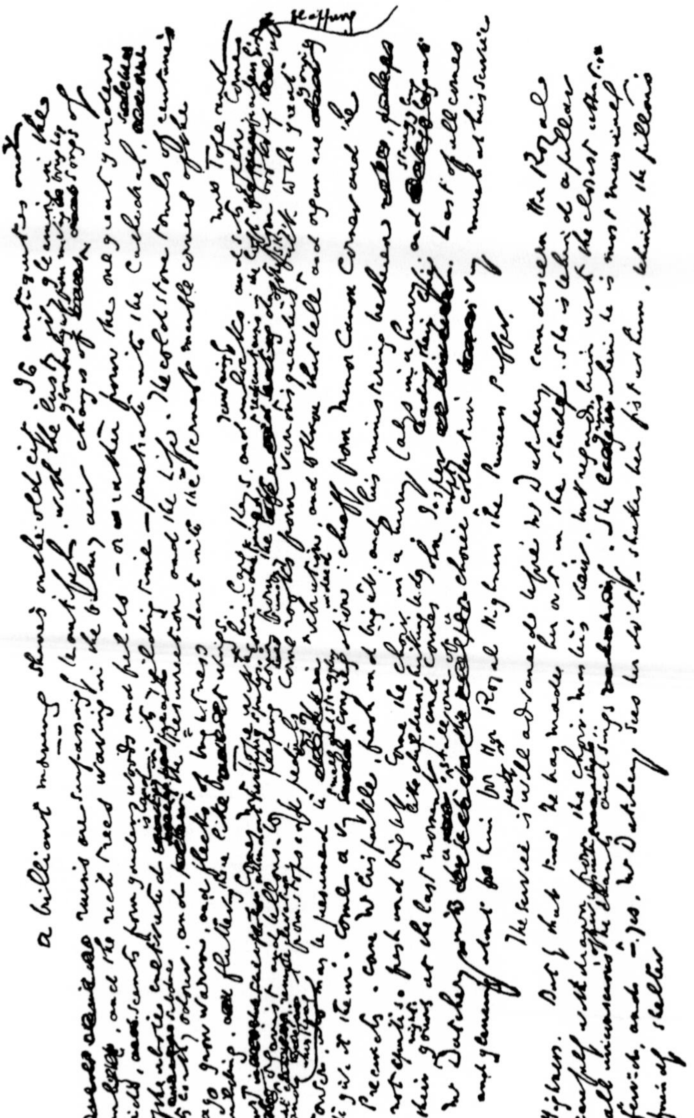

"No" - replied the Dodger "not here, for this ain't the shop for justice; besides which my attorney is a breakfasting this morning with the Wice President of the House of Commons, but I shall have something to say elsewhere, and so will he, and so will a wery numerous and respectable circle of acquaintance as'll make them beaks wish they'd never been born, or that they'd got their footman to hang 'em up to their own hat-pegs afore they let 'em come out this morning to try it on upon me. I'll —"

"There; he's fully committed" : interposed the clerk. "Take him away."

From *Oliver Twist*: written in 1837.

LONDON: 1869–70.

Probable reason for writing it in advance.

that he might have plunged too soon into the incidents leading on to the catastrophe, such as the Datchery assumption in the fifth number (a misgiving he had certainly expressed to his sister-in-law), it had occurred to him to open some fresh veins of character incidental to the interest, though not directly part of it, and so to handle them in connection with Sapsea as a little to suspend the final development even while assisting to strengthen it. Before beginning any number of a serial he used, as we have seen in former instances, to plan briefly what he intended to put into it chapter by chapter; and his first number-plan of *Drood* had the following: 'Mr. Sapsea. Old Tory jackass. 'Connect Jasper with him. (He will want a solemn donkey 'by and by):' which was effected by bringing together both Durdles and Jasper, for connection with Sapsea, in the matter of the epitaph for Mrs. Sapsea's tomb. The scene now discovered might in this view have been designed to strengthen and carry forward that element in the tale; and otherwise it very sufficiently expresses itself. It would supply an answer, if such were needed, to those who have asserted that the hopeless decadence of Dickens as a writer had set in before his death. Among the lines last written by him, these are the very last we can ever hope to receive; and they seem to me a delightful specimen of the power possessed by him in his prime, and the rarest which any novelist can have, of revealing a character by a touch. Here are a couple of people, Kimber and Peartree, not known to us before, whom we read off thoroughly in a dozen words; and as to Sapsea himself, auctioneer and mayor of Cloisterham, we are face to face with what before

*Ante*, 133-4.

A delightful specimen of Dickens's writing.

we only dimly realised, and we see the solemn jackass, in his business pulpit, playing off the airs of Mr. Dean in his Cathedral pulpit, with Cloisterham laughing at the impostor.

'HOW MR. SAPSEA CEASED TO BE A MEMBER OF 'THE EIGHT CLUB.

'TOLD BY HIMSELF.

'Wishing to take the air, I proceeded by a circuitous 'route to the Club, it being our weekly night of meeting. 'I found that we mustered our full strength. We were 'enrolled under the denomination of the Eight Club. We 'were eight in number; we met at eight o'clock during 'eight months of the year; we played eight games of four-'handed cribbage, at eightpence the game; our frugal 'supper was composed of eight rolls, eight mutton chops, 'eight pork sausages, eight baked potatoes, eight marrow-'bones, with eight toasts, and eight bottles of ale. There 'may, or may not, be a certain harmony of colour in the 'ruling idea of this (to adopt a phrase of our lively neigh-'bours) reunion. It was a little idea of mine.

Unpublished scene for *Edwin Drood.*

'A somewhat popular member of the Eight Club, was a 'member by the name of Kimber. By profession, a 'dancing-master. A commonplace, hopeful sort of man, 'wholly destitute of dignity or knowledge of the world.

'As I entered the Club-room, Kimber was making the 'remark: "And he still half-believes him to be very high '"in the Church."

'In the act of hanging up my hat on the eighth peg by 'the door, I caught Kimber's visual ray. He lowered it, 'and passed a remark on the next change of the moon. I 'did not take particular notice of this at the moment,

LONDON: 1869–70.

'because the world was often pleased to be a little shy of 'ecclesiastical topics in my presence. For I felt that I was 'picked out (though perhaps only through a coincidence) 'to a certain extent to represent what I call our glorious 'constitution in Church and State. The phrase may be 'objected to by captious minds; but I own to it as mine. 'I threw it off in argument some little time back. I said: '"OUR GLORIOUS CONSTITUTION in CHURCH and STATE."

Unpublished scene for *Edwin Drood*.

'Another member of the Eight Club was Peartree; also 'member of the Royal College of Surgeons. Mr. Peartree is not accountable to me for his opinions, and I say 'no more of them here than that he attends the poor 'gratis whenever they want him, and is not the parish 'doctor. Mr. Peartree may justify it to the grasp of *his* 'mind thus to do his republican utmost to bring an appointed officer into contempt. Suffice it that Mr. Peartree can never justify it to the grasp of *mine*.

'Between Peartree and Kimber there was a sickly sort 'of feeble-minded alliance. It came under my particular 'notice when I sold off Kimber by auction. (Goods taken 'in execution). He was a widower in a white under-waist-'coat, and slight shoes with bows, and had two daughters 'not ill-looking. Indeed the reverse. Both daughters 'taught dancing in scholastic establishments for Young 'Ladies—had done so at Mrs. Sapsea's; nay, Twinkleton's '—and both, in giving lessons, presented the unwomanly 'spectacle of having little fiddles tucked under their chins. 'In spite of which, the younger one might, if I am cor-'rectly informed—I will raise the veil so far as to say I 'KNOW she might—have soared for life from this degrading 'taint, but for having the class of mind allotted to what I 'call the common herd, and being so incredibly devoid of 'veneration as to become painfully ludicrous.

'When I sold off Kimber without reserve, Peartree (as 'poor as he can hold together) had several prime house-'hold lots knocked down to him. I am not to be blinded; 'and of course it was as plain to me what he was going to 'do with them, as it was that he was a brown hulking sort 'of revolutionary subject who had been in India with the 'soldiers, and ought (for the sake of society) to have his 'neck broke. I saw the lots shortly afterwards in Kim-'ber's lodgings—through the window—and I easily made 'out that there had been a sneaking pretence of lending 'them till better times. A man with a smaller knowledge 'of the world than myself might have been led to suspect 'that Kimber had held back money from his creditors, and 'fraudulently bought the goods. But, besides that I knew 'for certain he had no money, I knew that this would 'involve a species of forethought not to be made com-'patible with the frivolity of a caperer, inoculating other 'people with capering, for his bread.

Unpublished scene for *Edwin Drood.*

'As it was the first time I had seen either of those two 'since the sale, I kept myself in what I call Abeyance. 'When selling him up, I had delivered a few remarks—'shall I say a little homily?—concerning Kimber, which 'the world did regard as more than usually worth notice. 'I had come up into my pulpit, it was said, uncommonly 'like—and a murmur of recognition had repeated his '(I will not name whose) title, before I spoke. I had then 'gone on to say that all present would find, in the first

London: 1869–70.

'page of the catalogue that was lying before them, in the 'last paragraph before the first lot, the following words: '"Sold in pursuance of a writ of execution issued by a '"creditor." I had then proceeded to remind my friends, 'that however frivolous, not to say contemptible, the busi-'ness by which a man got his goods together, still his 'goods were as dear to him, and as cheap to society (if 'sold without reserve), as though his pursuits had been 'of a character that would bear serious contemplation. I 'had then divided my text (if I may be allowed so to call 'it) into three heads: firstly, Sold; secondly, In pursuance 'of a writ of execution; thirdly, Issued by a creditor; 'with a few moral reflections on each, and winding up 'with, "Now to the first lot" in a manner that was 'complimented when I afterwards mingled with my 'hearers.

Unpublished scene for *Edwin Drood.*

'So, not being certain on what terms I and Kimber 'stood, I was grave, I was chilling. Kimber, however, 'moving to me, I moved to Kimber. (I was the creditor 'who had issued the writ. Not that it matters.)

'"I was alluding, Mr. Sapsea," said Kimber, "to a '"stranger who entered into conversation with me in the '"street as I came to the Club. He had been speaking '"to you just before, it seemed, by the churchyard; and '"though you had told him who you were, I could hardly '"persuade him that you were not high in the Church."

'"Idiot!" said Peartree.

'"Ass!" said Kimber.

'"Idiot and Ass!" said the other five members.

'"Idiot and Ass, gentlemen," I remonstrated, looking

'around me, "are strong expressions to apply to a young '"man of good appearance and address." My generosity 'was roused; I own it.

'"You'll admit that he must be a Fool," said Peartree.

'"You can't deny that he must be a Blockhead," said 'Kimber.

'Their tone of disgust amounted to being offensive. 'Why should the young man be so calumniated? What 'had he done? He had only made an innocent and 'natural mistake. I controlled my generous indignation, 'and said so.

'"Natural?" repeated Kimber; "*He's* a Natural!"

Unpublished scene for *Edwin Drood.*

'The remaining six members of the Eight Club laughed 'unanimously. It stung me. It was a scornful laugh. 'My anger was roused in behalf of an absent, friendless 'stranger. I rose (for I had been sitting down).

'"Gentlemen," I said with dignity, "I will not remain '"one of this Club allowing opprobrium to be cast on an '"unoffending person in his absence. I will not so violate '"what I call the sacred rites of hospitality. Gentlemen, '"until you know how to behave yourselves better, I leave '"you. Gentlemen, until then I withdraw, from this '"place of meeting, whatever personal qualifications I '"may have brought into it. Gentlemen, until then you '"cease to be the Eight Club, and must make the best '"you can of becoming the Seven."

'I put on my hat and retired. As I went down stairs 'I distinctly heard them give a suppressed cheer. Such 'is the power of demeanour and knowledge of mankind. 'I had forced it out of them.

LONDON: 1869–70.

'II.

'Whom should I meet in the street, within a few yards 'of the door of the inn where the Club was held, but the 'self-same young man whose cause I had felt it my duty so 'warmly—and I will add so disinterestedly—to take up.

'"Is it Mr. Sapsea," he said doubtfully, "or is it——"

"'It is Mr. Sapsea," I replied.

"'Pardon me, Mr. Sapsea; you appear warm, sir."

'"I have been warm," I said, "and on your account." 'Having stated the circumstances at some length (my 'generosity almost overpowered him), I asked him his 'name.

Unpublished scene for *Edwin Drood*.

'"Mr. Sapsea," he answered, looking down, "your '"penetration is so acute, your glance into the souls of '"your fellow men is so penetrating, that if I was hardy '"enough to deny that my name is Poker, what would it '"avail me?"

'I don't know that I had quite exactly made out to a 'fraction that his name *was* Poker, but I daresay I had 'been pretty near doing it.

'"Well, well," said I, trying to put him at his ease by 'nodding my head in a soothing way. "Your name is '"Poker, and there is no harm in being named Poker."

'"Oh Mr. Sapsea!" cried the young man, in a very 'well-behaved manner. "Bless you for those words!" He 'then, as if ashamed of having given way to his feelings, 'looked down again.

'"Come, Poker," said I, "let me hear more about you. '"Tell me. Where are you going to, Poker? and where '"do you come from?"

'"Ah Mr. Sapsea!" exclaimed the young man. "Disguise from you is impossible. You know already that "I come from somewhere, and am going somewhere else. "If I was to deny it, what would it avail me?"

London: 1869–70.

Unpublished scene for *Edwin Drood.*

'"Then don't deny it," was my remark.

'"Or," pursued Poker, in a kind of despondent rapture, "or if I was to deny that I came to this town to see and "hear you sir, what would it avail me? Or if I was to "deny———"

The fragment ends there, and the hand that could alone have completed it is at rest for ever.

---

Some personal characteristics remain for illustration before the end is briefly told.

# CHAPTER XIX.

## PERSONAL CHARACTERISTICS.

1836—1870.

LONDON 1836–70.

OBJECTION has been taken to this biography as likely to disa ppoint its readers in not making them 'talk to Dickens 'as Boswell makes them talk to Johnson.' But where will the blame lie if a man takes up *Pickwick* and is disappointed to find that he is not reading *Rasselas?* A book must be judged for what it aims to be, and not for what it cannot by possibility be. I suppose so remarkable an author as Dickens hardly ever lived who carried so little of authorship into ordinary social intercourse. Potent as the sway of his writings was over him, it expressed itself in other ways. Traces or triumphs of literary labour, displays of conversational or other personal predominance, were no part of the influence he exerted over friends. To them he was only the pleasantest of companions, with whom they forgot that he had ever written anything, and felt only the charm which a nature of such capacity for supreme enjoyment causes every one around it to enjoy. His talk was unaffected and natural, never bookish in the smallest degree. He was quite up to the average of well read men, but as there was no ostentation of it in his writing, so neither was

Dickens not a bookish man.

Character of his talk.

there in his conversation. This was so attractive because so keenly observant, and lighted up with so many touches of humorous fancy; but, with every possible thing to give relish to it, there were not many things to bring away.

What determines a book's place.

Of course a book must stand or fall by its contents. Macaulay said very truly that the place of books in the public estimation is fixed, not by what is written about them, but by what is written in them. I offer no complaint of any remark made upon these volumes, but there have been some misapprehensions. Though Dickens bore outwardly so little of the impress of his writings, they formed the whole of that inner life which essentially constituted the man; and as in this respect he was actually, I have thought that his biography should endeavour to present him. The story of his books, therefore, at all stages of their progress, and of the hopes or designs connected with them, was my first care. With that view, and to give also to the memoir what was attainable of the value of autobiography, letters to myself, such as were never addressed to any other of his correspondents, and covering all the important incidents in the life to be retraced, were used with few exceptions exclusively; and though the exceptions are much more numerous in the present volume, this general plan has guided me to the end. Such were my limits indeed, that half even of those letters had to be put aside; and to have added all such others as were open to me would have doubled the size of my book, not contributed to it a new fact of life or character, and altered materially its design. It would have been so much lively illustration added to the subject, but out of place here. The purpose here was

Why so much said of Dickens's books.

Why letters to one correspondent so largely used.

LONDON: 1836-70.

Dickens made to tell his own story.

to make Dickens the sole central figure in the scenes revived, narrator as well as principal actor; and only by the means employed could consistency or unity be given to the self-revelation, and the picture made definite and clear. It is the peculiarity of few men to be to their most intimate friend neither more nor less than they are to themselves, but this was true of Dickens; and what kind or quality of nature such intercourse expressed in him, of what strength, tenderness, and delicacy susceptible, of what steady level warmth, of what daily unresting activity of intellect, of what unbroken continuity of kindly impulse through the change and vicissitude of three-and-thirty years, the letters to myself given in these volumes could alone express. Gathered from various and differing sources, their interest could not have been as the interest of these; in which everything comprised in the successive stages of a most attractive career is written with unexampled candour and truthfulness, and set forth in definite pictures of what he saw and stood in the midst of, unblurred by vagueness or reserve. Of the charge of obtruding myself to which their publication has exposed me, I can only say that I studied nothing so hard as to suppress my own personality, and have to regret my ill success where I supposed I had even too perfectly succeeded. But we have all of us frequent occasion to say, parodying Mrs. Peachem's remark, that we are bitter bad judges of ourselves.

Intercourse with a friend.

A fault not consciously committed.

The other properties of these letters are quite subordinate to this main fact that the man who wrote them is thus perfectly seen in them. But they do not lessen the estimate of his genius. Admiration rises higher at the writer's mental forces, who, putting so much of himself into his work for the public, had still so much overflowing for such private intercourse. The sunny health of nature in them is manifest; its largeness, spontaneity, and manliness; but they have also that which highest intellects appreciate best. 'I have read them,' Lord Russell wrote to me, 'with delight and pain. His heart, his imagination, his 'qualities of painting what is noble, and finding diamonds 'hidden far away, are greater here than even his works 'convey to me. How I lament he was not spared to 'us longer. I shall have a fresh grief when he dies in 'your volumes.' Shallower people are more apt to find other things. If the bonhommie of a man's genius is obvious to all the world, there are plenty of knowing ones ready to take the shine out of the genius, to discover that after all it is not so wonderful, that what is grave in it wants depth, and the humour has something mechanical. But it will be difficult even for these to look over letters so marvellous in the art of reproducing to the sight what has once been seen, so natural and unstudied in their wit and fun, and with such a constant well-spring of sprightly runnings of speech in them, point of epigram, ingenuity of quaint expression, absolute freedom from every touch of affectation, and to believe that the source of this man's humour, or of whatever gave wealth to his genius, was other than habitual, unbounded, and resistless.

Lord Russell on Dickens's letters.

Shallower judgments.

Answer to detractors.

There is another consideration of some importance. Sterne did not more incessantly fall back from his works upon himself than Dickens did, and undoubtedly one of the impressions left by the letters is that of the intensity

LONDON: 1868.

and tenacity with which he recognized, realized, contemplated, cultivated, and thoroughly enjoyed, his own individuality in even its most trivial manifestations. But if any one is led to ascribe this to self-esteem, to a narrow exclusiveness, or to any other invidious form of egotism, let him correct the impression by observing how Dickens bore himself amid the universal blazing-up of America, at the beginning and at the end of his career. Of his hearty, undisguised, and unmistakeable enjoyment of his astonishing and indeed quite bewildering popularity, there can be as little doubt as that there is not a particle of vanity in it, any more than of false modesty or grimace.* While realizing fully the fact of it, and the worth of the fact, there is not in his whole being a fibre that answers falsely to the charmer's voice. Few men in the world, one fancies, could have gone through such grand displays of fireworks, not merely with so marvellous an absence of what the French call *pose*, but unsoiled by the smoke of a cracker. No man's strong individuality was ever so free from conceit.

No self-conceit in Dickens.

His bearing in America.

Other personal incidents and habits, and especially some matters of opinion of grave importance, will help to make

Fitz-Greene Halleck on Dickens in 1842.

* Mr. Grant Wilson has sent me an extract from a letter by Fitz-Greene Halleck (author of one of the most delightful poems ever written about Burns) which exactly expresses Dickens as he was, not only in 1842, but, as far as the sense of authorship went, all his life. It was addressed to Mrs. Rush of Philadelphia, and is dated the 8th of March 1842. 'You 'ask me about Mr. Boz. I am quite delighted with him. He is a thorough 'good fellow, with nothing of the author about him but the reputation, and 'goes through his task as Lion with exemplary grace, patience, and good 'nature. He has the brilliant face of a man of genius . . . His writings you 'know. I wish you had listened to his eloquence at the dinner here. It was 'the only real specimen of eloquence I have ever witnessed. Its charm was 'not in its words, but in the manner of saying them.'

his character better known. Much questioning followed a brief former reference to his religious belief, but, inconsistent or illogical as the conduct described may be, there is nothing to correct or to modify in my statement of it;* and, to what otherwise appeared to be in doubt, explicit answer will be afforded by a letter, written upon the youngest of his children leaving home in September 1868 to join his brother in Australia, than which none worthier appears in his story. 'I write this note to-day because your 'going away is much upon my mind, and because I 'want you to have a few parting words from me, to think 'of now and then at quiet times. I need not tell you that 'I love you dearly, and am very, very sorry in my heart 'to part with you. But this life is half made up of partings, 'and these pains must be borne. It is my comfort and 'my sincere conviction that you are going to try the life 'for which you are best fitted. I think its freedom and 'wildness more suited to you than any experiment in a 'study or office would have been; and without that train-'ing, you could have followed no other suitable occupation. 'What you have always wanted until now, has been a set, 'steady, constant purpose. I therefore exhort you to per-'severe in a thorough determination to do whatever you 'have to do, as well as you can do it. I was not so old as 'you are now, when I first had to win my food, and to do 'it out of this determination; and I have never slackened 'in it since. Never take a mean advantage of any one in

ii. 37–38.

Letter to his youngest son.

Pains of parting.

His own example.

* In a volume called *Home and Abroad*, by Mr. David Macrae, is printed a correspondence with Dickens on matters alluded to in the text, held in 1861, which will be found to confirm all that is here said.

LONDON: 1868.

'any transaction, and never be hard upon people who are 'in your power. Try to do to others as you would have 'them do to you, and do not be discouraged if they fail 'sometimes. It is much better for you that they should 'fail in obeying the greatest rule laid down by Our Saviour 'than that you should. I put a New Testament among 'your books for the very same reasons, and with the very 'same hopes, that made me write an easy account of it for 'you, when you were a little child. Because it is the best 'book that ever was, or will be, known in the world; and 'because it teaches you the best lessons by which any 'human creature, who tries to be truthful and faithful to 'duty, can possibly be guided. As your brothers have gone 'away, one by one, I have written to each such words as I 'am now writing to you, and have entreated them all to 'guide themselves by this Book, putting aside the inter-'pretations and inventions of Man. You will remember 'that you have never at home been harassed about religious 'observances, or mere formalities. I have always been 'anxious not to weary my children with such things, before 'they are old enough to form opinions respecting them. 'You will therefore understand the better that I now most 'solemnly impress upon you the truth and beauty of the 'Christian Religion, as it came from Christ Himself, and 'the impossibility of your going far wrong if you humbly 'but heartily respect it. Only one thing more on this 'head. The more we are in earnest as to feeling it, the 'less we are disposed to hold forth about it. Never abandon 'the wholesome practice of saying your own private prayers, 'night and morning. I have never abandoned it myself,

Advice to a son.

*Ante*, ii. 215.

Forms not realities in religion.

Personal prayer.

'and I know the comfort of it. I hope you will always be 'able to say in after life, that you had a kind father. You 'cannot show your affection for him so well, or make him 'so happy, as by doing your duty.' They who most intimately knew Dickens will know best that every word there is written from his heart, and is radiant with the truth of his nature.

LONDON: 1868.

To the same effect, in the leading matter, he expressed himself twelve years before, and again the day before his death; replying in both cases to correspondents who had addressed him as a public writer. A clergyman, the Rev. R. H. Davies, had been struck by the hymn in the Christmas tale of the Wreck of the Golden Mary (*Household Words*, 1856). 'I 'beg to thank you' Dickens answered (Christmas Eve, 1856) 'for your very acceptable letter—not the less gratifying to 'me because I am myself the writer you refer to. . . There 'cannot be many men, I believe, who have a more humble 'veneration for the New Testament, or a more profound 'conviction of its all-sufficiency, than I have. If I am ever '(as you tell me I am) mistaken on this subject, it is be'cause I discountenance all obtrusive professions of and 'tradings in religion, as one of the main causes why 'real Christianity has been retarded in this world; and 'because my observation of life induces me to hold in un'speakable dread and horror, those unseemly squabbles 'about the letter which drive the spirit out of hundreds 'of thousands.' In precisely similar tone, to a reader of *Edwin Drood* (Mr. J. M. Makeham), who had pointed out to him that his employment as a figure of speech of a line from Holy Writ in his tenth chapter might be subject

Hymn in a Christmas tale.

Letter to a clergyman in 1856.

London: 1868.

Letter to a layman, 8th June 1870.

to misconstruction, he wrote from Gadshill on Wednesday the eighth of June, 1870. 'It would be quite inconceiv-'able to me, but for your letter, that any reasonable reader 'could possibly attach a scriptural reference to that pas-'sage... I am truly shocked to find that any reader can 'make the mistake. I have always striven in my writings 'to express veneration for the life and lessons of our 'Saviour; because I feel it; and because I re-wrote that 'history for my children—every one of whom knew it, from 'having it repeated to them, long before they could read, 'and almost as soon as they could speak. But I have never 'made proclamation of this from the house tops.' *

A dislike of all display was rooted in him; and his objection to posthumous honours, illustrated by the instructions in his will, was very strikingly expressed two years before his death, when Mr. Thomas Fairbairn asked his help to a proposed recognition of Rajah Brooke's services by a memorial in Westminster Abbey. 'I am very strongly 'impelled' (24th of June 1868) 'to comply with any request 'of yours. But these posthumous honours of committee, 'subscriptions, and Westminster Abbey are so profoundly 'unsatisfactory in my eyes that—plainly—I would rather 'have nothing to do with them in any case. My daughter 'and her aunt unite with me in kindest regards to Mrs. 'Fairbairn, and I hope you will believe in the possession 'of mine until I am quietly buried without any memorial 'but such as I have set up in my lifetime.' Asked a year later (August 1869) to say something on the inauguration

Letter to Mr. Fairbairn.

Objection to posthumous honours.

* This letter is facsimile'd in *A Christmas Memorial of Charles Dickens by A. B. Hume* (1870), containing an Ode to his Memory written with feeling and spirit.

LONDON: 1836–70.

of Leigh Hunt's bust at his grave in Kensal-green, he told the committee that he had a very strong objection to speech-making beside graves. 'I do not expect or wish 'my feelings in this wise to guide other men; still, it is so 'serious with me, and the idea of ever being the subject of 'such a ceremony myself is so repugnant to my soul, that 'I must decline to officiate.'

Dislike of speech-making at a grave.

His aversion to every form of what is called patronage of literature * was part of the same feeling. A few months earlier a Manchester gentleman † wrote for his support to such a scheme. 'I beg to be excused,' was his reply, 'from complying with the request you do me the 'honour to prefer, simply because I hold the opinion that 'there is a great deal too much patronage in England. The 'better the design, the less (as I think) should it seek such 'adventitious aid, and the more composedly should it rest 'on its own merits.' This was the belief Southey held; it extended to the support by way of patronage given by such societies as the Literary Fund, which Southey also strongly resisted; and it survived the failure of the Guild whereby it was hoped to establish a system of self-help, under which men engaged in literary pursuits might be as proud to receive as to give. Though there was no project of his life into which he flung himself with greater eagerness than the

Too much 'patronage in England.

Source of quarrel with Literary Fund.

* I may quote here from a letter (Newcastle-on-Tyne, 5th Sept. 1858) sent me by the editor of the *Northern Express*. 'The view you take of the lite'rary character in the abstract, or of what it might and ought to be, expresses 'what I have striven for all through my literary life—never to allow it to be 'patronized, or tolerated, or treated like a good or a bad child. I am always 'animated by the hope of leaving it a little better understood by the thought'less than I found it.'—To James B. Manson, Esq.

As to treatment of literature.

† Henry Ryder-Taylor, Esq. Ph.D. 8th Sept. 1868.

LONDON: 1836–70.

Exertions for the Guild of Literature.

Guild, it was not taken up by the class it was meant to benefit, and every renewed exertion more largely added to the failure. There is no room in these pages for the story, which will add its chapter some day to the vanity of human wishes; but a passage from a letter to Bulwer Lytton at its outset will be some measure of the height from which the writer fell, when all hope for what he had so set his heart upon ceased. 'I do devoutly believe that this plan, 'carried by the support which I trust will be given to it, 'will change the status of the literary man in England, and 'make a revolution in his position which no government, 'no power on earth but his own, could ever effect. I have 'implicit confidence in the scheme—so splendidly begun '—if we carry it out with a stedfast energy. I have a 'strong conviction that we hold in our hands the peace 'and honour of men of letters for centuries to come, and 'that you are destined to be their best and most enduring 'benefactor. . . Oh what a procession of new years may 'walk out of all this for the class we belong to, after we 'are dust.'

What he hoped from it. 1850.

Vanity of human wishes.

These views about patronage did not make him more indulgent to the clamour with which it is so often invoked for the ridiculously small. 'You read that life of Clare?' he wrote (15th of August 1865). 'Did you ever see such 'preposterous exaggeration of small claims? And isn't it 'expressive, the perpetual prating of him in the book as '*the Poet?* So another Incompetent used to write to the 'Literary Fund when I was on the committee: "This '"leaves the Poet at his divine mission in a corner of the '"single room. The Poet's father is wiping his spectacles.

Small poets.

Huge pretensions.

'"The Poet's mother is weaving"—Yah!' He was equally intolerant of every magnificent proposal that should render the literary man independent of the bookseller, and he sharply criticized even a compromise to replace the half-profits system by one of royalties on copies sold. 'What 'does it come to?' he remarked of an ably-written pamphlet in which this was urged (10th of November 1866): 'what is the worth of the remedy after all? You and I 'know very well that in nine cases out of ten the author is 'at a disadvantage with the publisher because the publisher 'has capital and the author has not. We know perfectly 'well that in nine cases out of ten money is advanced by 'the publisher before the book is producible—often, long 'before. No young or unsuccessful author (unless he were 'an amateur and an independent gentleman) would make 'a bargain for having that royalty, to-morrow, if he could 'have a certain sum of money, or an advance of money. 'The author who could command that bargain, could com-'mand it to-morrow, or command anything else. For the 'less fortunate or the less able, I make bold to say—with 'some knowledge of the subject, as a writer who made 'a publisher's fortune long before he began to share in the 'real profits of his books—that if the publishers met next 'week, and resolved henceforth to make this royalty bar-'gain and no other, it would be an enormous hardship and 'misfortune because the authors could not live while they 'wrote. The pamphlet seems to me just another example of 'the old philosophical chess-playing, with human beings for 'pieces. "Don't want money." "Be careful to be born '"with means, and have a banker's account." "Your

As to writers and booksellers. 1866.

On 'royalty bargains.

Personal experience.

'"publisher will settle with you, at such and such long '"periods according to the custom of his trade, and you '"will settle with your butcher and baker weekly, in the '"meantime, by drawing cheques as I do." "You must be '"sure not to want money, and then I have worked it out '"for you splendidly."'

Editorship.

Less has been said in this work than might perhaps have been wished, of the way in which his editorship of *Household Words* and *All the Year Round* was discharged. It was distinguished above all by liberality; and a scrupulous consideration and delicacy, evinced by him to all his contributors, was part of the esteem in which he held literature itself. It was said in a newspaper after his death, evidently by one of his contributors, that he always brought the best out of a man by encouragement and appreciation; that he liked his writers to feel unfettered; and that his last reply to a proposition for a series of articles had been: 'Whatever you see your way to, I will see mine 'to, and we know and understand each other well enough 'to make the best of these conditions.' Yet the strong feeling of personal responsibility was always present in his conduct of both journals; and varied as the contents of a number might be, and widely apart the writers, a certain individuality of his own was never absent. He took immense pains (as indeed was his habit about everything) with numbers in which he had written nothing; would often accept a paper from a young or unhandy contributor, because of some single notion in it which he thought it worth rewriting for; and in this way, or by helping generally to give strength and attractiveness to the work of

Relations with contributors.

Work for others.

others, he grudged no trouble.* 'I have had a story' he wrote (22nd of June 1856) 'to hack and hew into some 'form for *Household Words* this morning, which has taken 'me four hours of close attention. And I am perfectly

Insertion in another man's contribution.

* By way of instance I subjoin an amusing insertion made by him in an otherwise indifferently written paper descriptive of the typical Englishman on the foreign stage, which gives in more comic detail experiences of his own already partly submitted to the reader (ii. 102–3). 'In a pretty piece at 'the Gymnase in Paris, where the prime minister of England unfortunately 'ruined himself by speculating in railway shares, a thorough-going English 'servant appeared under that thorough-going English name Tom Bob—the 'honest fellow having been christened Tom, and born the lawful son of Mr. 'and Mrs. Bob. In an Italian adaptation of DUMAS' preposterous play of 'KEAN, which we once saw at the great theatre of Genoa, the curtain rose upon 'that celebrated tragedian, drunk and fast asleep in a chair, attired in a dark 'blue blouse fastened round the waist with a broad belt and a most prodigious 'buckle, and wearing a dark red hat of the sugar-loaf shape, nearly three 'feet high. He bore in his hand a champagne-bottle, with the label RHUM, 'in large capital letters, carefully turned towards the audience; and two or 'three dozen of the same popular liquor, which we are nationally accustomed 'to drink neat as imported, by the half gallon, ornamented the floor of the 'apartment. Every frequenter of the Coal Hole tavern in the Strand, on that 'occasion, wore a sword and a beard. Every English lady, presented on the 'stage in Italy, wears a green veil; and almost every such specimen of our 'fair countrywomen carries a bright red reticule, made in the form of a 'monstrous heart. We do not remember to have ever seen an Englishman on 'the Italian stage, or in the Italian circus, without a stomach like Daniel 'Lambert, an immense shirt-frill, and a bunch of watch-seals each several 'times larger than his watch, though the watch itself was an impossible 'engine. And we have rarely beheld this mimic Englishman, without seeing 'present, then and there, a score of real Englishmen sufficiently characteristic 'and unlike the rest of the audience, to whom he bore no shadow of resem- 'blance.' These views as to English people and society, of which Count d'Orsay used always to say that an average Frenchman knew about as much as he knew of the inhabitants of the moon, may receive amusing addition from one of Dickens's letters during his last visit to France; which enclosed a cleverly written Paris journal containing essays on English manners. In one of these the writer remarked that he had heard of the venality of English politicians, but could not have supposed it to be so shameless as it is, for, when he went to the House of Commons, he heard them call out 'Places! Places!' 'Give 'us Places!' when the Minister entered!

Foreign views of English people.

Places! places!

LONDON: 1836–70.

'addled by its horrible want of continuity after all, and the 'dreadful spectacle I have made of the proofs—which look 'like an inky fishing-net.' A few lines from another letter will show the difficulties in which he was often involved by the plan he adopted for Christmas numbers, of putting within a framework by himself a number of stories by separate writers to whom the leading notion had before been severally sent. 'As yet' (25th of November 1859), 'not a story has come to me in the least belonging to the 'idea (the simplest in the world; which I myself described 'in writing, in the most elaborate manner); and everyone 'of them turns, by a strange fatality, on a criminal trial!' It had all to be set right by him, and editorship on such terms was not a sinecure.

Invention of Christmas numbers.

Editorial troubles.

Editorial pleasures.

It had its pleasures as well as pains, however, and the greatest was when he fancied he could descry unusual merit in any writer. A letter will give one instance for illustration of many; the lady to whom it was addressed, admired under her assumed name of Holme Lee, having placed it at my disposal. (Folkestone: 14th of August 1855.) 'I read your tale with the strongest emotion, and 'with a very exalted admiration of the great power dis-'played in it. Both in severity and tenderness I thought 'it masterly. It moved me more than I can express to 'you. I wrote to Mr. Wills that it had completely un-'settled me for the day, and that by whomsoever it was 'written, I felt the highest respect for the mind that had 'produced it. It so happened that I had been for some 'days at work upon a character externally like the Aunt. 'And it was very strange to me indeed to observe how

On a story by 'Holme 'Lee.'

'the two people seemed to be near to one another at 'first, and then turned off on their own ways so wide 'asunder. I told Mr. Wills that I was not sure whether 'I could have prevailed upon myself to present to a large 'audience the terrible consideration of hereditary mad-'ness, when it was reasonably probable that there must 'be many—or some—among them whom it would awfully, 'because personally, address. But I was not obliged to ask 'myself the question, inasmuch as the length of the story 'rendered it unavailable for *Household Words.* I speak 'of its length in reference to that publication only; rela-'tively to what is told in it, I would not spare a page of 'your manuscript. Experience shows me that a story in 'four portions is best suited to the peculiar requirements of 'such a journal, and I assure you it will be an uncommon 'satisfaction to me if this correspondence should lead to 'your enrolment among its contributors. But my strong 'and sincere conviction of the vigour and pathos of this 'beautiful tale, is quite apart from, and not to be influenced 'by, any ulterior results. You had no existence to me 'when I read it. The actions and sufferings of the cha-'racters affected me by their own force and truth, and left 'a profound impression on me.'* The experience there mentioned did not prevent him from admitting into his later periodical, *All the Year Round,* longer serial stories published with the names of known writers; and to his own interference with these he properly placed limits. 'When one of my literary brothers does me the honour

Plan pursued in *Household Words.*

Change of plan in *All the Year Round.*

* The letter is addressed to Miss Harriet Parr, whose book called *Gilbert Massenger* is the tale referred to.

LONDON: 1836–70.

'to undertake such a task, I hold that he executes it on 'his own personal responsibility, and for the sustainment 'of his own reputation; and I do not consider myself at 'liberty to exercise that control over his text which I claim 'as to other contributions.' Nor had he any greater pleasure, even in these cases, than to help younger novelists to popularity. 'You asked me about new writers last night. 'If you will read *Kissing the Rod*, a book I have read to-'day, you will not find it hard to take an interest in the 'author of such a book.' That was Mr. Edmund Yates, in whose literary successes he took the greatest interest himself, and with whom he continued to the last an intimate personal intercourse which had dated from kindness shown at a very trying time. 'I think' he wrote of another of his contributors, Mr. Percy Fitzgerald, for whom he had also much personal liking, and of whose powers he thought highly, 'you will find *Fatal Zero* a very 'curious bit of mental development, deepening as the 'story goes on into a picture not more startling than true.' My mention of these pleasures of editorship shall close with what I think to him was the greatest. He gave to the world, while yet the name of the writer was unknown to him, the pure and pathetic verse of Adelaide Procter. 'In the spring of the year 1853 I observed a 'short poem among the proffered contributions, very dif-'ferent, as I thought, from the shoal of verses perpetually 'setting through the office of such a periodical.'* The contributions had been large and frequent under an assumed

Mr. Edmund Yates.

Mr. Percy Fitzgerald.

Adelaide Procter's Poems.

* See the introductory memoir from his pen now prefixed to every edition of the popular and delightful *Legends and Lyrics*.

name, when at Christmas 1854 he discovered that Miss Mary Berwick was the daughter of his old and dear friend Barry Cornwall.

Adverse influences of periodical writing.

But periodical writing is not without its drawbacks, and its effect on Dickens, who engaged in it largely from time to time, was observable in the increased impatience of allusion to national institutions and conventional distinctions to be found in his later books. Party divisions he cared for less and less as life moved on; but the decisive, peremptory, dogmatic style, into which a habit of rapid remark on topics of the day will betray the most candid and considerate commentator, displayed its influence, perhaps not always consciously to himself, in the underlying tone of bitterness that runs through the books which followed *Copperfield.* The resentment against remediable wrongs is as praiseworthy in them as in the earlier tales; but the exposure of Chancery abuses, administrative incompetence, politico-economic shortcomings, and social flunkeyism, in *Bleak House, Little Dorrit, Hard Times,* and *Our Mutual Friend,* would not have been made less odious by the cheerier tone that had struck with much sharper effect at prison abuses, parish wrongs, Yorkshire schools, and hypocritical humbug, in *Pickwick, Oliver Twist, Nickleby,* and *Chuzzlewit.* It will be remembered of him always that he desired to set right what was wrong, that he held no abuse to be unimprovable, that he left none of the evils named exactly as he found them, and that to influences drawn from his writings were due not a few of the salutary changes which marked the age in which he lived; but anger does not improve satire, and it gave latterly, from

Earlier and later tone in his books.

Anger and satire.

LONDON: 1836–70.

the causes named, too aggressive a form to what, after all, was but a very wholesome hatred of the cant that everything English is perfect, and that to call a thing *un*English is to doom it to abhorred extinction.

'Member 'for No- 'where.'

'I have got an idea for occasional papers in *Household* '*Words* called the Member for Nowhere. They will con- 'tain an account of his views, votes, and speeches; and I 'think of starting with his speeches on the Sunday ques- 'tion. He is a member of the Government of course. The 'moment they found such a member in the House, they 'felt that he must be dragged (by force, if necessary) into 'the Cabinet.' 'I give it up reluctantly,' he wrote afterwards, 'and with it my hope to have made every man in 'England feel something of the contempt for the House of 'Commons that I have. We shall never begin to do any- 'thing until the sentiment is universal.' That was in August 1854; and the break-down in the Crimea that winter much embittered his radicalism. 'I am hourly 'strengthened in my old belief,' he wrote (3rd of February 1855) 'that our political aristocracy and our tuft-hunting 'are the death of England. In all this business I don't see 'a gleam of hope. As to the popular spirit, it has come to 'be so entirely separated from the Parliament and Govern- 'ment, and so perfectly apathetic about them both, that I 'seriously think it a most portentous sign.' A couple of months later: 'I have rather a bright idea, I think, for '*Household Words* this morning: a fine little bit of satire: 'an account of an Arabic MS. lately discovered very like 'the *Arabian Nights*—called the Thousand and One 'Humbugs. With new versions of the best known stories.'

Failures abroad.

Break-down at home.

'Thousand 'and One 'Hum- 'bugs.'

This also had to be given up, and is only mentioned as another illustration of his political discontents and of their connection with his journal-work. The influences from his early life which unconsciously strengthened them in certain social directions has been hinted at, and of his absolute sincerity in the matter there can be no doubt. The mistakes of Dickens were never such as to cast a shade on his integrity. What he said with too much bitterness, in his heart he believed; and had, alas! too much ground for believing. 'A country, he wrote (27th of April 1855) 'which 'is discovered to be in this tremendous condition as to its 'war affairs; with an enormous black cloud of poverty in 'every town which is spreading and deepening every hour, 'and not one man in two thousand knowing anything about, 'or even believing in, its existence; with a non-working 'aristocracy, and a silent parliament, and everybody for 'himself and nobody for the rest; this is the prospect, 'and I think it a very deplorable one.' Admirably did he say, of a notorious enquiry at that time: 'O what a fine 'aspect of political economy it is, that the noble professors 'of the science on the adulteration committee should have 'tried to make Adulteration a question of Supply and 'Demand! We shall never get to the Millennium, sir, by 'the rounds of that ladder; and I, for one, won't hold by 'the skirts of that Great Mogul of impostors, Master M'Culloch!' Again he wrote (30th of September 1855): 'I 'really am serious in thinking—and I have given as painful 'consideration to the subject as a man with children to live 'and suffer after him can honestly give to it—that representative government is become altogether a failure with

Opinions honestly (if mistakenly) formed.

Non-working aristocracy and silent parliament:

Not the way to the Millennium.

Failure of representative government.

LONDON: 1869.

'us, that the English gentilities and subserviences render 'the people unfit for it, and that the whole thing has broken 'down since that great seventeenth-century time, and has 'no hope in it.'

No thought of parliament for himself.

With the good sense that still overruled all his farthest extremes of opinion he yet never thought of parliament for himself. He could not mend matters, and for him it would have been a false position. The people of the town of Reading and others applied to him during the first half of his life, and in the last half some of the Metropolitan constituencies. To one of the latter a reply is before me in which he says: 'I declare that as to all 'matters on the face of this teeming earth, it appears to 'me that the House of Commons and Parliament alto- 'gether is become just the dreariest failure and nuisance 'that ever bothered this much-bothered world.' To a private enquiry of apparently about the same date he replied: 'I have thoroughly satisfied myself, having often 'had occasion to consider the question, that I can be far 'more usefully and independently employed in my chosen 'sphere of action than I could hope to be in the House of 'Commons; and I believe that no consideration would in- 'duce me to become a member of that extraordinary as- 'sembly.' Finally, upon a reported discussion in Finsbury whether or not he should be invited to sit for that borough, he promptly wrote (November 1861): 'It may save some 'trouble if you will kindly confirm a sensible gentleman who doubted at that meeting whether I was quite the 'man for Finsbury. I am not at all the sort of man; for I 'believe nothing would induce me to offer myself as a

No desire to enter the House of Commons.

Not the man for Finsbury.

'parliamentary representative of that place, or of any other 'under the sun.' The only direct attempt to join a political agitation was his speech at Drury-lane for administrative reform, and he never repeated it. But every movement for practical social reforms, to obtain more efficient sanitary legislation, to get the best compulsory education practicable for the poor, and to better the condition of labouring people, he assisted earnestly to his last hour; and the readiness with which he took the chair at meetings having such objects in view, the help he gave to important societies working in beneficent ways for themselves or the community, and the power and attractiveness of his oratory, made him one of the forces of the time. His speeches derived singular charm from the buoyancy of his perfect self-possession, and to this he added the advantages of a person and manner which had become as familiar and as popular as his books. The most miscellaneous assemblages listened to him as to a personal friend.

LONDON: 1869.

Reforms he took most interest in.

Chairmanship of meetings.

Two incidents at the close of his life will show what upon these matters his latest opinions were. At the great Liverpool dinner after his country readings in 1869, over which Lord Dufferin eloquently presided, he replied to a remonstrance from Lord Houghton against his objection to entering public life,* that when he took literature for

The Liverpool dinner in 1869.

* On this remonstrance and Dickens's reply the *Times* had a leading article of which the closing sentences find fitting place in his biography. 'If 'there be anything in Lord Russell's theory that Life Peerages are wanted 'specially to represent those forms of national eminence which cannot other- 'wise find fitting representation, it might be urged, for the reasons we have 'before mentioned, that a Life Peerage is due to the most truly national 'representative of one important department of modern English literature. 'Something may no doubt be said in favour of this view, but we are inclined 'to doubt if Mr. Dickens himself would gain anything by a Life Peerage. Mr. 'Dickens is pre-eminently a writer of the people and for the people. To our

LONDON: 1870.

his profession he intended it to be his sole profession; that at that time it did not appear to him to be so well understood in England, as in some other countries, that literature was a dignified profession by which any man might stand or fall; and he resolved that in his person at least it should stand 'by itself, of itself, and for itself;' a bargain which 'no consideration on earth would now induce him to break.' Here however he probably failed to see the entire meaning of Lord Houghton's regret, which would seem to have been meant to say, in more polite form, that to have taken some part in public affairs might have shown him the difficulty in a free state of providing remedies very swiftly for evils of long growth. A half reproach from the same quarter for alleged unkindly sentiments to the House of Lords, he repelled with vehement warmth; insisting on his great regard for individual members, and declaring that there was no man in England he respected more in his public capacity, loved more in his private capacity, or from whom he had received more remarkable proofs of his honour and love of literature, than Lord Russell.* In Birmingham shortly after, discoursing on education to the members of the Midland Institute, he

Reply to Lord Houghton's remonstrance.

Tribute to Lord Russell.

'thinking, he is far better suited for the part of the "Great Commoner" of 'English fiction than for even a Life Peerage. To turn Charles Dickens into 'Lord Dickens would be much the same mistake in literature that it was in 'politics to turn William Pitt into Lord Chatham.'

The living statesman he most honoured.

* One of the many repetitions of the same opinion in his letters may be given. 'Lord John's note' (September 1853) 'confirms me in an old im'pression that he is worth a score of official men; and has more generosity in 'his little finger than a Government usually has in its whole corporation.' In another of his public allusions, Dickens described him as a statesman of whom opponents and friends alike felt sure that he would rise to the level of every occasion, however exalted; and compared him to the seal of Solomon in the old Arabian story inclosing in a not very large casket the soul of a giant.

LONDON: 1857.

told them they should value self-improvement not because it led to fortune but because it was good and right in itself; counselled them in regard to it that Genius was not worth half so much as Attention, or the art of taking an immense deal of pains, which he declared to be, in every study and pursuit, the one sole, safe, certain, remunerative quality; and summed up briefly his political belief.—'My 'faith in the people governing is, on the whole, infinitesi- 'mal; my faith in the People governed is, on the whole, 'illimitable.' This he afterwards (January 1870) explained to mean that he had very little confidence in the people who govern us ('with a small p'), and very great confidence in the People whom they govern ('with a large P'). 'My 'confession being shortly and elliptically stated, was, with 'no evil intention I am absolutely sure, in some quarters 'inversely explained.' He added that his political opinions had already been not obscurely stated in an 'idle book or 'two'; and he reminded his hearers that he was the inventor 'of a certain fiction called the Circumlocution Office, said 'to be very extravagant, but which I *do* see rather fre- 'quently quoted as if there were grains of truth at the 'bottom of it.' It may nevertheless be suspected, with some confidence, that the construction of his real meaning was not far wrong which assumed it as the condition precedent to his illimitable faith, that the people, even with the big P, should be 'governed.' It was his constant complaint that, being much in want of government, they had only sham governors; and he had returned from his second American visit, as he came back from his first, indisposed to believe that the political problem had been solved in

The people governing and the People governed.

Reply to misconstruction.

Another explanation possible.

Last and first American experience.

LONDON: 1857.

Tone of last book.

the land of the free. From the pages of his last book, the bitterness of allusion so frequent in the books just named was absent altogether; and his old unaltered wish to better what was bad in English institutions, carried with it no desire to replace them by new ones.

Alleged offers from the Queen.

In a memoir published shortly after his death there appeared this statement. 'For many years past Her 'Majesty the Queen has taken the liveliest interest in Mr. 'Dickens's literary labours, and has frequently expressed a 'desire for an interview with him. . . This interview took 'place on the 9th of April, when he received her commands 'to attend her at Buckingham Palace, and was introduced 'by his friend Mr. Arthur Helps, the clerk of the Privy 'Council. . . Since our author's decease the journal with 'which he was formerly connected has said: "The Queen '"was ready to confer any distinction which Mr. Dickens's '"known views and tastes would permit him to accept, and '"after more than one title of honour had been declined, '"Her Majesty desired that he would, at least, accept a '"place in her Privy Council."' As nothing is too absurd*

Statements in vogue after Dickens's death.

* In a memoir by Dr. Shelton McKenzie which has had circulation in America, there is given the following statement, taken doubtless from publications at the time, of which it will be strictly accurate to say, that, excepting the part of its closing averment which describes Dickens sending a copy of his works to her Majesty by her own desire, *there is in it not a single word of truth.* 'Early in 1870 the Queen presented a copy of her book upon the 'Highlands to Mr. Dickens, with the modest autographic inscription, "from '"the humblest to the most distinguished author of England." This was 'meant to be complimentary, and was accepted as such by Mr. Dickens, who 'acknowledged it in a manly, courteous letter. Soon after, Queen Victoria 'wrote to him, requesting that he would do her the favour of paying her a 'visit at Windsor. He accepted, and passed a day, very pleasantly, in his 'Sovereign's society. It is said that they were mutually pleased, that Mr. 'Dickens caught the royal lady's particular humour, that they chatted together 'in a very friendly manner, that the Queen was never tired of asking questions

for belief, it will not be superfluous to say that Dickens knew of no such desire on her Majesty's part; and though all the probabilities are on the side of his unwillingness to accept any title or place of honour, certainly none was offered to him.

LONDON: 1870.

It had been hoped to obtain her Majesty's name for the Jerrold performances in 1857, but, being a public effort in behalf of an individual, assent would have involved 'either 'perpetual compliance or the giving of perpetual offence.' Her Majesty however then sent, through Colonel Phipps, a request to Dickens that he would select a room in the palace, do what he would with it, and let her see the play there. 'I said to Col. Phipps thereupon' (21st of June 1857) 'that 'the idea was not quite new to me; that I did not feel easy 'as to the social position of my daughters, &c. at a Court 'under those circumstances; and that I would beg her

*Ante*, 145.

Communication with her Majesty in 1857.

'about certain characters in his books, that they had almost a *tête-à-tête* 'luncheon, and that, ere he departed, the Queen pressed him to accept a 'baronetcy (a title which descends to the eldest son), and that, on his declin-'ing, she said, "At least, Mr. Dickens, let me have the gratification of '"making you one of my Privy Council." This, which gives the personal 'title of "Right Honorable," he also declined—nor, indeed, did Charles 'Dickens require a title to give him celebrity. The Queen and the author 'parted, well pleased with each other. The newspapers reported that a peer-'age had been offered and declined—*but even newspapers are not invariably 'correct.* Mr. Dickens presented his Royal Mistress with a handsome set of 'all his works, and, on the very morning of his death, a letter reached Gad's 'Hill, written by Mr. Arthur Helps, by her desire, acknowledging the present, 'and describing the exact position the books occupied at Balmoral—so placed 'that she could see them before her when occupying the usual seat in her 'sitting-room. When this letter arrived, Mr. Dickens was still alive, but 'wholly unconscious. What to him, at that time, was the courtesy of an 'earthly sovereign?' I repeat that the only morsel of truth in all this rigmarole is that the books were sent by Dickens, and acknowledged by Mr. Helps at the Queen's desire. The letter did not arrive on the day of his death, the 9th of June, but was dated from Balmoral on that day.

Rigmarole.

The only morsel of truth in it.

LONDON: 1870.

'Majesty to excuse me, if any other way of her seeing the 'play could be devised. To this Phipps said he had not 'thought of the objection, but had not the slightest doubt 'I was right. I then proposed that the Queen should come 'to the Gallery of Illustration a week before the subscrip-'tion night, and should have the room entirely at her own 'disposal, and should invite her own company. This, with 'the good sense that seems to accompany her good nature 'on all occasions, she resolved within a few hours to do.' The effect of the performance was a great gratification. 'My gracious sovereign' (5th of July 1857) 'was so pleased 'that she sent round begging me to go and see her and 'accept her thanks. I replied that I was in my Farce 'dress, and must beg to be excused. Whereupon she sent 'again, saying that the dress "could not be so ridiculous as '"that," and repeating the request. I sent my duty in 'reply, but again hoped her Majesty would have the kind-'ness to excuse my presenting myself in a costume and 'appearance that were not my own. I was mighty glad to 'think, when I woke this morning, that I had carried the 'point.'

Desire to see Dickens act.

Dickens sent for.

Declines to present himself in stage dress.

1858.

The opportunity of presenting himself in his own costume did not arrive till the year of his death, another effort meanwhile made having proved also unsuccessful. I was put 'into a state of much perplexity on Sunday' (30th of March 1858). 'I don't know who had spoken to my informant, 'but it seems that the Queen is bent upon hearing the '*Carol* read, and has expressed her desire to bring it 'about without offence; hesitating about the manner of it, 'in consequence of my having begged to be excused from

Her Majesty's wish to hear Dickens read.

'going to her when she sent for me after the *Frozen* '*Deep*. I parried the thing as well as I could; but being 'asked to be prepared with a considerate and obliging 'answer, as it was known the request would be preferred, I 'said, "Well! I supposed Col. Phipps would speak to me '"about it, and if it were he who did so, I should assure him '"of my desire to meet any wish of her Majesty's, and should '"express my hope that she would indulge me by making '"one of some audience or other—for I thought an audi-'"ence necessary to the effect." Thus it stands: but it 'bothers me.' The difficulty was not surmounted, but her Majesty's continued interest in the *Carol* was shown by her purchase of a copy of it with Dickens's autograph at Thackeray's sale;* and at last there came, in the year of his death, the interview with the author whose popularity dated from her accession, whose books had entertained larger numbers of her subjects than those of any other contemporary writer, and whose genius will be counted among the glories of her reign. Accident led to it. Dickens had brought with him from America some large and striking photographs of the Battle Fields of the Civil War, which the Queen, having heard of them through Mr. Helps, expressed a wish to look at. Dickens sent them at once; and went afterwards to Buckingham Palace with

Queen's interest in the *Carol*.

How the interview with her Majesty originated.

* The book was thus entered in the catalogue. 'DICKENS (C.), A CHRISTMAS CAROL, in prose, 1843; *Presentation Copy*, inscribed "*W. M. Thackeray, from Charles Dickens* (*whom he made very happy once a long way* '"*from home*)."' Some pleasant verses by his friend had affected him much while abroad. I quote the Life of Dickens published by Mr. Hotten. 'Her Majesty expressed the strongest desire to possess this presentation 'copy, and sent an unlimited commission to buy it. The original published 'price of the book was 5*s*. It became Her Majesty's property for £25 10*s*., 'and was at once taken to the palace.'

Purchase of Thackeray's copy of the *Carol*.

LONDON: 1870.

Mr. Helps, at her Majesty's request, that she might see and thank him in person.

It was in the middle of March, not April. 'Come now 'sir, this is an interesting matter, do favour us with it,' was the cry of Johnson's friends after his conversation with George the Third; and again and again the story was told to listeners ready to make marvels of its commonplaces. But the romance even of the eighteenth century in such a matter is clean gone out of the nineteenth. Suffice it that the Queen's kindness left a strong impression on Dickens.

Account of it.

Upon her Majesty's regret not to have heard his Readings, Dickens intimated that they were become now a thing of the past, while he acknowledged gratefully her Majesty's compliment in regard to them. She spoke to him of the impression made upon her by his acting in the *Frozen Deep*; and on his stating, in reply to her enquiry, that the little play had not been very successful on the public stage, said this did not surprise her, since it no longer had the advantage of his performance in it. Then arose a mention of some alleged discourtesy shown to Prince Arthur in New York, and he begged her Majesty not to confound the true Americans of that city with the Fenian portion of its Irish population; on which she made the quiet comment that she was convinced the people about the Prince had made too much of the affair. He related to her the story of President Lincoln's dream on the night before his murder. She asked him to give her his writings, and could she have them that afternoon? but he begged to be allowed to send a bound copy. Her Majesty then took from a table her own book upon the Highlands, with an autograph inscription 'to

*Ante*, 386–8.

'Charles Dickens'; and, saying that 'the humblest' of writers would be ashamed to offer it to 'one of the greatest' but that Mr. Helps, being asked to give it, had remarked that it would be valued most from herself, closed the interview by placing it in his hands. 'Sir,' said Johnson, 'they 'may say what they like of the young King, but Louis the 'Fourteenth could not have shown a more refined courtli-'ness'; and Dickens was not disposed to say less of the young King's granddaughter. That the grateful impression sufficed to carry him into new ways, I had immediate proof, coupled with intimation of the still surviving strength of old memories. 'As my sovereign desires' (26th of March 1870) 'that 'I should attend the next levee, don't faint with amaze-'ment if you see my name in that unwonted connexion. I 'have scrupulously kept myself free for the second of April, 'in case you should be accessible.' The name appeared at the levee accordingly, his daughter was at the drawing-room that followed, and Lady Houghton writes to me 'I never 'saw Mr. Dickens more agreeable than at a dinner at our 'house about a fortnight before his death, when he met the 'King of the Belgians and the Prince of Wales at the 'special desire of the latter.' Up to nearly the hour of dinner, it was doubtful if he could go. He was suffering from the distress in his foot; and on arrival at the house, being unable to ascend the stairs, had to be assisted at once into the dining-room.

What passed at the interview.

Dickens's grateful impression from it.

Going to a levee!

i. 91, 129.

Meeting the Prince of Wales.

The friend who had accompanied Dickens to Buckingham Palace, writing of him * after his death, briefly but with

* 'In Memoriam' by Arthur Helps, in *Macmillan's Magazine* for July 1870.

LONDON: 1870.

'In Memoriam' by Arthur Helps.

admirable knowledge and taste, said that he ardently desired, and confidently looked forward to, a time when there would be a more intimate union than exists at present between the different classes in the state, a union that should embrace alike the highest and the lowest. This perhaps expresses, as well as a few words could, what certainly was always at his heart; and he might have come to think it, when his life was closing, more possible of realisation some day than he ever thought it before.

A hope at the close of life.

The hope of it was on his friend Talfourd's lips when he died, and his own most jarring opinions might at last have joined in the effort to bring about such reconcilement. More on this head it needs not to say. Whatever may be the objection to special views held by him, he would, wanting even the most objectionable, have been less himself. It was by something of the despot seldom separable from genius, joined to a truthfulness of nature belonging to the highest characters, that men themselves of a rare faculty were attracted to find in Dickens what Sir Arthur Helps has described, 'a man to confide in, and 'look up to as a leader, in the midst of any great peril.'

Mr. Layard at Gadshill, 1866–7.

Mr. Layard also held that opinion of him. He was at Gadshill during the Christmas before Dickens went for the last time to America, and witnessed one of those scenes, not infrequent there, in which the master of the house was pre-eminently at home. They took generally the form of cricket matches; but this was, to use the phrase of his friend Bobadil, more popular and diffused; and of course he rose with the occasion. 'The more you want of 'the master, the more you'll find in him,' said the gasman

GADSHILL: 1867.

employed about his readings. 'Footraces for the villagers,' he wrote on Christmas Day, 'come off in my field 'to-morrow. We have been all hard at work all day, 'building a course, making countless flags, and I don't know 'what else. Layard is chief commissioner of the domestic 'police. The country police predict an immense crowd.' There were between two and three thousand people; and somehow, by a magical kind of influence, said Layard, Dickens seemed to have bound every creature present, upon what honour the creature had, to keep order. What was the special means used, or the art employed, it might have been difficult to say; but that was the result. Writing on New Year's Day, Dickens himself described it to me. 'We 'had made a very pretty course, and taken great pains. 'Encouraged by the cricket matches experience, I allowed 'the landlord of the Falstaff to have a drinking-booth 'on the ground. Not to seem to dictate or distrust, I gave 'all the prizes (about ten pounds in the aggregate) in 'money. The great mass of the crowd were labouring men 'of all kinds, soldiers, sailors, and navvies. They did not, 'between half-past ten, when we began, and sunset, displace 'a rope or a stake; and they left every barrier and flag as 'neat as they found it. There was not a dispute, and there 'was no drunkenness whatever. I made them a little speech 'from the lawn, at the end of the games, saying that please 'God we would do it again next year. They cheered most 'lustily and dispersed. The road between this and Chatham 'was like a Fair all day; and surely it is a fine thing to 'get such perfect behaviour out of a reckless seaport town. 'Among other oddities we had A Hurdle Race for

New Year's Day in the meadow.

Games for the villagers.

Dickens's description.

GADSHILL: 1867.

A winner in the games.

'Strangers. One man (he came in second) ran 120 yards 'and leaped over ten hurdles, in twenty seconds, *with a 'pipe in his mouth, and smoking it all the time.* "If it '"hadn't been for your pipe," I said to him at the winning-'post, "you would have been first." "I beg your pardon, '"sir,' he answered, "but if it hadn't been for my pipe, I '"should have been nowhere."' The close of the letter had this rather memorable announcement. 'The sale of 'the Christmas number was, yesterday evening, 255,380.' Would it be absurd to say that there is something in such a vast popularity in itself electrical, and, though founded on books, felt where books never reach?

Home enjoyments.

It is also very noticeable that what would have constituted the strength of Dickens if he had entered public life, the attractive as well as the commanding side of his nature, was that which kept him most within the circle of home pursuits and enjoyments. This 'better part' of him had now long survived that sorrowful period of 1857–8, when, for reasons which I have not thought myself free to suppress, a vaguely disturbed feeling for the time took possession of him, and occurrences led to his adoption of other pursuits than those to which till then he had given himself exclusively. It was a sad interval in his life; but, though changes incident to the new occupation then taken up remained, and with them many adverse influences which brought his life prematurely to a close, it was, with any reference to that feeling, an interval only; and the dominant impression of the later years, as of the earlier, takes the marvellously domestic home-loving shape in which also the strength of his genius is found. It will not do to draw

Same in late as in early years.

round any part of such a man too hard a line, and the writer must not be charged with inconsistency who says that Dickens's childish sufferings,* and the sense they burnt into him of the misery of loneliness and a craving for joys of home, though they led to what was weakest in him, led also to what was greatest. It was his defect as well as his merit in maturer life not to be able to live alone. When the fancies of his novels were upon him and he was under their restless influence, though he often talked of shutting himself up in out of the way solitary places, he never went anywhere unaccompanied by members of his family. His habits of daily life he carried with him wherever he went. In Albaro and Genoa, at Lausanne and Geneva, in Paris and Boulogne, his ways were as entirely those of home as in London and Broadstairs. If it is the property of a domestic nature to be personally interested in every detail, the smallest as the greatest, of the four walls within which one lives, then no man had it so essentially as Dickens. No man was so inclined naturally to derive his happiness from home concerns. Even the kind of interest in a house which is commonly confined to women, he

What was weakest and greatest in him.

Habits of life everywhere.

* An entry, under the date of July 1833, from a printed but unpublished Diary by Mr. Payne Collier, appeared lately in the *Athenæum*, having reference to Dickens at the time when he first obtained employment as a reporter, and connecting itself with what my opening volume had related of those childish sufferings. 'Soon afterwards I observed a great difference in C. D.'s dress, 'for he had bought a new hat and a very handsome blue cloak, which he threw 'over his shoulder *à l'Espagnole* . . . We walked together through Hunger-'ford Market, where we followed a coal-heaver, who carried his little rosy but 'grimy child looking over his shoulder; and C. D. bought a halfpenny-worth 'of cherries, and as we went along he gave them one by one to the little fellow 'without the knowledge of the father . . He informed me as he walked 'through it that he knew *Hunger*ford Market well . . . He did not affect to 'conceal the difficulties he and his family had had to contend against.'

C. D. in Hungerford-market: 1833.

LONDON: 1836–70.

Happiness in domestic concerns.

was full of. Not to speak of changes of importance, there was not an additional hook put up wherever he inhabited, without his knowledge, or otherwise than as part of some small ingenuity of his own. Nothing was too minute for his personal superintendence. Whatever might be in hand, theatricals for the little children, entertainments for those of larger growth, cricket matches, dinners, field sports, from the first new year's eve dance in Doughty Street to the last musical party in Hyde Park Place, he was the centre and soul of it. He did not care to take measure of its greater or less importance. It was enough that a thing was to do, to be worth his while to do it as if there was nothing else to be done in the world. The cry of Laud and Wentworth was his, alike in small and great things; and to no man was more applicable the German 'Echt,' which expresses reality as well as thoroughness. The usual result followed, in all his homes, of an absolute reliance on him for everything. Under every difficulty, and in every emergency, his was the encouraging influence, the bright and ready help. In illness, whether of the children or any of the servants, he was better than a doctor. He was so full of resource, for which every one eagerly turned to him, that his mere presence in the sick-room was a healing influence, as if nothing could fail if he were only there. So that at last, when, all through the awful night which preceded his departure, he lay senseless in the room where he had fallen, the stricken and bewildered ones who tended him found it impossible to believe that what they saw before them alone was left, or to shut out wholly the strange wild hope that he might again be suddenly

Centre and soul of his home.

Family dependence on him.

Night of the 8th of June, 1870.

among them *like* himself, and revive what they could not connect, even then, with death's despairing helplessness.

LONDON: 1836–70.

It was not a feeling confined to the relatives whom he had thus taught to have such exclusive dependence on him. Among the consolations addressed to those mourners came words from one whom in life he had most honoured, and who also found it difficult to connect him with death, or to think that he should never see that blithe face any more. 'It is almost thirty years,' Mr. Carlyle wrote, 'since my 'acquaintance with him began; and on my side, I may 'say, every new meeting ripened it into more and more 'clear discernment of his rare and great worth as a brother 'man: a most cordial, sincere, clear-sighted, quietly de- 'cisive, just and loving man: till at length he had grown 'to such a recognition with me as I have rarely had for 'any man of my time. This I can tell you three, for it is 'true and will be welcome to you: to others less concerned 'I had as soon *not* speak on such a subject.' 'I am pro- 'foundly sorry for *you*,' Mr. Carlyle at the same time wrote to me; 'and indeed for myself and for us all. It is an 'event world-wide; a *unique* of talents suddenly extinct; 'and has "eclipsed," we too may say, "the harmless gaiety '"of nations." No death since 1866 has fallen on me 'with such a stroke. No literary man's hitherto ever did. 'The good, the gentle, high-gifted, ever-friendly, noble 'Dickens,—every inch of him an Honest Man.'

Thomas Carlyle: 4th of July 1870.

The same: 11th of June 1870.

Of his ordinary habits of activity I have spoken, and they were doubtless carried too far. In youth it was all well, but he did not make allowance for years. This has had abundant illustration, but will admit of a few words more. To

Daily habits.

LONDON: 1836–70.

all men who do much, rule and order are essential; method in everything was Dickens's peculiarity; and between breakfast and luncheon, with rare exceptions, was his time of work. But his daily walks were less of rule than of enjoyment and necessity. In the midst of his writing they were indispensable, and especially, as it has often been shown, at night. Mr. Sala is an authority on London streets, and, in the eloquent and generous tribute he was among the first to offer to his memory, has described himself encountering Dickens in the oddest places and most inclement weather, in Ratcliffe-highway, on Haverstock-hill, on Camberwell-green, in Gray's-inn-lane, in the Wandsworth-road, at Hammersmith Broadway, in Norton Folgate, and at Kensal New Town. 'A 'hansom whirled you by the Bell and Horns at Brompton, 'and there he was striding, as with seven-league boots, 'seemingly in the direction of North-end, Fulham. The 'Metropolitan Railway sent you forth at Lisson-grove, and 'you met him plodding speedily towards the Yorkshire 'Stingo. He was to be met rapidly skirting the grim brick 'wall of the prison in Coldbath-fields, or trudging along the 'Seven Sisters-road at Holloway, or bearing, under a steady 'press of sail, underneath Highgate Archway, or pursuing 'the even tenor of his way up the Vauxhall-bridge-road.' But he was equally at home in the intricate byways of narrow streets and in the lengthy thoroughfares. Wherever there was 'matter to be heard and learned,' in back streets behind Holborn, in Borough courts and passages, in city wharfs or alleys, about the poorer lodging-houses, in prisons, workhouses, ragged-schools, police-courts, rag-shops, chand-

Street walks.

Mr. G. A. Sala in *Daily Telegraph*, June 1870.

London haunts.

lers' shops, and all sorts of markets for the poor, he carried his keen observation and untiring study. 'I was among the 'Italian Boys from 12 to 2 this morning,' says one of his letters. 'I am going out to-night in their boat with the 'Thames Police,' says another. It was the same when he was in Italy or Switzerland, as we have seen; and when, in later life, he was in French provincial places. 'I walk miles away 'into the country, and you can scarcely imagine by what 'deserted ramparts and silent little cathedral closes, or how 'I pass over rusty drawbridges and stagnant ditches out 'of and into the decaying town.' For several consecutive years I accompanied him every Christmas Eve to see the marketings for Christmas down the road from Aldgate to Bow; and he had a surprising fondness for wandering about in poor neighbourhoods on Christmas-day, past the areas of shabby genteel houses in Somers or Kentish Towns, and watching the dinners preparing or coming in. But the temptations of his country life led him on to excesses in walking. 'Coming in just now,' he wrote in his third year at Gadshill, 'after twelve miles in the rain, I was so wet 'that I have had to change and get my feet into warm 'water before I could do anything.' Again, two years later: 'A south-easter blowing, enough to cut one's throat. I am 'keeping the house for my cold, as I did yesterday. But 'the remedy is so new to me, that I doubt if it does me 'half the good of a dozen miles in the snow. So, if this 'mode of treatment fails to-day, I shall try that to-morrow.' He tried it perhaps too often. In the winter of 1865 he first had the attack in his left foot which materially disabled his walking-power for the rest of his life. He supposed

Our old walk on Christmas Eve.

Walks on Christmas Day.

In rain and snow.

First attack of lameness. 1865.

its cause to be overwalking in the snow, and that this had aggravated the suffering is very likely; but, read by the light of what followed, it may now be presumed to have *Ante*, 272. had more serious origin. It recurred at intervals, before America, without any such provocation; in America it came back, not when he had most been walking in the snow, but when nervous exhaustion was at its worst with him; after America, it became prominent on the eve of the occurrence at Preston which first revealed the progress that disease had been making in the vessels of the brain; and in the last year of his life, as will immediately be seen, it was a constant trouble and most intense suffering, extending then gravely to his left hand also, which had before been only slightly affected.

How the lameness came on.

It was from a letter of the 21st of February 1865 I first learnt that he was suffering tortures from a 'frost-bitten' foot, and ten days later brought more detailed account. 'I 'got frost-bitten by walking continually in the snow, and 'getting wet in the feet daily. My boots hardened and 'softened, hardened and softened, my left foot swelled, and 'I still forced the boot on; sat in it to write, half the day; 'walked in it through the snow, the other half; forced the 'boot on again next morning; sat and walked again; and 'being accustomed to all sorts of changes in my feet, took 'no heed. At length, going out as usual, I fell lame on the 'walk, and had to limp home dead lame, through the snow, 'for the last three miles—to the remarkable terror, by-the-'bye, of the two big dogs.' The dogs were Turk and Linda.

How it affected his large dogs: *ante*, 191–3.

Boisterous companions as they always were, the sudden change in him brought them to a stand-still; and for the rest of the journey they crept by the side of their master as slowly as he did, never turning from him. He was greatly moved by the circumstance, and often referred to it. Turk's look upward to his face was one of sympathy as well as fear, he said; but Linda was wholly struck down.

Right things to be done for their own sake.

The saying in his letter to his youngest son that he was to do to others what he would that they should do to him, without being discouraged if they did not do it; and his saying to the Birmingham people that they were to attend to self-improvement not because it led to fortune, but because it was right; express a principle that at all times guided himself. Capable of strong attachments, he was not what is called an effusive man; but he had no half-heartedness in any of his likings. The one thing entirely hateful to him, was indifference. 'I give my heart to very few 'people; but I would sooner love the most implacable 'man in the world than a careless one, who, if my place 'were empty to-morrow, would rub on and never miss me.' There was nothing he more repeatedly told his children than that they were not to let indifference in others appear to justify it in themselves. 'All kind things,' he wrote, 'must 'be done on their own account, and for their own sake, 'and without the least reference to any gratitude.' Again he laid it down, while he was making some exertion for the sake of a dead friend that did not seem likely to win proper appreciation from those it was to serve. 'As 'to gratitude from the family—as I have often remarked 'to you, one does a generous thing because it is right and 'pleasant, and not for any response it is to awaken in 'others.' The rule in another form frequently appears

The thing most hateful.

LONDON: 1836–70.

in his letters; and it was enforced in many ways upon all who were dear to him. It is worth while to add his comment on a regret of a member of his family at an act of self-devotion supposed to have been thrown away: 'Nothing of what is nobly done can ever be lost.' It is also to be noted as in the same spirit, that it was not the loud but the silent heroisms he most admired. Of Sir John Richardson, one of the few who have lived in our days entitled to the name of a hero, he wrote from Paris in 1856. 'Lady Franklin sent me the whole of that Rich-'ardson memoir; and I think Richardson's manly friend-'ship, and love of Franklin, one of the noblest things I 'ever knew in my life. It makes one's heart beat high, 'with a sort of sacred joy.' (It is the feeling as strongly awakened by the earlier exploits of the same gallant man to be found at the end of Franklin's first voyage, and never to be read without the most exalted emotion.) It was for something higher than mere literature he valued the most original writer and powerful teacher of the age. 'I would 'go at all times farther to see Carlyle than any man alive.'

The silent heroisms.

One of his heroes.

Another.

Of his attractive points in society and conversation I have particularized little, because in truth they were himself. Such as they were, they were never absent from him. His acute sense of enjoyment gave such relish to his social qualities that probably no man, not a great wit or a professed talker, ever left, in leaving any social gathering, a blank so impossible to fill up. In quick and varied sympathy, in ready adaptation to every whim or humour, in help to any mirth or game, he stood for a dozen men. If one may say such a thing, he seemed to be always the more

At social meetings.

himself for being somebody else, for continually putting off his personality. His versatility made him unique. What he said once of his own love of acting, applied to him equally when at his happiest among friends he loved; sketching a character, telling a story, acting a charade, taking part in a game; turning into comedy an incident of the day, describing the last good or bad thing he had seen, reproducing in quaint, tragical, or humorous form and figure, some part of the passionate life with which all his being overflowed. 'Assumption has charms for me 'so delightful—I hardly know for how many wild reasons— 'that I feel a loss of Oh I can't say what exquisite foolery, 'when I lose a chance of being some one not in the re- 'motest degree like myself.' How it was, that, from one of such boundless resource in contributing to the pleasure of his friends, there was yet, as I have said, so comparatively little to bring away, may be thus explained. But it has been also seen that no one at times said better things, and to happy examples formerly given I will add one or two of a kind he more rarely indulged. 'He is below par 'on the Exchange,' a friend remarked of a notorious puffing actor; 'he doesn't stand well at Lloyds.' 'Yet no one 'stands so well with the under-writers,' said Dickens; a pun that Swift would have envied. 'I call him an Incubus!' said a non-literary friend, at a loss to express the boredom inflicted on him by a popular author. 'Pen-and-ink-ubus, 'you mean,' interposed Dickens. So, when Stanfield said of his midshipman son, then absent on his first cruise, 'the 'boy has got his sea-legs on by this time!' 'I dont know, remarked Dickens, 'about his getting his sea-legs on; but

His delight in 'as- 'sump- 'tion.'

Agreeable pleasantries.

Puns.

LONDON: 1836–70.

'if I may judge from his writing, he certainly has not got 'his A B C legs on.'

Other agreeable pleasantries might be largely cited from his letters. 'An old priest' (he wrote from France in 1862), 'the express image of Frederic Lemaitre got up for the 'part, and very cross with the toothache, told me in a 'railway carriage the other day, that we had no antiquities 'in heretical England. "None at all?" I said. "You '"have some ships however." "Yes; a few." "Are they '"strong?" "Well," said I, "your trade is spiritual, my '"father: ask the ghost of Nelson." A French captain 'who was in the carriage, was immensely delighted with 'this small joke. I met him at Calais yesterday going 'somewhere with a detachment; and he said—Pardon! But 'he had been so limited as to suppose an Englishman in-'capable of that bonhommie!' In humouring a joke he was excellent, both in letters and talk; and for this kind of enjoyment his least important little notes are often worth preserving. Take one small instance. So freely had he admired a tale told by his friend and solicitor Mr. Frederic Ouvry, that he had to reply to a humorous proposal for publication of it, in his own manner, in his own periodical. 'Your modesty is equal to your merit. . . I 'think your way of describing that rustic courtship in middle 'life, quite matchless. . . . A cheque for £1000 is lying 'with the publisher. We would willingly make it more, 'but that we find our law charges so exceedingly heavy.' His letters have also examples now and then of what he called his conversational triumphs. 'I have distinguished 'myself' (28th of April 1861) 'in two respects lately. I took

A cross old priest.

Humouring a joke.

To Frederic Ouvry.

Two unlucky hits.

'a young lady, unknown, down to dinner, and, talking to 'her about the Bishop of Durham's nepotism in the matter 'of Mr. Cheese, I found she was Mrs. Cheese. And I ex-'patiated to the member for Marylebone, Lord Fermoy, 'generally conceiving him to be an Irish member, on the 'contemptible character of the Marylebone constituency 'and Marylebone representation.'

Ghost stories.

Among his good things should not be omitted his telling of a ghost story. He had something of a hankering after them, as the readers of his briefer pieces will know; and such was his interest generally in things supernatural that, but for the strong restraining power of his common sense, he might have fallen into the follies of spiritualism. As it was, the fanciful side of his nature stopped short at such pardonable superstitions as those of dreams, and lucky days, or other marvels of natural coincidence; and no man was readier to apply sharp tests to a ghost story or a haunted house, though there was just so much tendency to believe in any such, 'well-authenticated,' as made perfect his manner of telling one. Such a story is related in the 125th number of *All the Year Round*, which before its publication both Mr. Layard and myself saw at Gadshill, and identified as one related by Lord Lytton. It was published in September, and in a day or two led to what Dickens will relate. 'The artist himself 'who is the hero of that story' (to Lord Lytton, 15th of September 1861) 'has sent me in black and white his 'own account of the whole experience, so very original, so 'very extraordinary, so very far beyond the version I have 'published, that all other like stories turn pale before it.'

Story of a portrait painter.

LONDON: 1870.

The ghost thus reinforced came out in the number published on the 5th of October; and the reader who cares to turn to it, and compare what Dickens in the interval (17th of September) wrote to myself, will have some measure of his readiness to believe in such things. 'Upon the publica-

Portrait painter's own account.

'tion of the ghost story, up has started the portrait-painter 'who saw the phantoms! His own written story is out of 'all distance the most extraordinary that ever was produced; 'and is as far beyond my version or Bulwer's, as Scott is 'beyond James. Everything connected with it is amazing; 'but conceive this—the portrait-painter had been engaged 'to write it elsewhere as a story for next Christmas, and not 'unnaturally supposed, when he saw himself anticipated in '*All the Year Round*, that there had been treachery at his

Marvels of coincidence.

'printer's. "In particular," says he, "how else was it '"possible that the date, the 13th of September, could '"have been got at? For I never told the date, until I '"wrote it." Now, *my* story had NO DATE; but seeing, 'when I looked over the proof, the great importance of 'having *a* date, I (C. D.) wrote in, unconsciously, the exact 'date on the margin of the proof!' The reader will

*Ante*, 151.

remember the Doncaster race story; and to other like illustrations of the subject already given, may be added this dream. 'Here is a curious case at first-hand' (30th of May 1863). 'On Thursday night in last week, being at the 'office here, I dreamed that I saw a lady in a red shawl 'with her back towards me (whom I supposed to be E.). 'On her turning round I found that I didn't know her,

A dream.

'and she said "I am Miss Napier." All the time I was 'dressing next morning, I thought—What a preposterous 'thing to have so very distinct a dream about nothing! and 'why Miss Napier? for I never heard of any Miss Napier. 'That same Friday night, I read. After the reading, came 'into my retiring-room, Mary Boyle and her brother, and '*the* Lady in the red shawl whom they present as "Miss '"Napier!" These are all the circumstances, exactly told.'

LONDON: 1870.

Another kind of dream has had previous record, with no superstition to build itself upon but the loving devotion to one tender memory. With longer or shorter intervals this was with him all his days. Never from his waking thoughts was the recollection altogether absent; and though the dream would leave him for a time, it unfailingly came back. It was the feeling of his life that always had a mastery over him. What he said on the sixth anniversary of the death of his sister-in-law, that friend of his youth whom he had made his ideal of all moral excellence, he might have said as truly after twenty-six years more. In the very year before he died, the influence was potently upon him. 'She is so much in my thoughts at all times, especially 'when I am successful, and have greatly prospered in any-'thing, that the recollection of her is an essential part of 'my being, and is as inseparable from my existence as the 'beating of my heart is.' Through later troubled years, whatever was worthiest in him found in this an ark of safety; and it was the nobler part of his being which had thus become also the essential. It gave to success what success by itself had no power to give; and nothing could consist with it, for any length of time, that was not of good report and pure. What more could I say that was not better said from the pulpit of the Abbey where he rests?

ii. 122-5. i. 98, 386.

Predominant impression of his life.

Effects on his career

LONDON: 1870.

'He whom we mourn was the friend of mankind, a philan-'thropist in the true sense; the friend of youth, the friend 'of the poor, the enemy of every form of meanness and 'oppression. I am not going to attempt to draw a portrait 'of him. Men of genius are different from what we sup-'pose them to be. They have greater pleasures and greater 'pains, greater affections and greater temptations, than the 'generality of mankind, and they can never be altogether 'understood by their fellow men. . . But we feel that a 'light has gone out, that the world is darker to us, when 'they depart. There are so very few of them that we cannot 'afford to lose them one by one, and we look vainly round 'for others who may supply their places. He whose loss 'we now mourn occupied a greater space than any other 'writer in the minds of Englishmen during the last thirty-'three years. We read him, talked about him, acted him; 'we laughed with him; we were roused by him to a con-'sciousness of the misery of others, and to a pathetic inte-'rest in human life. Works of fiction, indirectly, are great 'instructors of this world; and we can hardly exaggerate 'the debt of gratitude which is due to a writer who has led 'us to sympathize with these good, true, sincere, honest 'English characters of ordinary life, and to laugh at the 'egotism, the hypocrisy, the false respectability of religious 'professors and others. To another great humourist who 'lies in this Church the words have been applied that his 'death eclipsed the gaiety of nations. But of him who 'has been recently taken I would rather say, in humbler 'language, that no one was ever so much beloved or so 'much mourned.'

Doctor Jowett in Westminster Abbey.

# CHAPTER XX.

## THE END.

### 1869—1870.

GADSHILL: 1869.

Mr. and Mrs. Fields.

THE summer and autumn of 1869 were passed quietly at Gadshill. He received there, in June, the American friends to whom he had been most indebted for unwearying domestic kindness at his most trying time in the States. In August, he was at the dinner of the International boat-race; and, in a speech that might have gone far to reconcile the victors to changing places with the vanquished, gave the healths of the Harvard and the Oxford crews. He went to Birmingham, in September, to fulfil a promise that he would open the session of the Institute; and there, after telling his audience that his invention, such as it was, never would have served him as it had done, but for the habit of commonplace, patient, drudging attention, he declared his political creed to be infinitesimal faith in the people governing and illimitable faith in the People governed. In such engagements as these, with nothing of the kind of strain he had most to dread, there was hardly more movement or change than was necessary to his enjoyment of rest.

Harvard and Oxford.

At Birmingham. *Ante*, 460-1.

He had been able to show Mr. Fields something of the

LONDON: 1869.

Places shown to visitor.

Where *Pickwick* was begun.

An opium den. *Ante*, 427.

Last paper in *All the Year Round*.

*Ante*, 415.

interest of London as well as of his Kentish home. He went over its 'general post-office' with him, took him among its cheap theatres and poor lodging-houses, and piloted him by night through its most notorious thieves' quarter. Its localities that are pleasantest to a lover of books, such as Johnson's Bolt-court and Goldsmith's Temple-chambers, he explored with him; and, at his visitor's special request, mounted a staircase he had not ascended for more than thirty years, to show the chambers in Furnival's Inn where the first page of *Pickwick* was written. One more book, unfinished, was to close what that famous book began; and the original of the scene of its opening chapter, the opium-eater's den, was the last place visited. 'In a miser-'able court at night,' says Mr. Fields, 'we found a haggard 'old woman blowing at a kind of pipe made of an old ink-'bottle; and the words which Dickens puts into the mouth 'of this wretched creature in *Edwin Drood*, we heard her 'croon as we leaned over the tattered bed in which she 'was lying.'

Before beginning his novel he had written his last paper for his weekly publication. It was a notice of my *Life of Landor*, and contained some interesting recollections of that remarkable man. His memory at this time dwelt much, as was only natural, with past pleasant time, as he saw familiar faces leaving us or likely to leave; and, on the death of one of the comedians associated with the old bright days of Covent Garden, I had intimation of a fancy that had never quitted him since the Cheltenham reading. 'I see in the paper to-day that Meadows is dead. I had 'a talk with him at Coutts's a week or two ago, when he 'said he was seventy-five, and very weak. Except for 'having a tearful eye, he looked just the same as ever. My 'mind still constantly misgives me concerning Macready. 'Curiously, I don't think he has been ever, for ten minutes 'together, out of my thoughts since I talked with Meadows 'last. Well, the year that brings trouble brings comfort 'too: I have a great success in the boy-line to announce 'to you. Harry has won the second scholarship at Trinity 'Hall, which gives him £50 a year as long as he stays 'there; and I begin to hope that he will get a fellowship.' I doubt if anything ever more truly pleased him than this little success of his son Henry at Cambridge. Henry missed the fellowship, but was twenty-ninth wrangler in a fair year, when the wranglers were over forty.

Macready.

Son Henry's scholarship. *Ante*, 42.

He finished his first number of *Edwin Drood* in the third week of October, and on the 26th read it at my house with great spirit. A few nights before we had seen together at the Olympic a little drama taken from his *Copperfield*, which he sat out with more than patience, even with something of enjoyment; and another pleasure was given him that night by its author, Mr. Halliday, who brought into the box another dramatist, Mr. Robertson, to whom Dickens, who then first saw him, said that to himself the charm of his little comedies was 'their unassuming form,' which had so happily shown that 'real wit could afford to put off any airs 'of pretension to it.' He was at Gadshill till the close of the year; coming up for a few special occasions, such as Procter's eighty-second birthday; and at my house on new-year's eve he read to us, again aloud, a fresh number of his book. Yet these very last days of December had not been

Author of *Caste* and *School.*

LONDON: 1869–70.

without a reminder of the grave warnings of April. The pains in somewhat modified form had returned in both his left hand and his left foot a few days before we met; and they were troubling him still on that day. But he made so light of them himself; so little thought of connecting them with the uncertainties of touch and tread of which they were really part; and read with such an overflow of humour Mr. Honeythunder's boisterous philanthropy; that there was no room, then, for anything but enjoyment. His only allusion to an effect from his illness was his mention of a now invincible dislike which he had to railway travel. This had decided him to take a London house for the twelve last readings in the early months of 1870, and he had become Mr. Milner-Gibson's tenant at 5, Hyde Park Place.

A reading of *Edwin Drood.*

House for a season.

St. James's Hall was to be the scene of these Readings, and they were to occupy the interval from the 11th of January to the 15th of March; two being given in each week to the close of January, and the remaining eight on each of the eight Tuesdays following. Nothing was said of any kind of apprehension as the time approached; but, with a curious absence of the sense of danger, there was certainly both distrust and fear. Sufficient precaution was supposed to have been taken* by arrangement for the presence, at

The additional readings. *Ante*, 423.

* I desire to guard myself against any possible supposition that I think these Readings might have been stopped by the exercise of medical authority. I am convinced of the contrary. Dickens had pledged himself to them; and the fact that others' interests were engaged rather than his own supplied him with an overpowering motive for being determinedly set on going through with them. At the sorrowful time in the preceding year, when, yielding to the stern sentence passed by Sir Thomas Watson, he had dismissed finally the staff employed on his country readings, he had thus written to me. 'I do believe (3rd of

Motive for these readings.

each reading, of his friend and medical attendant, Mr. Carr Beard; but this resolved itself, not into any measure of safety, the case admitting of none short of stopping the reading altogether, but simply into ascertainment of the exact amount of strain and pressure, which, with every fresh exertion, he was placing on those vessels of the brain where the Preston trouble too surely had revealed that danger lay. No supposed force in reserve, no dominant strength of will, can turn aside the penalties sternly exacted for disregard of such laws of life as were here plainly overlooked; and though no one may say that it was not already too late for any but the fatal issue, there will be no presumption in believing that life might yet have been for some time prolonged if these readings could have been stopped.

Medical attendance at readings.

Penalty of disregarding fixed laws.

'I am a little shaken,' he wrote on the 9th of January, 'by my journey to Birmingham to give away the Institution's prizes on Twelfth Night, but I am in good heart; 'and, notwithstanding Lowe's worrying scheme for collecting a year's taxes in a lump, which they tell me is 'damaging books, pictures, music, and theatres beyond 'precedent, our "let" at St. James's Hall is enormous.' He opened with *Copperfield* and the *Pickwick Trial;* and I

*Ante*, 461.

May 1869) 'that such people as the Chappells are very rarely to be found in 'human affairs. To say nothing of their noble and munificent manner of 'sweeping away into space all the charges incurred uselessly, and all the im'mense inconvenience and profitless work thrown upon their establishment, 'comes a note this morning from the senior partner, to the effect that they 'feel that my overwork has been "indirectly caused by them, and by my great '"and kind exertions to make their venture successful to the extreme." There 'is something so delicate and fine in this, that I feel it deeply.' That feeling led to his resolve to make the additional exertion of these twelve last readings, and nothing would have turned him from it as long as he could stand at the desk.

Tribute to Messrs. Chappell.

LONDON: 1870.

may briefly mention, from the notes taken by Mr. Beard and placed at my disposal, at what cost of exertion to himself he gratified the crowded audiences that then and to the close made these evenings memorable. His ordinary pulse on the first night was at 72; but never on any subsequent night was lower than 82, and had risen on the later nights to more than 100. After *Copperfield* on the first night it went up to 96, and after *Marigold* on the second to 99; but on the first night of the *Sikes and Nancy* scenes (Friday the 21st of January) it went from 80 to 112, and on the second night (the 1st of February) to 118. From this, through the six remaining nights, it never was lower than 110 after the first piece read; and after the third and fourth readings of the *Oliver Twist* scenes it rose, from 90 to 124 on the 15th of February, and from 94 to 120 on the 8th of March; on the former occasion, after twenty minutes' rest, falling to 98, and on the latter, after fifteen minutes' rest, falling to 82. His ordinary pulse on entering the room, during these last six nights, was more than once over 100, and never lower than 84; from which it rose, after *Nickleby* on the 22nd of February, to 112. On the 8th of February, when he read *Dombey*, it had risen from 91 to 114; on the 1st of March, after *Copperfield*, it rose from 100 to 124; and when he entered the room on the last night it was at 108, having risen only two beats more when the reading was done. The pieces on this occasion were the *Christmas Carol*, followed by the *Pickwick Trial*; and probably in all his life he never read so well. On his return from the States, where he had to address his effects to audiences composed of immense numbers of people, a

Excitement incident to readings.

After *Oliver Twist* scenes.

Last night of all.

LONDON: 1870.

certain loss of refinement had been observable; but the old delicacy was now again delightfully manifest, and a subdued tone, as well in the humorous as the serious portions, gave something to all the reading as of a quiet sadness of farewell. The charm of this was at its height when he shut the volume of *Pickwick* and spoke in his own person. He said that for fifteen years he had been reading his own books to audiences whose sensitive and kindly recognition of them had given him instruction and enjoyment in his art such as few men could have had; but that he nevertheless thought it well now to retire upon older associations, and in future to devote himself exclusively to the calling which had first made him known. 'In but two short weeks from this time I hope that you 'may enter, in your own homes, on a new series of read'ings at which my assistance will be indispensable; but 'from these garish lights I vanish now for evermore, with 'a heartfelt, grateful, respectful, affectionate farewell.' The brief hush of silence as he moved from the platform; and the prolonged tumult of sound that followed suddenly, stayed him, and again for another moment brought him back; will not be forgotten by any present.

Farewell address.

Effect produced.

Little remains to be told that has not in it almost unmixed pain and sorrow. Hardly a day passed, while the readings went on or after they closed, unvisited by some effect or other of the disastrous excitement shown by the notes of Mr. Beard. On the 23rd of January, when for the last time he met Carlyle, he came to us with his left hand in a sling; on the 7th of February, when he passed with us his last birthday, and on the 25th, when he read

Results of over excitement.

LONDON: 1870.

the third number of his novel, the hand was still swollen and painful; and on the 21st of March, when he read admirably his fourth number, he told us that as he came along, walking up the length of Oxford-street, the same incident had recurred as on the day of a former dinner with us, and he had not been able to read, all the way, more than the right-hand half of the names over the shops. Yet he had the old fixed persuasion that this was rather the effect of a medicine he had been taking than of any grave cause, and he still strongly believed his other troubles to be exclusively local. Eight days later he wrote: 'My uneasiness 'and hemorrhage, after having quite left me, as I supposed, 'has come back with an aggravated irritability that it has 'not yet displayed. You have no idea what a state I am 'in to-day from a sudden violent rush of it; and yet it has 'not the slightest effect on my general health that I know 'of.' This was a disorder which troubled him in his earlier life; and during the last five years, in his intervals of suffering from other causes, it had from time to time taken aggravated form.

*Ante*, 411.

Return of an old malady.

*Ante*, 283; i. 263.

Last appearances in public.

His last public appearances were in April. On the 5th he took the chair for the Newsvendors, whom he helped with a genial address in which even his apology for little speaking overflowed with irrepressible humour. He would try, he said, like Falstaff, 'but with a modification almost 'as large as himself,' less to speak himself than to be the cause of speaking in others. 'Much in this manner they 'exhibit at the door of a snuff-shop the effigy of a High-'lander with an empty mull in his hand, who, apparently 'having taken all the snuff he can carry, and discharged

At Newsvendors' Dinner.

'all the sneezes of which he is capable, politely invites his 'friends and patrons to step in and try what they can do in 'the same line.' On the 30th of the same month he returned thanks for 'Literature' at the Royal Academy dinner, and I may preface my allusion to what he then said with what he had written to me the day before. Three days earlier Daniel Maclise had passed away. 'Like you 'at Ely, so I at Higham, had the shock of first reading at 'a railway station of the death of our old dear friend and 'companion. What the shock would be, you know too 'well. It has been only after great difficulty, and after 'hardening and steeling myself to the subject by at once 'thinking of it and avoiding it in a strange way, that I 'have been able to get any command over it or over 'myself. If I feel at the time that I can be sure of the 'necessary composure, I shall make a little reference to it 'at the Academy to-morrow. I suppose you won't be there.'* The reference made was most touching and manly. He told those who listened that since he first entered the public lists, a very young man indeed, it had been his constant fortune to number among his nearest and dearest friends members of that Academy who had been its pride;

LONDON: 1870.

At Royal Academy Dinner.

Death of Daniel Maclise.

* I preserve also the closing words of the letter. 'It is very strange—you 'remember I suppose ?—that the last time we spoke of him together, you said 'that we should one day hear that the wayward life into which he had fallen 'was over, and there an end of our knowledge of it.' The waywardness, which was merely the having latterly withdrawn himself too much from old friendly intercourse, had its real origin in disappointments connected with the public work on which he was engaged in those later years, and to which he sacrificed every private interest of his own. His was only the common fate of Englishmen, so engaged, who do this; and when the real story of the 'Fresco-painting 'for the Houses of Parliament' comes to be written, it will be another chapter added to our national misadventures and reproaches in everything connected with Art and its hapless cultivators.

An old story.

LONDON: 1870.

and who had now, one by one, so dropped from his side that he was grown to believe, with the Spanish monk of whom Wilkie spoke, that the only realities around him were the pictures which he loved, and all the moving life but a shadow and a dream. 'For many years I was one 'of the two most intimate friends and most constant 'companions of Mr. Maclise, to whose death the Prince of 'Wales has made allusion, and the President has referred 'with the eloquence of genuine feeling. Of his genius in 'his chosen art, I will venture to say nothing here; but 'of his fertility of mind and wealth of intellect I may con-'fidently assert that they would have made him, if he had 'been so minded, at least as great a writer as he was a 'painter. The gentlest and most modest of men, the freshest 'as to his generous appreciation of young aspirants and the 'frankest and largest hearted as to his peers, incapable of 'a sordid or ignoble thought, gallantly sustaining the true 'dignity of his vocation, without one grain of self-ambition, 'wholesomely natural at the last as at the first, "in wit a '"man, simplicity a child,"—no artist of whatsoever deno-'mination, I make bold to say, ever went to his rest leaving 'a golden memory more pure from dross, or having devoted 'himself with a truer chivalry to the art-goddess whom 'he worshipped.' These were the last public words of Dickens, and he could not have spoken any worthier.

*Ante*, i. 157-8.

Eulogy well deserved.

Dickens's last public words.

Upon his appearance at the dinner of the Academy had followed some invitations he was led to accept; greatly to his own regret, he told me on the night (7th of May) when he read to us the fifth number of *Edwin Drood;* for he was now very eager to get back to the quiet of Gadshill.

Temptations of London.

He dined with Mr. Motley, then American minister; had met Mr. Disraeli at a dinner at Lord Stanhope's; had breakfasted with Mr. Gladstone; and on the 17th was to attend the Queen's ball with his daughter. But she had to go there without him; for on the 16th I had intimation of a sudden disablement. 'I am sorry to report, that, in 'the old preposterous endeavour to dine at preposterous 'hours and preposterous places, I have been pulled up by 'a sharp attack in my foot. And serve me right. I hope 'to get the better of it soon, but I fear I must not think 'of dining with you on Friday. I have cancelled every-'thing in the dining way for this week, and that is a very 'small precaution after the horrible pain I have had and 'the remedies I have taken.' He had to excuse himself also from the General Theatrical Fund dinner, where the Prince of Wales was to preside; but at another dinner a week later, where the King of the Belgians and the Prince were to be present, so much pressure was put upon him that he went, still suffering as he was, to dine with Lord Houghton.

LONDON: 1870.

Another attack in the foot.

*Ante*, ii. 195.

*Ante*, 469.

We met for the last time on Sunday the 22nd of May, when I dined with him in Hyde Park Place. The death of Mr. Lemon, of which he heard that day, had led his thoughts to the crowd of friendly companions in letters and art who had so fallen from the ranks since we played Ben Jonson together that we were left almost alone. 'And none 'beyond his sixtieth year,' he said, 'very few even fifty.' It is no good to talk of it, I suggested. 'We shall not 'think of it the less' was his reply; and an illustration much to the point was before us, afforded by an incident

Our last meeting.

LONDON: 1870.

deserving remembrance in his story. Not many weeks before, a correspondent had written to him from Liverpool describing himself as a self-raised man, attributing his prosperous career to what Dickens's writings had taught him at its outset of the wisdom of kindness, and sympathy for others; and asking pardon for the liberty he took in hoping that he might be permitted to offer some acknowledgment of what not only had cheered and stimulated him through all his life, but had contributed so much to the success of it. The letter enclosed £500. Dickens was greatly touched by this; and told the writer, in sending back his cheque, that he would certainly have taken it if he had not been, though not a man of fortune, a prosperous man himself; but that the letter, and the spirit of its offer, had so gratified him, that if the writer pleased to send him any small memorial of it in another form he would gladly receive it. The memorial soon came. A richly worked basket of silver, inscribed 'from one who has been cheered and stimulated 'by Mr. Dickens's writings, and held the author among his 'first remembrances when he became prosperous,' was accompanied by an extremely handsome silver centrepiece for the table, of which the design was for figures representing the Seasons. But the kindly donor shrank from sending Winter to one whom he would fain connect with none but the brighter and milder days, and he had struck the fourth figure from the design. 'I never look at it,' said Dickens, 'that I don't think most of the Winter.'

Note-worthy incident.

Tribute of gratitude for his books.

'Con-'spicuous' by absence.

A matter discussed that day with Mr. Ouvry was briefly resumed in a note of the 29th of May, the last I ever received from him; which followed me to Exeter, and closed thus. 'You and I can speak of it at Gads by and by. 'Foot no worse. But no better.' The old trouble was upon him when we parted, and this must have been nearly the last note written before he quitted London. He was at Gadshill on the 30th of May; and I heard no more until the telegram reached me at Launceston on the night of the 9th of June, which told me that the 'by and by' was not to come in this world.

GADSHILL: 1870.

Last letter from him.

The few days at Gadshill had been given wholly to work on his novel. He had been easier in his foot and hand; and, though he was suffering severely from the local hemorrhage before named, he made no complaint of illness. But there was observed in him a very unusual appearance of fatigue. 'He seemed very weary.' He was out with his dogs for the last time on Monday the 6th of June, when he walked with his letters into Rochester. On Tuesday the 7th, after his daughter Mary had left on a visit to her sister Kate, not finding himself equal to much fatigue, he drove to Cobham-wood with his sister-in-law, there dismissed the carriage, and walked round the park and back. He returned in time to put up in his new conservatory some Chinese lanterns sent from London that afternoon; and, the whole of the evening, he sat with Miss Hogarth in the dining-room that he might see their effect when lighted. More than once he then expressed his satisfaction at having finally abandoned all intention of exchanging Gadshill for London; and this he had done more impressively some days before. While he lived, he said, he should like his name to be more and more associated with the place; and he had a notion that when he

Last days.

*Ante*, 189.

GADSHILL: 1870.

died he should like to lie in the little graveyard belonging to the Cathedral at the foot of the Castle wall.

Writing in the Châlet.

On the 8th of June he passed all the day writing in the Châlet. He came over for luncheon; and, much against his usual custom, returned to his desk. Of the sentences he was then writing, the last of his long life of literature, a portion has been given in facsimile on a previous page; and the reader will observe with a painful interest, not alone its evidence of minute labour at this fast-closing hour of time with him, but the direction his thoughts had taken. He imagines such a brilliant morning as had risen with that eighth of June shining on the old city of Rochester. He sees in surpassing beauty, with the lusty ivy gleaming in the sun, and the rich trees waving in the balmy air, its antiquities and its ruins; its Cathedral and Castle. But his fancy, then, is not with the stern dead forms of either; but with that which makes warm the cold stone tombs of centuries, and lights them up with flecks of brightness, 'fluttering there like wings.' To him, on that sunny summer morning, the changes of glorious light from moving boughs, the songs of birds, the scents from garden, woods, and fields, have penetrated into the Cathedral, have subdued its earthy odour, and are preaching the Resurrection and the Life.

Thoughts on his last day of consciousness.

Wednesday evening, 8th of June.

He was late in leaving the Châlet; but before dinner, which was ordered at six o'clock with the intention of walking afterwards in the lanes, he wrote some letters, among them one to his friend Mr. Charles Kent appointing to see him in London next day; and dinner was begun before

Miss Hogarth saw, with alarm, a singular expression of trouble and pain in his face. 'For an hour,' he then told her, 'he had been very ill;' but he wished dinner to go on. These were the only really coherent words uttered by him. They were followed by some, that fell from him disconnectedly, of quite other matters; of an approaching sale at a neighbour's house, of whether Macready's son was with his father at Cheltenham, and of his own intention to go immediately to London; but at these latter he had risen, and his sister-in-law's help alone prevented him from falling where he stood. Her effort then was to get him on the sofa, but after a slight struggle he sank heavily on his left side. 'On the ground' were the last words he spoke. It was now a little over ten minutes past six o'clock. His two daughters came that night with Mr. Beard, who had also been telegraphed for, and whom they met at the station. His eldest son arrived early next morning, and was joined in the evening (too late) by his younger son from Cambridge. All possible medical aid had been summoned. The surgeon of the neighbourhood was there from the first, and a physician from London was in attendance as well as Mr. Beard. But all human help was unavailing. There was effusion on the brain; and though stertorous breathing continued all night, and until ten minutes past six o'clock on the evening of Thursday the 9th of June, there had never been a gleam of hope during the twenty-four hours. He had lived four months beyond his 58th year.

GADSHILL: 1870.

The close.

*Ante*, 474.

Thursday, 9th of June.

The excitement and sorrow at his death are within the

LONDON: 1870.

memory of all. Before the news of it even reached the remoter parts of England, it had been flashed across Europe; was known in the distant continents of India, Australia, and America; and not in English-speaking communities only, but in every country of the civilised earth, had awakened grief and sympathy. In his own land it was as if a personal bereavement had befallen every one. Her Majesty the Queen telegraphed from Balmoral 'her deepest regret at the sad news of Charles Dickens's 'death;' and this was the sentiment alike of all classes of her people. There was not an English journal that did not give it touching and noble utterance; and the *Times* took the lead in suggesting* that the only fit resting-place for the remains of a man so dear to England was the Abbey in which the most illustrious Englishmen are laid.

General mourning.

Wish to bury him in the Abbey.

With the expression thus given to a general wish, the Dean of Westminster lost no time in showing ready compliance; and on the morning of the day when it appeared

Friday, 10th of June.

Monday, 13th of June.

* It is a duty to quote these eloquent words. 'Statesmen, men of science, 'philanthropists, the acknowledged benefactors of their race, might pass away, 'and yet not leave the void which will be caused by the death of Dickens. 'They may have earned the esteem of mankind; their days may have been 'passed in power, honour, and prosperity; they may have been surrounded by 'troops of friends; but, however pre-eminent in station, ability, or public 'services, they will not have been, like our great and genial novelist, the in-'timate of every household. Indeed, such a position is attained not even by 'one man in an age. It needs an extraordinary combination of intellectual and 'moral qualities . . before the world will thus consent to enthrone a man as 'their unassailable and enduring favourite. This is the position which Mr. 'Dickens has occupied with the English and also with the American public for 'the third of a century. . . Westminster Abbey is the peculiar resting-place 'of English literary genius; and among those whose sacred dust lies there, 'or whose names are recorded on the walls, very few are more worthy than 'Charles Dickens of such a home. Fewer still, we believe, will be regarde 'with more honour as time passes and his greatness grows upon us.'

S. L. Fildes — J. Saddler.

THE GRAVE

was in communication with the family and representatives. The public homage of a burial in the Abbey had to be reconciled with his own instructions to be privately buried without previous announcement of time or place, and without monument or memorial. He would himself have preferred to lie in the small graveyard under Rochester Castle wall, or in the little churches of Cobham or Shorne; but all these were found to be closed; and the desire of the Dean and Chapter of Rochester to lay him in their Cathedral had been entertained, when the Dean of Westminster's request, and the considerate kindness of his generous assurance that there should be only such ceremonial as would strictly obey all injunctions of privacy, made it a grateful duty to accept that offer. The spot already had been chosen by the Dean; and before midday on the following morning, Tuesday the 14th of June, with knowledge of those only who took part in the burial, all was done. The solemnity had not lost by the simplicity. Nothing so grand or so touching could have accompanied it, as the stillness and the silence of the vast Cathedral. Then, later in the day and all the following day, came unbidden mourners in such crowds, that the Dean had to request permission to keep open the grave until Thursday; but after it was closed they did not cease to come, and 'all day long,' Doctor Stanley wrote on the 17th, 'there was a constant pressure to the spot, 'and many flowers were strewn upon it by unknown 'hands, many tears shed from unknown eyes.' He alluded to this in the impressive funeral discourse delivered by him in the Abbey on the morning of Sunday the 19th,

LONDON: 1870.

His own wish.

The Burial.

Unbidden mourners.

LONDON: 1870.

pointing to the fresh flowers that then had been newly thrown (as they still are thrown, in this fourth year after the death), and saying that 'the spot would thenceforward 'be a sacred one with both the New World and the Old, 'as that of the representative of the literature, not of this 'island only, but of all who speak our English tongue.' The stone placed upon it is inscribed

CHARLES DICKENS.

BORN FEBRUARY THE SEVENTH 1812. DIED JUNE THE NINTH 1870.

The Grave.

The highest associations of both the arts he loved surround him where he lies. Next to him is RICHARD CUMBERLAND. Mrs. PRITCHARD'S monument looks down upon him, and immediately behind is DAVID GARRICK'S. Nor is the actor's delightful art more worthily represented than the nobler genius of the author. Facing the grave, and on its left and right, are the monuments of CHAUCER, SHAKESPEARE, and DRYDEN, the three immortals who did most to create and settle the language to which CHARLES DICKENS has given another undying name.

FINIS.

# APPENDIX.

## I.

## THE WRITINGS OF CHARLES DICKENS.

### 1835.

SKETCHES BY BOZ. Illustrative of Every-day Life and Every-day People. (The detached papers collected under this title were in course of publication during this year, in the pages of the *Monthly Magazine* and the columns of the *Morning* and the *Evening Chronicle.*) i. 76; 83–84; 86; 92–3.

### 1836.

SKETCHES BY BOZ. Illustrative of Every-day Life and Every-day People. Two volumes: Illustrations by George Cruikshank. (Preface dated from Furnival's Inn, February 1836.) John Macrone.

THE POSTHUMOUS PAPERS OF THE PICKWICK CLUB. Edited by Boz. With Illustrations by R. Seymour and Phiz (Hablot Browne). (Nine numbers published monthly from April to December.) Chapman and Hall.

SUNDAY UNDER THREE HEADS. As it is; as Sabbath Bills would make it; as it might be made. By Timothy Sparks. Illustrated by H. K. B. (Hablot Browne). Dedicated (June 1836) to the Bishop of London. Chapman & Hall. i. 128.

THE STRANGE GENTLEMAN. A Comic Burletta, in two acts. By "Boz." (Performed at the St. James's Theatre, 29th of September 1836, and published with the imprint of 1837.) Chapman & Hall. i. 95.

THE VILLAGE COQUETTES. A Comic Opera, in two acts. By Charles Dickens. The Music by John Hullah. (Dedication to Mr. Braham is dated from Furnival's Inn, 15th of December 1836.) Richard Bentley. i. 95.

SKETCHES BY BOZ. Illustrated by George Cruikshank. Second Series. One volume. (Preface dated from Furnival's Inn, 17th of December 1836.) John Macrone.

### 1837.

THE POSTHUMOUS PAPERS OF THE PICKWICK CLUB. Edited by Boz. (Eleven numbers, the last being a double number, published monthly from January to November. Issued complete in the latter month, with Dedication to Mr. Serjeant Talfourd dated from Doughty-street, 27th of September, as *The Posthumous Papers of the Pickwick Club. By Charles Dickens.*) Chapman & Hall. i. 86–91; 104–111. iii. 310–11.

Oliver Twist; or the Parish Boy's progress. By Boz. Begun in *Bentley's Miscellany* for January, and continued throughout the year. Richard Bentley.

1838.

Oliver Twist. By Charles Dickens, Author of the Pickwick Papers. With Illustrations by George Cruikshank. Three volumes. (Had appeared in monthly portions, in the numbers of *Bentley's Miscellany* for 1837 and 1838, with the title of *Oliver Twist; or the Parish Boy's Progress.* By Boz. Illustrated by George Cruikshank. The Third Edition, with Preface dated Devonshire-terrace, March 1841, published by Messrs. Chapman & Hall.) Richard Bentley. i. 100; 103–5; 130–142. iii. 4–5; 311; 338–9.

Memoirs of Joseph Grimaldi. Edited by "Boz." Illustrated by George Cruikshank. Two volumes. (For Dickens's small share in the composition of this work, his preface to which is dated from Doughty-street, February 1838, see i. 120–2.) Richard Bentley.

Sketches of Young Gentlemen. Illustrated by Phiz. Chapman & Hall. i. 128.

Life and Adventures of Nicholas Nickleby. By Charles Dickens. With Illustrations by Phiz (Hablot Browne). (Nine numbers published monthly from April to December.) Chapman & Hall.

1839.

Life and Adventures of Nicholas Nickleby. (Eleven numbers, the last being a double number, published monthly from January to October. Issued complete in the latter month, with dedication to William Charles Macready.) Chapman & Hall. i. 124; 142–156. ii. 76–7; 79. iii. 311.

Sketches by Boz. Illustrative of Every-day Life and Every-day People. With forty Illustrations by George Cruikshank. (The first complete edition, issued in monthly parts uniform with *Pickwick* and *Nickleby*, from November 1837 to June 1839, with preface dated 15th of May 1839.) Chapman & Hall. i. 100–103.

1840.

Sketches of Young Couples; with an urgent Remonstrance to the Gentlemen of England, being Bachelors or Widowers, at the present alarming crisis. By the Author of Sketches of Young Gentlemen. Illustrated by Phiz. Chapman & Hall. i. 128.

1840–1841.

MASTER HUMPHREY'S CLOCK. By Charles Dickens. With Illustrations by George Cattermole and Hablot Browne. Three volumes. (First and second volume, each 306 pp. ; third, 426 pp.) For the account of this work, published in 88 weekly numbers, extending over the greater part of these two years, see i. 168–180 ; 215 ; 256-7. In addition to occasional detached papers and a series of sketches entitled MR. WELLER'S WATCH, occupying altogether about 90 pages of the first volume, 4 pages of the second, and 5 pages of the third, which have not yet appeared in any other collected form, this serial comprised the stories of The Old Curiosity Shop and Barnaby Rudge ; each ultimately sold separately in a single volume, from which the pages of the *Clock* were detached. Chapman and Hall.

I. OLD CURIOSITY SHOP (1840).

Began at p. 37 of vol. i. ; resumed at intervals up to the appearance of the ninth chapter ; from the ninth chapter at p. 133, continued without interruption to the close of the volume (then issued with dedication to Samuel Rogers and preface from Devonshire-terrace, dated September 1840) ; resumed in the second volume, and carried on to the close of the tale at p. 223. i. 177–193. iii. 312.

II. BARNABY RUDGE (1841).

Introduced by brief paper from Master Humphrey (pp. 224–8), and carried to end of Chapter XII. in the closing 78 pages of volume ii., which was issued with a preface dated in March 1841. Chapter XIII. began the third volume, and the story closed with its 82nd chapter at p. 420 ; a closing paper from Master Humphrey (pp. 421–426) then winding up the Clock, of which the concluding volume was published with a preface dated November 1841. i. 113–14 ; 126–7 ; 139–41 ; 200–202 ; 208–23.

1841.

THE PIC-NIC PAPERS by Various Hands. Edited by Charles Dickens. With Illustrations by George Cruikshank, Phiz, &c. Three volumes. (To this Book, edited for the benefit of Mrs. Macrone, widow of his old publisher, Dickens contributed a preface and the opening story, the *Lamplighter*.) Henry Colburn. i. 103 ; 160 ; 215–16.

1842.

AMERICAN NOTES FOR GENERAL CIRCULATION. By Charles Dickens. Two volumes. Chapman and Hall. ii. 1–18 ; 29.

1843.

THE LIFE AND ADVENTURES OF MARTIN CHUZZLEWIT. With Illustrations by Hablot Browne. (Begun in January, and, up to the close of the year, twelve monthly numbers published). Chapman & Hall.

A CHRISTMAS CAROL IN PROSE. Being a Ghost Story of Christmas. By Charles Dickens. With Illustrations by John Leech. (Preface dated December 1843.) Chapman & Hall. ii. 38–39 ; 49–50 ; 62–69.

1844.

THE LIFE AND ADVENTURES OF MARTIN CHUZZLEWIT. With Illustrations by Hablot Browne. (Eight monthly numbers issued, the last being a double number, between January and July ; in which latter month the completed work was published, with dedication to Miss Burdett Coutts, and Preface dated 25th of June.) Chapman & Hall. ii. 22–4 ; 29–30 ; 41–3 ; 52–62 ; 76–79. iii. 313.

EVENINGS OF A WORKING MAN. By John Overs. With a Preface relative to the Author, by Charles Dickens. (Dedication to Doctor Elliotson, and preface dated in June.) T. C. Newby. ii. 85 and 86.

THE CHIMES : a Goblin Story of some Bells that Rang an Old Year out and a New Year in. By Charles Dickens. With illustrations by Maclise R.A., Stanfield R.A., Richard Doyle, and John Leech. Chapman & Hall. ii. 118–22 ; 126–32 ; 135–7 ; 149–50 ; 156.

1845.

THE CRICKET ON THE HEARTH. A Fairy Tale of Home. By Charles Dickens. With Illustrations by Maclise R.A., Stanfield R.A., Edwin Landseer R.A., Richard Doyle, and John Leech. (Dedication to Lord Jeffrey dated in December 1845.) Bradbury & Evans (for the Author). ii. 176–8 ; 189 ; 414–5.

1846.

PICTURES FROM ITALY. By Charles Dickens. (Published originally in the *Daily News* from January to March 1846, with the title of 'Tra- 'velling Letters written on the Road.') Bradbury & Evans (for the Author). ii. 66 ; 82 ; 138–42 ; 165 ; 193–4.

DEALINGS WITH THE FIRM OF DOMBEY AND SON, WHOLESALE, RETAIL, AND FOR EXPORTATION. By Charles Dickens. With Illustrations by Hablot Browne. (Three monthly numbers published, from October to the close of the year.) Bradbury & Evans. (During this year Messrs. Bradbury & Evans published 'for the Author,' in numbers uniform with the other serials, and afterwards in a single volume, *The Adventures of Oliver Twist, or the Parish Boy's Progress.* By Charles Dickens. With 24 Illustrations by George Cruikshank. A new Edition, revised and corrected.)

THE BATTLE OF LIFE. A Love Story. By Charles Dickens. Illustrated by Maclise R.A., Stanfield R.A., Richard Doyle, and John Leech. (Dedicated to his 'English Friends in Switzerland.') Bradbury & Evans (for the Author). ii. 204 ; 215–16 ; 252–3 ; 257–8 ; 259–62 ; 266–70 ; 276–84.

1847.

DEALINGS WITH THE FIRM OF DOMBEY AND SON. (Twelve numbers published monthly during the year.) Bradbury & Evans.

FIRST CHEAP ISSUE OF THE WORKS OF CHARLES DICKENS. An Edition, printed in double columns, and issued in weekly three-halfpenny numbers. The first number, being the first of *Pickwick*, was issued in April 1847; and the volume containing that book, with preface dated September 1847, was published in October. New prefaces were for the most part prefixed to each story, and each volume had a frontispiece. The first series (issued by Messrs. Chapman and Hall, and closing in September 1852) comprised Pickwick, Nickleby, Curiosity Shop, Barnaby Rudge, Chuzzlewit, Oliver Twist, American Notes, Sketches by Boz, and Christmas Books. The second (issued by Messrs. Bradbury & Evans, and closing in 1861) contained Dombey and Son, David Copperfield, Bleak House, and Little Dorrit. The third, issued by Messrs. Chapman & Hall, has since included Great Expectations (1863), Tale of Two Cities (1864), Hard Times and Pictures from Italy (1865), Uncommercial Traveller (1865), and Our Mutual Friend (1867). Among the Illustrators employed for the Frontispieces were Leslie R.A., Webster R.A., Stanfield R.A., George Cattermole, George Cruikshank, Frank Stone A.R.A., John Leech, Marcus Stone, and Hablot Browne. See ii. 299 and 359.

1848.

DEALINGS WITH THE FIRM OF DOMBEY AND SON: WHOLESALE, RETAIL, AND FOR EXPORTATION. (Five numbers issued monthly, the last being a double number, from January to April; in which latter month the complete work was published with dedication to Lady Normanby and preface dated Devonshire-terrace, 24th of March.) Bradbury & Evans. ii. 79; 84; 193–4; 204; 215; 238; 251; 253–5; 307–8; 309–338. iii. 313.

THE HAUNTED MAN AND THE GHOST'S BARGAIN. A Fancy for Christmas Time. By Charles Dickens. Illustrated by Stanfield R.A., John Tenniel, Frank Stone A.R.A., and John Leech. Bradbury & Evans. ii. 253; 359–60; 389; 412–16; 436.

1849.

THE PERSONAL HISTORY OF DAVID COPPERFIELD. By Charles Dickens. With Illustrations by Hablot Browne. (Eight parts issued monthly from May to December.) Bradbury & Evans.

1850.

THE PERSONAL HISTORY OF DAVID COPPERFIELD. By Charles Dickens. Illustrated by Hablot Browne. (Twelve numbers issued monthly, the last being a double number, from January to November; in which latter month the completed work was published, with inscription to Mr. and Mrs. Watson of Rockingham, and preface dated October.) Bradbury & Evans. ii. 79 ; 392–3 ; 403–4 ; 408 ; 417 ; 431–4 ; 452–5 ; 462. iii. 1–19 ; 315–6.

HOUSEHOLD WORDS. On Saturday the 30th of March in this year the weekly serial of HOUSEHOLD WORDS was begun, and was carried on uninterruptedly to the 28th of May 1859, when, its place having been meanwhile taken by the serial in the same form still existing, HOUSEHOLD WORDS was discontinued. ii. 175–7 ; 418–25. iii. 211 ; 452–60.

CHRISTMAS NUMBER of *Household Words*. CHRISTMAS. To this Dickens contributed A CHRISTMAS TREE.

1851.

CHRISTMAS NUMBER of *Household Words*. WHAT CHRISTMAS IS. To this Dickens contributed WHAT CHRISTMAS IS AS WE GROW OLDER.

1852.

BLEAK HOUSE. By Charles Dickens. With Illustrations by Hablot Browne. (Ten numbers, issued monthly, from March to December.) Bradbury & Evans.

CHRISTMAS NUMBER of *Household Words*. STORIES FOR CHRISTMAS. To this Dickens contributed THE POOR RELATION'S STORY, and THE CHILD'S STORY.

1853.

BLEAK HOUSE. By Charles Dickens. Illustrated by Hablot Browne. (Ten numbers issued monthly, the last being a double number, from January to September, in which latter month, with dedication to his 'Companions in the Guild of Literature and Art,' and preface dated in August, the completed book was published.) Bradbury & Evans. ii. 313 ; 411. iii. 5–9 ; 20–32 ; 37–8 ; 313.

A CHILD'S HISTORY OF ENGLAND. By Charles Dickens. Three vols. With frontispieces from designs by F. W. Topham. (Reprinted from *Household Words*, where it appeared between the dates of the 25th of January 1851 and the 10th of December 1853. It was published first in a complete form with dedication to his own children, in 1854. Bradbury & Evans. iii. 37.

CHRISTMAS NUMBER of *Household Words*. CHRISTMAS STORIES. To this Dickens contributed THE SCHOOL BOY'S STORY, and NOBODY'S STORY.

1854.

HARD TIMES. FOR THESE TIMES. By Charles Dickens. (This tale appeared in weekly portions in *Household Words*, between the dates of the 1st of April and the 12th of August 1854; in which latter month it was published complete, with inscription to Thomas Carlyle.) Bradbury & Evans. iii. 44–9.

CHRISTMAS NUMBER of *Household Words:* THE SEVEN POOR TRAVELLERS. To this Dickens contributed three chapters. I. IN THE OLD CITY OF ROCHESTER; II. THE STORY OF RICHARD DOUBLEDICK; III. THE ROAD. iii. 131.

1855.

LITTLE DORRIT. By Charles Dickens. Illustrated by Hablot Browne. The first number published in December. Bradbury & Evans.

CHRISTMAS NUMBER of *Household Words.* THE HOLLY-TREE. To this Dickens contributed three branches. I. MYSELF; II. THE BOOTS; III. THE BILL. iii. 131; 380.

1856.

LITTLE DORRIT. By Charles Dickens. Illustrated by Hablot Browne. (Twelve numbers issued monthly, between January and December.) Bradbury & Evans.

CHRISTMAS NUMBER of *Household Words.* THE WRECK OF THE GOLDEN MARY. To this Dickens contributed the leading chapter: THE WRECK. iii. 447.

1857.

LITTLE DORRIT. By Charles Dickens. Illustrated by Hablot Browne. (Seven numbers issued monthly, the last being a double number, from January to June, in which latter month the tale was published complete, with preface, and dedication to Clarkson Stanfield.) Bradbury & Evans. iii. 51; 54; 75; 93; 131–141; 246–8.

THE LAZY TOUR OF TWO IDLE APPRENTICES, in *Household Words* for October. To the first part of these papers Dickens contributed all up to the top of the second column of page 316; to the second part, all up to the white line in the second column of page 340; to the third part, all except the reflections of Mr. Idle (363–5); and the whole of the fourth part. All the rest was by Mr. Wilkie Collins, iii. 146–152; 318.

CHRISTMAS NUMBER of *Household Words.* THE PERILS OF CERTAIN ENGLISH PRISONERS. To this Dickens contributed the chapters entitled THE ISLAND OF SILVER-STORE, and THE RAFTS ON THE RIVER.

THE FIRST LIBRARY EDITION OF THE WORKS OF CHARLES DICKENS. The first volume, with dedication to John Forster, was issued in December 1857, and the volumes appeared monthly up to the 24th, issued in November 1859. The later books and writings have been added in subsequent volumes, and an edition has also been issued with the illustrations. To the second volume of the Old Curiosity Shop, as issued in this edition, were added 31 'REPRINTED PIECES' taken from Dickens's papers in *Household Words:* which have since appeared also in other collected editions. Chapman & Hall. iii. 208.

AUTHORIZED FRENCH TRANSLATION OF THE WORKS OF DICKENS. Translations of Dickens exist in every European language; but the only version of his writings in a foreign tongue authorized by him, or for which he received anything, was undertaken in Paris. Nickleby was the first story published, and to it was prefixed an address from Dickens to the French public dated from Tavistock-house the 17th January 1857. Hachette. iii. 99; 103.

1858.

CHRISTMAS NUMBER of *Household Words.* A HOUSE TO LET. To this Dickens contributed the chapter entitled GOING INTO SOCIETY.' iii. 222; 231.

1859.

ALL THE YEAR ROUND, the weekly serial which took the place of HOUSEHOLD WORDS. Began on the 30th of April in this year, went on uninterruptedly until Dickens's death, and is continued under the management of his son. iii. 211–225; 425; 452–60.

A TALE OF TWO CITIES. By Charles Dickens. Illustrated by Hablot Browne. This tale was printed in weekly portions in *All the Year Round,* between the dates of the 30th of April and the 26th of November 1859; appearing also concurrently in monthly numbers with illustrations, from June to December; when it was published complete with dedication to Lord John Russell. iii. 215; 249; 320–27.

CHRISTMAS NUMBER of *All the Year Round.* THE HAUNTED HOUSE. To which Dickens contributed two chapters. I. THE MORTALS IN THE HOUSE; II. THE GHOST IN MASTER B'S ROOM. iii. 218.

1860.

HUNTED DOWN. A Story in two Portions. (Written for an American newspaper, and reprinted in the numbers of *All the Year Round* for the 4th and the 11th of August.) iii. 224; 248–9.

THE UNCOMMERCIAL TRAVELLER. By Charles Dickens. (Seventeen papers, which had appeared under this title between the dates of 28th of January and 13th of October 1860 in *All the Year Round,* were published at the close of the year, in a volume, with preface dated December. A later impression was issued in 1868, as a volume of what was called the Charles Dickens Edition; when eleven fresh papers, written in the interval, were added; and promise was given, in a preface dated December 1868, of the Uncommercial Traveller's intention 'to take to 'the road again before another winter sets in' Between that date and the autumn of 1869, when the last of his detached papers were written, *All the Year Round* published seven 'New Uncommercial Samples' which have not yet been collected. Their titles were, i. Aboard ship (which opened, on the 5th of December 1868, the New Series of *All the Year Round*) ; ii. A Small Star in the East ; iii. A Little Dinner in an Hour ; iv. Mr. Barlow ; v. On an Amateur Beat ; vi. A Fly-Leaf in a Life ; vii. A Plea for Total Abstinence. The date of the last was the 5th of June 1869 ; and on the 24th of July appeared his last piece of writing for the serial he had so long conducted, a paper entitled *Landor's Life.* iii. 219–224 ; 428.

CHRISTMAS NUMBER of *All the Year Round.* A MESSAGE FROM THE SEA. To which Dickens contributed nearly all the first, and the whole of the second and the last chapter: THE VILLAGE, THE MONEY, and THE RESTITUTION ; the two intervening chapters, though also with insertions from his hand, not being his.

GREAT EXPECTATIONS. By Charles Dickens. Begun in *All the Year Round* on the 1st of December, and continued weekly to the close of that year.

## 1861.

GREAT EXPECTATIONS. By Charles Dickens. Resumed on the 5th of January and issued in weekly portions, closing on the 3rd of August, when the complete story was published in three volumes and inscribed to Chauncy Hare Townshend. In the following year it was published in a single volume, illustrated by Mr. Marcus Stone. Chapman & Hall. iii. 217 ; 229 ; 230 (the words there used 'on Great Expectations 'closing in June 1861' refer to the time when the Writing of it was closed : it did not close in the Publication until August, as above stated) ; 327–336.

CHRISTMAS NUMBER of *All the Year Round.* TOM TIDDLER'S GROUND. To which Dickens contributed three of the seven chapters. I. PICKING UP SOOT AND CINDERS ; II. PICKING UP MISS KIMMEENS ; III. PICKING UP THE TINKER. iii. 217.

## 1862.

CHRISTMAS NUMBER of *All the Year Round.* SOMEBODY'S LUGGAGE. To which Dickens contributed four chapters. I. HIS LEAVING IT TILL CALLED FOR ; II. HIS BOOTS ; III. HIS BROWN-PAPER PARCEL ; IV. HIS WONDERFUL END. To the chapter of His Umbrella he also contributed a portion. iii. 318 ; 336–7.

## 1863.

CHRISTMAS NUMBER of *All the Year Round.* MRS. LIRRIPER'S LODGINGS. To which Dickens contributed the first and the last chapter. I. HOW MRS. LIRRIPER CARRIED ON THE BUSINESS ; II. HOW THE PARLOURS ADDED A FEW WORDS. iii. 337.

1864.

OUR MUTUAL FRIEND. By Charles Dickens. With Illustrations by Marcus Stone. Eight numbers issued monthly between May and December. Chapman & Hall.

CHRISTMAS NUMBER of *All the Year Round*: MRS. LIRRIPER'S LEGACY: to which Dickens contributed the first and the last chapter. I. MRS. LIRRIPER RELATES HOW SHE WENT ON, AND WENT OVER; II. MRS. LIRRIPER RELATES HOW JEMMY TOPPED UP. iii. 337.

1865.

OUR MUTUAL FRIEND. By Charles Dickens. With Illustrations by Marcus Stone. In Two Volumes. (Two more numbers issued in January and February, when the first volume was published, with dedication to Sir James Emerson Tennent. The remaining ten numbers, the last being a double number, were issued between March and November, when the complete work was published in two volumes. Chapman & Hall. iii. 241; 249–51; 269–70.

CHRISTMAS NUMBER of *All the Year Round.* DOCTOR MARIGOLD'S PRESCRIPTIONS. To this Dickens contributed three portions. I. TO BE TAKEN IMMEDIATELY; II. TO BE TAKEN FOR LIFE; III. The portion with the title of TO BE TAKEN WITH A GRAIN OF SALT, describing a Trial for Murder, was also his. iii. 345–6.

1866.

CHRISTMAS NUMBER of *All the Year Round.* MUGBY JUNCTION. To this Dickens contributed four papers. I. BARBOX BROTHERS; II. BARBOX BROTHERS AND CO.; III. MAIN LINE—THE BOY AT MUGBY; IV. No. 1 BRANCH LINE—THE SIGNAL-MAN. iii. 346 (where a slight error is made in not treating *Barbox* and the *Mugby Boy* as parts of one Christmas piece).

1867.

THE CHARLES DICKENS EDITION. This collected edition, which had originated with the American publishing firm of Ticknor and Fields, was issued here between the dates of 1868 and 1870, with dedication to John Forster, beginning with Pickwick in May 1867, and closing with the Child's History in July 1870. The REPRINTED PIECES were with the volume of AMERICAN NOTES, and the PICTURES FROM ITALY closed the volume containing HARD TIMES. Chapman & Hall.

CHRISTMAS NUMBER of *All the Year Round.* NO THOROUGHFARE. To this Dickens contributed, with Mr. Wilkie Collins, in nearly equal portions. With the new series of *All the Year Round,* which began on the 5th of December 1868, Dickens discontinued the issue of Christmas Numbers. iii. 346.

1868.

A HOLIDAY ROMANCE. GEORGE SILVERMAN'S EXPLANATION. Written respectively for a Child's Magazine, and for the Atlantic Monthly, published in America by Messrs. Ticknor and Fields. Republished in *All the Year Round* on the 25th of January and the 1st and 8th of February 1868. iii. 289, 346.

1870.

THE MYSTERY OF EDWIN DROOD. By Charles Dickens, with twelve illustrations by S. L. Fildes. (Meant to have comprised twelve monthly numbers, but prematurely closed by the writer's death in June.) Issued in six monthly numbers, between April and September. Chapman & Hall. iii. 424–439.

---

II.

## THE WILL OF CHARLES DICKENS.

'I, CHARLES DICKENS, of Gadshill Place, Higham in the county of 'Kent, hereby revoke all my former Wills and Codicils and declare this to 'be my last Will and Testament. I give the sum of £1000 free of legacy 'duty to Miss Ellen Lawless Ternan, late of Houghton Place, Ampthill 'Square, in the county of Middlesex. I GIVE the sum of £19 19 0 to 'my faithful servant Mrs. Anne Cornelius. I GIVE the sum of £19 19 0 'to the daughter and only child of the said Mrs. Anne Cornelius. I GIVE 'the sum of £19 19 0 to each and every domestic servant, male and 'female, who shall be in my employment at the time of my decease, and 'shall have been in my employment for a not less period of time than one 'year. I GIVE the sum of £1000 free of legacy duty to my daughter 'Mary Dickens. I also give to my said daughter an annuity of £300 a 'year, during her life, if she shall so long continue unmarried; such 'annuity to be considered as accruing from day to day, but to be payable 'half yearly, the first of such half-yearly payments to be made at the 'expiration of six months next after my decease. If my said daughter 'Mary shall marry, such annuity shall cease; and in that case, but in that 'case only, my said daughter shall share with my other children in the 'provision hereinafter made for them. I GIVE to my dear sister-in-law 'Georgina Hogarth the sum of £8000 free of legacy duty. I also give to 'the said Georgina Hogarth all my personal jewellery not hereinafter men-'tioned, and all the little familiar objects from my writing-table and my 'room, and she will know what to do with those things. I ALSO GIVE to 'the said Georgina Hogarth all my private papers whatsoever and where-'soever, and I leave her my grateful blessing as the best and truest friend 'man ever had. I GIVE to my eldest son Charles my library of printed 'books, and my engravings and prints; and I also give to my son Charles 'the silver salver presented to me at Birmingham, and the silver cup pre- 'sented to me at Edinburgh, and my shirt studs, shirt pins, and sleeve 'buttons. AND I BEQUEATH unto my said son Charles and my son Henry 'Fielding Dickens, the sum of £8000 upon trust to invest the same, and 'from time to time to vary the investments thereof, and to pay the annual 'income thereof to my wife during her life, and after her decease the said 'sum of £8000 and the investments thereof shall be in trust for my chil- 'dren (but subject as to my daughter Mary to the proviso hereinbefore 'contained) who being a son or sons shall have attained or shall attain the 'age of twenty-one years or being a daughter or daughters shall have 'attained or shall attain that age or be previously married, in equal shares 'if more than one. I GIVE my watch (the gold repeater presented to me 'at Coventry), and I give the chains and seals and all appendages I have 'worn with it, to my dear and trusty friend John Forster, of Palace Gate 'House, Kensington, in the county of Middlesex aforesaid; and I also 'give to the said John Forster such manuscripts of my published works as 'may be in my possession at the time of my decease. AND I DEVISE 'AND BEQUEATH all my real and personal estate (except such as is vested 'in me as a trustee or mortgagee) unto the said Georgina Hogarth and the 'said John Forster, their heirs, executors, administrators, and assigns 'respectively, upon trust that they the said Georgina Hogarth and John 'Forster, or the survivor of them or the executors or administrators of such 'survivor, do and shall, at their, his, or her uncontrolled and irresponsible 'direction, either proceed to an immediate sale or conversion into money 'of the said real and personal estate (including my copyrights), or defer 'and postpone any sale or conversion into money, till such time or times 'as they, he, or she shall think fit, and in the meantime may manage and 'let the said real and personal estate (including my copyrights), in such 'manner in all respects as I myself could do, if I were living and acting 'therein; it being my intention that the trustees or trustee for the time 'being of this my Will shall have the fullest power over the said real and 'personal estate which I can give to them, him, or her. AND I DECLARE 'that, until the said real and personal estate shall be sold and converted 'into money, the rents and annual income thereof respectively shall be 'paid and applied to the person or persons in the manner and for the pur- 'poses to whom and for which the annual income of the monies to arise 'from the sale or conversion thereof into money would be payable or ap- 'plicable under this my Will in case the same were sold or converted into 'money. AND I DECLARE that my real estate shall for the purposes of 'this my Will be considered as converted into personalty upon my decease. 'AND I DECLARE that the said trustees or trustee for the time being, do 'and shall, with and out of the monies which shall come to their, his, or 'her hands, under or by virtue of this my Will and the trusts thereof, pay 'my just debts, funeral and testamentary expenses, and legacies. AND I 'DECLARE that the said trust funds or so much thereof as shall remain 'after answering the purposes aforesaid, and the annual income thereof, 'shall be in trust for all my children (but subject as to my daughter Mary 'to the proviso hereinbefore contained), who being a son or sons shall have 'attained or shall attain the age of twenty-one years, and being a daughter 'or daughters shall have attained or shall attain that age or be previously 'married, in equal shares if more than one. PROVIDED ALWAYS, that, as 'regards my copyrights and the produce and profits thereof, my said 'daughter Mary, notwithstanding the proviso hereinbefore contained with 'reference to her, shall share with my other children therein whether she 'be married or not. AND I DEVISE the estates vested in me at my decease 'as a trustee or mortgagee unto the use of the said Georgina Hogarth and 'John Forster, their heirs and assigns, upon the trusts and subject to the 'equities affecting the same respectively. AND I APPOINT the said GEOR-'GINA HOGARTH and JOHN FORSTER executrix and executor of this my 'Will, and GUARDIANS of the persons of my children during their respective 'minorities. AND LASTLY, as I have now set down the form of words 'which my legal advisers assure me are necessary to the plain objects of 'this my Will, I solemnly enjoin my dear children always to remember 'how much they owe to the said Georgina Hogarth, and never to be want-'ing in a grateful and affectionate attachment to her, for they know well 'that she has been, through all the stages of their growth and progress, 'their ever useful self-denying and devoted friend. AND I DESIRE here 'simply to record the fact that my wife, since our separation by consent, 'has been in the receipt from me of an annual income of £600, while all 'the great charges of a numerous and expensive family have devolved 'wholly upon myself. I emphatically direct that I be buried in an inexpen-'sive, unostentatious, and strictly private manner; that no public announce-'ment be made of the time or place of my burial; that at the utmost not 'more than three plain mourning coaches be employed; and that those who 'attend my funeral wear no scarf, cloak, black bow, long hat-band, or 'other such revolting absurdity. I DIRECT that my name be inscribed in 'plain English letters on my tomb, without the addition of "Mr." or '"Esquire." I conjure my friends on no account to make me the subject 'of any monument, memorial, or testimonial whatever. I rest my claims 'to the remembrance of my country upon my published works, and to the 'remembrance of my friends upon their experience of me in addition 'thereto. I commit my soul to the mercy of God through our Lord and 'Saviour Jesus Christ, and I exhort my dear children humbly to try to 'guide themselves by the teaching of the New Testament in its broad spirit, 'and to put no faith in any man's narrow construction of its letter here or 'there. IN WITNESS whereof I the said Charles Dickens, the testator, 'have to this my last Will and Testament set my hand this 12th day of 'May in the year of our Lord 1869.

| | |
|---|---|
| 'Signed published and declared by the above-'named Charles Dickens the testator as and for his 'last Will and Testament in the presence of us '(present together at the same time) who in his 'presence at his request and in the presence of each 'other have hereunto subscribed our names as 'witnesses. | CHARLES DICKENS. |

'G. HOLSWORTH,
'26 Wellington Street, Strand.

'HENRY WALKER,
'26 Wellington Street, Strand.

'I, CHARLES DICKENS of Gadshill Place near Rochester in the county of 'Kent Esquire declare this to be a Codicil to my last Will and Testament 'which Will bears date the 12th day of May 1869. I GIVE to my son 'Charles Dickens the younger all my share and interest in the weekly 'journal called "All the Year Round," which is now conducted under 'Articles of Partnership made between me and William Henry Wills and 'the said Charles Dickens the younger, and all my share and interest in 'the stereotypes stock and other effects belonging to the said partnership, 'he defraying my share of all debts and liabilities of the said partnership 'which may be outstanding at the time of my decease, and in all other 'respects I confirm my said Will. IN WITNESS whereof I have hereunto 'set my hand the 2nd day of June in the year of our Lord 1870.

| | |
|---|---|
| 'Signed and declared by the said CHARLES 'DICKENS, the testator as and for a Codicil to his 'Will in the presence of us present at the same 'time who at his request in his presence and in the 'presence of each other hereunto subscribe our 'names as witnesses. | CHARLES DICKENS. |

'G. HOLSWORTH,
'26 Wellington Street, Strand.

'H. WALKER,
'26 Wellington Street, Strand.'

---

The real and personal estate,—taking the property bequeathed by the last codicil at a valuation of something less than two years' purchase; and of course before payment of the legacies, the (inconsiderable) debts, and the testamentary and other expenses,—amounted, as nearly as may be calculated, to £93,000.

## III.

## CORRECTIONS MADE IN THE THIRTEENTH THOUSAND OF THE SECOND VOLUME.

I REGRET to have had no opportunity until now (May, 1873) of making the corrections which appear in this impression of my second volume. All the early reprints having been called for before the close of 1872, the only change I at that time found possible was amendment of an error at p. 368, as to the date of the first performance at Devonshire House, and of a few others of small importance at pp. 235, 265, 292, 331, 414, and 416.

Premising that additional corrections, also unimportant, are now made at pp. 36, 110, 111, 116, 274, 302, 375, 414, and 451, I proceed to indicate what may seem to require more detailed mention.

P. 28. 'Covent-garden' is substituted for 'Drury-lane.' The *Chronicle* atoned for its present silence by a severe notice of the man's subsequent appearance at the Haymarket; and of this I am glad to be reminded by Mr. Gruneisen, who wrote the criticism.

29. The son of the publican referred to (Mr. Whelpdale of Streatham), pointing out my error in not having made the Duke of Brunswick the defendant, says he was himself a witness in the case, and has had pride in repeating to his own children what the Chief Justice said of his father.

92. The 'limpet on the rock' and the 'green boots' refer to a wonderful piece by Turner in the previous year's Academy, exhibiting a rock overhanging a magnificent sea, a booted figure appearing on the rock, and at its feet a blotch to represent a limpet: the subject being Napoleon at St. Helena.

143. 'Assumption' is substituted for 'Transfiguration.'

156. Six words are added to the last note.

167–8. An error in my former statement of the circumstances of Mr. Fletcher's death, which I much regret to have made, is now corrected.

169. The proper names of the ship and her captain are here given, as the Fantôme, commanded by Sir Frederick (now Vice-Admiral) Nicolson.

203. A correspondent familiar with Lausanne informs me that the Castle of Chillon is not visible from Rosemont, and that Dickens in these first days must have mistaken some other object for it. 'A long mass of mountain hides Chillon from view, and it only

'becomes visible when you get about six miles from Lausanne 'on the Vevay road, when a curve in the road or lake shows it 'visible behind the bank of mountains.' The error at p. 230, now corrected, was mine.

P. 220. 'Clinking,' the right word, replaces 'drinking.'

235-6. A passage which stood in the early editions is removed, the portrait which it referred to having been not that of the lady mentioned, but of a relative bearing the same name.

240-1. I quote a letter to myself from one of the baronet's family present at the outbreak goodnaturedly exaggerated in Mr. Cerjat's account to Dickens. 'I well remember the dinner at Mr. Cerjat's alluded 'to in one of the letters from Lausanne in your Life of Dickens. 'It was not however our first acquaintance with the "distin- '"guished writer," as he came with his family to stay at a Pension 'on the border of the Lake of Geneva where my father and his 'family were then living, and notwithstanding the gallant cap- 'tain's "habit" the families subsequently became very intimate.'

242. Lord Vernon is more correctly described as the fifth Baron, who succeeded to the title in 1835 and died in 1866 in his 64th year.

255. The distance of Mont Blanc from the Neuchâtel road is now properly given as sixty not six miles.

313, line 21. Not 'subsequent' but 'modified' is the proper word.

368. In mentioning the painters who took an interest in the Guild scheme I omitted the distinguished name of Mr. E. M. Ward, R.A., by whom an admirable design, taken from Defoe's life, was drawn for the card of membership.

425. In supposing that the Child's Dream of a Star was not among Dickens's Reprinted Pieces, I fell into an error, which is here corrected.

436. I did not mean to imply that Lady Graham was herself a Sheridan. She was only connected with the family she so well 'represented' by being the sister of the lady whom Tom Sheridan married.

---

The incident at Mr. Hone's funeral quoted at pp. 11–12 from a letter to Mr. Felton written by Dickens shortly after the occurrence (2nd of March, 1843), and published, a year before my volume, in Mr. Field's *Yesterdays with Authors* (pp. 146–8), has elicited from the 'Independent clergyman' referred to a counter statement of the alleged facts, of which I here present an abridgement, omitting nothing that is in any way material. 'Though it is 'thirty years since . . several who were present survive to this day, and 'have a distinct recollection of all that occurred. One of these is the writer 'of this article—another, the Rev. Joshua Harrison . . The Independent 'clergyman never wore bands, and had no Bible under his arm . . An 'account of Mr. Hone had appeared in some of the newspapers, containing 'an offensive paragraph to the effect that one "speculation" having failed, 'Mr. Hone was disposed, and persuaded by the Independent clergyman, 'to try another, that other being "to try his powers in the pulpit." This 'was felt by the family to be an insult alike to the living and the dead . . 'Mr. Harrison's account is, that the Independent clergyman was observed 'speaking to Miss Hone about something apparently annoying to both, and 'that, turning to Mr. Cruikshank, he said "Have you seen the sketch of '"Mr. Hone's life in the *Herald?*" Mr. C. replied "Yes." "Don't you '"think it very discreditable? It is a gross reflection on our poor friend, '"as if he would use the most sacred things merely for a piece of bread; '"and it is a libel on me and the denomination I belong to, as if we could '"be parties to such a proceeding." Mr. C. said in reply, "I know some-'"thing of the article, but what you complain of was not in it originally—'"it was an addition by another hand." Mr. C. afterwards stated that he 'wrote the article, "but *not* the offensive paragraph." The vulgar non-'sense put into the mouth of the clergyman by Mr. Dickens was wound up, 'it is said, by "Let us pray" . . but this *cannot* be true; and for this 'reason, the conversation with Mr. Cruikshank took place before the do 'mestic service, and that service, according to Nonconformist custom, is 'always begun by reading an appropriate passage of Scripture . . Mr. 'Dickens says that while they were kneeling at prayer Mr. Cruikshank 'whispered to him what he relates. Mr. C. denies it; and I believe him . . 'In addition to the improbability, one of the company remembers that Mr. 'Dickens and Mr. Cruikshank did not sit together, and could not have 'knelt side by side." The reader must be left to judge between what is said of the incident in the text and these recollections of it after thirty years.

---

At the close of the corrections to the first volume, prefixed to the second, the intention was expressed to advert at the end of the work to information, not in correction but in illustration of my text, forwarded by obliging correspondents who had been scholars at the Wellington House Academy (i. 54). But inexorable limits of space prevent, for the present, a fulfilment of this intention.

J. F.

PALACE GATE HOUSE, KENSINGTON,
*22nd of January* 1874.

# INDEX.

BRADBURY, AGNEW, & CO., PRINTERS, WHITEFRIARS.

Lightning Source UK Ltd.
Milton Keynes UK
UKOW051857181111

182311UK00001B/1/P